WITHDRAWN

LENSEN

Japanese Recognition of the U.S.S.R

OTHER BOOKS BY GEORGE ALEXANDER LENSEN

Report from Hokkaido: The Remains of Russian Culture in Northern Japan

Russia's Japan Expedition of 1852 to 1855

The Russian Push Toward Japan; Russo-Japanese Relations, 1697–1875

The World Beyond Europe: An Introduction to the History of Africa, India, Southeast Asia, and the Far East

Russia's Eastward Expansion (edited)

Revelations of a Russian Diplomat: the Memoirs of Dmitrii I. Abrikossow (edited)

Korea and Manchuria Between Russia and Japan 1895–1904: The Observations of Sir Ernest Satow, British Minister to Japan and China (edited)

The Soviet Union: An Introduction

The d'Anethan Dispatches From Japan, 1894–1910. The Observations of Baron Albert d'Anethan, Belgian Minister Plenipotentiary and Dean of the Diplomatic Corps (translation and edited)

The Russo-Chinese War

Trading under Sail off Japan, 1860–99. The Recollections of Captain John Baxter Will, Sailing-Master and Pilot (edited)

Faces of Japan: A Photographic Study

Russian Diplomatic and Consular Officials in East Asia. A Handbook (compiled)

Japanese Diplomatic and Consular Officials in Russia. A Handbook (compiled)

Yoshizawa and Karakhan at Peking.

Japanese Recognition of the U. S. S. R.

Soviet-Japanese Relations
1921–1930

GEORGE ALEXANDER LENSEN

SOPHIA UNIVERSITY · TOKYO
IN COOPERATION WITH
THE DIPLOMATIC PRESS
TALLAHASSEE · FLORIDA

PUBLISHED BY
SOPHIA UNIVERSITY
7, KIOI-CHŌ, CHIYODA-KU
TOKYO
IN COOPERATION WITH
THE DIPLOMATIC PRESS, INC.
1102 BETTON ROAD
TALLAHASSEE, FLORIDA
Copyright in Japan 1970, by Sophia University, all rights reserved
Library of Congress Catalog Card No. 70-95263
ISBN 910512-09-4

DS
849
R7
L37

PRINTED IN JAPAN
THE VOYAGERS' PRESS, TOKYO

To the memory of
WEYMOUTH TYREE JORDAN
friend, colleague, and distinguished historian

Contents

Preface	1
Chapter One: The Dairen Conference	5
Chapter Two: The Changchun Conference	49
Chapter Three: The Gotō-Ioffe Talks	85
Chapter Four: The Ioffe-Kawakami Talks	127
Chapter Five: The Karakhan Yoshizawa Talks	141
Chapter Six: The Basic Convention	177
Chapter Seven: Exchange of Official Representatives	203
Chapter Eight: Concession Contracts	227
Chapter Nine: Fishery Talks	241
Chapter Ten: The Fishery Convention	271
Chapter Eleven: Expanding Contacts	317
Chapter Twelve: Lingering Mistrust	343
Epilogue	363
Appendix	375
Source Notes	385
Bibliography	403
Index	409

昨日の敵は今日の友　　*Kinō no teki wa Kyō no tomo.*
(Yesterday's enemies [are] today's friends.)

—from a Japanese song, popular after the Russo-Japanese War.

Not one state, after recognizing our government, was so friendly in its expressions toward us as the Japanese one. Satō [the Japanese chargé d'affaires] in his meetings with me is the very embodiment of friendliness. Your reports about the receptions at the crown prince, the empress dowager and the like also point to a strikingly, even exceptionally strikingly, underlined friendliness. What is the meaning of this? That is what one must decipher. What do they expect? Do they want territory for immigration, do they want concessions, or do they want a safe rear for the coming war with the United States?

—from a letter of Foreign Commissar Chicherin to Ambassador Kopp in Tokyo, dated June 23, 1925.

Preface

THE Soviet Union is Japan's closest neighbor. On a clear day Russian-held islands can be seen from Hokkaido with the naked eye. Soviet waters abound in marine life coveted by Japanese fishermen and the vast resources of Siberia beckon Japanese industrialists.

Prior to the Pacific War Japan had important concessions in the Soviet Far East; these she lost in 1945. Since the reestablishment of diplomatic relations with the U.S.S.R. in 1956, Japan has tried to restore economic cooperation with the latter. The unprecedented growth of the Japanese economy has revived hopes in Tokyo and Moscow for renewed Japanese participation in the development of Siberia. There is little debate whether such cooperation is desirable, merely on what terms it could be accomplished.

Two basic questions occupy Japanese and Soviet negotiators: (1) Can a satisfactory profit sharing arrangement be worked out between private Japanese companies and the Soviet state? and (2) What constitutes a fair ratio of investment on the part of the two sides in the exploitation of a given concession?

The defeat of Japan has turned back the clock of history to the third quarter of the nineteenth century in the sense that the possession of some of the Kuril Islands is once more in dispute, at least from the Japanese point of view. It is to the 1920's, however, that we must turn for historical precedents for the economic and political questions now under discussion. Yet little has been written on the history of Soviet-Japanese relations from 1922 to 1930. Inexplicably A. N. Heifets's detailed study of Soviet diplomacy and the peoples of the East from 1921 to

1927, published under the auspices of the Academy of Sciences of the U.S.S.R. in 1968, ignores this topic.

It was my intention originally to cover this period more briefly as part of a general history of Soviet-Japanese relations. But the more I delved into the documents of the time, the more I was reminded of points which I had discussed with Japanese and Russian diplomats in Tokyo in 1968 in an attempt to assess the state of contemporary Soviet-Japanese relations. The arguments which Ambassador Oleg Aleksandrovich Troianovskii adduced in a speech at the Foreign Correspondents' Club in May of 1968 to show how Japan, which had recently moved to first place among capitalist countries in trade volume with the U.S.S.R., could profit by closer economic ties with the Soviet Union were identical with those advanced by his father, Ambassador Aleksandr Antonovich Troianovskii, forty years earlier. For example, in 1928 Troianovskii Sr. asserted that the Soviet Union constituted "the most solid and reliable buyer and payer"; in 1968 Troianovskii Jr. depicted the Soviet foreign trade organizations as "reliable, dependable and honest partners with whom good business is possible." In 1928 Troianovskii Sr. saw the key to successful economic relations in the avoidance of ideological disputation: "Don't touch on economic systems, talk as little as possible about principles and as much as possible about business." In 1968 Troianovskii Jr. declared: "One of the reasons which contributed to the successful promotion of our trade and economic relations was the fact that neither of our countries has ever made these relations depend on any current political considerations." I was struck also by the similarity of questions that are bound to arise in connection with the recognition of the Communist regime in Peking by Washington as well as Tokyo.

In the belief that a detailed reconstruction of the negotiations leading to Japanese recognition of the U.S.S.R., the conclusion of the various concession agreements, and the difficulties experienced in their execution will be of more than academic interest today, I have written this separate volume, and have included the full text of the major conventions and related correspondence in the body of the work. I have given direct quotes (in my own translation) particularly when dealing with telegrams, letters and other documents not yet published by either side. (It may be of interest to note parenthetically that while my research has taken me both to the Soviet Union and to Japan, the texts of many of the Russian dispatches—including those sent by special courier—were found in Japanese archives.)

Whatever one's political convictions may be, it is sad to note that the two leading Soviet diplomats who served their country so well in the negotiations with Japan were to perish within a few years in their fatherland—Ioffe by his own hand, Karakhan by the hand of an executioner. This is the more intriguing if one recalls that Kawaji Toshiakira, the Japanese diplomat with whom Vice Admiral Putiatin had concluded the very first treaty between Russia and Japan seventy years earlier, in 1855, also committed suicide—ironically upon learning that the Tokugawa forces had been defeated by adherents of the imperial regime with which Ioffe and Karakhan were to deal.

I have followed traditional usage in giving Japanese surnames first; they are transliterated according to the new Kenkyūsha system. Russian names follow the Library of Congress style.

I acknowledge with thanks the support of the Inter-University Committee on Travel Grants, which sponsored my research in the Soviet Union, and of the National Endowment for the Humanities, which awarded me a senior fellowship for research in Japan. I am grateful also to the American Philosophical Society and to the Research Council of the Florida State University for providing me with funds for the acquisition of source materials. Last but not least, I am deeply indebted to Professor Earl R. Beck, Dean Robert O. Lawton, and my colleagues in the Department of History at the Florida State University for making my repeated research in Japan possible.

GEORGE ALEXANDER LENSEN

Kyoto, June, 1969.

CHAPTER ONE

The Dairen Conference

THERE is a thin line between love and hate. In the decade following the Russo-Japanese War Tsarist Russia and Japan abruptly shed their hostility and became friends. It was a turnabout, reminiscent in retrospect of the dramatic reversal of Japanese-American feelings after the Pacific War. In 1916 Tsarist Russia and Japan launched a partnership that might have altered the entire course of East Asian international relations. In desperate need of supplies for her struggle with Germany and on the verge of collapse at home, the Tsarist government purchased enormous quantities of war materials and food from Japan; in fact, Japan sold to Russia all stocks of ammunition not needed for her own defense and geared the entire output of several government arsenals and private factories to her demands. In the process Russia ran up a staggering debt to Japan, part of which she met by extensive economic concessions to the latter in the Russian Far East.

The Communist *coup d'état* of November 7, 1917, gave a fatal blow to the Russo-Japanese alliance. Bolshevik cancellation in February of 1918 of the obligations and debts of the Tsarist and Provisional governments, including the vast sums owed to Japan, were a serious violation of Japanese interests; at the same time the temporary prostration of her mighty neighbor was too great an opportunity for Japanese militarists to ignore. Furnished by the United States, Great Britain and France with the pretext of safeguarding military stores in Siberia from seizure by liberated German prisoners of war and of rescuing Czechoslovak soldiers stranded in Russia, the Japanese poured into the Russian Far East in April of 1918 as participants in the Allied Intervention. Unlike the other Allies, they became involved in the Civil War, supporting anti-Communist leaders in an attempt to create a buffer state between their possessions and Soviet Russia. Bitter clashes between Red partisans and Japanese troops occurred, and the passions of hate once again overwhelmed those of love.

Yet while the Bolsheviks were dedicated to the overthrow of capitalist governments everywhere, they wished to modify rather than terminate their relations with the powers. As early as December 1, 1917—less than a month after the *coup d'état* and almost half a year before the landing of Japanese troops—the People's Commissariat of Foreign Affairs (*Narkomindel*) had approached the Japanese ambassador in Petrograd through Third Secretary[a] Ueda Sentarō 上田仙太郎 concerning the review of all treaty relations between the two countries; it had proposed the conclusion of a new commercial and economic agreement and of a convention concerning the state of affairs in the Far East and along the Pacific coast. Ambassador Uchida Yasuya 内田康哉 had agreed to convey the matter to Tokyo, but the imperial government had made no reply. Nor had Japan responded to a renewed proposal made by Deputy Commissar for Foreign Affairs Lev Mikhailovich Karakhan through Ueda in the spring of 1918.[1]

The Japanese intervention did not still Soviet desires for an accomodation with Japan; on the contrary, it had made it the more urgent. In April of 1919 the Far Eastern representative of the Foreign Commissariat, V. D. Vilenskii-Sibiriakov, expressed his government's desire for negotiating an agreement with Japan to Matsudaira Tsuneo 松平恒雄, chief of the civil affairs section of the Vladivostok expeditionary force; again there was no response from the Japanese government.[2] In May of the same

[a] Leonid Kutakov, who bases his account on reference to the communication in a later note from Commissar Chicherin, dated February 24, 1920, to the Japanese Foreign Office identifies Ueda (as did Chicherin) as consul; Tanaka Bunichirō notes in parentheses that he was secretary. Tanaka is correct. Neither Kutakov nor Tanaka give the full name of Ueda or any name of the ambassador. Such information in this and other instances was obtained from George Alexander Lensen (comp.), *Japanese Diplomatic and Consular Officials in Russia* (Tokyo and Tallahassee: Sophia University in cooperation with the Diplomatic Press, 1968).

year specific proposals for the regulation of relations between the two countries were handed to Chargé d'Affaires *ad interim* Marumo Naotoshi 丸毛直利 at Vologda, where the Allied diplomats had moved from Petrograd in February of 1918. There was no reply. Although the Soviets were prepared to recognize that Japan had special economic and commercial interests in the (Russian) Far East, Japan still had hopes of greater gains by direct military action or by the support of anti-communist forces.[3]

The Soviet commisar for foreign affairs, Georgii Vasil'evich Chicherin, was a colorful figure. An old aristocrat and diplomat from Tsarist times, fluent in three languages, and an able negotiator and talented politician, he had a broad outlook and seemed to desire a peaceful resolution of the differences inherent in the Soviet and capitalist systems. In dealing with foreign diplomats he showed great flexibility, the ability to maneuver and to find compromise formulas. On February 24, 1920, he cabled to the Japanese ambassadors in France and Sweden that Soviet Russia wanted peace with Japan. He assured them that his government had no hostile intentions toward Japan and would not interfere in her domestic affairs; it recognized Japan's preeminent economic and commercial interests in the (Russian) Far East.[4]

> The Peoples of Russia cherish no aggressive designs against Japan [Chicherin declared]. The Soviet government has no intention of interfering in the internal affairs of the Japanese people. It fully recognizes the special economic and commercial interests of Japan in the [Russian] Far East, interests surpassing in several respects those of other countries. It is equally interested in concluding an agreement on this subject which will be useful and beneficial to both parties.
>
> The Soviet government wishes to establish a *modus vivendi* guaranteeing peace between Russia and Japan, and guaranteeing the reciprocal advantages to both countries which would result from the relations to be established between them. . . .
>
> The People's Commissariat therefore proposes to the Japanese

government to engage in peace negotiations, in order to insure for the two peoples peaceful coexistence, friendly neighborly relations, and mutual satisfaction of reciprocal interests.[5]

On March 9, 1920, the Foreign Commissariat's diplomatic representative for the Far East and Siberia at Irkutsk forwarded to Foreign Minister Uchida Kōsai 內田康哉 a cable from Commissar of Foreign Affairs Georgii Vasil'evich Chicherin, seeking the commencement of negotiations between Russia and Japan to terminate hostilities and restore amicable relations.[6]

That month Communist partisans attacked the town of Nikolaevsk on the Amur River and massacred half the population, including the Japanese consul and most Japanese residents. There were many conflicting accounts of the event, but its essence was summarized in an article in the *Contemporary Review*.

> ... on February 28th, 1920, an armistice was concluded between the Bolsheviks and the White Guards, the latter laying down their arms after being given a pledge that they would be treated as prisoners of war. In spite of this, all the White Guards were murdered by the Bolshevik faction, who then demanded that the Japanese contingent should also lay down their arms. This they refused to do, and from March 12th to March 17th fierce attacks were made by the Bolsheviks on the Japanese Consulate and the barracks which the troops were holding. On March 17th, in face of overwhelming odds, the surviving Japanese troops, some 120 men, capitulated. They were thrown into prison, and finally shared the fate of the Russian White Guards, being murdered to a man under revolting circumstances. It was not until June 3rd that the Japanese reinforcements, so long overdue, arrived at Nikolaevsk, to find the city practically reduced to ashes. It was then discovered that the Bolsheviks, on learning of the approach of the Japanese relief force towards the end of May, had murdered every Japanese man, woman and child in the city, the victims numbering nearly seven hundred, including the officers and men of the garrison and

the Japanese Consul with his wife and children. The bodies of all these unfortunate people had been dismembered and flung into the river.[7, b]

Whether the atrocity had been the mad act of a half-crazed commissar, as thought by some, or the nervous response of the partisans to a treacherous Japanese attack, as claimed by the Soviet government later, the incident provided the Japanese military with a cause. They erected a monument with the figure of Justice, eyes covered and scales in hand, and the inscription that the murder of the Japanese at Nikolaevsk would never be forgotten. The massacre served to bolster the argument for Japanese annexation of a portion of the Russian Far East to shield the inhabitants of Manchuria and Korea from similar destruction. The Japanese did not accept Chicherin's contention that the incident, on the contrary, was a compelling reason for the cessation of Japanese-Russian hostilities. The surest way to avoid such incidents, Chicherin had vainly cabled to the Japanese foreign minister on March 22, was to initiate the peace talks proposed by the Soviet government.[8]

To avoid a full-scale confrontation with Japan as the Red Army was

[b] According to the memoirs of Petr Mikhailovich Nikiforov, chairman of the council of ministers of the Far Eastern Republic, the Japanese consul had collected all Japanese (civilian) subjects with their wives and children in the consulate and had opened fire at the advancing partisans. "Suddenly an explosion occurred in the consular building, smoke billowed from the windows, and the consulate burst into flames. Attempts by the partisans to penetrate into the building of the consulate in order to carry out the children were met by machine-gun fire." Yet Nikiforov mentions that "anarchists of the Triapitsyn detachment" had committed "criminal acts" during the withdrawal from Nikolaevsk and that Triapitsyn, chief of staff Nina Lebedeva, and their accomplices were tried by a people's court and shot when Triapitsyn tried to liquidate some Communists who had disclosed his misdeeds. (P. M. Nikiforov, *Zapiski prem'era DVR. Pobeda Leninskoi politiki v bor'be s interventsiei na Dal'nem Vostoke* [1917–1922 gg.] [Memoirs of the premier of the Far Eastern Republic. Victory of the Lenin policy in the struggle with the intervention in the Far East (1917–1922)] [Moscow: Gosudarstvennoe izdatel'stvo politicheskoi literatury, 1963] pp. 186–87.)

pushing eastward in the Civil War, toward the regions occupied by the Japanese, the Central Committee of the Russian Communist Party decided to create a temporary buffer state in the territory east of Lake Baikal. A resolution of the Congress of Toilers of the Baikal Region, dated March 28, 1920, stated that it was "expedient and necessary" to form "an independent autonomous government" and a week and a half later, on April 6, the Far Eastern Republic was proclaimed by the Congress.

The Far Eastern Republic, whose capital was first at Verkhneudinsk (Ulan-Ude) and later at Chita, was the prototype of a "People's Republic." Its government began as a democratic coalition of socialist parties and public organizations.

On April 17, 1920, Vilenskii-Sibiriakov reiterated to the commander of the Japanese expeditionary force that the Soviet government had no hostile intentions toward Japan and did not intend to interfere in her domestic affairs; he stated again that the Communist regime recognized Japan's special economic and commercial interests in the Far East. Once more Vilenskii-Sibiriakov called for the revision of the old treaties and the conclusion of new ones, for consideration of the abrogation of the liabilities incurred by the previous governments, an exchange of views on Russo-Japanese peace talks and for the establishment of commercial relations. He also pressed for the withdrawal of Japanese troops, pledged by an imperial proclamation two and a half weeks earlier, on March 31. Japan's reluctance to give a concrete reply reaffirmed the wisdom of the plan to deal with Japan indirectly, through the Far Eastern Republic.[9]

On July 15, 1920, the Far Eastern Republic succeeded in signing an armistice with the Japanese; she pledged in a joint declaration the next day not to adopt Communism as the basis of her social system. The idea of a non-Communist buffer state between Soviet Russia and her own empire appealed to Japan. She had hopes at first of gaining control of its government by support of anti-Communist Russians like Ataman Grigorii Mikhailovich Semenov, but even when she realized that such efforts were doomed to failure and that she would not be able to chart its destiny, she welcomed a buffer state as an Eastern *cordon sanitaire* to contain the spread of Bolshevism.

The Far Eastern Republic established commercial relations with the Allies and in 1922 was to send a delegation to the Washington Conference to plead for the evacuation of Japanese forces from Siberia. An American trade mission in the summer of 1921 was to pressure Japanese representatives in Chita into holding a secret conference with the government of the Far Eastern Republic to solve various problems between the F. E. R. and Japan and to prepare for the establishment of diplomatic relations between them. An earlier American note to Tokyo demanding Japanese withdrawal from Siberia and North Sakhalin had already given rise to fear in Tokyo of a Russo-American alliance against Japan. Yet in the fall of 1921 the Far Eastern Republic was to threaten the United States that if her trade mission were not admitted to the U.S., she would be forced to conclude an agreement with Japan even if it meant ceding North Sakhalin, where concessions had recently been granted to Americans. Although the Far Eastern Republic had neither the intention nor the authority of ceding North Sakhalin to another power, the note typified Soviet efforts to strengthen the Russian position by playing Japan and the United States against each other. In due time the Far Eastern Republic was to shed its democratic façade, emerge as a Communist regime, and rejoin the Russian Soviet Federated Socialist Republic (hereafter simply called Soviet Russia), but by then its mission had been accomplished. As Vladimir Il'ich Lenin, who had proposed the creation of the temporary buffer state, later boasted, the withdrawal of the Japanese from Siberia was gained not by Soviet military strength but by Soviet diplomacy, by exploiting Japanese-American differences and by making diplomatic use of the United States. Soviet diplomacy, he said, had succeeded not only in postponing war with Japan but in avoiding it altogether.[10]

The government of the Far Eastern Republic repeatedly called on the Japanese to withdraw from Siberia; at the same time it stressed its interest in the resumption of commercial relations. The foreign minister of the Far Eastern Republic addressed the Japanese foreign minister directly; the deputy foreign minister spoke to the Japanese chief of the political affairs section in Vladivostok. In December of 1920 Deputy Foreign Minister I. S. Kozhevnikov asked what Japan's conditions were for the promised evacuation and the normalization of Russo-Japanese relations. On January 18, 1921, Foreign Minister A. Krasnoshchekov wrote a lengthy letter to the Japanese foreign minister in which he restated the need for Japan to "adhere to the principle of absolute non-interference in the internal affairs of the Far Eastern Republic and desist from rendering assistance to the separate groups of the population in their inner struggles" and to set a definite date for the ending of the Japanese occupation. He added:

> Considering the fact that upon the territory of the Far Eastern Republic there is at present a Japanese diplomatic mission, the Government is kindly asking to be informed whether the Japanese Imperial Government will agree to receive our mission at Tokio upon the just principle of reciprocity with the aim to speedily establish political and economic relations based on such treaties that will be for the mutual benefit and friendship of both the Japanese and Russian peoples. We trust that this would speed the long hoped for day of mutual understanding and peaceful neighborly relations between the two peoples.[11]

In March Deputy Foreign Minister Kozhevnikov expressed the desire to proceed to Tokyo himself to exchange views with Foreign Office officials. At a time when Great Britain had already established relations with Soviet Russia and Italy was about to do so, it was a pity, he said, that Japan was not yet on friendly terms with the Far Eastern Republic.

The fact that the other powers were beginning to negotiate with Soviet Russia alarmed Tokyo. Germany too had concluded a trade agreement; Belgium, Sweden, Norway, Denmark, China and Italy were negotiating or preparing to negotiate; the United States and France which had participated in the intervention were not yet ready for official relations but they did not prohibit private commercial transactions; Great Britain was already studying conditions in the Chita region. There was mounting danger, if not certainty, the Japanese realized, that to continue to ignore Soviet overtures would leave Japan at a disadvantage in comparison with the other powers. The Soviets had created the Far Eastern Republic in order to approach Japan and they had made repeated offers for friendly relations; if Japan failed to deal with the Soviets before they reestablished their strength she might find American and British nationals in commanding economic positions.[12] Furthermore, Japan's continued occupation of Siberia had aroused mounting suspicion and antagonism in Europe and in the United States, and there was the possibility that Japan would be pressured into leaving without the opportunity to "stabilize the situation" if she delayed further in coming to an agreement with the Far Eastern Republic. Japan was particularly concerned over Chinese efforts to take advantage of Russia's weakness and difficulties to obtain from the Soviets the Chinese Eastern Railway as well as full control of the Sungari and Amur rivers. To protect her own interests in these regions Japan had to join hands with the actual authorities in Russia, rather than with impotent opposition groups.[13] Also by entering into negotiations with the Far Eastern Republic somewhere in Asia, she could avoid discussion of the evacuation question at the Washington Conference.[14]

On May 13, 1921, the Japanese cabinet agreed on the conditions for the withdrawal of Japanese forces and the establishment of commercial relations with the Far Eastern Republic: The government of the Far Eastern Republic was to put into effect east of the Selenga River the "propertied, democratic system" which it had already proclaimed; it was to refrain from radical propaganda in Korea and the Japanese homeland and to prevent acts by Koreans and other nationals in the Far Eastern Republic aimed at causing disturbances in Korea;[c] it was to respect the

---

[c] A Foreign Office spokesman expressed the fear that rebellious Koreans in and around Vladivostok might injure Japanese. He asserted that many Koreans were enlisted in the Bolshevik army and that "certain Koreans who were in collusion with the Bolsheviks had actually attempted an armed invasion of the Korean border and burned a Japanese Consulate." (Japanese Archives, MT 251.106.3: 647) Erich von Salzmann, representative of the *Kölnische Zeitung* and the Ullstein publishing house of Berlin, informed the Japanese in September of 1922 that according to the Soviet★

treaty rights of Japan and the life, property and vested rights of Japanese subjects including fishery rights and contracts between Japanese subjects and local governments; it was to give foreigners in general freedom of entry and exit as well as of residence and work and to allow them to own or to lease land in perpetuity; it was to dismantle fortifications and not construct military facilities threatening to Japan; it was to convert Vladivostok into a purely commercial port and was to make separate arrangements concerning the exchange of diplomatic personnel and military attachés and the establishment of trade. The question of measures connected with the Nikolaevsk incident was to be left for later discussion. Japan also desired access to the Amur and Sungari rivers, navigation of which was restricted to Russians and Chinese, and reannexation by the Far Eastern Republic of Kamchatka and other territory which it had ceded to Soviet Russia at the end of 1920.[15]

Continued Japanese protection, if not support, of "counterrevolutionary" bands prompted an intemperate letter from Ignatii L. Iurin, foreign minister of the Far Eastern Republic, to the Japanese foreign minister, dated June 2, 1921. Charging that "disorder in the Far Eastern Republic is evident only where there are Japanese troops, and where there are no Japanese troops one feels as safe as in America," Iurin posed five questions, to which he demanded "a straightforward and definite answer":

1. Do the Japanese Government and the Japanese people consider just the constant interference of the Japanese Command with Russian affairs against the will of the Russian people of the Far East?
2. Will the Japanese Government continue to help the criminals and brigands of the bands of Semenoff, Ungern etc., and put obstacles in the way of the authorities of the Far Eastern Republic in their struggle against those bandits?

*diplomat Rigin "the main object" of propaganda schools in Moscow, Tomsk, Omsk, Irkutsk and Tashkent was "to stir up Korea against Japanese rule." (Japanese Archives, MT 251.106.7: 2605)

3. Does the Japanese Government consider it necessary to establish friendly neighbourly relations with the Government of the Far Eastern Republic?
4. Does the Japanese Government consider it necessary to protect the interest of the Japanese merchants in the territory of the Far Eastern Republic in the only possible way, namely, to enter into a commercial treaty with the Government of the Far Eastern Republic?
5. Does the Japanese Government intend to withdraw from the territory of the Far Eastern Republic its army of occupation, the presence of which in Russian territory, [as] has been sufficiently proved during the last three years, has in no way helped to establish friendly relations nor to secure any privileges for Japanese residents, but on the contrary has been the source of a growing hatred toward Japan?[16]

When no reply ensued, Iurin wrote to the Japanese foreign minister:

> The disregard with which our note had been received, leaves no alternative but to conclude that the Japanese Government is prepared to acknowledge the misconduct of their officials, in which case, we are willing to dismiss the matter with indulgence, being sensible of the fact that the Japanese Government has been forced into a somewhat awkward position in this affair.
>
> At the same time we entertain earnest confidence that Japan will endeavour to find means to replace the irrational connections of to-day by cordial good-will and natural trust, instead of the animosity which has prevailed in the relations of the two people in recent years.

Iurin reiterated the desire of his government for business dealings with Japan. "It is no fault of ours that up to now we had been restrained by Japanese bayonets," he added. He called for the opening of direct negotiations in Chita or in Tokyo, whichever the Japanese government preferred.[17]

While Iurin pushed for direct talks in either capital, a number of meetings took place in Harbin from June 8 to July 20, 1921, between the Japanese Vice-Consul Shimada 島田 (Masaharu 正靖 of the Vladivostok Consulate General?) on one hand and Deputy Foreign Minister Kozhevnikov and Councilor Somov of the Far Eastern Republic on the other hand. According to Russian sources Shimada called on Kozhevnikov, who was passing through the city, and proposed the calling of a conference between representatives of the Japanese government and the Far Eastern Republic, a proposal that was accepted by the Russians.[18] According to Japanese sources it was the representatives of the Far Eastern Republic who took the initiative. They proposed mutual refraining from propaganda; the granting of land leases for about 60 years to Japanese subjects in the main cities of the Far Eastern Republic; the revision of the fishery agreement (during the Intervention the Japanese had greatly expanded their activity without permission); the granting of lumber and other concessions to Japan on North Sakhalin; purchase by the Far Eastern Republic of Japanese vessels on the Amur and Sungari rivers; the granting of a loan by Japan to the Far Eastern Republic; the surrender of Russian official residences, properties and vessels in Japan; the withdrawal of Japanese forces; and the convening of a conference at Dairen[d] on August 15 to negotiate an agreement on the basis of these points.

Since the proposal was close to Japanese thinking in a number of respects, Japan agreed to negotiations at Dairen. In accordance with a decision made by the cabinet and the Foreign Policy Research Board on July 12, Matsushima Hajime 松島肇, chief of the Political Affairs Section of the Vladivostok expeditionary force who had been in charge of civilian affairs at Vladivostok, was sent to Dairen to confer with the delegates of the Far Eastern Republic. Characteristically his mission was hidden from the Japanese public under the guise of a tour of inspection of Manchuria.[19] Matsushima had experience in dealing with Rus-

---

[d] Dairen 大連 is the Japanese name for Talien (Chinese); while in Russian hands (1898–1905), it was known as Dalny (Dal'nii).

sians and spoke the language. He had served in the Japanese embassy in St. Petersburg before the revolution, from 1908 to 1917, as attaché and second interpreter, then third, and eventually second secretary.

The Dairen Conference opened at the Yamato Hotel on August 26, 1921. Matsushima was assisted by Shimada, who had been involved in the preliminary talks at Harbin, and by General Takayanagi 高柳, chief of staff of the Japanese forces in the Russian Far East.[e] The Far Eastern Republic was represented briefly by Ignatii Iurin, its foreign minister and concurrently its representative in Peking, who arrived late because Japanese secret agents went through his luggage with meticulous care,[20] and then, from the beginning of September, by Dr. Fedor Nikolaevich Petrov, deputy chairman of the Council of Ministers of the Far Eastern Republic, assisted by Kozhevnikov and Anokhin.

Petrov was a physician and an old Communist. An active participant in the military uprising of 1905, he had been imprisoned in Warsaw for a year, had been confined to almost a decade of hard labor in the Shlisselburg fortress near St. Petersburg (1907–1915), then had been exiled "for life" to Siberia. A participant in the "February" and "October" revolutions, he had become deputy chairman of the Council of Ministers as well as Minister of Health and the Interior of the provisional government of the Far Eastern Republic in the autumn of 1920, and deputy chairman of the Council of Ministers (i.e. deputy prime minister) and member of the government of the permanent government of the republic in the spring of 1921.[f]

---

[e] According to Vasilii Konstantinovich Bliukher, who joined the conference.

[f] Later, from 1927 on, Dr. Petrov became intimately connected with the publication of *Bol'shaia sovetskaia entsiklopediia,* the big Soviet encyclopedia, and eventually was named director of the Sovetskaia Entsiklopediia Institute. His revolutionary outlook imbued his scholarship as it had his diplomacy. "The encyclopedia constitutes the strongest ideological weapon, reflecting the interests of the class which created it," Petrov wrote in his memoirs. Recalling the labor involved in "cleansing" the old scholarly data of its ideological foundations, Pavlov declared that scientific articles must "convey scientific information not only correctly but examine it also★

A hard-line revolutionary rather than a diplomat, Petrov found the situation at the conference "rather complicated." As he asserted in his memoirs, the Japanese diplomatic service resorted to "blackmail, threats, slander, and a highhanded disdainful attitude toward its partner [in the negotiations]." "Matsushima, the leader of the Japanese delegation, was an old, experienced diplomat," Petrov stated. "Small of stature, with sly, shifty eyes and a smile which appeared and disappeared on his face as if by order, he knew how to present the most impudent proposals in a deceivingly mild form...."[21]

Almost at once the negotiators were at loggerheads. It was the position of the Far Eastern Republic that Japan withdraw her forces from Siberia before any agreement was concluded. The Japanese, on the other hand, demanded the conclusion of a treaty prior to evacuation. On September 6 the representatives of the Far Eastern Republic presented a draft agreement of twenty-nine articles in which they made the compromise proposal that the Japanese begin their withdrawal at once but complete it within one month after the signature of the agreement. The draft read:

> The government of the Far Eastern Republic on one hand and the Imperial Japanese Government on the other hand, moved by the mutual desire for the development and strengthening of friendly and good-neighborly relations between the Japanese and Russian peoples and for the strengthening and growth of economic relations, have decided to conclude an agreement of peace, friendship and trade on the foundations of reciprocity, equal rights, justice and mutual benefits, as well as on the basis of full reciprocal recognition of the supreme prerogatives and sovereignty of each of the states on the expanse of its entire territory and have appointed for this purpose as their representatives:

---

*from the standpoint of dialectical materialism." (F. N. Petrov, *65 let v riadakh Leninskoi partii. Vospominaniia* [65 years in the ranks of Lenin's party. Memoirs] [Moscow, 1962], pp. 139–40.

HIS MAJESTY THE EMPEROR OF JAPAN

THE GOVERNMENT OF THE FAR EASTERN REPUBLIC

who, empowered upon reciprocal communication of their powers, recognized as having been drawn up in the appropriate and legal manner, have stipulated and concluded the following articles:

ARTICLE I

Let there be permanent peace between the Government of the Far Eastern Republic and the Imperial Japanese Government, as well as between the Japanese and Russian peoples in the Far East without any exception for places or persons.

ARTICLE II

The Government of Japan and the Far Eastern Republic have agreed, on the basis of the principle of the recognition of the sovereign rights of each people to its territories, not to interfere in the affairs of the opposite party. The two Governments commit themselves not to allow in their territory the existence and activity of any kind of groups and organizations pretending to the role of Government as well as groups having as their objective the overthrow of the Government of the other party.

ARTICLE III

The citizens of the Far Eastern Republic and of Japan have the right of free arrival, travel and residence at any place whatever in the territory of the other contracting party, subject to the observance of its laws, both for purposes of trade, profession and earning as well as for their personal needs.

ARTICLE IV

The personal safety and inviolability of property of the citizens of Japan staying in the Far Eastern Republic and of citizens of the

Far Eastern Republic staying in the territory of Japan will always be under the patronage and protection of the laws of each of the said states.

ARTICLE V

The citizens of Japan have the right in the entire territory of the Far Eastern Republic and the citizens of the Far Eastern Republic in the entire territory of Japan to engage unhindered in their professions as well as to trade freely in all objects in which trade is permitted.

ARTICLE VI

Citizens of Japan departing for any purposes for the Far Eastern Republic and citizens of the Far Eastern Republic departing for the territory of Japan must have with them passports for foreign travel, issued by the [legally] constituted authorities, certifying their citizenship. When citizens of Japan proceed to the Far Eastern Republic and back the passports must be visaed by consuls.

ARTICLE VII

The citizens of the Far Eastern Republic during their residence in the territory of Japan and the citizens of Japan during their residence in the territory of the Far Eastern Republic enjoy the rights of the free profession of their religious and political convictions.

ARTICLE VIII

Each of the contracting parties has the right to have in the territory of the other, where it considers it of benefit for the interests of its citizens and trade, its consular representatives, consuls general, viceconsuls and consular agents. Until such time as a special agreement is concluded between the contracting parties the consular service is regulated by the standards customary in international relations and international practice.

ARTICLE IX

In criminal and civil cases the citizens of the two contracting parties are subject to the court of the country, in the territory of which the given case has arisen.

ARTICLE X

The Governments of the contracting parties mutually stipulate the inviolability of person of the citizens of one of the contracting parties during the entire period of their stay in the territory of the other. The citizens of either party may be arrested during their residence in the alien territory only by order of the appropriate judicial establishment and only upon accusation of having committed a criminal act. Every arrest must be reported to the nearest consul within 24 hours.

ARTICLE XI

The contracting parties pledge in the near future, not later than two months from the day of the signature of the present agreement, to call together a conference of its representatives for the working out of a special agreement about the extradition of persons, who having been prosecuted or convicted for specific crimes, committed in the territory of one of the contracting parties, take refuge in the territory of the other party.

ARTICLE XII

There must be free trade and navigation between the possessions of the contracting parties.

ARTICLE XIII

The citizens of the Far Eastern Republic in the territory of Japan and the citizens of Japan in the territory of the Far Eastern Republic are subject to any sort of state, provincial and municipal duties and taxes connected with the character of their activity.

The citizens of the contracting parties must not be forced to pay other or higher taxes than those that are paid at the given time or in the future will be paid by native citizens.

ARTICLE XIV

For the purpose of working out a mutually beneficial customs tariff the Governments of the contracting parties have agreed to the immediate establishment of a mixed commission for the working out of a tariff and of general decisions concerning the application of customs regulations, whose decisions, upon proper confirmation by both Governments will have force as supplementary articles to this agreement.

ARTICLE XV

In those localities of the contracting Governments where a considerable number of their citizens are concentrated, the [above-] mentioned persons can, in full compliance with local laws, establish their commercial and industrial associations, open stock exchanges, chambers of commerce, trade and other unions, clubs and schools for their compatriots.

ARTICLE XVI

The governments of the contracting parties mutually pledge to grant the right of free entry of the commercial vessels of one party into all open ports of the other. Not one of the vessels of the Far Eastern Republic in the ports of Japan nor one of the vessels of Japan in the ports of the Far Eastern Republic nor their cargo and ship's property can under any conditions and circumstances be subject to detainment or seizure.

ARTICLE XVII

The Governments of the contracting parties have stipulated the formation of a special commission of representatives of the contracting parties for the detailed working out of regulations governing the sailing of vessels between the ports of the contracting parties. The time for [its] formation will be determined by mutual agreement between the Governments, but [will be] not later than three months from the day of the signature of this agreement.

ARTICLE XVIII

The contracting parties have agreed to the immediate opening of post-and-telegraph communications between Japan and the Soviet Union and for their regulation to form immediately upon signature of this agreement a commission of representatives of both states. For the purpose of regulating questions connected with the sending of correspondence both to the Russian Soviet Federated Socialist Republic from Japan and the other way around, to propose at the conference of the commission that representatives of the Russian Soviet Federated Socialist Republic participate also.

ARTICLE XIX

The Governments of Japan and the Far Eastern Republic, upon signature of the present agreement, have to begin the immediate joint discussion of a commercial treaty on the principles laid down in the present agreement.

ARTICLE XX

The Governments of Japan and the Far Eastern Republic have decided to begin at once revision of the fishery conventions. Since these conventions were concluded between the Government of Japan and the Imperial Government of Russia and since the Russian Soviet Federated Socialist Republic is interested in them, the Governments of the contracting parties consider essential the participation of representatives of Soviet Russia in the contemplated conferences.

ARTICLE XXI

Recognizing the principle of the Open Door, the Government of the Far Eastern Republic will show full cooperation to all Japanese enterprisers in granting them concessions on bases mutually beneficial to both parties, on condition that the laws of the country be observed.

ARTICLE XXII

The Imperial Japanese Government immediately begins to withdraw its forces from the territory of the Far Eastern Republic and completes this withdrawal during the period technically required for the completion of the evacuation, but not later than one month from the day of the signature of the present agreement.

ARTICLE XXIII

It has been agreed that the two Governments of Japan and the Far Eastern Republic will appoint their representatives who will have the responsibility of assisting the evacuation of the Japanese forces, the preservation and transfer intact to the legal[ly constitued] authorities of the property belonging to the Far Eastern Republic.

ARTICLE XXIV

The Governments of the contracting parties take measures for the prompt establishment of normal diplomatic relations. The Governments pledge to conclude the negotiations concerning the establishment of regular diplomatic missions within a period of three months.

ARTICLE XXV

The present agreement is enacted for ten years from the day of the exchange of ratifications; if six months before the terms of this agreement neither contracting party expresses the desire for any changes in it or [for any] additions, all present stipulations remain in force for another decade.

ARTICLE XXVI

Each contracting party pledges to recognize and respect the flag and emblem [*gerb*] of the other party as the emblem [*emblem*] of a friendly state. The design of the flag and emblem, as well as changes in them, should they follow, will be communicated reciprocally through diplomatic channels.

ARTICLE XXVII

The decision of all commissions, formed on the basis of the given agreement will, upon confirmation by both Governments, have force as supplementary articles of the present treaty.

ARTICLE XXVIII

Concerning all questions, in connection with which the supplementing or elaboration of any stipulations of this treaty is required, the above-mentioned parties may upon mutual agreement conclude articles supplementary to this [treaty].

ARTICLE XXIX

This treaty must be ratified by the two high contracting parties in compliance with their respective constitutions and the ratifications must be exchanged in the city of Tokyo as soon as possible, but not later than one month from this day. In witness whereof we, the undersigned, by virtue of our respective powers have signed this treaty in two copies, each in the Russian language, and have attached our respective seals.
Done in two copies in the city of Dairen, the . . . day of the . . . month of the year 1921.

Signed. . . .
Signed. . . .[22]

The Japanese refused to commit themselves to a specific time limit for their evacuation. They proposed an amendment of the article which would have left the time of withdrawal at their own discretion. When the delegates of the Far Eastern Republic rejected this, the Japanese asked for a two-week recess.[23]

In late September or early October[g] the Japanese presented to the representatives of the Far Eastern Republic a counter-draft, phrased in 17 public articles—hence commonly called "the Seventeen Demands"—and 3 secret articles. The Japanese draft embodied the conditions for withdrawal decided upon at the cabinet meeting of May 13; it went further in demanding a pledge that the Far Eastern Republic would never keep any naval forces in the Pacific and scrap those vessels which it had, that North Sakhalin be leased to Japan for a period of 80 years as compensation for the Nikolaevsk incident, and that the Far Eastern Republic remain strictly neutral in the event of a conflict between Japan and a third power (be it even Soviet Russia).

Japan's policy in Siberia was a reflection of Japanese policy toward China. The Seventeen Demands were similar in tone to the infamous Twenty-one Demands which sought to convert the Chinese Republic into a Japanese satellite. When they became public knowledge later, the *North China Star* proclaimed that they unveiled "the true designs of Japanese militarism in no lesser degree than the 21 points presented by them to China, and no State, unless it openly agrees to become a colony of Japan, will ever accept them." So important were they as an indicator of Japanese ambitions, that they deserve to be quoted in full:

[g] Russian sources and studies based on Russian sources say October. (See, for example, *Diplomaticheskii slovar'*, vol. I, p. 419; Xenia Joukoff Eudin and Robert C. North, *Soviet Russia and the East 1920–1927. A Documentary Survey* (Stanford: Stanford University Press, 1957), p. 134; and John A. White, *The Siberian Intervention* (Princeton: Princeton University Press, 1950), p. 411. But Japanese sources specifically state September 26. (Japan, Gaimushō [Foreign Office], *Nihon gaikō nempyō narabi ni shuyō bunsho* 日本外交年表竝主要文書 (Chronology and main documents of Japanese diplomacy) (Tokyo, 1965), vol. I, p. 253; Tanaka Bunichirō 田中文一郎, *Nisso Koshō-shi* 日ソ交渉史 (History of Negotiations between Japan and the Soviet Union) (Tokyo: Foreign Office, Europe and Asia Bureau, 1942), vol. IIIA, pp. 47-48.

THE DAIREN CONFERENCE

1. The government of the Far Eastern Republic shall convert Vladivostok into a purely commercial port, placing it under foreign control and taking no measures interfering with trade.
2. The two governments bind themselves, after signing this treaty, to review the Russo-Japanese fishing convention, increasing the rights of Japanese fishers and extending the rights of Japanese in Russian coastwise trade.
3. The two governments bind themselves, immediately on the signing of this treaty, to reach an agreement concerning postal and telegraph connections.
4. The two governments mutually recognize freedom of trade, communications, and navigation, and will not place citizens or ships of the other government in a less favorable position than those of a third nation. Details in this connection shall be specified in a separate agreement on trade and navigation.
5. Both contracting sides bind themselves to conclude, on the signing of this treaty, an agreement concerning tariff regulations and tariff duties, on the basis of Article 4.
6. Citizens of each country, living in the other, shall have the right of protection for their persons and inviolability of their property, and shall not be placed in a less favorable position than citizens of the other government or of a third government.
7. Citizens of each country may engage on the territory of the other in commerce, industry, manufacturing, handicrafts, professional and other occupations, and shall not be placed in a less favorable position as regards trade and industry than citizens of the other government or of a third government; as concerns industries, professions and trade, they shall be in the same position as citizens of a third government.
8. Citizens of each country shall have the right of entering the territory of the other and of freely traveling and living in

the other country in accordance with its laws. On entering the other country national passports must be presented.

9. Each country binds itself not to carry on hostilities against the other, and to abstain from any propaganda which might be dangerous to the other, and to take steps to prevent the entrance to the other country and the activity of all organizations attempting to carry on activities hostile to the other country. The procedure for turning over such persons to the other country shall be determined in a special agreement.

10. The government of the Far Eastern Republic guarantees the Japanese government that it will never introduce the communistic regime on its territory and will always maintain the principle of private property not only in connection with Japanese subjects but also with its own citizens.

11. Recognizing the principle of the Open Door, the government of the Far Eastern Republic must rescind in connection with Japanese subjects all restrictions existing on its territory, and not establish such restrictions in the future, concerning the mining industry, agriculture, the timber industry, or, in general, concerning any extracting industry, and shall give to Japanese subjects freedom in trade and industry, putting them in the same position as its own citizens, and the Far Eastern Republic also binds itself to allow Japanese subjects the right of owning land and full freedom in coastwise trade under the Japanese flag.

The government of the Far Eastern Republic binds itself to allow to Japanese subjects freedom of navigation on the Amur River under the Japanese flag and agrees to declare to the Chinese government its desire that Japanese subjects be given the rights of navigation on the Sungari River under the Japanese flag. This article applies only to Japanese subjects, and the rights acquired hereunder may not be extended to other foreigners.

THE DAIREN CONFERENCE

12. Each country shall send to the other its representatives with the rights of legation, and shall establish points for the residence of consuls.
13. Both governments recognize the treaties and conventions existing between the Japanese government and the old Russian government, and both governments agree that all rights acquired by citizens of the other government before the signing of this treaty shall remain as they are.
14. The government of the Far Eastern Republic [obliges] itself to take down and if necessary blow up all forts and fortifications along the whole Pacific coast, in the region of Vladivostock and along the Korean border, and never to re-establish these, and also to undertake no military operations in the regions bordering on Korea and Manchuria.

    The government of the Far Eastern Republic must admit the official residence and travel of special Japanese military missions and of individual Japanese military officers throughout its whole territory.

    The government of the Far Eastern Republic obliges itself never to maintain a naval fleet in the Pacific and to destroy the existing fleet.
15. In settling the Nikolaievsk question, the government of the Far Eastern Republic binds itself to give to the Japanese Government the northern half of Sakhalin as a lease for eighty years, as compensation of the losses suffered by Japanese subjects at the time of the Nikolaievsk incident.
16. The present treaty shall be effective from the moment of its ratification by the two contracting governments and remain in force until the conclusion in the future of a perpetual treaty.
17. The present treaty shall be drawn up in both the Russian and Japanese languages, both of which shall be considered official.

SECRET ARTICLES

1. In case of an armed conflict between Japan and a third power, the government of the Far Eastern Republic binds itself to observe strict neutrality.
2. The Japanese government will evacuate its troops from the Maritime Province at the time which in its own judgment will be convenient, when this shall be necessary.
3. The evacuation of Sakhalin will take place after the northern half of the island has actually been received in lease according to Article 15 of the treaty.[24,h]

The public articles did not stipulate any time for the withdrawal of the Japanese forces. At first the Japanese had wished to make no mention of the subject at all. It was their attitude that they had intervened with the noblest of intentions and would withdraw with similar goodwill. A secret clause eventually left the matter to the discretion and convenience of the Japanese. In vain the Japanese negotiators tried to reassure the representatives of the Far Eastern Republic about the deletion of a definite date for the evacuation of Siberia, asserting that once a general agreement had been concluded the Japanese forces would withdraw voluntarily, since with the conclusion of the agreement the menace to Korea and to Japanese residents and transportation would have been removed; all that would be needed then would be a military agreement to make the necessary arrangements for withdrawal.

The Japanese had in mind the evacuation of mainland territory; they did not envisage withdrawal from North Sakhalin, which, as stated, was to be leased for eighty years. Any talk about Sakhalin and Kamchatka was complicated, of course, by the fact that it was questionable whether the authority of the Far Eastern Republic extended to these regions. Nor could the delegates of the Far Eastern Republic make commitments concerning fishery and economic matters affecting Soviet Russia.[25]

[h] English wording received by U.S. State Department from Tokyo through official channels.

Negotiations at Dairen were soon deadlocked and virtually halted for a month. On November 6 Iakov Davidovich Ianson, who had succeeded Iurin as minister of foreign affairs of the Far Eastern Republic, wrote a letter to the foreign minister of Japan in which he reiterated the desire of his government to create amicable commercial intercourse between the two countries. But he decried the continuance of "brutal activities" on the part of "counter-revolutionary Russian organizations" in Japanese-held territory and noted that his government was "forced to hold responsible for it, though indirectly, the Japanese Military Command, who by maintaining the expeditionary army in the Maritime Privince and by the support and protection extended to the Russian White Guard organizations operating in that Province create the possibility for the violations committed against the peaceful Russian population to remain unpunished." "The Government of the Far Eastern Republic believes," Ianson concluded, "that the negotiations now proceeding at Dairen may be brought to a mutually favorable conclusion and may lead to the establishment of friendly [?] economic relations between the contracting parties only on the actual evacuation of the Japanese troops from the territory of the Far Eastern Republic, the Japanese Government thus proving the sincerity of her friendly intentions toward the Far Eastern Republic."[26]

The same day, on November 6, the Russian side suggested the resumption of the Dairen talks with Soviet participation in the discussion of fishery and other economic questions. On November 12 General Vasilii Konstantinovich Bliukher, commander-in-chief and minister of war of the Far Eastern Republic, arrived to advise Petrov; discussions were resumed on the 14th.[27,i]

Matsushima had stated that the matter of evacuation would have to

---

[i] Bliukher (spelled also Blücher, alias Galin, Galen and Galents) later was to play an important role in Chiang K'ai-shek's conquest of northern China; in 1929 he commanded the Eastern Special Army of the Soviet Union in the war with China over the Chinese Eastern Railway. He was dismissed during the purges of 1937–38 and "mysteriously disappeared." [Eudin and North, p. 457].

be worked out by the military. With the arrival of Bliukher the experts of the two sides met, but the Japanese generals, according to Petrov, were even more "arrogant" than their diplomats. "They did not even want to hear out our representatives, but met merely to dictate their demands." Under the circumstances it seemed useless to continue the meetings of the military experts and Bliukher soon returned to take command of military operations of the "People's Revolutionary Army" against the interventionists and white forces. "Your military are not inclined to negotiate," Petrov told Matsushima. "They prefer to fight. Our commander-in-chief has decided to give them the opportunity. You and we both will be waiting for good news."[28]

On November 27 Petrov requested deletion of the three secret clauses from the Japanese demands, and presented revised and supplementary articles. On December 5, when the Japanese notified him that they were about to relieve a part of the Vladivostok expeditionary force, he tried to get a commitment concerning complete evacuation and sought to settle the Nikolaevsk incident by giving to Japan industrial concessions in North Sakhalin. He took the opportunity to demand once more the participation of a representative of Soviet Russia on the fishery commission.[29] That day, on December 5, Iulian Iuzefovich Markhlevskii arrived in Dairen. A Polish Communist (his name was also spelled Marchlewski), he had a Ph. D. in economics from the University of Zürich. He had assisted Lenin in the establishment of the Marxist paper *Iskra* and had been a leader in the Communist movements in Poland and Germany. An agent of the Comintern, he was assigned to various important negotiations by the Soviet government.[j]

The Japanese had refused to admit a regular delegate from Soviet Russia, and Markhlevskii came ostensibly as an observer. What the Japanese did not know was that from the moment of his arrival the delegates of the Far Eastern Republic were surbordinate to him. The Central Committee of the Russian Communist Party had decreed at its

---

[j] Markhlevskii remained truly international until his very end. He died in 1925 in Italy and was buried in Germany; in 1950 his body was moved to Poland.

meeting of November 28, 1921: "From the moment of the arrival of Comrade Markhlevskii in Dairen, complete guidance of the negotiations is to be surrendered to him, regardless of the fact whether or not he will be admitted officially to the conference."[30] Official dispatches to Ianson were sent in the joint names of Markhlevskii and Petrov.

Petrov in his memoirs describes his relationship with Markhlevskii, an old friend from the days of his revolutionary activity in Warsaw, as follows:

> With Iu. Iu. Markhlevskii we discussed all points of our and the Japanese treaty drafts and with the aid of ciphers constantly consulted with the People's Commissar for Foreign Affairs G. V. Chicherin. In such a way the representatives of the People's Commissar for Foreign Affairs of the R.S.F.S.R. took an active part in the Dairen Conference.[31]

Insufficient data is available to determine the precise impact of the change in leadership on the Russian position at the Dairen Conference. Markhlevskii does seem to have bolstered opposition to Japanese demands. By February 20, 1922, the negotiations were deadlocked again.[32]

The Japanese seemed reluctant to give up the many rights which they had obtained during and after the First World War.

> Joker lies in article two [five?] [the correspondent of the *Chicago Tribune* wired on December 24, 1921], for this includes certain unspecified secret agreements with Kerensky, Kolchak and Merkuloff governments which believed give Japanese preferential rights maritime province also providing return money Japan advanced wherewith waged warfare against Chita government. It is over this article that hardest battle occurred. Great secrecy over this but reported deal entire Japanese method keeping province upset by playing financing one faction against other obtaining treaty promises in return.[33]

The failure of anti-Communist elements whom the Japanese supported to halt the advance of the Red Army on Vladivostok prompted the Japanese government after considerable deliberation to make another effort to come to an agreement with the Far Eastern Republic. On March 20, 1922, Foreign Minister Uchida cabled Matsushima to resume talks.

Before the end of the month full accord had been reached on the general agreement.[34] Its 16 articles were a great improvement over the Seventeen Demands. The full text of the "Trade and General Agreement," as the document was entitled, was as follows:

PREAMBLE

The Imperial Japanese government and the government of the Far Eastern Republic, desiring to establish between the two nations peaceful trade relations, as well as the development of economic and other intercourse, and realizing that it is necessary to conclude a preliminary agreement between the two governments prior to the conclusion in the future of a formal treaty defining the economic and the political relations between the two peoples, it was agreed to fix the following clauses:

I

Each of the high contracting parties undertakes to respect the sovereignty of the other, not to undertake hostile operations against one another, not to interfere in one another's affairs and not to carry on propaganda, direct or indirect, outside the borders of its own territory which might threaten the established order of State; each undertakes to take the necessary steps to prevent admission to its territory of any person or group of persons, and to disrupt all organizations and activity of such persons, groups and organizations aiming at the destruction of the existing order of things in the territory of the other.

II

The subjects or citizens of each of the high contracting parties have the right, in accordance with the laws of the given country, to stay, travel or to live within the borders of the other's territory.

Subjects or citizens of each of the high contracting parties intending to go to the territory of the other shall be provided with the passports issued by his or her country, issued by the proper authorities and must obtain visé of the representatives of the other country.

III

Subjects or citizens of each of the high contracting parties staying or residing within the territory of the other shall enjoy the full protection of the law of the country regarding personal safety and the inviolability of property on an equal footing with the subjects or citizens of that country or the subjects and citizens of a third country.

IV

Subjects or citizens of each of the high contracting parties shall enjoy full liberty as to religious practices and liberty of conscience, while in the territory of the other, in accordance with the laws of the country.

V

Subjects or citizens of each of the high contracting parties have the right to engage in commerce, trade, industry, and professions in the territory of the other and in the case of commerce and industry, subjects or citizens of each of the high contracting parties within the territory of the other shall enjoy all existing laws or such laws as may be enacted relating thereto on an equal footing with subjects or citizens of the most favored nation. Those engaged in the professions and trades shall be on an equal footing with the subjects or citizens of a third country. This article does not infringe upon the rights which are or may be granted to subjects or citizens of a country bound by convention with either of the high contracting parties.

VI

The governments of the two countries simultaneously recognize the laws of trade, communication and navigation existing in each other's country and each side agrees not to treat the subjects or citizens and vessels of the other country in an inferior manner to treatment given the subjects or citizens and vessels of any third country.

The governments of the two countries bind themselves immediately upon the signing of this agreement to conclude a pact relating to subjects of trade communication and navigation as well as tariffs and customs rules based upon the most favorable principles. This article does not apply to the rights now granted or which may be granted to subjects or citizens of any country now bound by an economic convention to either of the high contracting parties.

VII

The government of the Far Eastern Republic agrees to revise and improve those of the existing port rules at Vladivostok and other conditions which hinder trade and navigation.

VIII

The governments of the high contracting parties bind themselves, immediately upon the signing of this agreement, to reach an understanding about the opening of postal and telegraphic communications between the two countries.

IX

The governments of the high contracting parties bind themselves to begin negotiations, immediately upon the signing of this agreement, with the intention of revising the Russo-Japanese Fishing Convention and the conclusion of a temporary pact replacing the above-mentioned convention, having agreed to cancel those clauses detrimental to the fishing industry of both countries, inasmuch as this does not interfere with the aims of guarding the living wealth of the waters, as well as to add to the convention such clauses as might benefit the fishing industry of both countries and the successful protection of the waters.

The Government of the Far Eastern Republic also agrees to discuss the question regarding the granting to the Japanese vessels of the right of coast navigation in so far as it is necessary for the promotion of the fishing industry, based on the above-mentioned item in this clause.

X

The Far Eastern Republic will recognize the principle of the open door, and will abolish, for Japanese subjects, the restrictions which have hitherto been imposed on foreigners in regard to mining, forestry, agriculture, industry, commerce and other occupations within its borders, nor will it impose such restrictions again in future. It will grant the right of land leasehold for a period not exceedingly 36 years, and will also agree to the participation of Japanese subjects in companies engaged in coastwise trade of 'the Far Eastern Republic.'

XI

The governments of the two high contracting parties will enter into negotiations with a view to revising all pacts, conventions and agreements concluded between the Imperial Japanese government and former recognized Russian governments.

The governments of the high contracting parties are binding themselves to recognize all rights which were acquired by subjects or citizens of both parties in the same form as at present, provided these rights do not, by virtue of their nature or the circumstances of acquisition, conflict with the laws of the land where they originated.

Rights acquired by the Japanese subjects, as from August 26 to the moment of the extension of the jurisdiction of the Far Eastern Republic over the territory remaining during this period outside its sphere of influence are not to be recognized.

XII

The governments of the high contracting parties may send to the territory of the other representatives and persons responsible to them who will enjoy the rights of diplomatic representatives. The governments may also send to one another's territory such persons as will fulfil the functions of consuls and will enjoy such special rights as defined by International Law. Details of the number and places of residence of such representatives will be arranged by special agreement between the two governments.

XIII

The articles of this agreement are to come into force from the moment of signature of the same and continue until the conclusion of a formal treaty as indicated in the preamble of this agreement.

XIV

All arrangements entered into and based on this agreement and all documents attached thereto as additional clauses are considered as having the same force as this agreement.

XV

In case of the necessity of explaining any circumstances relating to this agreement, the governments of the high contracting parties may by mutual consent conclude additional clauses to this agreement.

XVI

This agreement is drawn up in both Japanese and Russian languages and in its interpretation both texts are authentic.[35,k]

---

[k] The text of the entire agreement was made public by V. G. Antonov of Dal'ta. The Japanese Foreign Office agreed that the text was accurate, except for article X. The Japanese version of article X has been used here. The Russian version read: *

Petrov rejected Japanese demands for joint Japanese-Russian enterprises on the Sungari and Amur rivers on the grounds that this would have been in violation of the Treaty of Aigun of 1858 which allowed navigation on these rivers to Russians and Chinese only. In their report to Ianson, dated March 27, 1922, Petrov and Markhlevskii wrote that the Japanese wished to conclude also various other agreements pertaining to China, if only the Russians would be willing to talk to them about these questions "openly and full of trust." The contention that Russia recognized the sovereignty of the Chinese republic and would not discuss such matters without Chinese representation evoked only derogatory remarks about the Chinese from the Japanese delegation, according to an interview later given by Markhlevskii in Shanghai.[36]

Petrov repeated the demand that Soviet Russia be represented on the fishery commission. He proposed simultaneous signature of the general agreement and such agreements as the evacuation of Japanese forces from the Maritime Province and North Sakhalin and the settlement of the Nikolaevsk incident. He also asked that a military commission be set up to review the situation in the Maritime Province.

Meanwhile new instructions from Foreign Minister Uchida, dated March 27, reached Matsushima. He was to show the Russian representatives a draft military agreement which allegedly had taken the interests of the Far Eastern Republic into consideration both in the matter of the

* The government of the Far Eastern Republic, notwithstanding the laws of the Republic, will grant to Japanese subjects concessions of mining and forest industries and others on conditions favorable to both parties subject to the observance of the laws of the country. In its efforts to develop coastwise shipping, the Far Eastern Republic will grant to Japanese subjects the right to participate in Russian companies.

The Foreign Office spokesman claimed that the Russian version was proposed to make it appear that the Japanese wanted vested rights in Siberia. ". . . what was really Chita's proposition, which has not been acceded to by Japan, was published as Japan's, and moreover in a manner to make it appear as if it were one which had been rejected by Chita. This is proof of the extent to which Chita has not scrupled to go in falsification and propaganda." (*Japan Advertiser*, April 22, 1922).

disposition of confiscated arms and railroad work equipment and in the reduction in the Japanese defense area; at the same time he was to warn the Russian representatives that Japan would break off the talks unless the basic and the military agreements were signed by April 15. Armed with these instructions, Matsushima explained the Japanese conditions on March 30, and conveyed the threat of terminating the talks.

Japanese willingness to promise withdrawal from the Maritime Province within three months of the signing of an evacuation agreement was accompanied by too many qualifications to satisfy the Russians. (One reporter labeled the draft military agreement a "truly Asian document.") The most ominous qualification was that the time fixed for the beginning of the evacuation was to be calculated from the moment when arrangements had been completed by a joint commission of military experts in the face of the fact that no time limit had been set for the work of the commission.[37] The Russian representatives insisted that they would not sign a general agreement unless Japan promised to evacuate North Sakhalin by the end of the current navigation season and would not oppose the entry of the forces of the Far Eastern Republic into Vladivostok.[38]

At the sessions on April 1 and 3 the representatives of the Far Eastern Republic presented to Matsushima the revised draft of a military agreement, a draft document stating that the Japanese would not obstruct entry of the forces of the Far Eastern Republic into Vladivostok, a draft document concerning private property, a draft protocol stating that the Japanese forces would be withdrawn from North Sakhalin by the end of the navigation season, and a draft statement concerning the dismantling of fortifications. Although the officials of the Far Eastern Republic expressed the wish to conclude all agreements within five days, after prolonged discussion the two sides could agree only on the draft concerning private property and the draft concerning the fortifications.

On April 5 the imperial government decided at a cabinet meeting to break off negotiations if the Far Eastern Republic did not bow to Japanese demands by April 15, the deadline previously announced. The various units of the expeditionary force were to be relieved as scheduled.[1] The

The 8th and 11th divisions were duly exchanged that month.

government would bide its time to await changes in the Far Eastern situation and withdraw its forces at a favorable opportunity.

On April 6 and 9 the Japanese made a last effort to persuade the Russians to accept the Japanese terms, but the Russians objected to the indefinite ending of the Japanese occupation; they insisted that the Japanese agree to withdraw from the Maritime Province within 45 days from the signing of the basic agreement.

When it became clear that the conference would founder over the evacuation issue, the Japanese side suddenly introduced modifications in the provisions of the trade and general agreement, so that the breakdown could be attributed technically to dispute over the latter. "The modifications, as far as can be made out," the *Peking Daily News* observed, "raised whole questions of principle that had as a matter of fact already been agreed upon, and that they should have been raised at all suggests that they were raised merely as an excuse for the breaking-off of the negotiations, and to save the reputation of the militarist dictators of Japan, who had been unable to support the idea of a prompt evacuation of the Maritime Province."[39]

On April 15 the delegates of the Far Eastern Republic rejected the Japanese demand that they accept all of their proposals and tossed back the ultimatum; if the Japanese failed to respond favourably to their demands within 24 hours, they would leave. The following day the delegates of the Far Eastern Republic proposed to extend the time period for Japanese evacuation from 45 to 50 days and to do so (as a face saver) by secret agreement. Matsushima rejected this and pronounced the conference terminated. Petrov and his delegation left that very night for the north. The Japanese delegates politely bowed them off at the railway station, then departed themselves on the 20th.[40]

The Dairen Conference had failed for a number of reasons. With a general to "assist" Matsushima, the Japanese chief delegate's hands may have been tied, for the military were determined to stay in the Russian Far East. Certainly the changing complexion of the Far Eastern Republic had been a major factor. As long as the republic had appeared to be a democratic, non-Communist creation, there had been hope that it might accept the Japanese demand that Communism be kept out of Siberia, but as it turned obviously red, it became plain that the Japanese demand would never be accepted and that the negotiations were doomed to failure.[41] The Russians made little effort to hide the fact that the Far Eastern Republic was the mouthpiece of Moscow. As Mikhail Krichevskii wrote concerning the rupture of negotiations in the Soviet journal *Mezhdunarodnaia zhizn'* (International life) in May of 1922, the lengthy conference between the representatives of Japan and the representatives of the Far Eastern Republic "had in fact been a conference between Japan and Soviet Russia." He remarked that it was evident from the polemics in the Japanese press that this had been realized not only by the Far Eastern Republic but also by Japan.[42]

It was said that when Matsushima bade farewell to Petrov he expressed surprise that such a small state as the Far Eastern Republic had rejected the proposals of a great power like Japan, for Japan herself had accepted the demands of greater powers at the Washington Conference with little discussion. Petrov had allegedly replied that behind the Far Eastern Republic stood Soviet Russia, which was as great a power as those whose demands Japan had accepted at Washington.[43]

Both sides blamed each other for the collapse of the Dairen Conference, which, with some interruptions, had continued for eight months. Pointing the finger at the Far Eastern Republic, a Japanese Foreign Office spokesman asserted that her demand for a fixed time limit for the complete withdrawal of Japanese troops implied "unwarranted distrust."

> Whereas Japan has . . . throughout the negotiations maintained a sincere and conciliatory attitude [the Foreign Office official declared], the Chita delegate entirely ignored the spirit in which she offered concessions and brought up one demand after another, thereby trying to gain time. Not only did he refuse to entertain Japanese proposals, but declared that he would drop the negotiations and return to Chita immediately.
>
> The only conclusion from this attitude of the Chita Govern-

ment being that they lacked the sincerity with which to try to bring the negotiations to fruition, the Japanese Government have instructed their delegate to quit Dairen.[44]

The Russians did not deny their mistrust of the Japanese; they thought it warranted, however. "The methods of the Japanese command in the occupied region," V. G. Antonov, Tokyo manager of Dal'ta (Far Eastern Telegraph Agency), the official organ of the Far Eastern Republic, declared on April 21, "made the Far Eastern Republic government distrustful of vague assurances that evacuation would take place 'as soon as possible.' "[45] When the Japanese negotiators, visibly offended by Russian mistrust, spoke of samurai honor and pride, the Russians responded that samurai pride could not take the place of a document in international relations.[46]

Many Japanese failed to understand Russian mistrust; they really believed that their occupation of Russian territory was a worthy and unselfish cause and not an imperialistic scheme. A statement issued by the Japanese on January 7, 1922, reflected their exasperation:

> Japan, retaining her troops in Eastern Siberia from the sheer necessity of self-protection, strictly maintains neutrality in regard to Russian domestic strifes, and as repeatedly stated in the declarations of the Imperial Government, it is their desire that the time will soon come when the local political condition recovering itself they may be enabled to evacuate there. It is complexing beyond comprehension that in spite of this state of things, there should be Russians, who, whenever anything occurs that may prove disadvantageous to their party or faction insinuatingly find fault with the attitude of Japan, the more reckless of them going the length of making mischievous propaganda against her on the strength of nothing more authentic than pure fabrications.
>
> When in May last year, a political upheaval occured in Vladivostok, sweeping away the influence of the Chita Government, rumor was set afloat alleging that the Japanese force was behind the "White Army." On the other hand, the meeting, later, of the

Dairen Conference, the secret visit of Zetlin to Vladivostok, and the refusal of the Japanese Army to supply arms to the Merkouloff Government, gave rise to another rumour purporting this time, that the Japanese troops were helping the Red Army. These malicious rumours were utterly devoid of foundation, the Japanese Army having throughout maintained strict neutrality and positively unpartial attitude. . . .

The allegation that the Japanese troops are supplying the White Army with arms and are helping civil strife, in order to make it a pretext of retaining the troops in Siberia, is too ludicrous to be seriously taken. Japan has no desire but to hope that the Russians will cease their internal strifes and peace and order may be established in the Far Eastern Russia as soon as possible, so that she may withdraw her troops with a sense of relief. What the Japanese Army at Vladivostok have done is that in compliance with the request of the local Consular body, they have handed to the local administrative body a minimum supply of arms absolutely necessary for the maintenance of order, to be used by a fixed number of private policemen, whose existence has for some time been recognised. It is absolutely untrue to say that the Japanese troops have ever supplied the White Army with any arms. The truth of what has just been said must be quite clear from the fact that the Merkouloff "Government" is blaming Japan for her refusal to grant them any warlike implements, the Japanese troops having nothing whatever to do with the latest activity of the White Army. . . .

The circular [allegedly distributed by the Chita government] declares further that "Japan has at the Dairen Conference made a demand of such nature as the cession of the shores of the Tartary Strait". Facts could not be more outrageously distorted. The principal object of Japan at the Dairen Conference is to obtain assurances in connection with the security of the life and property of Japanese subjects, the elimination of dangers to communication and the menace to the Empire of Japan and the freedom of commerce and industry, in the Far Eastern Russia, thereby to be enabled to effect the withdrawal of her troops from the Maritime Province, and Japanese Government harbours no other motives or wishes.[47]

To the Russians it seemed that the Japanese were insincere, that they had participated in the Dairen Conference only to curb discussion of the Siberian question in Washington. They believed that Japan had increased the tempo of the negotiations had shown apparent willingness to come to an agreement only while the Washington Conference had lasted (November 12, 1921, to February 6, 1922).[m] Foreign Minister Ianson asserted in a letter to Foreign Minister Uchida on April 22, that the breakdown of the negotiations had been "entirely the fault of the Japanese government."

Ianson wrote that full agreement had been reached toward the beginning of April on all provisions of a treaty of commerce as well as on a number of questions concerning relations between the two sides. The wording of the text of all the points of the trade agreement and of all supplements pertaining to other economic and political questions had been worked out. The two sides thus had seemed on the verge of the establishment of commercial relations. Agreement had not been reached only on the question of the evacuation of Japanese troops from the Maritime Province. Whenever this question had been raised during the Dairen talks, Ianson stated, the Japanese delegation had declared that this question would be solved concretely and positively and that evacuation would take place as soon as the possibility would arise for the conclusion of a general agreement between both sides. When, however, by the beginning of April such a possibility emerged very definitely, it became necessary to work out a written act about the evacuation; as the two

[m] In his memoirs Petrov recalls that the position of his side had been stiffened by orders directly from Lenin. At the time of the Washington Conference Lenin had sent a directive to the negotiators at Dairen through Chicherin instructing them to take into consideration the clash of interests of the imperialists at the Washington Conference and to continue adhering to the hard line at Dairen. (Petrov, 91).

delegations were considering it, it became evident that the Japanese government had changed its original opinion about the need of evacuating the Japanese troops from the Maritime Province. The Far Eastern Republic could not accept the continuation of the Japanese occupation, which made the reestablishment of commercial and other economic relations between Japan and the Far Eastern Republic practically impossible and the treaty of commerce meaningless.

> The government of the Far Eastern Republic believes that there can be peace in the Russian Far East and economic cooperation between Japan on one hand and the Russian Far East and Siberia on the other hand only in the event of the complete evacuation of Russian territory by Japanese troops [Ianson reiterated]. The government of the Far Eastern Republic will strive by all means to achieve this end; it declares, however, that further contacts between the two governments will be successful only if the Japanese government will show a similar inclination.[48]

The Japanese government rebutted Ianson's note. It argued:

> Since the Imperial Japanese Government has taken the decision to evacuate, there is not the slightest doubt that it will carry it out; this can be seen from the evacuation of the Transbaikal and Amur regions, which has already taken place. In spite of this the Chita Government does not believe in our sincerity and has formed a mistaken opinion about the Imperial Government's intentions concerning the evacuation. The Imperial Government must explain such an attitude by Chita as being due either to the mistaken views of their representatives in Dairen concerning the Japanese Government or to the deliberate evasion of the concluding of any agreement whatsoever.[49]

The foreign press voiced conflicting views. The *North China Star* accused Japanese diplomacy of "wilyness" and "the capacity for perversion of the truth" and charged the Japanese delegates with "bad faith and insincerity."[50] The *North China Standard*, on the other hand, declared that Japan had displayed a "conciliatory attitude," and attributed the failure of the conference to the "peremptory tone" of the Chita delegation. Referring to the "ultimatum" of the Far Eastern Republic that the Japanese evacuate the Maritime Province in forty-five days, including preliminary arrangements, and to the various other demands made on the Japanese, the *North China Standard* commented that "no self-respecting Government could have accepted such an ultimatum unless under stress of force." It added: "Whatever may be thought of the Bolsheviks and their methods they have long since proved that they are no diplomats. With brutal force and recklessness no negotiations can be carried through."[51]

Tanaka Bunichirō 田中文一郎, a diplomat with long experience in Russia, who years later analyzed the failure of the Dairen Conference for the edification of his colleagues in the Foreign Office, believed that it was the Russian government that had lost interest in the conclusion of an agreement between the Far Eastern Republic and Japan, in fact gradually had come to think one undesirable. Tanaka attributed the change in Soviet attitude to the change in Russia's international position. At the outset of the negotiations, in the summer of 1921, Russia had been completely isolated from the rest of Europe and her need for consumer goods had been desperate; she had desired trade with Japan at any price. Following the conclusion of commercial agreements with Great Britain, Italy and Germany and the import of American and Chinese goods, the need for trade with Japan had become less acute and the position of the Far Eastern Republic correspondingly stronger. While the Far Eastern Republic had been established originally as a coalition buffer state for the purpose of approaching Japan as well as of avoiding conflict with her, its government had eventually become Communist-dominated and in effect Moscow-ruled. As the chances of Soviet Russia's recognition by the other powers increased and the likelihood of their recognition of the Far Eastern Republic as an autonomous state declined, Moscow deemed it best not to complicate matters by an agreement between Japan and the Far Eastern Republic, recognizing the independence of the latter. Tanaka observed furthermore that the delegate of the Far Eastern Republic had insufficient knowledge of law and treaties to understand the Japanese proposals fully and that he was not a man of compromise. Last but not least, Tanaka realized, the representative of the Far Eastern Republic suspected the intentions of the Japanese military and did not have faith in their vague pledge of withdrawal.[52]

CHAPTER TWO

The Changchun Conference

ON May 20, 1922, V. G. Antonov, former head of the Communist government of Vladivostok and now manager of the Tokyo office of Dal'ta, the official news agency of the Far Eastern Republic, sounded out Matsudaira Tsuneo, now director of the Bureau of European and American Affairs of the Japanese Foreign Office, about the resumption of negotiations between Russia and Japan.[a] Matsudaira must have been encouraging, for on June 12 Antonov returned to convey that the government of the Far Eastern Republic wished to resume negotiations and had entrusted him with discussing the date and place for such a new conference. The Far Eastern Republic made two conditions for the resumption of talks: that a representative of the Soviet government be allowed to participate and that Japan fix a time for the evacuation of her forces from the Russian Far East.

At a meeting of the cabinet on June 23 and of the Foreign Policy Research Board on June 24 the Japanese government decided to withdraw its forces from the Maritime Province, including the coast opposite Sakhalin, by the end of October, before freezing, and made a public statement to this effect. It was the feeling of the Japanese statesmen not only that the red terror had abated in Europe and in Siberia but that relations between Soviet Russia and the other powers had improved to such an extent that the latter might insist on Japanese evacuation and

---

[a] According to journalist Albert Maybon, Antonov's appointment as manager of the news agency had been a blind; he had been sent specifically to pave the way for talks between Tokyo and Chita. (*L'Asie Française*, May 1923, in Japanese Archives, MT 251.106.14: 387-391)

Japan would risk the embarrassment of having to withdraw in response to such demands if she continued the occupation. Deeming it desirable to conclude an agreement with the Far Eastern Republic prior to evacuation, the Japanese government informed Antonov that it would fix a date for the evacuation of the Maritime Province and would allow the participation of Soviet representatives in the proposed negotiations in order to obtain immediate Soviet approval of an agreement between the Far Eastern Republic and Japan. The Japanese added that points settled at Dairen should be left untouched, discussion to proceed speedily on items where there had been differences of opinion. They thought that talks would be held again at Dairen. As an inducement for a speedy conclusion of an agreement, they stated that if the government of the Far Eastern Republic signed the Japanese proposals for the basic agreement and other points by August 15, the war stores held by them would be handed over to it (rather than to anti-Communist forces).[1]

Antonov left Tokyo on June 29 to convey the Japanese views to the government at Chita. The announcement of Japan's decision to evacuate her forces from the Maritime Province came as a complete surprise to the Far Eastern Republic. But welcome as the news was, the feeling of relief was mixed with the conviction that the Japanese would now seek to reward themselves for the "voluntary" withdrawal.[2]

While the Japanese were waiting to hear from Antonov again, E. K. Ozarnin, the extraordinary representative of the Far Eastern Republic in the Chinese Eastern Railway zone at Harbin, handed to Consul General Yamanouchi Shirō 山内四郎 a letter from Foreign Minister Ianson to the Japanese foreign minister, dated June 30. In it Ianson officially repeated the demand that Japan specify the date of withdrawal from the territory of the Far Eastern Republic and allow Soviet participation in negotiations between the two countries, noting that Russia would participate in "a joint delegation with the F.E.R." Ianson expressed the hope that the negotiations would take place and would "open the way to the wide economic development and commercial relations between the Russian Far East and Japan."[3] Expecting word from Antonov, the imperial government merely had Yamanouchi answer orally that it agreed in principle to the resumption of negotiations. When more time elapsed without any communication from Antonov, Japan replied in a written note from the Foreign Office to the People's Commissariat for Foreign Affairs, dated July 18 and transmitted by Yamanouchi to Ozarnin the following day, that withdrawal of the forces from the Maritime Province would be completed "not later than November 1" and that it had consented to Soviet participation in the coming conference "under conditions regulating the formulation of the agreement." The government remarked that the details of this question had been discussed between Matsudaira and Antonov. "As a place for the conference," the note concluded, "it would be desirable to select Harbin or Dairen."[4]

Meanwhile a reply from Antonov to Matsudaira arrived in Harbin and was conveyed by Ozarnin to Yamanouchi on the same day as the note from the Foreign Office to the People's Commissariat for Foreign Affairs:

> The official resolution of the Imperial Japanese Government concerning evacuation makes it possible to suppose that this question will be solved at the forthcoming Conference in a spirit satisfactory to both sides and that a way will be found to formulate this question in such manner as not to create difficulties for the Japanese Delegation [Antonov wrote]. The matter of the participation of delegates of the Russian [Soviet Federated Socialist] Republic is discussed in the note of Ia. D. Ianson [of June 30]. The question of the working out of an agreement and its final drawing up can be left for the Conference itself, since it is impossible to decide in advance by means of the exchange of telegrams and fragmentary negotiations.[5]

The desirability of a reasonable compromise between the Soviet Union and Japan was noted by the *Peking Tientsin Times:*

> It is politic for Russia to leave passion aside, and to give sympathetic consideration to Japan's economic desires, while resisting, as she must, if she is determined to preserve Russian sovereignty

over Eastern Siberia, her more threatening political pretensions. It is ridiculous to suppose that either the Chita Government or the Moscow Government will be able to develop the resources of Northern Sakhalin unaided. And it is equally patent that the subjects of no other foreign Power will be prepared to sink the large amount of capital needed for the exploitation of Northern Sakhalin in an attempt to develop its resources if such enterprise evokes the hostility of Japan.

Referring to reports from Tokyo that Japan was weighing the possibility of purchasing North Sakhalin from the Soviet Union, the paper regarded this, if true, as "a bold bid not only for amicable liquidation of the whole Siberian adventure, but for Russian political friendship." "If the renewal of Russian friendship is the fundamental motive animating the Japanese Government," the *Peking Tientsin Times* concluded, "the Katō Ministry, if it does nothing else of constructive value, but achieves that, will have deserved well of its country."[6]

Such a view was not shared by various White Russian groups which protested against Japanese dealings with the Communists. The Council of National State Associations (Sovet Natsional'no-Gosudarstvennykh Ob'edinenii) in the city of Harbin, for example, warned that negotiations with the Bolsheviks could lead to the destruction of Japan's own military might and the loss of her significance in the Far East. "The negotiations and the agreement and treaty about commercial relations with the Bolsheviks stemming from them will arouse general outrage among the Russian people, and they will not recognize the force of a treaty concluded with their tyrants, murderers and executioners of . . . Russia."[7]

On July 28 Yamanouchi reiterated to Ozarnin that his government wished to complete an agreement by August 15.[7, b] The following day, on July 29, the representative of the Far Eastern Republic at Harbin handed Yamanouchi a letter, dated July 25 and signed jointly by Lev

---

[b] Tanaka states that Japan pressed Russia for a reply on July 27. It is possible that instructions were sent to Yamanouchi from Tokyo on the 27th; he then spoke to the Russian official the next day.

THE CHANGCHUN CONFERENCE 53

Mikhail Karakhan, Deputy People's Commissar of Foreign Affairs of Russia, and by Iakov Davidovich Ianson, Minister of Foreign Affairs of the Far Eastern Republic. In it they acknowledged the decision of the imperial Japanese government "to carry out the complete evacuation of Japanese forces from Russian territory in the Far East." They expressed the satisfaction of the governments of Russia and of the Far Eastern Republic with the decision of the Japanese government to evacuate its troops from the Russian Far East by November 1, 1922.

In view of the mutual agreement of Russia and the Far Eastern Republic on one hand, and Japan on the other hand, to start negotiations for the establishment of peaceful and friendly relations [the note continued], the governments of Soviet Russia and the Far Eastern Republic are of the opinion that at the coming conference Russia, the Far Eastern Republic, and Japan should be represented upon a basis of equality, and that the coming agreement should be signed in the name of each of the governments represented at the conference.

Russia and the Far Eastern Republic considered Chita or Moscow as the most appropriate place for the conference; they pledged to secure for the Japanese delegation "all necessary comfort for the negotiations and particularly good connection by direct wire with all points on the mainland." If Japan had any objections to Chita or Moscow, the two governments were prepared to agree to Peking or Tokyo, preferably the latter, provided satisfactory communication with Chita and Moscow could be guaranteed.

In conclusion the note named the delegates who had been appointed to represent Soviet Russia and the Far Eastern Republic: Adol'f Abramovich Ioffe, member of the All-Russian Central Executive Committee, and Ianson, minister of foreign affairs of the Far Eastern Republic.[8]

The letter from Karakhan and Ianson, although transmitted to Yamanouchi after his demand for a reply, had not been the awaited response. On August 1 Yamanouchi handed to the deputy representative of the Far Eastern Republic in Harbin a note in which he stated that he had received instructions that day to seek a prompt answer to his request of July 28. Reiterating that Japan would prefer to meet again at Dairen, he declared that if this were unacceptable, Japan would be willing to meet in Harbin; she was unable to agree to Tokyo or Chita.[c]

Yamanouchi noted that Japan had repeatedly declared that an agreement must be concluded before she could evacuate her troops. He asserted that most points had been settled at Dairen; questions which had not been considered at Dairen, such as the fishery problem and the Nikolaevsk incident, could be discussed only after the signature of the basic treaty. Yamanouchi observed that all this had already been communicated to the Far Eastern Republic through Antonov and repeated that the agreement must be concluded not later than August 15.[9]

On August 10 the representative of the Far Eastern Republic handed to Yamanouchi a note from Karakhan and Ianson, dated August 6, in reply to the statement of the Japanese government, conveyed by him. Karakhan and Ianson wrote that their governments shared the desire for a speedy conclusion of an agreement but that they doubted that this could be done by the 15th of the same month; the representatives of both sides could hardly get together by that time, particularly since agreement had not yet been reached on a place of meeting. For the sake of saving time the governments of Soviet Russia and the Far Eastern Republic agreed to the Japanese proposal that a general agreement be considered and signed first, and that more detailed and concrete questions be examined after the signature at the same conference. The two governments felt that with mutual goodwill such a general basic treaty could be concluded quickly in view of the negotiations that had taken place at Dairen.[d]

---

[c] The Russians felt that there was much popular support in Japan for the resumption of Russo-Japanese relations and that the Japanese government had refused to meet in Tokyo for fear of political demonstrations in support of the Soviet delegation. (Mikhail Pavlovich [Vel'tman], *Sovetskaia Rossia i imperialisticheskaia Iaponiia* [Soviet Russia and imperialist Japan] [Moscow, 1923], p. 83)

[d] It is curious to note a discrepancy in the text published by the Soviet Foreign Office in 1961 on the basis of the wording that appeared in *Izvestiia* on August 10,*

Since Japan had turned down Moscow and Chita as places of negotiation, the two governments felt that they could no longer insist on Tokyo. Inasmuch as Japan had not objected to Peking, the governments of Soviet Russia and the Far Eastern Republic "insist[ed] on this city," which had the added advantage that the Russian delegate, who had been appointed was at the same time the extraordinary plenipotentiary representative of the R.S.F.S.R. to China and was already en route to Peking.[10]

On August 14 the Japanese government expressed its satisfaction with the consent of the Far Eastern Republic to sign a general treaty before a detailed consideration of separate questions and agreed to extend the dealine for concluding such an agreement "for some time" beyond August 15. It fully concurred with the view that the general agreement could be concluded quickly and declared that if the signature of the agreement took place shortly, it would be prepared to settle all matters that might arise in connection with the evacuation of the Japanese troops. It refused to hold the conference at Peking, however, on the grounds that it was inconvenient to conduct negotiations in such an international city on foreign territory, and instead proposed Harbin, Dairen, Mukden or Changchun. It promised good communication with Chita and stated that it would not object to the transfer of further negotiations to another place upon mutual agreement. It concluded with the hope that the Far Eastern Republic would accept the Japanese proposal without much loss of time on preliminary selection of a place for the negotiations.[11]

The Russian side replied in a note, dated August 24, signed jointly by Karakhan and Ianson, and transmitted through the Japanese con-

---

*1922, and the typewritten copy, preserved in the Japanese Foreign Office Archives. The text published by the Soviet side states: "The governments of the R.S.F.S.R. and the F.E.R. suppose that such a general basic treaty, in view of the negotiations that had taken place in Dairen, can with mutual goodwill be signed [*podpisan*] in the shortest period." The text in the Japanese Foreign Office has "worked out" [*pyrabotan*] instead of "signed."

sulate general in Harbin. The note pointed out that Peking was not an international city but a Chinese city and that Harbin, Mukden and Changchun were on the same "foreign" Chinese soil. Yet in order not to delay further with debates about a place of meeting, the Russian side stated, it agreed to Changchun on condition that further negotiations would be held at a more convenient place. It gave notice that its delegation, counting experts and technical personnel, would number about 25 persons, and insisted on a direct telegraph line to Chita. It asked, furthermore, that the Japanese government set a definite time for the beginning of the negotiations, taking into consideration the fact that Ioffe would not be able to leave Peking for Changchun before August 30.[12]

On August 29 the Russians received a reply from the Japanese government proposing that negotiations begin at Changchun on September 4.[13] Changchun was at the junction of the Japanese South Manchurian Railway and the Russian Chinese Eastern Railway. It was a place equally distant and convenient from Japan and Russia and at the same time well protected by Japanese guards so that both sides could meet in absolute safety.

The Japanese government announced that Matsudaira Tsuneo would be its chief delegate. Matsudaira was a diplomat of higher position and greater experience than Matsushima. As noted above, he was director of the Bureau of European and American Affairs of the Foreign Office. He had been one of the Japanese delegates to the Washington Conference and had been the civilian representative in Siberia in matters relating to railways.[e] Matsushima Hajime, who had been the chief delegate at Dairen and now was consul general at Vladivostok, was to assist Matsudaira.[14]

"The Japanese delegates at the Conference may be expected fully to appreciate that every argument they use, every demand they make, and

[e] Later Matsudaira was to become Minister of the Imperial Household and in 1936 almost was assassinated by ultranationalists. After the Pacific War he was to be first chairman of the Diet under the new constitution.

every demand they refrain from making, will go to shape the future course of the relations between Japan and Russia, the *Peking Tientsin Times* wrote. Reporting that the Japanese press favored the restoration of friendly relations between the two countries and that even *Kokumin*, the imperialist organ, advocated the political recognition of the Soviet government, the paper expressed satisfaction at the dispersion of "all the hypocrisy" of Japan's pronouncements of Siberia. "One feels the better for the disappearance of all the nauseating insincerity with which Japan sought to cover her tracks."

> It is good to know [the *Peking Tientsin Times* continued] that Japan is now looking beyond Governments, and remembers that while they come and go the people remain, and that in the last analysis, whether under democracies, autocracies, or oligarchies, the people's opinion is the determining factor in the larger issues of international politics. A new, strong spirit of Nationalism is reviving in Russia, and is impregnating even the present Government, once the apostles of Internationalism. It will flame higher as the torch of revolutionary ardour flickers and fails, and if legitimate national grievances blow upon it, it will be a menace to the peace of the world.[15]

Yet the consensus of press prophesies held out little hope for the success of the pending pourparlers. "Summed up, the general observations seem to indicate that Changchun will produce certain understandings on commerce and allied subjects if treated separately but matters like the Nikolaevsk massacre, Soviet recognition and political questions, if made indispensible bases of agreement, are likely to wreck the conference."[16]

The Japanese delegates arrived at Changchun on September 2; the delegates of Russia and the Far Eastern Republic on the morning of the 4th. A preliminary meeting took place at the Japanese consulate that day to discuss procedural questions. The delegations of the R.S.F.S.R. and the F.E.R. proposed that the plenary sessions be opened to the press, but the Japanese turned this down on the ground that it would delay the course of negotiations. They feared that if the press were admitted, the Soviets would use the plenary sessions as a propaganda platform. The Japanese also rejected the Russian proposal to release joint summaries to the press after every meeting. But they had not reckoned with the persistence of newspaper correspondents, who had come to Changchun from all over the world after the announcement of a Russo-Japanese conference, and had to reverse themselves soon on this point. Joint communiqués were issued after every meeting.[17]

The conference formally opened on September 5. As decided the previous day, the first order of business was the exchange of credentials. To the apparent surprise of the Japanese, Ioffe and Ianson represented both Russia and the Far Eastern Republic concurrently, with Ioffe portraying himself as the chief representative and doing most of the talking. The letter from Karakhan and Ianson had been so couched that the predominant role of Ioffe and his representation of both states had not been obvious. While the Japanese had agreed to Soviet participation in the conference they had not realized that Ioffe would be the spokesman for both governments.[18] In the words of Dmitrii Ivanovich Abrikossow,[f] who at that time was chargé d'affaires of the old embassy in Tokyo: "The curtain had lifted and Moscow stood in plain view. There was nothing for the Japanese to do but enter into direct negotiations with the Soviet government, and soon the myth of the Far Eastern Republic was forgotten."[19]

Ioffe (alias Viktor Krymskii) was a very able and well educated diplomat. A physician by training, he had been an associate of Leon Trotskii, editing with him the newspaper *Pravda* in Vienna (1908–12) and switching together with him from the Mensheviks to the Bolsheviks in 1917. He had been head of the Soviet delegation to the Brest-Litovsk peace conference and was concurrently member of the All-Russian Central

---

[f] The spelling preferred by Abrikossow himself, who later immigrated to the United States; a more accurate transliteration would be "Abrikosov."

Executive Committee, special plenipotentiary to China and special plenipotentiary to Japan.[g]

The Japanese Foreign Office naturally had sought information about the Russian diplomats. Such information was difficult to obtain. "The names of nearly all the members of the Soviet Mission to China cannot be fixed; they all have changed their names since 1917," the German journalist Erich von Salzmann wrote to the Japanese minister in Peking. "Nearly everyone of the members has disappeared from time to time, and they all refuse plainly to have any knowledge about the life of one of their fellow members. Suspicion among them is terrible. They all are in great fear of spies and treachery."[20] All that von Salzmann could learn at first about Ioffe was that he had studied medicine—"he has not passed examine [sic], and the Russians here doubt his degree as a Doctor" —and that he had been a member of the Brest-Litovsk commission. In another report von Salzmann added: "Mr. Joffe has the same sickness as Mr. Lenin. It is a general nervous breakdown. He has sometimes so much pain that he can even not walk or lift up his arms."[21, h]

A typed copy of an interview with Ioffe by the correspondent of the *Tientsin Times* in Harbin in early August, also in the Foreign Office archives, gives a more personal touch: "The first impression of Mr. Joffe was decidedly favourable," the journalist wrote. "He has the appearance of a German bourgeois rather than that of a Russian Communist, being well-built and well fed, with a pleasant countenance and a short beard. He has a quiet way of speaking and is perfectly frank and open in his

[g] Within a few years Ioffe was to be dead by his own hand. He was an ill man, as will be seen later, and was to undergo prolonged psychiatric treatment. But there was more to his suicide than bodily distress. He strongly supported Trotskii in the intra-party struggle of 1925-27 and took his life when Stalin gained the upper hand.

[h] Von Salzman was correct in the symptoms of Ioffe's illness but not in its nature. Von Salzman also furnished data to the Soviet mission, trading information for information as enterprising newsmen often do. He boasted that he had been the only man in Peking who had prophesied to the Soviet mission correctly in the summer of 1922 what would transpire in China.

conversation, showing no signs of hesitation when answering any questions."[21] A French newspaper added: "Monsieur Joffe is plain-dealing and has a sense of humor, qualities which are not disliked in Japan. And he talks business, a language which pleases."[22]

A hint of what was in store for the Japanese should have come from the answers given by Ioffe to a lengthy list of questions presented to him by Furuno Inosuke 古野伊之助 of the Kokusai News Agency in Peking. The queries ranged the gamut from "What is the percentage of illiteracy in Russia today as compared with that before the Revolution?" to "What is the latest information about Mr. Lenin's condition? Will he be able to come back to his office soon?" The questions were dated August 22, 1922, and Ioffe's reply August 26. Typewritten copies of the exchange found their way into the Foreign Office, though it is not clear when.

The questions and answers concerning the forthcoming Russo-Japanese negotiations deserve to be quoted in full:

1. What is the latest information as to where and when the Russo-Japanese negotiations take place?

    The latest negotiations have been proceeding as to the place of the Russo-Japanese Conference. We had proposed to Japan Moscow, Tchita [Chita], Tokyo and Peking. However, Japan declined our hospitality and refused us her own. At last she counter-proposed Harbin, Chanchun [sic] and Mukden. Unwilling to indulge in further controversies, we have finally fixed Chanchun, notwithstanding the fact that, from our viewpoint, this place is unsuitable—which opinion has been conveyed to Japan. It is now to be hoped that negotiations will soon be opened.

2. Are you going to personally represent both Soviet Russia and the Far Eastern Republic at the coming conference with Japan or is Mr. Yanson or anybody else coming to represent the Far Eastern Republic?

    I have been empowered to negotiate in the name of both the Russian Socialist Federative Soviet Republic [sic] and the

Far Eastern Republic, just in the same way as Mr. Yanson, the Minister of Foreign Affairs of the Far Eastern Republic, who also [is] vested with double authority. At the same time I have been appointed to be Chairman by both the Government of the R.S.F.S.R. and F.E. Republic.

3. When the Russo-Japanese conference is resumed do you propose to adopt as the basis of discussion the trade agreement of seventeen points, which was agreed upon at the Dairen Conference or is it your idea to start discussions afresh regardless of the results of the Dairen Conference?

We took no part in the drafting of the Dairen agreement, for Markhlevsky watched the Conference in the capacity only of an onlooker. Therefore we cannot consider the Dairen draft agreement binding for us. But still we think that such long negotiation cannot be considered as having no significance.

4. Upon what principles and along what lines do you propose to conduct the coming negotiations with Japan?

In my view, negotiations can be conducted only on the basis of full equality of rights of the parties concerned, the interests of each side must be safeguarded and both parties must be willing to make mutual concessions in case of necessity.

5. What are your views on the Nikolaevsk affair? Is the Soviet Government ready to take responsibility for the settlement of the affair?

I consider that the responsibility for the Nikolaevsk episode must be laid altogether on Japan. Any Government bringing their troops into foreign territory must be ready to reckon with possible consequences.[24]

Not only did the Japanese learn in the ensuing talks that Ioffe spoke for the Far Eastern Republic as well as for Soviet Russia, but that he had considerably wider powers than expected. It was the view of the Japanese that the Dairen Conference had failed primarily because they had not been willing to set a date for the evacuation of Japanese forces from Siberia. Now that they had made a specific commitment in their note of July 19, they felt that the various points on which agreement had been reached more or less after eight months of negotiations would be accepted without further debate.[25]

On September 5 or during the next session—the date is not clear[i]—Matsudaira conveyed a declaration of the Japanese government to the effect that it intended to enter into negotiations with the Far Eastern Republic (and not with Soviet Russia) for the purpose of securing a guarantee of the safety of Japanese persons and property, the removal of any direct threat to the border of the Far Eastern Republic and Japan, and the removal of previous restrictions on Japanese industrial enterprise in the (Russian) Far East. The declaration reiterated the position that agreement had been reached at Dairen on almost all points and that the conference had broken down because no date had been set for the evacuation; now that withdrawal had begun, the Dairen draft should be signed, opinions being exchanged on the unsettled questions.[26]

The idea that the talks at Changchun be confined to unresolved issues had been introduced by the Japanese during the informal preliminary talks. They were taken aback, therefore, when Ioffe insisted on the right to reopen all questions, including those which had seemed to have been settled, and when he asserted that the declaration of the imperial government was so contrary in scope and purpose of establishing good neighborly relations between Japan and the Far Eastern Republic and Soviet Russia that he could not negotiate on that basis and must seek new instructions. Ioffe implied that the conference could not continue unless the Japanese plenipotentiaries obtained wider powers.[27]

The negotiations ground to a halt, but Karakhan approved of Ioffe's considerations. As he wired him on September 9: "The position must be firm, no concessions beyond those fixed in the previous instructions. Russia is participating in general and not for the purpose of countersign-

[i] On September 6 according to Russian documents, but the session sounds very much like the one described by Tanaka as having taken place on the 5th. Occasionally —not always—the Japanese and Russian sources differ by one day.

THE CHANGCHUN CONFERENCE 63

ing the signature of the Far Eastern Republic and solving fishery questions. Give to understand that Russia has returned to the Pacific Ocean and that all illusions about our weakness and the possibility of slighting us as an unequal power are fruitless." Karakhan added, however, that although a rupture of the negotiations was not directly dangerous for Russia and that Russia could wait for the conclusion of a treaty, all measures should be taken not to let it come to a breakdown.[28]

When talks were resumed on September 10, Ioffe declared in the name of Soviet Russia and the Far Eastern Republic that the desire of the Japanese delegation to limit discussion to questions concerning the F.E.R. and to conclude an agreement solely with the F.E.R. was completely unexpected. Confining consideration merely to Far Eastern questions would mean to solve only those issues in which Japan was interested. The economic and political intimacy of Soviet Russia and the Far Eastern Republic was so close that separate and independent examination of questions with each of them in turn was impossible. The fixing of rights of Japanese citizens in the territory of the Far East would be tantamount to the fixing of the rights of Japanese subjects in the territory of all of Russia, which was unthinkable without the consent of the latter.

Ioffe stated that in spite of the Intervention the Russian people harbored no hostility toward Japan and were willing to let bygones be bygones. But the governments of Soviet Russia and the Far Eastern Republic could not agree to negotiations which would insure the interests of one side only. The evacuation of Japanese troops and the return of Russian property seized by the Japanese forces were insufficient compensation for the two governments which he represented, since the evacuation had been a prior condition for the talks and the property was subject to return to its rightful owners, the Russian people, regardless of the course of the negotiations. In conclusion Ioffe said that he did not object to the making of a general agreement first, leaving the discussion of particulars for later, but he could not accept the mere repetition of the Dairen draft as the basic agreement; its scope must be widened, for the Dairen draft had been negotiated between Japan and the Far Eastern Republic only, while now at Changchun Russia was a participant.

The Japanese waxed impatient at Ioffe's attempts to broaden the scope of the negotiations. They particularly denied his contention that they were making their evacuation from the Russian Far East and the transfer of war stores subject to the conclusion of an agreement.[29]

That night, at midnight, Ioffe handed a letter to a courier. It was addressed to Deputy Foreign Commissar Litvinov, with a copy designated for the chairman of the government of the Far Eastern Republic. It read as follows:

> Dear Fedor Nikolaevich,[j]
> Our negotiations with the Japanese delegates[k] are dragging out; the sessions are stormy with many debates. I see the reason for this in the motto of the Japanese delegates "to take but not to give [*vziat', no ne dat'*]." Nonetheless I hope to gain the time of the evacuation of the Japanese troops from the Maritime Province and its liquidation.
> All this would no doubt facilitate my work not only in Changchun, but also in China. At the unofficial meeting which took place this September 10 in the building of the Japanese consulate at 19:00 hours, the Japanese delegates made an out-of-order declaration in

---

[j] The patronymic of Litvinov, to whom the letter was addressed, was Maksim Maksimovich. His revolutionary pseudonyms had been "Papasha," Kuznetsov, Maksimovich, Luvin'e, Feliks and Nits but not Fedor Nikolaevich. The chairman of the government of the Far Eastern Republic was A. M. Krasnoshchekov and later N.M. Matveev. The only Fedor Nikolaevich who comes to mind is Petrov, deputy chairman of the Council of Ministers of the Far Eastern Republic and Ioffe's predecessor in the negotiations with the Japanese. If the letter was written to him, copies were sent both to Krasnoshchekov and Litvinov.

[k] Soviet correspondence abounds in abbreviations, such as "iapdelegaty," "iapvoiska" and "iappra." I have refrained from translating them as "Jap delegates," "Jap troops" and "Jap government" lest a derogatory meaning be implied. The Soviets referred to their own government as "sovpra." I have supplied the various telegrams with punctuation and missing words without subjecting the reader to the original Russian "tchk" ("*tochka*" or "stop"), "dvtchk" ("*dvoinaiia tochka*" or "colon"), "kvtchk" ("*kovychka*" or "quote") and "zpt" ("*zapetaia*" or "comma").

which they hinted to me rather transparently at the insincerity of the Soviet government toward Japan and showed their indignation at the insincerity of the propaganda work [*agitrabota*] of our agents against Japan. At the same time they raised the immutable question of the impossibility of direct negotiations with me as delegate extraordinary of the R.S.F.S.R. and they asked to enlighten them about the question of the merging of the Russian delegations. All these questions gave rise to heated debates, from which I saw that the merging of our delegations, as not done according to the Japanese recipe was not to the taste of the Japanese delegates.

As I had expected, the Japanese delegates at their risk [*na svoi risk i strakh*] agreed "conditionally" until receipt of instructions from Tokyo to subject a number of questions outside the framework of the Dairen draft to preliminary private discussion. The essence of these questions boiled down to the following: (1) The leasing of the northern part of Sakhalin not for 30 years, as there was talk earlier, but for 33 years; (2) revision of the Russo-Japanese fishery convention, the matter to be discussed simultaneously with the question about Kamchatka; (3) the Nikolaevsk question was to be discussed independently of the question of leasing Sakhalin; (4) the destruction of the Vladivostok fortress with all resultant consequences and the removal of any direct and indirect danger to the borders of the F.E.R. and Japan; (5) concerning concessions; (6) about the disbandment of our army in the F.E.R.

Not even going into a discussion of the [above-] mentioned questions, since in my opinion the Japanese delegates merely wished to learn our views concerning them, Iakov Davidovich [Ianson] and I proposed preliminary discussion of four counter-questions: (1) abrogation of the Russo-Japanese military convention of 12 April 1920 and the conclusion of a new Russo-Japanese agreement according to which only the armies of the F.E.R. will have the right to be in the neutral zone and to enter into Vladivostok; in this connection Iakov Davidovich pointed out to the Japanese delegates that at the present time the White detachments have been transferred from Vladivostok to Nik[ol'sk] Ussur[iisk], while the Japanese armies have not yet been evacuated; (2) about the fate of the Russian arms in Vladivostok; (3) about the liquidation of the Dietrichs adventure and the end of dealings between the Japanese government and him;¹ (4) complete non-interference of Japan in Russian affairs.

A delay in the solution of these questions, I said, will force the governments of the F.E.R. and the R.S.F.S.R. to doubt the sincerity of the Japanese government and to suppose that it is evading the solution of the given questions for the assurance of the conclusion of a treaty before the end of the evacuation. By mutual agreement a four-day official recess in work was decided upon so that during this time each delegation would seek instructions from its government concerning the questions broached. Until that time it was decided to have private conferences. Shall act[m] strictly in accordance with the instructions of Vladimir Il'ich [*Lenin*]. I have already gained a definite impression of the Changchun Conference. Although I do not count on brilliant benefits from it, I am confident nevertheless, that in return for broad commercial concessions on our part the Japanese will agree to a number of political concessions in general and the "bloodless" liquidation of Dietrichs in particular. . . .[n]

    With comradely greeting, A. Ioffe
    Delegate Extraordinary [*Chrezdelegat*] [of the] R.S.F.S.R.[30]

A dispatch from Ianson to the chairman of the government of the Far Eastern Republic, written the next day, elaborated on the heated debates to which Ioffe had referred. For example, when the Japanese

---

¹ M. K. Dietrichs was one of the generals who vainly tried to unify the various White forces in opposition to the Soviet regime.

[m] The text reads "*budu deistvitel'no tochno*"; no doubt it should read "*budu deistvovat' tochno*."

[n] The remainder of the letter pertained to Russian relations with China.

delegates had warned that the Changchun conference might come to naught if Russian agents did not cease their agitation against the Japanese government, Ioffe had fulminated: "You say that you have reliable information [about Soviet agitation against the Japanese government]. Share it with us and I would show you that you were misled by enemies of the Russian people, who profess for the fifth year now to be true patriots but continue to shed the blood of their own brothers and to ruin Russia, and it is not their fault if they have not succeeded in doing so until this time."

Another acid exchange came over the question of the scope of the conference. Ianson reported:

> Matsudaira once again stated: "I have told you gentlemen repeatedly that until we receive instructions from Tokyo we must in our negotiations with you remain within the framework of the Dairen draft; we are willing at our risk to give partial preliminary consideration to a number of questions outside the framework of the Dairen draft."
>
> Adol'f Abramovich [Ioffe] interrupts Matsudaira declaring: "This question is raised by you Messrs. delegates regularly at every meeting. I find it necessary to inform you again that in the correspondence which preceded the negotiations the Soviet Government nowhere expressed agreement to the conduct of the negotiations within the framework of the Dairen draft; on the contrary it proposed to conduct negotiations about a general agreement and independently. . . . Now, gentlemen, not only will the Dairen treaty not satisfy the Russian people, but it will hardly satisfy the Japanese people either as it leaves unsolved a whole series of questions which interest both sides.

Ioffe's letter revealed that he had had instructions from Lenin himself. Ianson's dispatch disclosed that while Ioffe professed that his government "desires the most prompt signature of an agreement" and the request for the four-day recess had come from the Japanese, it was Ioffe who had engineered the delays by his excessive demands. "By our breaks in the negotiations we shall be able to gain time, awaiting the end of the Japanese evacuation and the advance of our armies to the south of the Maritime Province," Ianson wrote. "I suppose that neither Matsushima nor Matsudaira have realized that we are delaying the conference, since we have insisted continuously on the speediest solution of all questions."

Ioffe and Ianson seemed to feel that their task had been needlessly complicated by their predecessors. "Adol'f Abramovich sees the main reason [for the difficulties encountered] in the unwise policy of our diplomats at Dairen," Ianson concluded. "The Far Eastern Bureau made a great mistake when it assigned Petrov to Dairen. But Iurin too proved no better."[31, o]

On September 13 the Japanese side reiterated that the agreement which they were now discussing was bilateral, concerning Japan and the Far Eastern Republic only, but at the same time expressed willingness to make a trade agreement with the Soviet Union following the conclusion of the agreement with the F.E.R.[32]

During the meeting of September 15 an argument ensued about the wording of the preamble of the treaty. Matsudaira insisted that mention be made first that negotiations had taken place between Soviet Russia and the Far Eastern Republic on one hand and Japan on the other hand, but that then the agreement had been concluded actually between Japan and the Far Eastern Republic only. Ioffe retorted that although Russia had consented against its better judgment to try to reach agreement first on problems concerning the Far Eastern Republic only, this did not mean that it could approve of the conclusion of a separate treaty between the Far Eastern Republic and Japan. Ioffe demanded that even in the case of questions concerning Japan and the Far Eastern Republic only, Russia be officially a negotiating party.

o It is curious that neither of these two interesting dispatches was published by the Soviets in *Dokumenty vneshnei politiki SSSR*. It is even more fascinating to speculate how copies, typed in Russian on stationary of the Japanese Consulate General in Harbin, found their way into the Foreign Office Archives. Yet in spite of occasional typographical and grammatical errors (which may be blamed on the copyist) I see no reason to doubt their authenticity.

During the debate Ioffe pointed to article 1 as an illustration of the problem. In that article Japan pledged not to support any individuals or groups who planned to fight against the Far Eastern Republic. If the article were confined to the Far Eastern Republic there would be nothing to prevent the Japanese from supporting the same White groups, if only they declared that their activity was directed not against the F.E.R. but against the R.S.F.S.R. The Japanese could put them on vessels and dispatch them against Okhotsk. To this the Russian side could not agree. Matsudaira admitted that he understood Soviet objections and would seek new instructions on this point; meanwhile he suggested that deliberations on the other articles continue, to which Ioffe agreed.[33]

On September 15 agreement was reached on most articles, except articles 5 and 10,[34] presumably of the sixteen-article "Trade and General Agreement" discussed at Dairen, i.e. concerning the rights of Japanese subjects in the Russian Far East, river and coastal navigation, and the principle of the Open Door. On September 18 Matsudaira announced that the Japanese government consented to the conclusion of an agreement with both the Far Eastern Republic and Soviet Russia, but on matters concerning the Far East only.

Negotiations to extend the provisions to the R.S.F.S.R. could be begun upon conclusion of the agreement. Ioffe replied that he had queried Moscow and Chita about the acceptability of such a scheme but had not yet received a reply.

During the session on the 18th there was discussion about the abovementioned reciprocal rights of citizens of each country to engage in trade or professional activity in the territory of the other, as well as about reciprocal freedom of trade and river and sea navigation, and about the revision of the Russo-Japanese fishery convention. In connection with a report in the press that the Japanese delegation had received instructions to agree with only such corrections as did not change the essence of the Dairen agreement, Ioffe reminded the delegates that he had repeatedly stated that the Dairen draft was unacceptable because circumstances had changed since that time.[35]

On September 19, apparently in reply to Ioffe's cable of September 15,

Karakhan asked that Ioffe communicate to him the Japanese proposals in the formulation that went into the records, i.e. verbatim rather than in his own words, "since it was difficult to make a decision if the Japanese delegation changed its point of view from one session to another." Karakhan expressed the feeling that Matsudaira's method of negotiation was not serious. If the Japanese government found it necessary to give the impression that the negotiations were continuing in order to allay the press and public opinion, Karakhan cabled, Russian public opinion judged the negotiations by results. It was senseless to mark time on questions on which agreement had been reached in the preliminary exchange of notes. "We agreed to negotiate, after having put forth a number of conditions, which we consider to have been accepted, and deem it useless to discuss them anew. (1) Either the treaty is signed by Japan with the R.S.F.S.R. and the F.E.R. or there will be no treaty at all. (2) The Dairen draft facilitates negotiations, but does not bind us." Karakhan stated that Russia was correcting and supplementing the Dairen draft, taking into consideration Japanese interests. He concluded on a note of irritation: "This is our point of view, which was known to you when you left and which must remain unchanged your guide now too."[36]

At the morning session on September 19 Matsudaira made public the new instructions which he had received. They stated, as he had said the day before, that the preamble of the agreement must stipulate that the agreement was limited to the territory of the Far Eastern Republic and that all articles themselves must be formulated as an agreement between the F.E.R. and the R.S.F.S.R. on one hand and Japan on the other hand. Matsudaira reiterated that only editorial changes would be allowed in the articles of the treaty agreed upon at Dairen.

Ioffe retorted that no agreement had been signed at Dairen and what was not signed was not binding; he regarded the Dairen draft merely as a basis for negotiation. He reserved the right not only to modify some of the articles on which agreement had been reached at Dairen, but to reject them completely.

Matsudaira thereupon expressed the hope that no debate would ensue in connection with the articles that had been settled at Dairen, apparently accepting the Soviet position that the articles were subject to discussion.

Considerable controversy arose again concerning article 1 in so far as it applied to the Far Eastern Republic only. Repeating the argument he had made on September 15, that it would leave Japan free to support all White guards who declared that they were hostile not to the Far Eastern Republic but to Soviet Russia, Ioffe reasserted once more that he could not accept this wording. Matsudaira responded that while the article legally would apply only to the relations between Japan and the Far Eastern Republic, Japan had in fact no intention to support any organization hostile to Soviet Russia.

The preamble of the new Japanese draft stated that the treaty concerning the Far Eastern Republic would go into effect immediately upon signature, regardless of the beginning of the negotiations concerning questions relating to all of Russia. Ioffe objected. When Matsudaira asked when Ioffe thought the treaty would take legal effect, Ioffe replied: "When not a single Japanese soldier will be left on Russian soil."

In response to a direct question, Matsudaira declared that Japan planned to evacuate the Priamur region by the end of September and the Maritime Province by the end of October; North Sakhalin would be cleared only after the settlement of the Nikolaevsk question. Rhetorically Ioffe asked what relationship North Sakhalin had to the Nikolaevsk question; Matsudaira made no reply. When Ioffe inquired when it was contemplated to settle the Nikolaevsk question, Matsudaira stated that it would not be done at this conference and that at any rate it could be settled only with a government which had been recognized at least *de facto*. In view of Japan's continued non-recognition of his government, Ioffe queried sarcastically how it was possible then to solve issues favorable to Japan with a government that had not been recognized *de facto*; again Matsudaira did not give a straight answer.[37, p]

---

p Ioffe was struck by another contradiction, which he later noted in an article. By wanting the Far Eastern Republic to assume responsibility for the Nikolaevsk*

At the evening session on September 19 Ioffe declared that it was absolutely clear from the debate that morning that the Japanese government did not consider it possible to commit itself formally not to undertake hostile action against Soviet Russia or to deny support to groups and organizations seeking to disturb Russian law and order. Furthermore, a new, unexpected point had emerged from the debate, namely that Japan planned to continue the occupation of North Sakhalin indefinitely, since the date of evacuation was made dependent on the settlement of the Nikolaevsk incident which was not subject to examination at the conference. Ioffe proposed, therefore, to adjourn the conference temporarily to give him time to make a report to his government and obtain new instructions.

Matsudaira agreed to a recess saying that he foresaw no difficulty in resolving the first point, as Japan truly had no intention to support elements hostile to Russia or engage in hostile action herself. As regarded the occupation of North Sakhalin on the other hand, Matsudaira expressed surprise at Ioffe's statement that this was a new element, saying that the whole world knew Japan's position that the evacuation of North Sakhalin depended on the solution of the Nikolaevsk question.[38]

Karakhan's suspicion that the Japanese were not serious in negotiating but conferred merely for the sake of public opinion and the press was reciprocated by the Japanese. Reviewing the attitude of the plenipotentiaries of the Far Eastern Republic and Soviet Russia, Tanaka wrote on the basis of Japanese sources: "It became increasingly clear that they were insincere, and the inference grew deeper that they were interested mainly in scoring points in domestic and foreign propaganda."

Believing that the other side was waiting merely for a convenient pretext to break off the negotiations the Japanese plenipotentiaries recommended to the Foreign Office that it do so first. On September 23 Foreign Minister Uchida instructed Matsudaira to terminate negotiations if Ioffe continued quibbling and procrastinating and did not give

---

*incident, the Japanese in effect tried to solve the question which they were unwilling to discuss. (Ioffe, p. 10)

a clear answer by the end of the month; at the same time the delegates were to make it clear that the responsibility for breaking off the negotiations rested entirely with the Russian side.[39]

Negotiations were resumed on September 23. Ioffe declared that he had received new instructions. The governments of Soviet Russia and the Far Eastern Republic agreed to the Japanese proposal that there be two consecutive treaties and consented that the first treaty, to be concluded between Soviet Russia and the Far Eastern Republic on one hand and Japan on the other, settle only questions concerning the Far Eastern Republic and Japan with the understanding that this treaty contain the obligation for Japan to enter into negotiations with Soviet Russia concerning trade relations, pertaining to the entire territory of the R.S.F.S.R. The governments of Soviet Russia and the Far Eastern Republic could not accept, however, that the mutual restraint from hostile action be confined to the Far Eastern Republic and Japan and insisted that the very first treaty include a guarantee extending to Soviet Russia. Nor could the two governments concur under any circumstances with the formulation that the evacuation of North Sakhalin depended on the solution of the Nikolaevsk question, for they could not accept responsibility for the events at Nikolaevsk. They expressed the supposition that this question together with questions about the losses inflicted on Russian citizens during the Japanese occupation of Siberia as well as the question of Japanese interests on Sakhalin and questions about any other Japanese or Russian interests could be the subject of consideration by the negotiating parties, but insisted categorically that the date for the evacuation of North Sakhalin and all other Russian territory must be fixed in the first treaty or in an appendix that formed an integral part of the treaty, without reference to any other questions.

The Japanese agreed to the extension of the non-aggression pledge to Soviet Russia in a separate set of documents which would be regarded as forming part of the general agreement. But they did not budge on the tie-in of the evacuation of North Sakhalin with the Nikolaevsk question and would not set a date for evacuation, and requested new instructions from Tokyo.[40] They were provoked by Ioffe's assertion that he had not known about the Japanese contention that the Japanese occupation of North Sakhalin had been a "guaranty" occupation and by his statement that it was impossible to continue the conference in such a state of affairs; they replied that the Russians must have known the Japanese position even during the preliminary talks and that it was too late to listen to such assertions.[41]

During the session of September 25,[q] Matsudaira stated that the decision of the Japanese government to limit the application of the general agreement to relations between Japan and the Far Eastern Republic, to make the agreement effective immediately upon signature and to leave the negotiation of other matters until after the signing of this general agreement, had been final. Both negotiating parties had agreed on this at Dairen and again during the preliminary talks leading to the Changchun Conference.

Matsudaira reiterated that the delegates of Soviet Russia and the Far Eastern Republic must have known from repeated statements by the Japanese government and the Japanese delegation at the Dairen Conference that the occupation of North Sakhalin was a guaranty for the settlement of the Nikolaevsk events. It was crystal clear from the document attached to the general agreement worked out at Dairen as well as from the preliminary talks concerning the Changchun Conference that both sides had agreed on this. "If the Russian delegation now, in demanding the fixing of a date for the evacuation of Sakhalin, insists that it does not know that the occupation of Sakhalin is a guaranty of the settlement of the Nikolaevsk events, it merely shows the desire of the delegation to annul the agreement, attained by the preliminary negotiations," Matsudaira asserted. "So long as the delegation of the R.S.F.S.R. and the F.E.R. adheres to such a line of conduct, the Japanese government considers it impossible to continue the present negotiations, not to speak of the inopportuneness to consider these questions, which were raised by the Russian delegation for the first time at the session of September 23."

---

[q] According to Japanese sources; September 26 according to Russian sources.

Ioffe denied that there had been any preliminary understanding by both sides that the occupation of Sakhalin was related to the settlement of the Nikolaevsk affair. No such agreement could have existed, if for no other reason than that the Dairen Conference had broken up over this very issue. There had been Dairen talks but not a Dairen agreement. Ioffe argued that Soviet Russia and the Far Eastern Republic had made many concessions to Japan, had even accepted Japan's "strange, incomprehensible, suspicion-arousing demand" that separate agreements be made with the Far Eastern Republic and Soviet Russia. Denouncing the manner in which the Japanese evacuation was being carried out—without coordination with the Soviet military command, so that the organization of counterrevolutionary elements was assisted and bloodshed rather than peace resulted—Ioffe declared that Russia had shown its sincere desire to come to an agreement with Japan by not insisting that negotiations begin with the consideration of Japanese evacuation. But Soviet Russia had to reject a treaty which satisfied the interests of one side only and did not even guarantee the establishment of peace in the Far East.

Ioffe noted that he had repeatedly stated that no consideration could be given to any declarations and statements that could be known to the other side only from newspaper reports. In the official correspondence between the two governments there was no mention that Japan would insist at Changchun on the occupation of North Sakhalin as a guaranty of the settlement of the Nikolaevsk affair. Official notification thereof was made to the delegation of Soviet Russia and the Far Eastern Republic only at the session on September 19; hence they could not react to it until then. "The Russian and Far Eastern Republics, which occupy not less than one sixth of the surface of the globe and have a population of 150 million cannot tolerate that their territory be occupied by foreigners as a guaranty of [the settlement of] any sort of controversy," Ioffe declared. "A treaty, by which the R.S.F.S.R. and the F.E.R. do not even achieve the freeing of their territory from Japanese occupation, is of no value to Russia and the F.E.R."

Ioffe commented that the American Secretary of State Charles Evans Hughes had expressed the same view as the two governments at the

Washington Conference. He was confident that "if even such an enemy of Soviet Russia as Hughes" had independently developed this position there would be widespread support for it among the laboring classes throughout the world, including Japan. Referring back to Matsudaira's assurance that the Japanese people harbored no hostile feelings toward the Russian people and desired friendly relations with them, Ioffe expressed the hope that even though an agreement was not possible now, some day the Japanese people would induce their government to reopen negotiations, which would truly correspond to the friendly feelings of the two peoples.

Matsudaira, in accordance with Uchida's instructions, had presented Ioffe and Ianson with an ultimatum; unless they changed their point of view, the conference would be ended. "We must repeat," Ioffe declared, "that we cannot change our line on this question and that we, like the Japanese delegation, shall have to leave Changchun." Ioffe concluded by asking that the Japanese prolong their hospitality for another two to three days to permit them to wind up their affairs. Thus the Changchun Conference collapsed after thirteen sessions or twenty-one days.[42, r]

In a public statement made on September 25, Matsudaira reviewed the course of the Changchun talks. He accused the Russian side of "a complete ignoring of the circumstances attending the conference and the upsetting of the understanding arrived at in the preliminary negotiations." While he declared that "the entire responsibility for the breakup of the conference rests with the Russians," he expressed the "confident belief" of his government that the collapse of the conference would in no wise effect "the sympathy and kind feeling entertained by the Government and people of Japan towards the Russian people."[43]

Foreign Minister Uchida declared on September 27 that the failure of the Changchun Conference meant no change in the Japanese policy of

---

[r] According to a dispatch from Moscow, printed in the *Deutsche Allgemeine Zeitung* on October 4, 1922, Ioffe's departure was delayed by illness. The Japanese delegation called on Ioffe to express their sympathy and to assure him that the end of the conference was merely a temporary break in Russo-Japanese negotiations.

withdrawal from Siberia: "The withdrawal from Vladivostok and other mainland points will be concluded by the end of October. As for Saghalien, our retirement from the northern or Russian half of the island will take place, as repeatedly stated, as soon as the Nikolaevsk affair has been settled. The Japanese Government has no territorial design in this or any other connection."

Uchida restated the objectives with which Japan had come to the conference:

> It was made clear in advance that we sought a working arrangement with the Chita Government which would protect our frontiers from lawless incursions, terminate hostile propaganda, and give protection to Japanese and Koreans residing lawfully in Siberia. We hoped to obtain the recognition of the rights of private ownership of property for our people and freedom to trade and conduct their affairs: and these things, we believed, would benefit the unfortunate Russians in Siberia as well as the approximately ten thousand Japanese and the Koreans, who still reside and attempt to conduct their business there by right of treaty with the former Government of Russia.

Uchida asserted that in dealing with the Moscow representatives the Japanese diplomats had encountered "difficulties of the same character" as their European colleagues and expressed doubt, in view of Soviet Russia's denial of private ownership of property in European Russia, of "the sincerity of the Soviet intentions at Changchun." Yet like Matsudaira he ended on a note of goodwill, proclaiming that "the Japanese Government in accordance with the wishes of the Japanese people deeply sympathizes with the affllicted Russian people and profoundly desires that peace and order may be maintained in Siberia."[44]

Analyzing the failure of the Changchun talks on the basis of Japanese archival material, Tanaka made mention of the fact that the Russians had had frequent contact with Japanese newspapermen. They did so, he felt, not only to spread propaganda but also to gather information about conditions in Japan. One of the reasons the talks collapsed, Tanaka felt, was that the Russians concluded from what they had heard from the newspapermen that there was much internal opposition to the government's policy in Japan and that with time internal pressure from Japanese businessmen and workers would force the Japanese government come to more favorable terms with Soviet Russia. Sooner or later the Japanese would evacuate their forces from the Maritime Province anyway. They felt that the days of the Far Eastern Republic were numbered and that it would soon be incorporated in the Russian Soviet Federated Socialist Republic with Vladivostok too reverting to Russian rule. It thus was to their advantage to wait until the situation was more favorable rather than to sign an immediate agreement that entailed considerable sacrifice.[45]

Ioffe's high regard for newspapers and their use was common knowledge. In a speech at Peking he himself had referred to the press of Europe as "the great power" and to the press of China as "the prime great power."[46] Soviet contact with Japanese journalists is borne out by Russian sources, which tell of a secret memorandum that was handed to the Russian delegation by a Japanese newspaperman. The journalist stated that the failure of the conference would be a disaster for both Russia and Japan. Asserting that he was sympathetic toward Russia, he proposed two ways in which the conference could be concluded successfully, a step he deemed necessary for the recognition of the Soviet regime by Japan. He promised to use the influence of the Japanese press to hasten recognition, if either of the two proposals were accepted by the Soviets. Briefly, the journalist stated that Russia could either accept the Japanese proposals of the Dairen Conference promptly and thereby gain Japanese goodwill, obtain the confiscated war stores and soon recognition, or it could insist on the abolition of the Dairen agreement and on the start of negotiations for the conclusion of a commercial agreement not only between Japan and the Far Eastern Republic but also with Russia. To overcome opposition to the latter course, Russia would have a choice of either offering to sell to Japan North Sakhalin or at least of guaranteeing that she would cede neither Sakhalin nor the Maritime Province to a third power, since Japan feared American seizure of Asia. The journalist

THE CHANGCHUN CONFERENCE 79

suggested, furthermore, that Soviet Russia pledge not to incite Koreans to seek independence from Japan.[47]

Reviewing the collapse of the second round of talks from the Soviet standpoint, Ioffe did not regard the Changchun Conference as the culmination of the Dairen Conference in the sense that all that had remained to be done was for the Russian delegates to add a few finishing touches and sign the agreement hammered out earlier. In his view the international situation had changed dramatically, and the idea of "bufferism," which had been tied closely to the Siberian intervention, could no longer play a role at the conference. The Russian delegation, therefore, was prepared for an all-out fight to regain for Russia her proper place on the Pacific. When it became apparent that Japan's attitude toward the Soviet regime had not changed and that it was regarded as just as weak and beleaguered as it had been in the early days of the Revolution, Ioffe realized that the talks were as yet premature and that the Changchun Conference would be as fruitless as the Dairen Conference had been.

The Japanese had come to Changchun to discuss only trade and other problems between Japan and the Far Eastern Republic and questions such as fishery, relating to the Russian Far East; they had not been ready for a general agreement with Soviet Russia. Matsudaira had frankly stated to Ioffe that the Japanese people had come to trust the Far Eastern Republic, where there was a democratic regime rather than a Communist one, and that they were willing to establish economic relations with it. It had been found at Dairen that Soviet participation in negotiations was necessary to solve such problems as fishery, but Japan was not yet ready to make a more far-reaching agreement with the R.S.F.S.R., though it thought that the projected agreement with the Far Eastern Republic would pave the way for a later agreement with Soviet Russia.

In the eyes of Ioffe Japanese diplomacy was unique in that it did not consider it necessary to compromise the points of view of the two negotiating parties in the conclusion of an agreement. Japanese diplomacy, he wrote, was concerned exclusively with Japanese interests and was not even interested in knowing and understanding the interests of the other side. In his words:

> Japanese diplomacy puts forth its demands. If they are categorically rejected, and it becomes necessary to retreat, Japanese diplomacy merely moderates its appetite without going out to meet the other side, i.e. it does not seek to make compromises in the direction of the interest of the other side but merely gives in herself, limiting her own interests. To be sure, a compromise results, but there is an enormous difference, since in the case of the Japanese tactics there remains quite often till the end a lack of understanding what the other side wishes, in what it is interested.[48]

Ioffe felt that the Japanese had lost their sense of reality. During the Civil War the Soviets had been greatly interested in the disposition of the military stores, the safeguarding of which had been one of the pretexts for the Intervention. By this time, however, they believed that the most valuable part of the supplies had been shipped to Japan, that Siberia had been sufficiently pacified to an extent that the arms could no longer be effectively used against them, and that the Japanese would surrender the remainder to White forces anyway, regardless of any agreement. Thus Ioffe thought it to have been unrealistic for the Japanese to try to blackmail his government with these military stores into agreeing to their terms. Ioffe attributed the Japanese loss of a sense of reality to prolonged Japanese dealings with weak Siberian governments and individual adventurers who depended on Japanese support. They had forgotten how delegates of a government representing all of Russia conducted themselves.[49]

The Japanese had tried to hold the Russian government responsible for the Nikolaevsk incident. Ioffe had argued that the incident did not give Japan any grounds for claims against the Russian government, because at the time of its occurrence neither the government of Soviet Russia nor the government of the Far Eastern Republic had extended its authority to this region. Japan's struggle here had not been with regular Russian troops but with local partisans operating on their own.

Neither at Dairen nor at Changchun had the Japanese stated what compensation they desired for the Nikolaevsk incident; they had merely declared that they continued to occupy North Sakhalin as a guaranty that compensation would be made. The Russian delegates countered that the occupation of territory as a guaranty was unbefitting relations between civilized states; at the same time they suspected that Japan had no intention of withdrawing from North Sakhalin in view of its economic and strategic importance, even liberal Japanese politicians talking of the importance of the island to Japan.[50]

In a statement about the Far Eastern situation, published in *Izvestiia* on October 25, 1922, Foreign Commissar Chicherin stated the official Soviet position that the negotiations with Japan had failed because "the appetites of the Japanese imperialists are still so great, that an understanding with them for us at that time was still impossible." Alleging that Japan intended to annex North Sakhalin, which came so close to the mainland and particularly to the mouth of the Amur River that its surrender would mean the exposure of navigation on the Amur to foreign domination, he declared: "The estuary of Siberia's most important river would practically be in Japanese hands. We cannot agree to this under any circumstances, and if the Japanese government will not retract this demand, there will not only be no agreement with Japan, but there will remain in existence a source of future complications."[51]

On November 11 Ioffe, who had returned to his post in Peking, followed up Chicherin's pronouncement with a note to the Japanese Minister Obata Torikichi 小幡酉吉, which stated that the worker-peasant government of Soviet Russia protested "in the most determined and energetic way" against the continuation of the "completely illegal and absolutely inadmissable occupation by Japanese forces of the Russian part of Sakhalin." Yet at the same time Ioffe held open the door for renewed talks by reminding the Japanese government that he had stated definitely at Changchun in the name of his government that Japanese economic interests on Sakhalin could be satisfied in another way, by granting appropriate concessions in the northern part of the island, and that Russia, true to her word was still willing to do so.[52]

The rupture of negotiations had been agreeable to both sides, so much so that the question arose whether anyone cared for the Changchun Conference.

> Whether it is a success or failure, it does not seem to bother either the Russians or the Japanese [the *Peking Daily News* reported]. The Japanese delegates have shown, in a statement by their official spokesman, that degree of eagerness to return to Tokio that one is induced to think that it was a serious blunder on their part to have been ever at Changchun at all. The Russians have been equally firm in their resolution not to continue the useless bickerings with the representatives from Tokio—so much so that it seemed absolutely foolish to have ever undertaken what is obviously next to impossibility.[53]

Yet while neither the Japanese nor the Soviets wanted to drag the conference out further when it became evident that no agreement could be reached, both sides left convinced that this was not a final break but merely a temporary interruption in a continuing dialogue.

The Japanese negotiators had been encouraged in their opposition by letters from military and civilian White Russian organizations, which protested against any accomodation with the Communists. To win Japanese support they inveighed against the danger which Bolshevism posed for Japan, one of the few remaining pillars of law and civilization in their eyes. White Russian officers and soldiers reminded the Japanese that their blood had run together in the common struggle against the Reds and called upon them not to take the "insane step" of surrendering the war materials in Vladivostok. "The time has come," Major General Tkachev wrote to the Japanese delegates at the Changchun Conference, "when the enemies of mankind are directing their blows in your direction too and long to raise the flag of the International atop sacred Mt. Fuji."[54]

The foreign press again was divided as to which side was responsible for the collapse of the negotiations. The *Peking Daily News* put the responsibility squarely on the shoulders of Japan. It regarded the demand

THE CHANGCHUN CONFERENCE 83

for a definite date for Japanese withdrawal from North Sakhalin as "a natural question for the Russian representatives to ask and . . . a fair question for the Japanese representatives to answer."[55] The *North China Standard*, on the other hand, once more blamed the Russians:

> Again the failure was due to the overbearing attitude of the Bolsheviks on the one hand and their dishonest—we cannot find a milder word—practices on the other. For a man of the position of Mr. Yoffe to come all the way from Moscow to start negotiations which are supposed to be undertaken with a view to conclude a friendly agreement and then to stand up and declare that he has never heard of the most fundamental conditions upon which these negotiations are based is more than bluff, it is sheer impudence.[56]

The *North China Daily News* held out hopes for the successful resumption of negotiations because of changes in Japanese public opinion. "It is more than interesting to note quite a considerable feeling in Japan favoring the enlargement of the scope of the Conference, and naturally in the great industrial centre of Osaka, where people are probably more interested in trade than politics, this sentiment has been especially pronounced." The paper remarked that "in the new condition of opinion in Japan, as mirrored in the press there, one finds so great a desire to have finished with the Siberian business that compromise hitherto deemed out of the question seems to-day almost possible." A week later the paper added: "Looking to the diplomatic methods pursued in other parts of the world by the Soviet representatives, we have very little doubt that before long they will be prepared with fresh proposals by which the Japanese can again be brought to the conference table."[57]

In November of 1922 the Japanese evacuation of the Maritime Province was completed and, with the Japanese armies gone, the *raison d'être* for the Far Eastern Republic had vanished. The Popular Assembly repealed the constitution, renounced its power and requested and the same month obtained reincorporation of the Far Eastern Republic into the Russian Soviet Federated Socialist Republic. On December 30 the various republics of Russia joined in the Union of Soviet Socialist Republics.[58]

The "menace" of Japan, which had been the reason for the creation of an ostensibly democratic buffer state had been also used as an argument for its liquidation. In its final declaration the Popular Assembly asserted that Japan had sought to take advantage of the sovereignty of the Far Eastern Republic and of its separation from Soviet Russia to gain complete freedom for Japanese capital in the Russian Far East, which would have made possible the colonization of this region by Japan. The Popular Assembly declared that the democratic constitution of the Far Eastern Republic had not protected it from the inroads of Japanese and other imperialists. "We learned from our experience that the talk of bourgeois democratic governments about democracy and freedom are words, hiding their rapacious imperialistic yearnings for the seizure and plundering of weaker countries and colonies."[59]

CHAPTER THREE

The Gotō-Ioffe Talks

AMONG the Japanese who spoke out for a Russo-Japanese rapprochement was Gotō Shimpei 後藤新平, formerly foreign minister and currently lord mayor of Tokyo. Viscount Gotō was no Communist-sympathizer; his advocacy of Russo-Japanese collaboration antedated the Revolution. In the decade following the Russo-Japanese War Gotō had advocated Russo-Japanese collaboration as a means of blocking American penetration into the Far East. He had served as president of the South Manchurian Railway (1906–08), had negotiated with Tsarist representatives concerning economic cooperation between the two countries (1909–10) and in 1915–16 had conferred with the Tsarist minister about the conclusion of an alliance.

Gotō was connected with shipping and railway enterprises which had far-reaching interests in the Russian Far East before the Revolution. He was a highly effective, popular orator, dubbed at one time the "Japanese [Teddy] Roosevelt." He associated with men of diverse political views. In the words of his biographer: "His right arm embraced even those patriots who belonged to the extreme right wing, while his left arm reached those socialists who were on the extreme left wing. Just as Bismarck, while enforcing an absolute government on one hand, met with Lassalle, an extreme leftist, and utilized his wisdom and tactics on the other hand, so the Count's arm was extended to the extreme left wing in spite of the fact that the Count himself was regarded as belonging to the bureaucratic establishment."[1] In his advocacy of Japanese recognition of the Soviet regime and of renewed Russo-Japanese collaboration Gotō thus reflected at once the feeling of businessmen and of workers; recognition of Soviet Russia was one of the planks of the Japanese federation of labor at its convention in 1922.

Gotō realized that the difficult economic situation in which Russia found herself in the wake of the Revolution presented a great opportunity for Japan to utilize the vast territory of the Soviet Far East to further her own development; he argued also that prompt conclusion of a treaty between Japan and Russia would forestall the normalization of Russo-American and Russo-Chinese relations, either of which might leave Japan dangerously isolated.[a] Gotō brushed aside political differences, noting that the foundations of foreign policy were land and people, not ideology. He deemed economic collaboration between Japan and Russia not only desirable but necessary. "The resources of the eastern part of the Russian territory seem to be waiting for our help in their exploitation."

Gotō did not confine his advocacy of a Japanese-Soviet rapprochement to words. When he learned that Ioffe, who had been the chief Soviet delegate at Changchun, had fallen ill, he decided to take the opportunity to invite him to Japan for a cure and in the process to reopen informal talks. Like Ioffe, Gotō was a physician by training—he had received an M.D. in Germany—and had been director of the Public Health Bureau and chief inspector of army hygiene. He was also president of the Russo-Japanese Association. It was natural, therefore, for him to communicate with Ioffe in terms of his health as well as of the state of Soviet-Japanese relations.

While Soviet sources suggest that the invitation was Gotō's idea, some Japanese sources assert that Ioffe had conveyed to Gotō his desire to visit Japan for recuperation and sightseeing and that Gotō extended the invitation in response to this. At any rate, Gotō cleared the matter with Premier Katō Tomosaburō 加藤友三郎;[b] in fact, they secretly agreed

---

[a] While the Soviet Union did not yet present a formidable opponent, she could have been dangerous to Japan as an ally of the United States, the latter having emerged from World War I as the most serious opponent of Japanese expansion by championing the territorial integrity of Russia and China.

[b] Admiral Katō Tomosaburō, chief assistant of Admiral Tōgō Heihachirō during the Russo-Japanese War and chief delegate of Japan at the Washington Naval Conference, was premier from June 12, 1922 to August 25, 1923. Do not confuse with Katō Takaaki, who became premier in June of 1924.

that the private talks would eventually become unofficial negotiations.² When Gotō released to the press that the premier approved of the invitation to Ioffe, Foreign Minister Uchida spoke up against the resumption of negotiations in this manner, but by this time Gotō and his followers had publicized Katō's support so widely that the premier could not reverse himself. At last the Foreign Office concurred on condition that Ioffe would come as a private person. So long as Japan did not recognize the Soviet Union she could not extend to Ioffe diplomatic status and privileges. On January 16, 1923, Gotō cabled to Ioffe: "I extend my sincere sympathy for your health and suggest whether you cannot spend some time in Japanese hot springs for cure that might help clear misunderstandings between our two nations."³

Meanwhile the Japanese Ambassador to Poland, Kawakami Toshitsune 川上俊彦[c], on his way through the Soviet Union told Foreign Commissar Chicherin that the cession of North Sakhalin to Japan would make possible the normalization of Russo-Japanese relations and the *de jure* recognition of Soviet Russia by Japan. Although Chicherin flatly rejected Kawakami's suggestion and refused to consider the cession of any part of Russian territory as subject to discussion, he had Ioffe accept the Japanese invitation to visit Tokyo and enter into negotiations about the normalization of Soviet-Japanese relations. He made it clear, however, that this would be done without any prior commitment whatsoever.⁴ On January 23, 1923, Ioffe arrived in Shanghai and cabled to Gotō: "I beg you to accept my sincere thanks for your kind invitation which mark of attention I may be permitted to consider as expression of feelings of Japanese people reciprocated by Russian people. Am leaving Shanghai for Tokyo Saturday twenty-seventh."⁵

The following day, on January 24, Consul General Tanaka wired that Ioffe had met Sun-Yat-sen, head of the revolutionary Kuomintang government; two days later, on January 26, a joint Soviet-Chinese communiqué was made public. In it Ioffe assured Sun that China had "the warmest sympathy of the Russian people and can count on the support of Russia"

---

[c] Also known as Toshihiko.

in its quest for national unification. As Cornelius Vanderbilt Jr. had written in October of 1922: "And Japan is frightened—far more badly frightened than ever before in her history—for, should Russia and China enter into military alliance against Japan, all the fruits of Nipponese victories in the field, on the sea and at the conference tables would become pyrrhic victories."[6]

Home Minister Mizuno Rentarō 水野錬太郎 warned the Japanese consulate at Shanghai that there might be an attempt on the life of Ioffe, particularly by a relative of one of the Japanese massacred at Nikolaevsk, and expressed the wish that Ioffe could be dissuaded from coming. Foreign Minister Uchida, who had opposed Ioffe's visit from the very beginning, instructed Tanaka to inform Ioffe that his visit at the present time was undesirable; he repeated Mizuno's assertion that "various elements" were vociferously opposed to his coming and that, although the police would do their best to protect him, there was danger of an attack on his person. Gotō cabled Ioffe to give serious thought to the matter in order to avoid misunderstandings. When Tanaka tried once more to dissuade him from proceeding to Japan, Ioffe retorted that he must interpret this as a change in the position of the Japanese government and warned that this would make a most unfavorable impression in Moscow. Unable to accept the responsibility for the repercussions that might ensue, Tanaka declared that the desire of his government to normalize relations with the Soviet Union had not changed and that he did not object to the trip. Booking passage on the American steamer *Empress of Asia*, Ioffe reached Nagasaki on January 29 and Yokohama on February 1. He was accompanied by his young wife Mary and their four year old son Vladimir and by his private secretary Levin.[7, d]

Gotō's secretary Mori Kōzō 森孝三 had joined Ioffe at Kobe. He accompanied Ioffe and his party to Tokyo, where they arrived at 12:40 p.m.

---

[d] "Mr. Levin is a member of the so-called *extraordinary commission* with privileges and special rights. He reports directly to Moscow; he is the controller of Mr. Joffe, and seems to me more important as [than] Joffe himself," von Salzmann had reported from Peking. (Japanese Archives, MT 251.106. 7:2600 and MT 251.106.15:573)

on February 1. They proceeded from the station to the Tsukiji-Seiyoken Hotel where Gotō and Ioffe met for the first time and talked for three hours. The following day Ioffe paid a return visit to Gotō at his residence, then left for the hot spring resort of Atami where he was to confer with Gotō in a relaxed atmosphere while recuperating.[8]

Japanese reaction to Ioffe's visit was mixed. Gotō had welcomed him warmly and a large crowd of well-wishers had greeted him at Tokyo Station. Capitalists who desired new markets because of the decline in trade with China since 1915 and fishermen who longed for legal access to Russian waters were as relieved by Ioffe's arrival "as if they had met Buddha in Hell." To some people, on the other hand, the shout "Ioffe is coming!" sounded like "The Mongols are coming!" The police secretly went through Ioffe's baggage while he was sightseeing in Yokohama and spied on him so clumsily that Ioffe remarked in irritation that in no other country of the world could he have encountered "so many and such disagreeable things as in Japan." When popular excitement prompted queries on the Diet floor, Foreign Minister Uchida replied that Ioffe's visit was purely personal in nature, and Home Minister Mizuno promised to do his best to insure the safety of the Russians.

There were those who thought that Gotō had turned red. On February 5 members of the Sekkabōshidan 赤化防止団 (The Anti-Bolshevik League) forced their way into Gotō's residence in Azabu (Sakura-chō), demanded an interview with the viscount and when they learned that he was not in, smashed his furniture, sliding doors and various articles. They returned three weeks later, on February 28, and bloodied the head of Gotō's eldest son, Ichizō 一蔵, who met them in place of his father.[9]

In the archives of the Japanese Foreign Office there is the English text of a letter which Ioffe wrote to Gotō from Atami. Although very long, it is worth reproducing in full for the light it throws not only on the events related but on the personality and approach of the writer.

Atami,
February 7th 1923

Dear Viscount Gotō,

Insofar as I can judge by the Japanese papers that I am in a position to read (and by these I mean, consequently, mostly the English written ones), there exists a large misunderstanding on the part of the Japanese Government and the Japanese public at large in their conception of the Russian Far-Eastern policy.

I agreed perfectly with you when you gave out as a motive of your courteous invitation to me to come to Japan for recuperating also the hope that my stay in this country could help to clear the misunderstandings that exist between Russia and Japan.

Most grateful as I am to you for your kind attention and hospitality shown to me, I would not care to let an opportunity pass by of clearing up misunderstandings where such exist, as it seems to me. It can be perfectly clearly surmised from reports having appeared in the above-mentioned papers that the Japanese Government, or rather the Ministry of Foreign Affairs, believe there exist several different points of view among ruling circles in Russia on questions of foreign policy in general and with regard to Japan, in particular.

Mr. Kawakami, Japanese Minister Plenipotentiary and Envoy Extraordinary to Warsaw, declared, in an interview, that though Mr. Yoffe's influence and importance in Russia were very great, yet he could surmise from conversations with Russian statesmen that the policy of Mr. Yoffe at Changchun did not meet with approval.

At the same time, one of the Japanese papers openly declares that the question of Russo-Japanese relations and of the so-called third Russo-Japanese Conference is one of *personality*, or, in other words, that this question depends on what persons the Japanese Government will have to deal with; and there are many Japanese papers which report the view of the Ministry of Foreign Affairs purporting to say as if in Russia, in her foreign policy, there were also with regard to Japan a certain current, headed by Messrs. Krassin and Karakhan, which is supposed to be much more prone to compromise than the one which I represent. A few hints contained in the papers seem also to convey the impression that there is a belief that it is possible to conclude solely a trade agreement precisely with this more compromising current, and this—regardless of the question of the Japanese occupation of Northern Saghalien.

May I be allowed, esteemed Viscount Goto, in the interest of the elucidation of truth, to assure you categorically that all this is pure misunderstanding and does not in the least correspond to the real situation as it stands.

Since, on principle, the Workers and Peasants' Government does not recognise secret diplomacy, there can never in general be any currents in the foreign policy of Soviet Russia, and this policy must always and wholly represent the true interests of the majority of the people, i.e. the toiling masses, of Russia. Russian diplomacy is *people's* diplomacy and there are not, nor can there be, any dissensions among us within the group engaged in diplomatic work.

Mr. Krassin is People's Commissary of Foreign Trade, and, as such does not take part in diplomatic work specially, being in charge of matters of foreign trade. True, Mr. Karakhan is Member of the Collegium of the People's Commissariat of Foreign Affairs and one of the Assistant-"Remplacants" of Mr. Chicherin; however, he has never held any special position of his own, nor has he ever had too much influence on Russian foreign policy, in any special direction for these two reasons: first, owing, as already stated above, to the fact there exist no dissensions whatsoever by us within our diplomatic milieux, and then, secondly, because by us as, also, anywhere also, Plenipotentiary Envoys represent all the Republic and not alone the People's Commissariat of Foreign Affairs.

While I was conducting negotiations at Changchun in the name of the R.S.F.S.R., I was in the closest contact with my Government and communicated with the latter on every serious question. Each serious question was discussed by all the Government as a whole, and so was too the opinion of the Delegation on such question, and the voice of the Department concerned in a given question always carried special weight.

As the negotiations were all through a matter of public knowledge in Russia, the broad masses too had the possibility of expressing their views on the questions under discussion at Changchun, and I may safely advance that, perhaps, there never had yet existed such solidarity between the Delegates, the Government and the peoples as at the time of the Changchun Conference. Not only is there no dissatisfaction being felt in Russia with my Changchun policy, but, on the contrary, "my" policy at Changchun was and still is nothing but the policy of my people and my Government.

All the peoples of Russia and the whole of her Government were altogether indignant at the conquering notes in which the Japanese Delegation conducted negotiations at Changchun, and all shared this point of view that until the evacuation of Northern Saghalien by the Japanese no negotiations were at all possible with Japan. On the other hand, the Russian Delegation at Changchun had, in the name of their people and Government, declared quite unambiguously their willingness to meet half-way Japanese economic interests in Saghalien too, doing it in some other way, without acts of violence on the part of Japan.

It would be out of place here to dwell more in detail on all the phases of the Changchun Conference and the causes of its disruption: I promised to write you another letter on this matter, and, though the state of my health be a big obstacle thereto, I will yet write this letter.

At the present time, however, I may call your attention to the fact that even after the failure of the Changchun Conference, the friendly attitude of Russia towards Japan has not at all been changed. After the occupation of the Maritime and the Amur provinces by the Red troops, the Japanese consuls were left everywhere on their posts, although up till now there are no Russian consuls yet in Japan, and despite the fact that in this matter the international law upholds very strictly the point of view of reciprocity. Nor was the attitude of the Russian authorities to the Japanese residents on the spots also after the rupture of the negotiations such as would correspond to relations that should set in between hostile States, this attitude, on the contrary, being then and still remaining extremely friendly. I may likewise remark that yet on the 11th of November 1922, acting in the name and upon the instruction of my Government, I handed to the Japanese Government, through the Japanese Minister to Peking, a Note of protest against the continued occupation of Saghalien, in which Note it was once again and more definitely yet pointed out that Russia was willing to grant concessions to Japan in Northern Saghalien. However, no answer was forthcoming to this Note, and, on the contrary, the Japanese Government continued its strongly hostile policy vis-à-vis Russia, ignoring her altogether and being, apparently, foremostly anxious lest anyone would take Japan under for being willing to recognise Russia and show her even some primitive courteousness.

Just the reverse: when the well-known and quite inadmissible act of piracy of Japanese ships against Russian had taken place, when many peaceful Russian citizens were slaughtered and their property was seized, and when, again in the name and on the instruction of my own Government, I sent, through Mr. Obata, a Note to the Japanese Government, this Note was first very courteously accepted (just as the first one had been) in the Japanese Legation at Peking, and then, after a few days it was brought back to the Russian Plenipotentiary Mission by a Secretary of the Japanese Legation, who declared that the latter had no right to receive it, and that the only way of having this Note sent to the Legation was by mail. When, however, this course was followed, a few days later the same Secretary of the Japanese Legation brought the Note to the Russian Mission again, declaring he had made a mistake, and that the Note could not be accepted either by mail. Although this Note might very well have been refused immediately, seeing that when it had come by post it was quite clear that the mail came from the Russian Mission, and it was more than easy to guess what the parcel contained, this wavering and ambiguous policy was continued further.

When your kind invitation to me was received to come to Japan for recuperation, and Mr. Fujita, who was sent by you, announced that the Japanese Government accepted all those conditions which had been set by me during preliminary conversations, namely that the Government guaranteed diplomatic immunity for myself and the party, the freedom of moving in Japan, the immunity of correspondence and the right to use secret code and have couriers—my staff, who, after the incident with the piracy Note, had been directed by me to discontinue all relations with the Japanese Legation at Peking, requested Messrs. Fujita and Taguchi to inquire whether the Japanese Government was actually granting to me all the above-enumerated guarantees. Both your representatives brought from the Legation an answer in the affirmative and left Peking to see me at Shanghai, where I was preparing to go from for the South of China.

At Shanghai, the Acting Japanese Consul General confirmed to my Secretary, in the presence of your representatives, quite officially, that your Government actually gives all the above guarantees, while he enumerated each of these guarantees. Then I decided to accept your courtesy and come to Japan. However, some three or four days later, the Acting Consul General telephoned to my Secretary to the effect that his Government could not give the above-mentioned guarantees. I then informed your representatives that this being so, I would not go to Japan. They answered this was a misunderstanding, for the Acting Consul General had in view this fact alone that the guarantees in question could not be given in writing, but that in fact they remained in force; at the same time a letter was received from the Acting Consul General, saying the attitude of the Japanese Government had not changed and that everything he himself had declared was still perfectly valid.

My answer was that I never demanded written declarations from official representatives of Governments, for in my relations with other Governments I am used to consider verbal statements as made by their representatives quite as valid as written ones, but, however, for more clearness' sake, I requested your representatives to lay down in writing all that had been declared to them, and also to my Secretary in their presence, by official representatives of the Japanese Government.

However, just before boarding the ship leaving for Japan, the Acting Consul General communicated to me a telegram received from the Japanese Ministry of Interior Affairs, stating that there had been discovered a plot against me, and that, therefore, the Government could not guarantee my personal safety.

Although I was rather astonished that the Japanese Government, which is so susceptible in the matter of all international *usus*, could have admitted that the Home Office should address itself directly—although all relations with foreigners, as according to international usus, go always through the medium of the Foreign Office—and although it made me absolutely astounded how a plot that had been *discovered* could yet be dangerous, however, being used to risking my own life, while in this telegram there was no refusal on the part of the Japanese Government of the guarantees that were granted to me and while, at the same time, I had already booked my tickets and my baggage was already on board the ship—there thus remained nothing for me to do but to be grateful to the Home Minister for his kind care for my person and go on board the ship. And so that was exactly what I did do.

It was at Yokohama that the first case of violation of guarantees given took place: in the absence of any one of my representatives, my baggage was opened with skeleton keys and examined carefully, while even private letters were read.

It was only following upon your statement to me, dear Viscount

Gotō, to the effect that this event really took place by accident, and the promise that this case would be investigated, that I decided to stay in Japan and not to leave immediately. Next, however, the Government broke also the guarantee given for the cipher code, while it changed three times its attitude regarding the couriers. Out of respect for you, I decided to give way in the secret code question, but I cannot compromise in the matter of couriers.

On the other hand, the Japanese Government has surrounded me with such a wall of spies that, instead of the freedom promised, I find myself as in prison; all my correspondence is evidently being perlustrated, as letters reach me with a delay of some four or five days, besides with roughly visible signs of their having been opened before they reached me, which signs cannot fail to fly in my face, as I have behind me an experience of fifteen years of work under the Czarist regime, and, consequently, have been used to methods much more perfect technically of the Czar's secret police.

During one month that I have been staying in Japan, where I was invited to come to by the Lord Mayor of the capital of this country and one of her most prominent high officials, besides having received preliminarily so courteously guarantees from the Japanese Government, I have gathered the impression that not in any single country of the world could I have had so many and such disagreeable things as in Japan. During the five years' run of our power I have had the opportunity both officially and informally to visit various countries and had to do with different Governments or their representatives—as well as those that recognise us both de jure and de facto, and those which do so only de facto, as those that do not recognise us at all. Now, I have also many a time had to do with representatives of countries with which we were in a state of war. Yet never and nowhere have I had to face such unfriendliness, hostility and sheer lack of tact as are shown towards me by the Japanese Government. And, indeed, on the background of a most friendly attitude of nearly all the layers of Japanese public, on the background of those expressions of deep sympathy which I receive almost every day in verbal or written form, such a conduct of the Japanese Government can have but one meaning. It is precisely for this reason, and not with a view to making a complaint that I have been writing to you all that has been laid down in the foregoing pages.

At Changchun the Japanese Delegation spoke to us in the language of conquerors to conquered, ignoring altogether Russian interests and setting forth only their own, and, owing to this, the Changchun parley was even more painful than the Brest-Litovsk negotiations, for while at the Brest Conference the Germans put their rapacious ultimatums, yet they clad them in a fitting form of reciprocity.

When I come to think now of the conduct of the Japanese Government vis-à-vis Russia, it seems to me that the former still maintains the old Changchun attitude of completely ignoring Russia as a sovereign Great Power. Recent facts only confirm this.

When my Government sent a protest to the Japanese against the arbitrary stationing, contrary to international usus, of Japanese warships in Russian territorial waters, reports appeared in the newspapers to the effect that the Japanese Government meant to ignore this protest and simply leave it unanswered. When there was some appearance that the question of fisheries in Russian waters could not be settled before the beginning of the spring fishing campaign, it was semi-officially reported in the papers as if the Japanese Government intended to allow Japanese fishermen to fish in Russian territorial waters under the protection of Japanese warships.

Whatever the attitude towards the Japanese press, but if the Government does not deny such *semi-official* reports, one may be induced to believe the latter are correct.

Now, all these facts and those mentioned above can be explained but in one way only: what the Japanese Government fears most is lest it be suspected of being willing to recognise the Soviet Government, and thus, in the attitude it assumes towards the latter, it overplays its hand and conducts such a policy as if, in general, Russia were not a sovereign State. The Japanese Government even forgets that there exists an immense difference as between last year and the current one, for if, last year, Japan could explain her behaving in Siberia arbitrarily and like at home by the fact she had agreements with local Governments, established by herself, this year—there already exist no more such Governments, there being but one single Government of Russia: i.e. the Moscow one—the only name that such acts as those of last year deserve as according to the international law is simply "piracy," and nowhere and on the part of no man will they meet with any sympathy at all.

As regards mutual relations with Russia, these acts rouse in the Russian people only feelings of deepest offense and rancour—which makes impossible for tens of years to come any agreement between the two peoples.

When I first came to the Far East, I heard much of the utmost susceptibility of Oriental peoples and the extremely big importance they attach to "saving face."

I can understand this in the case of China, where foreigners actually behave themselves like at home. But I utterly fail, however, to understand this with Japan. Indeed, Japan is one of the greatest Powers in the world, and no one could possibly take it into his mind to treat her as a party which has not equal rights.

On the other hand, Russia is, to a large extent, also an Oriental, Asiatic State, and for many reasons it is precisely Russia that has full right anyhow, much more than Japan to be susceptible in questions of her prestige. Not only is Japan recognised by all, but juridically she is allied with the greatest Powers. Russia was but yet quite recently an arena of a most arbitrary conduct within her territory of Great Powers, interfering in her internal affairs under the pretext of supporting various black-hundred [i.e. ultra-reactionary] generals and admirals, and, if we do not count the smaller States, up to now Russia has been recognised de jure by

Germany alone. On the other hand, Russia covers a territory larger than one seventh part of the earth, and as for her natural riches, she is wealthier than perhaps any other country in the world; her population is over 150 millions, and her army is perhaps the strongest that exists. There are at the same time a great many White Guards outside of Russia who do their best to criticize and throw blame on the Russian Government for everything; whenever Russia take up an uncompromising attitude towards other States, she comes in for blame for this same attitude, but if, on the contrary, she is conciliating, then a hue and cry is raised and people go on saying that "with the Czarist Government no one would ever have even dared speak in such a way."

Evidently Soviet Russia has more right than anyone else to be susceptible about her prestige and more right too than anyone else to be concerned with "saving her face," that is she has more right than all other States to demand full equality of rights in her international relations.

It is clear, therefore, that until the Japanese Government will understand this, all agreement between Russia and Japan becomes extremely difficult, if at all possible.

In conditions of new Russian diplomacy, when all the negotiations are conducted openly in the face of all the people, each and any Russian peasant or worker takes part, so to say, himself or herself in the negotiations and is especially sensitive to any affront made upon Russia by the other contracting party.

It must stare everyone in the face who is acquainted with the sentiments of the large popular masses in Russia what a difference there is between the attitude to-day, following upon the Japanese intervention in Siberia. All the hardships of the war of 1904-05 and the heavy bloodshed in that war did not rouse such indignation among the Russian people as exists to-day, after the Japanese intervention of recent years, and which is still aggravated by the above-described attitude towards Russia on the part of the Japanese Government.

In the conscience of the Russian people—due, probably, to these very reasons—France and Japan are considered as the worst enemies, and any action, in itself perhaps not even meant to be hostile, on the part of the Governments of these States calls forth immediately among the Russian people some suspicion of new inimical actions against Russia. The same thing is happening now, when newspapers are publishing reports about the Japanese Government planning to bring the White Guards from Gensan to Saghalien, and in Russia suspicion is being aroused generally that this means a new attempt at intervention against Russia from Saghalien.

Russia, on the other hand, does not in the least consider herself as a country beaten, while she esteems, on the contrary, that she came out as victor from the world capitalistic intervention against Russia.

The Russian people is proud thereof that, through its own efforts and sacrifice, there are no more foreign troops on Russian soil, and, therefore, takes especially painfully the occupation by the Japanese army of the Russian part of Saghalien. To let alone the fact that all the Russian people understands perfectly well the strategic and economic importance of Saghalien, its occupation makes the people lack the conscience of full pride of and full satisfaction at the unification of all the Russian territories under the Russian Red Flag.

If we were now to make concrete inferences from the foregoing, it will be evident that, from the *Russian point of view*, letting quite alone the question as to how far these stipulations are acceptable to Japan—the resumption of Russo-Japanese negotiations is possible only under the following stipulations:

1. Recognition of full equality of the rights of Russia with Japan, as well in the proceedings of the negotiations, i.e. in the setting forth of claims by the other party, as in the treaty itself, i.e. in the corresponding wording and laying down of the clauses themselves of the agreement.

2. Willingness to conduct negotiations not barely on a trade agreement, but on a full treaty, inclusive of the resumption of normal diplomatic relations, for there is a special decision in this reference of the Supreme Organ of the Russian Republic. When at the time of the Genoa Conference I made a report on the latter and also on the Russo-German Treaty (known as the Rapallo Treaty), the All-Russian Central Executive Committee of Soviets passed a resolution deciding that henceforth the Council of People's Commissaries shall not have the right to conclude half-way treaties of the Russo-British Trade Agreement type, while instructing it, on the contrary, to sign treaties of the Rapallo Treaty type. And this latter Treaty differs, as is known, in that in it: (1) both parties renounce any claims and accounts for the past, and (2) both parties mutually recognise one another both de facto and de jure.

When, after this Rapallo Treaty, a commercial treaty was concluded in Italy between this country and Russia, which did not contain such clauses, this latter treaty was, for that very reason, not ratified by the All-Russian Central Executive Committee of Soviets.

3. A date, which would be acceptable, must be fixed for the evacuation of Northern Saghalien by the Japanese troops.

As it was precisely on this question that the rupture of the Changchun Conference occurred, it is perfectly clear that this stipulation is an absolutely indispensable condition.

As, due to the altogether peculiar and unprecedented-in-history attitude taken up towards me by the Japanese Government, I have been now for about one month and a half cut off from Russia in general and my Government, in particular—I am not in a position to judge of the feelings actually prevailing in Russia vis-à-vis Japan. However, I would believe that this attitude could not get better, in view of the conduct of the Japanese Government referred to above, but, at the same time, I do not believe that the above-mentioned preliminary condition may have changed, which I laid down in the present letter on the basis of foregoing decisions of the Russian Government and my knowledge of the sentiments of the Russian people.

What are in this respect the Japanese stipulations, I do not know, for since I have been staying in this country, the larger part of the Japanese public and press demand simply an immediate recognition of Russia de jure and an immediate resumption of negotiations.

However, as much space is being given in the press to the so-called "Nikolaevsk Affair," I may remind that the Russian Delegates at Changchun never refused to take up this issue immediately, but, that, on the contrary, it was the Japanese Delegation that did not wish, declaring that this question, for some reason or other, in contrast to all the rest, could be discussed only with a Russian Government recognised by Japan, and insisting energetically on the connection between the question of the "Nikolaevsk Affair" and the occupation of Saghalien, or, in other words, exactly on such a proposition as, for the above-stated reasons of prestige of a sovereign State, was absolutely unacceptable to Russia.

Thus, this question having not been discussed at Changchun, no decision about it was taken in Russia.

Now, although it seems most strange to me that one party or the other should take upon herself the responsibility for events which must yet be investigated by both of these parties, I nevertheless believe that there does exist, however, with regard to this question one, though a far distant, precedent. When at Genoa our counter-partners claimed from us compensation for losses, we were willing on principle to accept such demand, conditional upon the recognition of our counter-claims. Although it may be true, however, that the above-mentioned decision of the All-Russian C.E.C. of Soviets to take the Rapallo Treaty, containing mutual renouncement of all accounts in the past, as prototype of all future treaties concluded by Russia—is in contradiction with that.

Personally I believe that the Rapallo decision ought to be considered as the most reasonable diplomatically, for mutual relations between peoples do not end, but begin, with the conclusion of treaties and if, for odious mercantile profits, both parties start turning over again all the horrors of a war already gone through and partly forgotten, this hardly contributes to the settling of friendly relations between corresponding peoples.

I beg to ask your pardon for this extended letter, but I hope, however, that I have been able to satisfy your desire, and have laid down objectively the possible Russian point of view on the resumption of the Russo-Japanese Conference.

I beg you, dear Viscount Gotō, to accept the assurance that whatever the future may have in store for Russo-Japanese mutual relations, personally for yourself I will always have feelings of profound esteem and heartfelt gratitude.

Yours most sincerely
(Signed) A. JOFFE[10]

Ioffe's contention that the Japanese were not living up to their obligations was supported in a telegram sent to him from Peking on February 19 by Davtian, who was in charge of the Soviet mission during his absence. "I strongly feel the lack of communication with you," Davtian cabled. "The conduct of the Japanese authorities violates the guarantees given [;] it is contrary to the courteous reception extended by Russia to Ambassador Kawakami."[11]

A month later, on March 2, Ioffe telegraphed: "The attitude here is the same as before—the kindness of Viscount Gotō is exceptional and the friendship and sympathy of all classes of society are clearly shown, but the government, which as all assert is becoming increasingly shaky, continues its arch-unfriendly line and resorts to chicanery at every step."[12]

The debate which ensued among Japanese statesmen as to whether or not to establish diplomatic relations with the Soviet Union is reminiscent of the debate that had raged over a century before whether or not to establish commercial and eventually diplomatic relations with Tsarist Russia. Premier Katō, who had been Admiral Togō Heihachirō's 東郷平八郎 chief assistant during the Russo-Japanese War, now served concurrently as minister of the navy. His support of Gotō's view that a Japanese-Soviet rapprochement was desirable was a reflection of naval thinking. The vice minister of the navy wrote in a secret letter to Tanaka Tokichi 田中都吉, vice minister of foreign affairs, on February 23, 1923: "The time has come to take steps for a rapprochement with Russia."[13] The navy regarded the oil concessions of North Sakhalin as vital to national defense and argued for the restoration of amicable relations; it urged that friendship between Japan and Russia not be endangered by dickering over minor issues or by indiscriminate fishing under the protection of the imperial navy."[14]

While the international position of Russia was gradually improving in 1922–23, that of Japan was deteriorating. Not only had her prolonged occupation of Siberia and her reluctance to withdraw from North Sakhalin increased American and British political opposition, but American and English businessmen had taken advantage of Japan's economic weakness (due partly to the cost of the Siberian venture) to regain the strong position which they had held in the markets of China, Manchuria and the South Pacific prior to the Russo-Japanese War. As Japanese trade in the South Pacific was cut into half between 1920 and 1923 and the import of Japanese goods by the United States dropped sharply, and as talk of war between Japan and the United States (on whom the former depended to a considerable degree economically) mounted, Japanese business circles turned their eyes on the Soviet neighbor, whose sprawling territory held forth the prospect of huge markets and vast sources of supply of raw materials.[15] The memories of large-scale sales to Russia during World War I were still fresh in the minds of Japanese capitalists.

The Ministry of War, on the other hand, opposed recognition of the U.S.S.R. in the desire to retain possession of North Sakhalin; the Home

Office was against it also for fear that it would contribute to the spread of revolutionary feeling inside Japan.

In the Foreign Office there was a division of opinion. Matsudaira, director of the Bureau of European and American Affairs, and various old diplomats including Obata, the minister to China, and Foreign Minister Uchida himself were against recognition of the Soviet Union, lest Japanese relations with the United States and England be adversely affected. On the other hand, Ambassador Kawakami and a number of younger diplomats, including Vice-Consul Shimada in Harbin and Consul General Matsushima, favored recognition of the U.S.S.R. and evacuation of Sakhalin. When Kawakami at a press conference labeled the old policy toward the Soviet Union ludicrous and outmoded, Uchida reprimanded him and not only told him not to express his personal views but forbade him to meet Ioffe on his arrival.

The question of recognition of the U.S.S.R. had become a domestic political issue. Access to Russian waters was vital for Japanese fishery. Soviet abrogation of Tsarist agreements, the collapse of Russian administration during the Civil War and the Intervention had provided Japanese with the opportunity for unrestricted fishing in Russian waters. But with the reunification of Russia and the prospective exclusion of poachers, the need for a new fishery agreement became obvious. While Uchida had admitted to a group of deputies of the Kōseikai party on December 6, 1922, before Ioffe's visit, that the fishery question might well become the object and cause of renewed negotiations and that Japan would be prepared to agree to a Russian proposal for a third conference if the Soviet Union genuinely desired one, he added: "But of this one cannot speak openly. We are taking some secret measures in this direction."

On January 22, 1923, the opposition party, the Kenseikai, adopted a resolution calling on the imperial government to take measures to establish control over radical ideas and to recognize the Soviet Union upon agreement with the other powers. Following Ioffe's arrival, resolutions were introduced (though not passed) in the Diet calling for the recognition of the Soviet regime, and there was considerable debate in and out of parliament about the course that Japan should steer. On one extreme were ultra-conservatives who regarded Ioffe's visit as an outright offense to the dignity of the imperial family. On the other extreme were those who felt that the Soviet Union and Japan had equal reason to dislike the West and thus were natural allies. No argument could have brought home more effectively the failure of current Japanese policy and the need to come to terms with the Soviet government than the fact that the Japanese occupation of North Sakhalin had not prevented the Russians from granting oil concessions in this area to the American firm of Harry Ford Sinclair.[16]

Although Ioffe had been informed before his departure from China that he would be regarded as a private visitor without diplomatic status and privileges, he raised the question again a fortnight after his arrival. He told Gotō on February 16 that he found it impossible to confer with him any further unless he be given the right to communicate with Moscow in code and to use diplomatic couriers. Gotō asked Katō to allow Ioffe's request, warning the premier of the danger of a Soviet-Chinese rapprochement in the event that Ioffe was rebuffed.

While the Japanese government was pondering what to do, Moscow put pressure on Japan in support of Ioffe's demands. So long as an anti-Communist government at Vladivostok had collaborated with the Japanese, the visas issued to Japanese nationals by the old Russian consulates in Japan had been honored. With the fall of Vladivostok to the Red forces such visas had lost validity overnight.[17]

Since Japan did not recognize the U.S.S.R. there were no Soviet diplomatic or consular officials in Japan who could issue visas to Japanese travelers. As a temporary expedient Soviet officials boarded vessels which arrived in Soviet ports and there gave visas to Japanese visitors. But on January 19, 1923, the Far Eastern Revolutionary Committee, which administered the Russian Far East, decreed that the procedure of issuing visas upon arrival be discontinued and so informed Matsumura Sadao 村松貞雄, the Japanese consul general at Vladivostok, on the 22nd. At his request they delayed enforcement for a while, but on March 6 refused landing permission to passengers of the *Koji Maru*, who had steamed into Vladivostok without the necessary permits. When Watanabe Riye 渡邊理惠, the Japanese acting consul general, wanted to discuss the problem, he was informed that the entire matter of Soviet-Japanese relations was being considered in Tokyo. The Russian action caused great alarm among banking, business and fishery circles and the government was showered with demands for the reestablishment of commercial and diplomatic relations with the neighboring state.[18]

On March 7 Ioffe reiterated to Gotō his government's conditions for the resumption of official talks: equal rights of the negotiating parties, consent of Japan to negotiate concerning the establishment of diplomatic as well as of commercial relations, and the fixing of an acceptable date for the evacuation of North Sakhalin. Matsudaira, to whom Gotō took the demands, replied on March 21 that Japan was willing to negotiate on an equal basis. As for recognition of the U.S.S.R., however, Japan made it conditional on the settlement of the Nikolaevsk incident and on the Soviet Union's honoring of its international obligations; the evacuation of North Sakhalin like the recognition of the U.S.S.R. depended on the settlement of the Nikolaevsk incident. Gotō conveyed the reply to Ioffe during his meetings with the later on March 29 and 30.[19]

Gotō talked also about the Japanese proposal of March 30 about the exchange of commercial agents who could perform consular functions until such time as diplomatic relations had been reestablished, although the proposal seems to have been conveyed officially through the Japanese consul general at Vladivostok. The Japanese proposal had been prompted by Soviet notification of Acting Consul General Watanabe on February 20, 1923, that his official authority would expire in three months unless he obtained a formal exequatur. An exequatur is a written authorization of a consular officer by the government to which he is accredited, and it was obvious that Watanabe could not be accredited to a government that was not recognized by his country.[20, e]

The Japanese envisaged that they would send commercial agents to Vladivostok, Nikol'sk-Ussuriisk, Chita, Blagoveshchensk, Nikolaevsk-

---

[e] The same demand was made of the American and British consuls, who consequently withdrew from Vladivostok in May of 1923.

on-the-Amur, Petropavlosvk and Moscow; Soviet officials would proceed to Yokohama, Nagasaki, Tsuruga, Hakodate and Gensan. The commercial agents were to have the same rights as consuls of third powers, including the right to use code in communication; they were to refrain from any political propaganda activity.[21]

In communicating the above to Ioffe, Deputy Foreign Commissar Karakhan cabled on April 6: "The Japanese proposal has much for and against it. Even if it were accepted in principle, it must be supplemented. We will give no answer whatever until we receive a ciphered reply from you. I hope the Japanese government will understand that if the proposal is serious, one must not deprive you of the right of [using] code."[22] Ioffe, therefore, informed the Japanese government the same day in the name of Karakhan that no matter of substance would be discussed by the Soviet Union until such time as the use of cipher was permitted.[23]

On April 10 Gotō, through whom Ioffe had no doubt conveyed the reply, called on Premier Katō and handed him a written memorandum in which he posed three questions: (1) was it worthwhile to continue negotiations on an unofficial level? (2) should one not allow the use of code and find out the views of the Russian government about the questions under negotiations? (3) should steps not be taken so that Ioffe would return to Moscow rather than to Peking? Katō answered through Uchida that he favored the continuation of unofficial talks, though he had no objection in principle to a third round of negotiations. He would permit Ioffe the use of code and would assign a Foreign Office official in the event that direct contact with the Japanese government would be required during the informal talks. He expressed the belief that agreement could be reached at least on the fishery question.[24]

Ioffe knew that more and more Japanese businessmen were clamoring for the resumption of Russo-Japanese trade and sought to take advantage of the situation. "The Chamber of Commerce of Kobe has resolved to demand of the Japanese government the immediate renewal of commercial relations with Russia and in this connection to delegate to Vladivostok two representatives together with technical personnel—a total of four to five persons—on condition that the Japanese government would grant access to the same number of persons from Russia to Kobe," Ioffe telegraphed to Moscow on April 4. "The president of the Chamber of Commerce is personally known to me in the most favorable light; all the years he and the chamber over which he presided carried out a policy for us." Ioffe strongly advised that the Japanese proposal be accepted and Russian representatives carefully selected.[25]

New arguments were raised by proponents of Russo-Japanese collaboration in support of their cause. "Many of the world Powers, while chanting peans to justice and humanity, do not really give equal treatment to different races, but Russia has no racial prejudice, and since the establishment of the Moscow dynasty 300 years ago equal rights have been extended to all races as an expression of the traditional spirit of the Russian people," Mochizuki Koraō, a member of parliament, wrote in *Taiyō*.

> I do not know the details of the negotiations held between Premier Katō and Viscount Gotō in November last, which led to the latter's invitation to Mr. Joffe to come to Japan [Mochizuki declared], but I think it narrow-minded for the Japanese Government not to allow Mr. Joffe to use private telegraphic code and the free exchange of diplomatic communications after once consenting to his sojourn in Japan. Some people are laboring under the misapprehension that Mr. Joffe has come to Japan to Bolshevise the nation. The national character of Japan and the traits of her people, which are unchanged since the foundation of the country, may be likened to the color of the sun that absorbs all colors, red or white, and in the veins of the 65,000,000 nationals there is not a drop of blood that forgets the nation, for the souls of the Imperial ancestors repose in them.... If the rulers of the country ... see to it that the living conditions of the people are stabilized, then a thousand Joffes are not to be feared.[26]

On April 13 the Soviet government backed its demand for use of code in communication by taking away that right from the Japanese consul general in Vladivostok, who had enjoyed it until then. On April

17 Watanabe transmitted an official protest from the Japanese government, asserting that the decision of the Soviet government was the expression of a "hostile attitude" toward Japan. He hinted that the action might have a negative effect on the solution of the fishery problem and force the Japanese to engage in unrestricted fishery. But on April 20, as public pressure at home mounted and Gotō and other advocates of the establishment of relations with the U.S.S.R. planned a rally in support of recognition, Foreign Minister Uchida agreed to grant Ioffe the use of code and to begin preliminary negotiations, still disguised as an exchange of personal views between Ioffe and Gotō, in preparation for a third round of official talks.27

Uchida informed Gotō that the Japanese government had no objection in principle to the holding of a third conference, but it wanted Gotō to ascertain first how Russia proposed to settle the Nikolaevsk and North Sakhalin questions, on the solution of which the success or failure of any negotiations hinged. Uchida repeated that Japanese recognition of the Soviet Union depended on the settlement of the Nikolaevsk incident and on Soviet fulfillment of Russia's international obligations.28

When Gotō discussed these maters with Ioffe on April 24 the way was cleared for the commencement of preliminary negotiations. Ioffe seemed to agree to the settlement of the Nikolaevsk affair as a condition for Japanese withdrawal from North Sakhalin; he was granted the right to use code;f and although he and Ioffe differed whether North Sakhalin should be leased to Japan or exploited by joint Soviet-Japanese concessions if it could not be sold, they agreed that the crux of the problem was the economic development of the region.

On April 25 Gotō resigned as lord mayor of Tokyo to devote himself

---

f In cabling this to Karakhan, Ioffe stated that he deemed it "very important now" to respond by extending the same rights to "the so-called Japanese consuls." (Japanese Archives, MT 251.106.15:1402) The Soviet ban on Japanese code was duly lifted but reimposed again on November 24. The privilege of receiving correspondence by diplomatic pouch, delivered by captains of Japanese vessels to special messengers of the consulate general, was suspended from November 6, 1923, until the reestablish-★

THE GOTŌ-IOFFE TALKS   111

full-time to the preliminary negotiations. On April 29, in response to a Japanese call for a reply to its proposals of March 30, repeated on April 24, that commercial agents be exchanged, the Soviet People's Commissariat of Foreign Affairs issued a public statement to the effect that the reply had been delayed because the use of code had been forbidden, but that now that the Soviet demand for the use of code had been met, it would take the matter under consideration after hearing about it from Ioffe.[29]

While the Japanese government delayed giving a reply to the three conditions for the resumption of official talks, posed by Ioffe on March 7 and conveyed to the premier apparently only on May 10, Ioffe communicated to Gotō the willingness of the Soviet government to assume *moral* responsibility for the Nikolaevsk incident if Japan in turn expressed regret about the action of Japanese forces in Siberia. In regard to the Soviet demand for the evacuation of North Sakhalin, Ioffe repeated the offer to grant to the Japanese economic concessions in that region. (The Soviet Union was willing to grant concessions here and in the Russian Far East not only to rid her land of the Japanese armies but because this seemed a speedy way of rebuilding the national economy.)

During the Gotō-Ioffe talks Japan elaborated on the demand that the Soviet government meet the international obligations of Russia in order to obtain Japanese recognition. The Tsarist and Provisional governments had purchased enormous quantities of war supplies from Japan in their struggle with Germany during the First World War and the Japanese wanted the Soviet regime to pay for them. Ioffe countered that the Soviet government had declared at the international conference at Genoa in the

---

*ment of treaty relations. Telegram service between Vladivostok and Korea (part of the Japanese empire) had been suspended from February 6, 1923, because the Japanese government had not renewed the agreement of 1914 and had not settled outstanding telegram accounts. Parcel post between the Soviet Union and Japan was halted in August of 1923; in February of 1924 first class mail service was discontinued also. (Tanaka, pp. 81–82)

summer of 1922 that it would not honor any of the obligations of its predecessor governments relating to war debts. As a price of recognition Japan demanded also Soviet acceptance of Japanese rights gained by her victory in the Russo-Japanese War, as stipulated in the Treaty of Portsmouth (1905) and the fishery convention of 1907. Ioffe countered that Japanese intervention in Siberia had been tantamount to war and had destroyed all previous treaties. Besides, he said, the Soviet government had already renounced all Tsarist treaties and agreements. But Ioffe left the door open for a reconsideration of this matter, stating that recognition of the articles of the Portsmouth treaty would depend on the course of the negotiations.

In an attempt to reach a compromise, Gotō suggested that the question of the debts of the Tsarist and Provisional governments be left until the international settlement of this question in general. As for North Sakhalin, he proposed that either it be sold to Japan or that concessions be granted to a Japanese-Russian syndicate. On other matters his view approximated that of Ioffe.

As mentioned above, the Japanese government had favored the continuation of the unofficial talks, feeling that at least the fishery question might be resolved in this way. Ioffe's talks with Gotō had been confined essentially to political issues. Fishery matters were discussed by Ioffe directly with Japanese fishery people from April 1923. His position was weakened by the fact that the U.S.S.R. did not have the means of keeping poachers at bay; many White Russian commanders had sailed their vessels into exile. Meanwhile Japanese warships violated Russian territorial waters in protection of Japanese fishing vessels. The Japanese would have preferred to operate legally and groups of fishery people proceeded to Vladivostok to try to negotiate an agreement with local officials. Ignoring their demand that Japanese be granted the same number of fishing grounds as in the preceding year, the Soviet government on March 2, 1923, annulled all fishery agreements concluded before the reunification of Soviet Russia and the Far Eastern Republic (November 14, 1922). Laying down new lease regulations, the government allowed foreigners from any country, not just Japan, to bid for the fishing grounds.^g To Japanese protests that the new regulations went counter to the Treaty of Portsmouth and the Fishery Convention of 1907, Ioffe replied that old treaties could not remain effective between governments that did not recognize each other *de jure* or *de facto*. He added that under no circumstances could the Soviets recognize agreements concluded by the Whites and that according to international law unauthorized fishery in Russian territorial waters under the protection of the Japanese fleet in the absence of Soviet warships was an act of piracy and that the Soviet government reserved the right to take appropriate measures to deal with the Japanese pirates.[30] When someone asked Ioffe whether it was true that Russia had submarines at Vladivostok for possible use against Japanese poachers, he replied that he did not know, but that he hoped so.[31] Ioffe stressed that the fishery question could not be resolved by itself but that the whole complex of Japanese-Soviet relations must be adjusted.

An agreement between Japanese fishery enterprisers and Soviet officials was concluded in Vladivostok on May 21, 1923. The Japanese agreed to pay back rental fees for the use of the fishing grounds in 1920–21 and in turn received the right to lease in 1923 255 out of 511 fishing grounds. In the eyes of Soviet historians the provisional fishery agreement was "a victory for Soviet diplomacy" since the fishery people thereby recognized the sovereignty of the Soviet state over these waters.[32] Uchida wanted to introduce modifications into the agreement, but the Soviets stood their ground.

On May 5 Ioffe moved—or to be more exact, was moved—from Atami to Tokyo at the insistence of Japanese doctors. Although his affliction had been used by Gotō and himself as a means of resuming Soviet-Japanese negotiations, it had not been a "diplomatic illness." Ioffe showed remarkable fortitude in carrying on his work in spite of fever, hurt and, no doubt, considerable anxiety. Japanese sources state that Japanese doctors eventually diagnosed Ioffe's illness as a nervous disorder which

---

^g The text of the decree is quoted in a dispatch from the Kremlin to Ioffe, dated March 2. See Japanese Archives, MT 251.106.15:1817–1818.

had gripped him after a bout with influenza, and that Ioffe experienced great pain in his legs.[33] Actually Ioffe could not move about. He telegraphed to his daughter Nadezhda in Moscow on March 8 that he continued to lie in bed, and Levin, on May 4, in announcing Ioffe's pending removal to Tokyo, cabled that Ioffe was unble to walk.[34]

> Besides my basic malady of polyneuritis I suddenly became sick toward the end of March with some new illness, during which the temperature goes up to almost 41°[h] [Ioffe telegraphed to Karakhan on April 20]. The doctor who has come [with?] me from Tokyo can make no diagnosis. Gotō and corresponding groups insist on my moving to Tokyo. I oppose this to some extent in the belief that my appearance in Tokyo on a stretcher, while I had come here with difficulty but unassisted, can be strongly exploited against the groups friendly to us. However, in view of Gotō's dispatch of famous Japanese doctors and their discovery of a new illness I hope thereby to weaken the possibility of an attack [on the pro-Russian groups] and, therefore, we shall probably move to Tokyo in the next few days thanks to the determined insistence of Japanese doctors and Japanese politicians close to us. In spite of the malady I have continued to work until now and have carried out all that was necessary.[35]

On April 26 Levin reported to Moscow that for the third day Ioffe's temperature had been below normal. Ioffe had experienced a "terrible drop in strength" and as before still had practically no appetite. "Last [few] days [feeling] better; do not worry. Papa," Ioffe wired to Nadezhda that day. But Levin pointed out in his cable that whereas Ioffe's blood test had been negative, the doctors still could not make a final diagnosis.[36]

On May 16 Ioffe disclosed that he had had a heart attack and would not be able to leave Japan for some time as the doctors felt that such a voyage would endanger his life.[37] On May 27 a telegram, signed jointly by Levin and Dr. Ettinger, reported that the following diagnosis had

---

[h] 41° Centigrade or 105° Fahrenheit.

been reached unanimously at a consultation with top Japanese professors that day:

(1) post-infection polyneuritis of the lower extremities; the nature of the infectious illness which had caused it has not yet been found; (2) the heart attack in April in Atami, known to you, has been identified as having definitely been an attack of angina pectoris. The prognosis: favorable for (1), since usually post-infection polyneuritis is curable; as regards (2), however, it is impossible to determine the length of the illness. Due to condition of health departure from Tokyo is regarded as impossible at the present time.[38]

The Japanese public meanwhile seemed to have warmed to the Russians. As Ioffe telegraphed to Karakhan on May 9 from the Tsukiji-Seiyoken Hotel in Tokyo, where he had moved a few days earlier:

Gotō reports an extraordinary change in the feeling of the Japanese people and even upper circles in favor of a rapprochement and recognition of Russia. The enthusiastic welcome given to me on [my] first arrival in Tokyo showed that then too the broad masses were disposed favorably toward us. Now everything was on a still much larger scale. A tremendous surging crowd almost crushed my stretcher. The formation of a whole string of organizations for the rapprochement with Russia is also indicative. Finally the following facts are extremely important: several days ago there was a meeting of many thousands in favor of a rapprochement at which speeches were made in favor of the recognition of Russia among others by a Japanese citizen whose son was killed in the Nikolaevsk incident. A most celebrated Japanese scholarly writer, who is the spiritual leader of conservatism and publishes the well-known journal *Japan and the Japanese* and who in his reactionism is compared with our Pobedonostev, recently gave a lecture to an audience of fifteen hundred, probably also reactionary, scientifically demonstrating the necessity of recognition, and as he did so there was not one voice in the entire audience against it.[i] The entire movement is primarily [one] of the intelligentsia and of commercial circles. Workers' organizations only once adopted a resolution for the immediate renewal of trade relations [and], according to inside information from those who know the situation, unanimously for the recognition of Russia; the latter applies also to the peasantry which similarly does not speak out publicly. I personally receive a mass of greetings, get-well wishes, and notes to the effect that friendship is necessary; there were resolutions from entire cities. Gotō underlines the change in feeling in favor of Russia in the highest circles, including the imperial family. He is now free of his duties as Lord Mayor [of Tokyo] and travels about the country [making] speeches.[39]

The mounting sentiment in favor of dealing with the U.S.S.R. evoked a violent response from the right. On May 21 a "patriot" attacked Taguchi Unzō 田口運藏, Ioffe's Japanese secretary, branding him a traitor. The police, which arrested the assailant, declared the attack to have been an attempt to foil the pending Russo-Japanese negotiations.[40]

Debate continued in government circles about the wisdom of recognizing the Soviet regime. Katō felt that Japan should chart her own course in this matter. Uchida and the minister of home affairs felt that recognition of the Soviet Union might alienate the other powers, notably the United States, with whom Japan had vital trade relations. At the same time Uchida did not want credit for an agreement to go to Gotō, a personal political rival, who claimed to be carrying out the late Meiji emperor's wishes in seeking to realize a Russo-Japanese rapprochement. When Gotō concluded that he had accomplished all that could be accomplished in unofficial talks and recommended that the negotiations

---

[i] The Japanese speaker was probably Miyake Setsurei 三宅雪嶺; his publication was called *Nihon oyobi Nihonjin* 日本及日本人. Although Miyake was dissatisfied with excessive Westernization and advocated Japanism, he cannot be written off simply as a "rectionary." Pobedonostev refers to Konstantin Petrovich Pobedonostev, adviser of Alexander III and Nicholas II.

be moved up to an official level, Katō agreed that the time had come to do so, but the cabinet was divided.

On June 5 Ioffe sent a long telegram to the People's Commissariat of Foreign Affairs:[j]

> After Gotō's refusal to continue unofficial preliminary talks with me on behalf of the Japanese government, pointing out to the latter that the business had matured to such a degree that the Japanese government must itself take it into its hands and to conduct official preliminary talks with me, the situation has become perhaps still more complicated. Gotō transmitted to Premier Katō my big letter to the former, dated May 10, in which I communicate:
>
> 1. Your first reply.
>   A—the consent of Russia to enter with Japan into new talks, i.e. the so-called third Russo-Japanese conference, provided that the Japanese government accepts my so-called three prior conditions, i.e. equality of the sides during the negotiation of the conference and in the treaty itself worked out by it, the agreement of Japan to the conduct by the conference of negotiations concerning the conclusion of a complete normal treaty with the restoration of normal diplomatic and consular relations, i.e. mutual *de jure* recognition without special declarations but deriving directly from the treaty, the official fixing of a period, acceptable to us, for the evacuation of Sakhalin, before the conference in the form of a separate article of the treaty. (According to newspaper reports the Japanese government has already evacuated from our side of Sakhalin over 800 soldiers.)

---

[j] This and preceding telegrams were dispatched in romanized Russian apparently uncoded, so that the Japanese Foreign Office, in whose archives copies were found, must have been aware of their contents. Shortly thereafter the Soviets began to use code and the Foreign Office Archives contain wire after wire, the texts of which have remained for the Japanese (and for me) mere combinations of numbers.

B—Your consent to conduct preliminary talks concerning the possibility of a third Russo-Japanese conference in general and of prior conditions for this possibility in particular.

C—Your consent that I conduct negotiations immediately concerning the above-mentioned preliminary conditions.

2. In the said big letter to Gotō of May 10 I try to give my personal opinion which, as I noted in my letter, must, I feel, be more or less acceptable to both sides, i.e. the Russian government and the Japanese government, regarding questions that, I gather from my previous talks and correspondence with Gotō, must be of particular interest to the Japanese government:

A—The Nikolaevsk question. In spite of the absence of our moral and jurisdictional guilt for the Nikolaevsk events, in view of the importance of this question in the public opinion of Japan, created by appropriate propaganda on the part of the Japanese government, our readiness to recognize our moral and material responsibility for the Nikolaevsk events provided that Japan accepts the same responsibility for analogous deeds committed in Siberia by the Japanese. (According to my information there took place the burning of whole villages with the killing of their entire population, there was a pogrom in Vladivostok with the plundering and killing of the peaceful population, the same in Blagoveshchensk, Spassk, etc. In order to prepare for the negotiations seriously, it is necessary at once to begin seriously to collect authentic material.)

B—The Sakhalin question: sale or concession. In connection with the question of its sale I adduce all possible considerations and arguments for the necessity of an extremely large sum; I personally come to the conclusion that it cannot be less than a billion. As regards the question of its concession, I point to the necessity of Japan bearing the cost of the

forfeiture, stipulated in the concession agreement, of the Sinclair Company [concession].
C—The question of international obligations. (The recognition of old debts is meant. My answer regards this claim unacceptable; it sets forth our position at [the international conference at] Genoa, especially the non-recognition of war debts as a matter of principle; the debt of 300 million to Japan is according to my information entirely military.)
D—The prior guarantee to Japan of rights earlier obtained by her. (What is meant especially is the Treaty of Portsmouth, which is regarded as a treaty of victory, and the rights obtained by the fishery convention.)

In my reply amazement is expressed why these guarantees were necessary, since the Dairen and Changchun conferences had proved how far Russia went out to meet the interests of Japanese citizens in the economic sphere, which is evidenced in particular by the actual situation today, when so many concessions have been made to Japanese citizens in spite of the absence of any treaties whatsoever and the absence not only of reciprocity but on the contrary, in the face of a permanently hostile attitude toward us on the part of the Japanese government, especially on the part of the Ministry of Foreign Affairs. The claim is essentially rejected in my memorandum (1) on [the grounds of] principle because Japan herself by the fact of war against us had destroyed all treaties and [because] we on our part had annulled all [treaties], not only the Japanese ones, by a general decree (2) from a practical point of view, because such claim cannot be the subject of a preliminary agreement and is an item to be discussed at a conference, where everything depends on the general atmosphere and mutual concessions. This memorandum of mine, which apparently became known to the press, at least in part, and for some reason is called "the proposal of the Russian government" was by and large received well, often being characterized as brilliantly convincing[?],[k] although individual items were variously evaluated by different organizations.

Gotō transmitted it to the premier together with his memorandum and the following proposals which were to soften the disagreement between me and the Japanese government, indicating to me that one of the major points was the question of the debts. Gotō's five compromise points were as follows:

1. The Sakhalin question is solved either by means of purchase or by concession to a Japanese syndicate;
2. the problem of fulfilling international obligations, independent of the question of recognition, must be left for future international settlement;
3. concerning the Nikolaevsk question Russia must recognize its moral and material responsibility; if she really proves that the Japanese army committed similar acts, the Japanese government accepts responsibility for them and compensates for losses. (Consequently this is not simply a liquidation of the Nikolaevsk events, but in the latter case the *onus probandi* [burden of proof] is placed on us. Although Gotō stated orally that he considers this merely another form of liquidation, my memorandum demands a secret written agreement that this formula constitutes liquidation of the Nikolaevsk events without compensation.
4. The evacuation of Japanese troops stationed on Sakhalin must be a voluntary act of the Japanese government.
5. Recognition, in accordance with my point of view, must begin from the moment of the commencement of negotiations and end with the moment of ratification of the treaty. These five points, especially the second, have evoked the full sympathy of the entire press, in individual cases even enthusiasm. Gotō gave a statement to the newspaper; I, in my interviews also

---

[k] "*chasto polutchaya kharakteristiku genialnoi ubedilnosti* [sic]."

explained my point of view. The Russian question, especially the question of recognition, has become the central [issue].

Our compliance in the fishery question has enormously increased my prestige in general and has changed the situation much stronger still in our favor even in official circles. Among the ministers themselves nobody now dares to speak out against negotiations concerning recognition, the newspaper which is regarded as a semi-official organ of the Ministry of Foreign Affairs wrote recently that it was incorrect to regard the Ministry of Foreign Affairs as an enemy of talks about recognition since actually the opposite [was true]; the Ministry of Foreign Affairs goes further than others in regards to Russia. The foreign minister, according to the newspapers, has allegedly said in an interview that in spite of the measures he has taken in connection with my arrival he was not an opponent of official negotiations concerning recognition. Even the leading parties of the upper and lower houses, the Kenkyūkai and Seiyūkai, have changed their attitude. Our freeing of arrested persons, popular in Japan, has further improved the situation.

On May 2 there was a banquet of several hundred leading Japanese citizens, politicians, scholars, writers, journalists and the like under the chairmanship of Miyake, an ardent reactionary, scholar and publicist known throughout Japan, for the purpose of assisting in the rapprochement of Russia and Japan and honoring me. In spite of my absence in view of my inability to get up from bed (at the request of the sponsors I was represented by my wife; my reply to the welcoming speech of Professor Miyake I sent by letter) the banquet passed with tremendous enthusiasm. One participant even made a wonderful welcoming speech in the name of the working people of Japan.

In all this absolutely wonderful relationship we are disturbed sometimes unfortunately by our newspapers which know nothing about Japan, do not understand the situation and therefore write a lot of nonsense. One leading article of *Izvestiia VTSIK* [the paper "News," published by the All-Russia Central Executive Committee], not noticed by me earlier, argued that the European states saw in the Japanese merely the yellow race and at any moment would expell them from their alliance; it explained that Japan did not understand her own interests which lay in a rapprochement with Russia. Reprinted here, [the article] aroused the strongest indignation. Please take [appropriate] measures.

I recapitulate: The general attitude is very much in our favor, the refusal of Gotō to continue unofficial talks forces the Japanese government to decide at once whether or not official negotiations should now take place at all, and if so, on what basis. (I told Gotō that his removal from the negotiations, even in the form of removing himself, will make a bad impression in Russia and will adversely affect the outcome of the discussions. The same is written openly by some newspapers.)

The Japanese government met three times and could not come to any decision. The question is really very difficult from the Japanese point of view:

1. Japanese diplomacy has the distinctive tradition of deciding its policy very slowly generally speaking, to proceed step by step, to give the opportunity for all questions to "digest." (This was reiterated to us constantly by the Japanese delegates at Changchun.)
2. There are many personal complications and intrigues. For example, the Ministry of Foreign Affairs cannot allow that the laurels of its province fall to the outsider Gotō. Furthermore, within the Ministry of Foreign Affairs itself there are many different political directions.
3. Not all members of the cabinet are equally acquainted with the situation, equally understand it. For example, when I declared at one interview that in the event of Japan's rejection of a third Russo-Japanese conference the present *status*

THE GOTŌ-IOFFE TALKS

quo could not remain, that it must lead to a complete change in the policy of Russia toward Japanese citizens, many were seriously indignant, began to speak of the insincerity for which the East was notorious, without even understanding the fact that such relations between two states could not remain long, where one, without any reciprocity without any treaty relations meets all the interests of the other, even after it refuses to negotiate concerning questions of interest to both sides.

4. It is the first time in Japanese history that negotiations are conducted while everything is openly discussed before the entire people. It is extremely difficult to risk such a step since it means for the future too the transfer of the entire foreign policy onto a completely new track.

5. The recognition by Japan of Russia *de jure* even according to the formula proposed by me, without a special declaration but as the first of the four great powers,[1] means for Japan also a complete rejection of all the past policy, since the old relations with these four powers are impossible and the orientation must be changed.

6. The present Japanese government,[m] not leaning on anyone strictly speaking, is so weak that it generally does not dare to take decisive measures and the Russian question is particularly risky for it.

I consider it possible, therefore, that the Japanese government in spite of the above-mentioned feelings of its people will not risk at this time official talks, even preliminary ones, but will try to delay them, particularly since there are already indications in the press that the Japanese government, assuming from the concessions that we have already made that we are particularly

---

[1] England, France, the United States and Japan.
[m] The Katō administration.

interested in the negotiations, has decided, notwithstanding the dishonorableness of such conduct, to wait further in the hope of getting new concessions from us. Considering the particular integrity and high morality generally attributed to the present premier and the strict conscientiousness of Foreign Minister Uchida, I personally do not think that they will stop to such infamy and would more readily, for the reasons mentioned above, risk an open break.

In the opinion of the newspapers which analyze all possibilities available to the government the following is the most likely course of action: The Japanese government, not really committed by the reply to my proposals since the negotiations so far have been unofficial, can propose to us for the recognition of Russia prior conditions of its own, independent of Gotō's, that are completely unacceptable and thereby delay the talks. I deem this more probable in spite of the immorality of this approach too. Although I do not regard the Japanese government so naive as not to understand that such a decision is no decision at all, since it would not delay the negotiations but destroy them completely, because after such deceit and the loss of prestige on the part of Russia, the latter will be forced for the sake of "saving face," as one always says in the East, to change its policy radically in regard to all interests of Japanese citizens and take the position of complete reciprocity in relations.

I write in such detail because the entire question after all is supposed to be decided by the Japanese government next week and we must likewise prepare ourselves for one or another result of the Japanese decisions, although in accordance with the opinion of the last [medical] consultation, I myself will under no circumstances be able to leave Tokyo very soon. It is necessary also to think about the replacement of Antonov, which is important in any case and particularly necessary in the event of my departure since while I am here Moscow has still had some information; without me, with Antonov alone here, you will have nothing except for brief disconnected telegrams, which in addition to all their shortcomings will distort the facts.[41]

The dilemma which plagued the Japanese authorities was illustrated by the arrest of about a hundred leftists, including university professors and prominent public leaders, on the charge of fomenting a Communist plot at the same time that announcement was made of the decision to go ahead with the negotiations with Ioffe. Commenting on this "striking paradox" in Japanese policy, a reporter for the *Chicago Daily News* wired that while the police authorities connected the alleged plot with agitation for the recognition of the U.S.S.R., the government by according Ioffe an official status in the negotiations was actually aiding the propagation of "dangerous thought." "The envoy's health is improving greatly, at least politically," the correspondent wired sarcastically. "Already the recent fishery agreement has furnished a pretext for introducing a large corps of Soviet agents into Japan on the ground that they are needed to examine fishermen's passports."[42]

On June 9, in the absence as yet of a cabinet decision on the Russian question, Katō proposed to Ioffe through Gotō that the unofficial preliminary talks be terminated and what might be called "official unofficial" preliminary negotiations be begun for the purpose of determining the prior conditions for a third Russo-Japanese conference.[n] The talks that had been conducted until then were to be regarded as not having taken place at all. The new informal talks concerning the prior conditions for the third Russo-Japanese conference were to differ in that they were to be conducted officially by specially empowered representatives. Katō declared that although it was understood that Ioffe was the representative for the entire Far East, the Japanese government had had no official knowledge thereof and requested appropriate notification by the Soviet Union. As a personal courtesy to Ioffe, the Japanese government rented

---

[n] In a letter to Ioffe, dated August 3, 1923, Kawakami actually used as Ioffe's title "*Predsedatel' R.S.F.S.R. na neoffitsial'nikh predvaritel'nykh peregovorakh, imeiushchikh tsel'iu otkrytie Iapono-Russkoi Konferentsii*"! (Japanese Archives, MT 251.106.11:673)

a conference room in his hotel and informed him that it had no objections to his conferring while lying down.

Ioffe accepted the proposal with the understanding that the three prior conditions which he had posed would remain in effect. He added, however, that he did not see what the Japanese proposal would accomplish. A new official start might give a temporary breather, but once discussions came to the Nikolaevsk question and Soviet recognition of Tsarist debts the old differences would reassert themselves. Ioffe expressed the concern that now that discussions were to proceed on an official level, such controversy might lead to a complete break.[43]

On June 16, 1923, Commissar Chicherin cabled to Count Uchida that Ioffe had been appointed as the Soviet plenipotentiary. The imperial government wired in reply a week later, on June 21, that Minister Kawakami Toshitsune would represent Japan. A large banquet, attended by over 600 persons, kicked off the official unofficial negotiations and on June 28 Ioffe and Kawakami got down to work.[44]

CHAPTER FOUR
The Ioffe-Kawakami Talks

KAWAKAMI Toshitsune, like Matsushima, Matsudaira and Gotō before him, had experience in dealing with Russians. A graduate of the Tokyo Foreign Language School in Russian (1884), he had served from 1892 to 1900 as chancelor and then second and eventually first interpreter in St. Petersburg, from 1900 to 1904 and again from 1906 to 1907 as commercial representative in Vladivostok, and from 1912 to 1914 as consul general in Moscow.[a]

On June 28, 1923, at the outset of the "informal preliminary negotiations," during which the groundwork was to be laid for an official Soviet-Japanese conference, Ioffe demanded as prior conditions for the convening of such a conference: (1) formal recognition of the U.S.S.R. by Japan, and (2) the fixing of a definite date for the evacuation of North Sakhalin. Kawakami parried the Soviet conditions with a set of Japanese counter-demands: (1) settlement of the North Sakhalin question, (2) settlement of the Nikolaevsk incident, and (3) Soviet fulfillment of international obligations.[1]

For twelve meetings Ioffe and Kawakami discussed the above points in detail.[b] The best solution of the Sakhalin question, Kawakami argued,

[a] Kawakami was minister to Poland from 1921 to 1923; subsequently he became director of the South Manchurian Railway and liaison officer with Russia. He served as president of the North Sakhalin Mining Company (1926) and later as president of the Nichi-Ro Fisheries Corporation, a Japanese-Russian joint venture.

[b] Accroding to Kutakov the counter-proposals were made in July, i.e. at a subsequent meeting, and included the demand for concessions in the Soviet Far East. Tanaka and Kutakov disagree on the general order in which the demands were presented. According to Tanaka, Ioffe began by demanding the recognition of the*

would be for Russia to sell the northern half of the island to Japan, since repeated disputes were bound to spring from joint possession. Kawakami asserted that studies made by Japanese scientists and experts found the economic value of the island limited; large sums of money would have to be invested to develop the natural resources. He offered, therefore, "150,000,000 yen or thereabouts" as a reasonable price. In the event that Japan purchased North Sakhalin, Kawakami declared, she would be willing to pledge not to fortify the island and to guarantee the free navigation of the Straits of Tatary and of La Perouse, stipulated in the Treaty of Portsmouth; Russia in turn would have to promise not to erect fortifications opposite the island.

Ioffe did not turn down the Japanese offer outright. He actually stated that he deemed the proposal acceptable in principle. He merely upped the "reasonable price" to one billion gold rubles and later, upon further instructions from Moscow, to one billion and a half.

Ioffe was more receptive to the alternative proposal for settling the Sakhalin question by granting to Japan long-term concessions for the development of natural resources, such as oil-fields, coal-mines and forests in North Sakhalin.

Kawakami asserted that the concessions desired by Japan differed in

*Soviet Union and the fixing of a date for the evacuation of North Sakhalin; Kawakami's points were "counter-demands." According to Kutakov, Ioffe raised these demands after a discussion of Kawakami's proposals; Kawakami replied that if the Russians accepted the six Japanese points, the Soviet Union's conditions for the holding of official talks would be agreeable.

Although Kutakov does not number them, the six points seem to have been: (1) the North Sakhalin question (sale or concessions); (2) concessions in the Russian Far East; (3) apology for the Nikolaevsk incident; (4) assumption of the obligations of the Tsarist and Provisional governments and compensation to those whose enterprises had been nationalized; (5) guarantee of personal safety and respect for private property and freedom of trade and industry in the forthcoming treaty of commerce; and (6) mutual restraint from propaganda. (Tanaka, p. 74; Leonid Nikolaevich Kutakov, *Istoriia sovetsko-iaponskikh diplomaticheskikh otnoshenii* (History of Soviet-Japanese diplomatic relations) [Moscow, 1962], pp. 36–37) character from the Tsarist lease of Port Arthur and Dairen; the Japanese wanted economic concessions for the exploitation of natural resources of a special nature within a fixed area in the territory and not political concessions entailing the lease of the entire region. Kawakami added that the Russian government could participate in the exploitation of the concessions; 5 to 6% of the net profit from the concessions might be paid to the Russian government. He expressed the hope of his government that the concessions would be for the term of 99 years, certainly of not less than 55 years.

Ioffe replied that the granting of long-term concessions was acceptable in principle, provided it was not construed as an indemnity for the Nikolaevsk incident. Various details would have to be worked out, of course, but, he felt sure, agreement could be reached on this matter.

The Nikolaevsk issue, on the other hand, evoked much controversy. Japan demanded that:

(A) Russia shall express her regrets at the massacre of the Japanese Consul, members of the Consulate and Japanese residents in Nikolaevsk.
(B) Russia shall recognize her obligations to indemnify the Japanese for losses incurred in connection with the Nikolaevsk Affair.[2]

In support of the Japanese demands Kawakami presented the Japanese side of the Nilolaevsk incident, in which the Japanese consul and members of the consulate and hundreds of Japanese military and civilians had been massacred.

> Such an atrocious act has no precedent in history and it could not but give rise to the intense indignation and excitement of the whole Japanese people. The murder of the peaceful Japanese residents admits of no justification on the plea of military necessity, any more than the murder of several thousand peaceful Russians, who had no relation whatever with the Japanese detachment [Kawakami is quoted to have stated in substance].
>
> Judging from various pieces of evidence that emanated from the

Russian side (for instance, the telegram dated March 23rd, 1920, addressed to Count Uchida, Foreign Minister, by M. Tchicherin [Chicherin]: the text of the judgment given at the People's Tribunal at the village of Kerbi on July 9th, 1920; etc.), the force led by Triapitsyn had connection not only with the Moscow Government but with the Headquarters of the Red Army at Khabarovsk and at Vladivostok, and Triapitsyn was publicly recognized as a commander in the Red Army and his force as a contingent of it. Therefore, the Russian Government cannot absolve itself from its responsibility for the Nikolaevsk Affair on the ground that the said massacre was committed by bandits, or Partisans, and Triapitsyn was executed by the judgment of a court of Russia.[3]

Bitter about the Japanese intervention in Siberia, Ioffe at first replied testily that it was the Japanese commander who had provoked the incident and that the Soviet Union would express regret at the massacre of Japanese at Nikolaevsk if the Japanese government would express its regret at similar crimes perpetrated by its forces in Siberia. But for the sake of furthering the negotiations Ioffe eventually modified his stand; he said that if the demand for compensation were dropped—if it were merely a matter of expressing regret—the Soviet Union could do so unilaterally. The Japanese replied that while compensation could not be waived completely, they were prepared, in view of Russia's financial plight, to try not to demand financial compensation in so far as possible, if the Soviet Union would settle the North Sakhalin problem to the satisfaction of Japan.[4]

The controversy now narrowed to the wording of the Soviet note of regret. The Russians did not deny the occurrence; yet while expressing their regret they wished to absolve their government and regular army from responsibility as a matter of national prestige; the Japanese desired Soviet assumption of such responsibility as a face-saving gesture for their withdrawal from North Sakhalin. After repeated revisions, agreement was reached on the first half of the third Soviet draft note in which Russia expressed "her most profound regret" to Japan for the "atrocious crime" committed at Nikolaevsk. "At that time, not only 351 Japanese officers and men but 384 peaceful Japanese residents including the Japanese Consul were massacred, without distinction of men, women and children, by a force led by Triapitsyn and, subsequently, the whole city of Nikolaevsk, with approximately 8,000 Russian inhabitants, was burnt to the ground by Triapitsyn," the note admitted. But Soviet attempts to add such clauses as "Russia was constrained to safeguard herself and the fruits of revolution in various places" or "no such incident is and can be possible any longer among the disciplined troops of the Red Army" were rejected by the Japanese who felt that whatever regret the Soviets expressed in the first part of the text they nullified in the second part. It was finally resolved to leave the matter for later consideration and to proceed to other issues.

Japan's desire for concessions on North Sakhalin has already been mentioned. Kawakami also pressed for concessions on the mainland. Ioffe consented. They concurred that "Russia shall agree to give the Japanese concessions for the development of natural resources such as forests and mines in Russia's territory in the Far East."[5]

No agreement could be reached on the question of Soviet assumption of the international obligations of the Tsarist and Provisional governments. In vain Kawakami argued that "according to the fundamental principle of international law, so long as a state continues to exist on the basis of its former territory and inhabitants, no internal political change can alter its international position." Ioffe countered that the old treaties were not adapted to the conditions of "these progressive times." Russia had paid her debts incurred before the war. She considered it "perfectly within her rights in not paying war debts from the viewpoint of international morality, since these debts did not bring any benefit to the Russian people" and since Russia had been excluded from the distribution of the spoils of the war. Kawakami retorted that Russia had brought the latter upon herself by her betrayal of the Allied cause in signing a separate peace.[6]

Kawakami stated eventually that Japan would be willing to substitute new agreements for the old ones, provided they incorporated the rights extended to her after her victory in the Russo-Japanese War. He offered to let the question of international obligations, including the many commitments to Japan assumed by Russia during World War I, ride till the question was settled by an international agreement. He did want a Soviet admission in principle that the debts incurred by the Tsarist and Provisional governments should be repaid, although Japan was willing to give a moratorium on their repayment and even to cancel some of them completely in view of Russia's difficult financial situation.

Kawakami proposed that the Soviet Union promise to protect the safety of the lives of Japanese subjects, respect their right of private ownership and assure them commercial and industrial freedom in the event of the conclusion of a commercial treaty. Ioffe said that he saw no objections so long as Soviet laws were observed. Ioffe also went along with Kawakami's demand that both states pledge themselves to refrain from propaganda and subversive activities, provided the statement could be made comprehensive and specific.[7]

On July 19 Ioffe received instructions from Moscow to obtain formulation of the Japanese demands. At the same time he was to propose the commencement of official negotiations; the Soviet Union was prepared to send special plenipotentiaries. In the event that the Japanese refused to open official negotiations, Ioffe was to declare that this meant the rupture of negotiations, a development for which the Japanese government must accept full responsibility. If it came to such a declaration, he was to underline again the illegality of the occupation of North Sakhalin by Japanese forces.

Ioffe duly requested a written statement of Japan's final proposals, but was unable to obtain it. The Japanese were not yet ready to enter into official negotiations. Uchida still opposed recognition of the U.S.S.R. and Kawakami, acting under his instructions, merely explored the Soviet position without committing Japan.

When another week passed without concessions from the Japanese, who continued to insist that the evacuation of North Sakhalin depended on the settlement of the Nikolaevsk incident, Ioffe was instructed by

Chicherin to break off the unofficial negotiations and to propose at the same time that official negotiations be begun as soon as possible.[8]

At the meeting on July 24 Ioffe declared orally that he wished to bring the negotiations to a quick conclusion.[9] Two days later, on July 26, he transmitted to Kawakami a resumé of the results of their informal talks.[c] In a cover letter he stated that he had no more questions to put to Kawakami for preliminary consideration, while Kawakami likewise was in no position to present any more questions of a preliminary nature. Accordingly, in his capacity as representative extraordinary and plenipotentiary for Far Eastern countries of the Russian Soviet Federated Socialist Republic, Ioffe considered it impossible to continue the informal negotiations and proposed the commencement of formal negotiations "on the basis of the informal negotiations, held from June 28 to July 24" on condition that Japan "voluntarily" announce her willingness to evacuate North Sakhalin immediately. Although this issue had wrecked the Changchun Conference, Ioffe noted that the preliminary negotiations had shown that the Sakhalin question could be solved without the prolongation of the occupation, which so strongly hindered the establishment of truly good-neighbor relations. Noting that resolved questions should be settled at the forthcoming conference, Ioffe expressed "every hope" that the fourth round of negotiations would at last bring success if the Japanese showed greater *"bona fides"*[d] than in the unofficial talks, now drawing to an end.[10]

Kawakami found the Soviet resumé generally inadequate in the presentation of the Japanese position and at times contrary to the Japanese minutes of the talks. At a final meeting on July 31 he made a number of corrections. Still dissatisfied, he prepared a Japanese summary and sent

[c] Kutakov's assertion that Chicherin's instructions were dated July 28 must be incorrect; Tanaka's statement that Ioffe's letter was written on July 27 also is in error. Ioffe's letter, preserved in the Japanese Archives, is dated July 26. It was received by Kawakami on the 27th. (Japanese Archives, MT 251.106.11:823–825; MT 251.106.11:269)

[d] Good faith; rendered as "sincerity" in the English translation of the Foreign Office.

it to Ioffe together with a letter of reply, dated August 3.[e] Kawakami did not agree that they had gone as far as they could in the preliminary discussions; "the claims and wishes of both sides have been made clear on the whole, yet there are not a few points on which concurrence of views has yet to be reached." He remarked that he had expected further consideration of the concrete means of settling the Nikolaevsk question as well as of the matter of Russia's international obligations and expressed regret that Ioffe had terminated the conversations so abruptly.

> With regard to the withdrawal of troops from North Sakhalien referred to in your Note [Kawakami continued] the Japanese Government will have no hesitation in making the necessary declaration in that respect, when the Nikolaevsk question and problems connected therewith are settled, but since the stationing of our troops in North Sakhalien is nothing but an occupation of guarantee with respect to the Nikolaevsk affair, no action can be taken in that regard unless, as has been repeatedly stated in the past, a complete understanding is reached regarding the solution of the various questions mentioned above. In occupying North Sakhalien Japan is actuated by no purpose whatever other than the above-mentioned object, and nothing is further from her intention to encroach unlawfully and improperly on the territorial rights of a foreign country, as I have repeatedly explained to you, and as, I trust, is still fresh in your memory.[11]

The ending of the talks was not unwelcome to the Japanese government. "The Foreign Office smiles gleefully at the miscarriage of the preliminary pourparlers and especially at the prospect of Moscow's replacement of Mr. Ioffe," a Japanese correspondent wrote in a scathing article in the *Japan Advertiser*. He sympathized with Ioffe's reported

---

[e] For the complete text of the two summaries, each prepared in double columns juxtaposing the Japanese proposals and Russian answers, see Japanese Archives, MT 251.106.11:470–477 and 452–467; summaries of the summaries may be found in Japanese Archives MT 251.106.11:380–386 and MT 251.106.16:548–554.

suspicion that if the Foreign Office had substituted "a blank sheet" for the conversations he had had with Count Gotō, it might do the same for the talks he had now been having with Kawakami. He noted that Ioffe must have been aware of the fact that he was personally disliked by the Foreign Office and that the latter had not wanted to negotiate with him, lest Gotō reap political benefit from the agreement.

Why then did the Foreign Office enter into negotiations with him at all? [the correspondent queried and then replied himself:] The Foreign Office was forced to it by the influence of public opinion. Viscount Gotō had worked public opinion to such a point that the Foreign Office had either to accept or refuse it. In both cases it was bound to lose face. The only way to get it out of the dilemma was to accept with the intention of refusing—to make naught of the Gotō-Ioffe preparations by taking them out of Gotō's hands. With his voluntary withdrawal and the entrance of the Foreign Office represented by Mr. Kawakami, public opinion took breath and tired by technical trivialities soon lost interest in the whole question. The time came then for deliberate professional propaganda to get to work. The propaganda of the Seiyūkai and the Foreign Office had the whole field open to its insiduous influence. The press was thenceforth served with practically nothing but the statements of the Foreign Office. Mr. Ioffe incautiously antagonized the pressmen in the earlier part of the pourparlers, so that the account of the proceedings from his side was not presented at all. The fickleness of public opinion and the lack of insight and initiative of the Japanese reporters have been strikingly illustrated in the last two months. Encouraged by such a turn in public sentiment, the Foreign Office stiffened its back and appears to observant critics to have deliberately worked for the miscarriage of the negotiations. Wittingly or unwittingly he fell into the snare by opposing technicality to technicality. In the meantime, the report that Mr. Karahan is to succeed Mr. Joffe has been persistently circulated. Whatever may be the motive that may have prompted Moscow to replace the envoy, it is exactly what the Foreign Office was most anxious to see and was deliberately soliciting for.[12]

Ioffe's departure did not still Gotō. On August 10 he wrote a letter to Chicherin in which he stated that he had a very frank exchange of opinions with Ioffe. They had conferred in a friendly manner and "each side, taking into consideration the natural geographical, historical and economic conditions of both countries and adhering to the most patriotic point of view," had striven to reestablish "friendly relations on the principles of justice and legality." As a result, Gotō asserted, Soviet-Japanese relations had improved radically—"as if we now live in another world." It was to the good of both countries, furthermore, that preliminary negotiations had begun.

> I always deeply regretted, considering the self-interests of the great powers [Gotō wrote], that after the [First] World War these powers decided during the peace talks to take a position, directed toward the exclusion of Russia from the world association and ignoring her. . . .
> The relations between Japan and Russia really differ greatly from the relations between Russia on one hand and England, America and the other states on the other hand. The time has already come for us, when not only the educated circles but likewise the broad layers of the population realize and understand that good relations between Japan and Russia will serve not only the happiness of both peoples, but at the same time [will] contribute to the stabilization of the neighboring state of China and its cultural existence, that they form the basis of peace in Eastern Asia and, finally, are in a position, together with America, to further the establishment of peace in the Pacific Ocean and thereby in the whole world.[13]

Gotō declared that since Japan and Russia were tied to each other by natural conditions they should not follow in the footsteps of England and

America in their policies but take the initiative in the formulation of relations. He said that he would try to obtain access to the economic resources of New Russia not only in view of the anti-Japanese movement in America, Africa, the South Seas and other British colonies but also because of the conviction "that the united strength of both peoples would be able to make up the shortcomings of the Versailles, Washington and other international conferences. . . ."

Gotō supported a proposal made by the Bank of Korea for the extension of credit to Siberia. He deemed the proposition in the interest of the further development of both countries, since the bank would function in the form of a mixed Russo-Japanese bank. He wrote that he had discussed with Ioffe the necessity of establishing a special credit bank in Siberia and asked that Chicherin obtain further information from [Ioffe's] private secretary, Mr. Levin, if Ioffe himself could not report about this personally.[14]

While Gotō waxed lyrical about the possibilities of Russo-Japanese collaboration, the authorities on both sides worried about espionage and subversion. In May of 1923 Soviet officials had arrested Japanese consular personnel and military attachés, an action repeated in February of 1924. Japanese authorities in Aomori meanwhile (in March of 1922) had refused landing permission to the captain and crew of a Russian steamer that had brought fresh herring to Aomori in accordance with a contract with a Japanese firm, lest they engage in propaganda on shore.

The extent of Japanese fear of Communist subversion is best illustrated by the reaction of Japanese officialdom to Soviet offers of help at a moment of national catastrophe. When news reached the Soviet Union about the great Tokyo-Yokohama earthquake of September 1, 1923, which claimed the lives of over 130,000 people and left two million homeless, the Russians rushed to be of assistance. The Soviet government in spite of its own financial difficulties appropriated 200,000 rubles in gold for relief and, setting up relief committes in various parts of the Soviet Union, raised generous contributions from individual workers as well as from Red Cross and party units. The government, furthermore, provided free transportation for Russian donated relief goods, waived export duty on Russian relief goods and reduced duty on relief goods in transit from Europe; it also offered lumber concessions and fishing grounds on exceedingly favorable terms to Japanese workers in need of assistance.[15]

But when the steamer *Lenin*—the first foreign relief vessel to reach Japan—arrived at Yokohama on September 12 with eleven units of the Red Cross, over 700,000 pounds of wheat, 180,000 pounds of rice, 100,000 pounds of fish and almost 800,000 pounds of other products, the Japanese would not let the Soviet representatives land. The Japanese were willing to accept the goods and distribute them themselves. They were unwilling to leave the distribution to the Russians, who, they feared, would take advantage of the prevailing misery and chaos to spread propaganda along with relief. When the Russians did not agree to this, wanting to surrender the goods to "representatives of groups of Japan's needy population which had suffered from the earthquake," they were ordered to depart. The Russians are a generous people; they are also easily offended. They were truly hurt by the Japanese rejection of Russian aid and vigorously protested in a note by Chicherin, conveyed through the Japanese consul general in Vladivostok.[16]

Chicherin wrote that the reports in the Japanese press that there had been Communist literature on the *Lenin* "are completely without foundation and do not correspond to fact." He pledged that should it be discovered that anyone on the vessels had overstepped the bounds of propriety toward the Japanese government, measures would be taken to prevent reoccurrence of such acts. Chicherin stated that the Soviet government categorically rejected the suspicion that in the present case it had any motives other than aid to the quake victims and accused the initiators of these accusations of showing an unwholesome attitude toward the establishment of better relations with the U.S.S.R.

In its reply, handed by the Japanese consul in Vladivostok to the representative of the Foreign Commissariat in that city on October 2, the Japanese government asserted that it had been informed by the local authorities at Yokohama that upon the arrival of the *Lenin* at Yokohama it had been publicly announced by the Russian representatives, that the relief goods aboard ship must be distributed only to workers and that they would undertake the distribution themselves. The local authorities had reported also that the Russian representatives had made speeches that, it was feared, could lead to disturbances among the population. The commander of the port, therefore, had taken it upon himself to order the departure of the vessel. Because communication with the central government had been very difficult at that moment in view of the destruction wrought by the earthquake, the sincere motives of the Japanese government could not be explained to the Russian ambassador. The note expressed the deep thanks of the government and people of Japan for the sympathy expressed by the Russian government and people, sympathy which it hoped would continue and would contribute to friendly relations between the two countries. The government reiterated that it would be glad to accept relief goods in the future, provided there would be no restrictions placed on the manner of their distribution.[17, f]

The offer of the Soviet government to assign fishing grounds to needy Japanese ran into similar difficulties. The Japanese government's desire to have the special leases worked by regular Japanese fishery enterprises, which then would contribute a share of the profit to the needy, was not acceptable to the Russians.

In a public statement on February 23, 1924, the foreign commissariat announced that the presidium of the Central Executive Committee of the U.S.S.R. was proposing to the Central Commission of Aid of Japan to stop organizational work for the showing of aid until conditions and relations were established between Japan and the Soviet Union "that would permit the working people of the U.S.S.R. to show direct aid to indigent Japanese citizens who had suffered from the earthquake."[18]

When the Soviet Union extended aid to Korean flood victims in August of 1925, it did so in the name of the Russian Red Cross; the latter sent 5,000 rubles to Ambassador Kopp with the request that he coordinate distribution with the Japanese Red Cross. (*Dokumenty vneshnei politiki* vol. VIII [Moscow 1963], p. 479)

CHAPTER FIVE

The Karakhan-Yoshizawa Talks

AT the beginning of September 1923 Lev Mikhailovich Karakhan succeeded Ioffe as plenipotentiary representative to China. Like Ioffe Karakhan had been a Menshevik until 1917 and like him had participated in the Brest-Litovsk negotiations, though in a subordinate capacity. He came from a once wealthy family, was well educated and had journalistic experience as a collaborator of Maksim Gorkii's semi-Menshevik newspaper *Novaia Zhizn.*' He had been assistant people's commissar for foreign affairs from 1918 to 1922, with a stint as ambassador in Poland (1921–22). He too was well versed in foreign affairs, therefore, and upon his arrival in Peking threw himself into the task of renewing Soviet-Japanese negotiations.

On September 22 Karakhan called on the Japanese minister in Peking, Yoshizawa Kenkichi 芳澤謙吉. He expressed his sympathy on the disaster that had befallen Japan and then asked whether the Japanese government, busy as it must be with problems of reconstruction, would be willing to begin official negotiations about the normalization of Russo-Japanese relations, as proposed by his government earlier. Yoshizawa reported the conversation to Tokyo, but a reply was delayed because a change in cabinet had occurred on September 2 and the government of Admiral Yamamoto Gombei 山本權兵衛 seemed opposed to recognition of the Soviet Union.[1, a]

---

[a] Yoshizawa in his frustratingly brief memoirs describes the meeting of September 22 as a courtesy call; he states that Karakhan raised the question of renewed relations between the two countries "one day in the last ten days of February" 1924, i.e. at the meeting of February 24, and that his discussions with Karakhan began in April. (Yo-★

On October 7 Karakhan wrote a very long letter to Viscount Gotō, who had become home minister in the new cabinet. Observing that the subject was dear to both of their hearts, Karakhan stated: "The Russo-Japanese problem, to which you have devoted so much valuable attention and strength, requires new efforts on the part of all who see in the friendship of our two peoples a guarantee of peace, order and prosperity in the Far East and [in] the Pacific Ocean [region] in general."

Karakhan observed that the earthquake catastrophe had inevitably delayed Japanese consideration of the Russo-Japanese problem, as all effort and thought went into relief and reconstruction at home. He was glad to bear witness that his countrymen had warmly come to the aid of the Japanese people, but saddened by the "feeling of offense and bitter taste" left by the "unworthy accusations" which had accompanied the expulsion of the relief ship *Lenin* from Yokohama. "We learned," he added, "that this was the work of the local military command and that the government in Tokyo found out about this *post factum*, that the Japanese people are not guilty in this insulting matter. It became clear to us, that just as in the past various military elements of Japan, who inspired and led the military expeditions in Siberia, brought much harm to Russo-Japanese relations, so now too they struck out with a careless and rash hand at the understanding that was coming into being between the two peoples." Expressing the conviction that "the stupid slander" directed against the vessel that had come to Yokohama "with brotherly help" had been the work of "enemies of a Russo-Japanese rapprochement," Karakhan attributed the major blame to "those numerous White emigrant elements, which have received undeserved refuge in your country."

Karakhan wrote that in spite of the negotiations that had taken place so far, Russo-Japanese relations were "to the highest degree abnormal"

★shizawa Kenkichi 芳澤謙吉, *Gaikō rokujū-nen* 外交六十年 [60 years of diplomacy] [Tokyo, 1958], pp. 73–74) The Soviet documents show that talks began earlier. Yoshizawa probably wrote part of his memoirs from memory and therefore was slightly off in his dates.

and demanded that they be straightened out as soon as possible lest further misunderstandings occur. Karakhan asserted that in the negotiations Russia had shown from the very beginning "great patience and the desire to make concessions to the Japanese people" even when this was not required either by necessity or by special interests. He pointed as an example to the provisional fishery agreement, which had been concluded that year in a favorable way for Japan. It had been Russia's hope that the negotiations conducted by Ioffe in Tokyo would be successful, but the Ioffe-Kawakami talks were without positive, formal results. "At the present time the negotiations have been interrupted, and it is not known when and under what circumstances they will be renewed; it must be clear to you, Mr. Viscount, as it is to me, that this time the negotiations either must not be begun or, once they have been begun, must have a final character and lead to the establishment of normal relations between the two countries."

Karakhan stated that he had been pleased to learn from Yoshizawa that the imperial government had not lost sight of the Russo-Japanese question in spite of the internal problems and he welcomed the news report that the new foreign minister, Iijūin Hikokichi, 伊集院彦吉, had declared that "for the establishment of friendly relations between neighborly countries official relations with Russia must be renewed." Admitting that he did not know how accurately the foreign minister had been quoted, he asserted that the reputed remarks concerning the beginning of official relations had been so "pythonic," that in spite of all his desire to understand what Ijūin had tried to say, Karakhan could not grasp as the result of what "energetic investigation" Japan would be ready to begin official negotiations.

Karakhan stressed the urgency of restoring official relations. He feared that the departure of the Japanese consul from Vladivostok could worsen Russo-Japanese relations and warned that the Russian authorities might not be in a position to solve the fishery problem in the coming season as favorably for Japan as they had during the current year. While he realized that such a prospect would be equally unpleasant for both countries, he stressed that "no one could say that the Russian authorities had acted wrongly, because in the absence of any relations whatsoever with the other side, one could hardly demand the right to make use of its natural resources."

Karakhan wrote that the urgency to restore official relations between Russia and Japan was even greater from the point of view of international relations in general in the light of the developing rivalry and power relationships in the whole world and particularly in the Pacific Ocean. "The interests of the world and the well-being of the peoples demand that the vacuum between our countries be filled both in their interest as well as even more in the interest of the peoples of the Pacific Ocean. Delay in this matter may give incorrigible and unexpected results." "Although I do not have the honor to be personally acquainted with you, I write to you as to an old acquaintance, since I know your evaluation of the world situation, from my friends and from your letters to them and to Mr. Chicherin."

"What divides the two neighboring countries?" Karakhan asked. "The Nikolaevsk events basically do not call forth disagreement; it is a matter of editing [the wording of the Soviet expression of regret]. Nor does the question of North Sakhalin evoke disagreement. The only point at issue is the question of debts and old treaties, concluded between Tsarist Russia and Japan."

Karakhan wrote that although Japan persistently strove for the recognition of the old debts and treaties, it was obvious that these two questions were not really of vital importance to the Japanese people, for the Japanese government did not demand the immediate payment of the debts, merely their recognition. It was interested in the matter, therefore, not as a matter of reality but as a matter of principle. But it was over this issue that the Soviet Union had broken off relations with all the great powers and it was unrealistic to expect now, when she was economically and militarily much stronger than when she had rejected the demands, that she would yield on this issue.

Karakhan gave the treaty of 1916 with its secret clauses as the example of a treaty that Soviet Russia could not accept. There might be items in the various treaties that would be retained, if Japan stated specifically what she wanted, but the blind retention of all the treaties in their entirety was impossible. "The most expedient solution of the Russo-Japanese problem would be the conclusion of a treaty that would have a basic [and] vital meaning for both peoples, a solution of the question that served a live people, and not dead formulas and dubious obligations of international solidarity." Karakhan felt that the new treaty should be like the Russo-German treaty of Rapallo, which had broken completely with the past. "All the old is behind, and the future of the two peoples must be built on new clear beginnings, which will not bear the traces of past wrongs and unnecessary considerations." Karakhan called this the principle of "mutual amnesty." Only agreements still of vital importance such as the fishery agreement, for example, should be retained.

When it came to vital issues rather than dead principles, Karakhan felt, the two peoples could go even farther than the Tsarist treaties had. Pointing to Gotō's letter of August 10 to Chicherin, in which Gotō had referred to the anti-Japanese movements in various parts of the world and the need for Japan to gain access to the resources of Russia, Karakhan stated that these raw materials were even more important to Japan now, after the great earthquake. It was alright for countries which were economically self-sufficient and thus did not feel the need for friendship with New Russia to keep insisting on dead formulas and old obligations, but Japan which had her own special interests in Russia, interests that were incomparable with those of the other powers, must go her own way. Apologizing for the length of his letter and for his outspokeness, Karakhan concluded with the hope that, notwithstanding influential anti-Soviet elements in Japanese politics, a Russo-Japanese rapprochement would find "sufficiently strong and authoritative advocates in Japan and that the work which Gotō had begun "with such success" would be completed.[2]

Two months later, on December 18, 1923, Foreign Commissar Chicherin replied to Gotō's letter of August 10. Chicherin thanked Gotō for his persistent efforts on behalf of better Russo-Japanese relations. "We expect very much from our future relations with Japan," he asserted.

"World interests are turning ever more to the Pacific Ocean, and the time is not far when Pacific interests will become dominant in the world. Siberia has a future of great promise and close collaboration with Japan forms the basic condition for the development of our Far Eastern regions."

Chicherin wrote that the serious illness of their friend Ioffe had been a heavy blow to a Russo-Japanese rapprochement. It was due to the illness that such matters as the establishment of banks and joint ventures had been delayed. He repeated the view that the great earthquake catastrophe made the establishment of friendly relations between the two countries more important than ever.[3]

Gotō replied to Chicherin somewhat more promptly. He wrote on January 30, 1924, that he fully shared his "wonderful thoughts concerning world politics", particularly the contention that Asia was becoming more and more the focus of attention and that world peace was tied most closely to peace in East Asia. Since Russo-Japanese relations played a major role in this, he deemed it a moral obligation of the leaders of both states to work for the quickest possible reestablishment of friendly relations between their countries. Gotō asserted that the movement begun by him and Ioffe for a rapprochement had been halted by the earthquake catastrophe and a resultant reactionary trend toward life; the dispute concerning the Russian relief shipment had contributed to this. But Gotō regarded this as a passing phenomenon and expected the negotiations to be renewed "in the not too distant future." On the other hand, the frequent change of persons in charge had meant delay because everyone of them had had to familiarize himself anew with the course of negotiations and to study the conditions for a treaty.

Gotō mentioned that he had been able to exchange opinions with Karakhan in Peking through his private secretary, Mr. Mori, and that he had always received Russian proposals with thanks. He concluded that Mr. Mori, whom he had now sent to Russia, would be furnished with the necessary information.[4]

That month, in January of 1924, Kiyoura Keigo 清浦奎吾 became premier[b] and Baron Matsui Keishirō 松井慶四郎 took over as foreign

[b] Yamamoto's administration was in power from September 2, 1923, until January*

minister. In mid-February Matsui suddenly found himself in the midst of a long-distance diplomatic duel with Karakhan. Karakhan began the exchange at a press interview in Peking with an attack on Matsui for various statements allegedly made in a speech at a gubernatorial conference in Tokyo. Matsui replied publicly "as if the opportunity were one for which he had been waiting with eager anticipation", as the *Japan Advertiser* put it. While it appeared that Karakhan had started the joust on the basis of a faulty account of Matsui's address, the exchange boiled down to Karakhan's contention that the ravages of the great earthquake had so weakened Japan that she would do well to make peace with Moscow and Matsui's retort that the seismic disaster had left the Japanese government unaffected in the formulation of its foreign policy.

In reporting the Karakhan-Matsui controversy, the *Japan Advertiser* added that at a meeting on February 20, the day that Matsui replied to Karakhan, the Japanese cabinet had "decided again to continue their policy of 'watchful waiting', a decision which apparently is being reached as a matter of ordinary routine at each successive meeting of the Cabinet Council these days" and concluded that "the Japanese policy of ignoring the existence of the Soviet Republic of Russia henceforth is to be maintained intact."[5] Yet actually the exchange with Karakhan may have prodded Matsui into action, for he instructed Minister Yoshizawa in Peking to meet with Karakhan and ascertain Soviet views concerning pending issues between the two countries.

Yoshizawa met Karakhan on February 24 and several times thereafter. He reported that Karakhan in turn had wished to learn the position of the Japanese government. On March 15 Matsui instructed Yoshizawa, therefore, to convey to Karakhan what problems must be settled before Japan could recognize the Soviet Union.[6]

On March 19 Yoshizawa informed Karakhan that the Japanese government had decided to recognize the Soviet government and had instructed him to enter into negotiations with him. Unlike Matsushima, Matsu-

---

*7, 1924; Kiyoura Keigo became premier on January 7, 1924, and remained in office until June 11 of the same year.

daira, and Kawakami, Yoshizawa did not speak Russian. He had graduated from Tokyo Imperial University with a degree in English literature. But he had been in the Foreign Ministry since the turn of the century, and had served as director of the Foreign Affairs Bureau before being appointed ambassador to China.[c]

Yoshizawa told Karakhan that he had a detailed draft of recognition, but before transmitting it to him needed Soviet consent to three prior conditions: (1) that the negotiations would be secret; (2) that the negotiations would not be labelled anything—neither informal talks nor a formal conference—but would simply be conducted between the two representatives in Peking; and (3) that the Soviet government would immediately, before recognition, settle the Vladivostok incidents—that it would free two Japanese officers still under arrest on a charge of espionage, would recognize the consul, and reestablish postal communication.

Karakhan retorted that the Soviet side had not asked to see the Japanese draft; the imperial government wanted to show it of its own volition. He could not agree to any prior conditions for accepting it. He told Yoshizawa that he had had no instructions to discuss this matter with him and would request none if the Japanese posed conditions.

On March 20 Yoshizawa seemingly withdrew the prior conditions and Karakhan promised to request Moscow to settle the Vladivostok incidents as soon as possible. He made it clear, however, that he could guarantee nothing and could accept no responsibility for the outcome. Karakhan further warned Yoshizawa before taking the draft that no negotiations could take place until he had received instruction from his government; it was possible that the Soviet government would reject talks or might demand the calling of an official conference. Acceptance of the draft did not commit the Russian side to anything.[7]

The plan of the Japanese government was as follows: (1) the Soviet

[c] Yoshizawa was to be Japan's delegate to the League of Nations at the time of the Manchurian Incident and the following year, in 1932, was to become Foreign Minister.

Union was to give a written expression of deep regret about the Nikolaevsk incident; (2) the Japanese government would forgo compensation for the incident on condition that it would receive favorable long-term concessions on Sakhalin; (3) the Portsmouth treaty was to remain in effect because of its historical importance for the Japanese people; (4) the Japanese government would renounce the debts of the Tsarist and Provisional governments in return for free, long-term concessions on Sakhalin and in Eastern Siberia; (5) the Soviet Union was to agree to the return of nationalized private property or to due compensation for it, though this matter could be left for future consideration if the most-favored-nation principle would be applied in the interim; (6) recognition was to be made in the draft that the future treaty of commerce would guarantee the safety of Japanese subjects in Russia and the protection of their property, private property as well as wide trade and industrial activity; (7) both sides were to pledge to refrain from propaganda and hostile activity; (8) Japan was to withdraw her forces from Sakhalin and formally recognize the Soviet Union.

Yoshizawa told Karakhan that the Japanese government was prepared to realize the above in any formulation—by an exchange of notes, a declaration, or an agreement. When Karakhan replied that it was his personal impression that the Japanese government had learned nothing and had no serious intention to adjust relations, Yoshizawa explained that he had merely made an oral communication and would send a written text for Karakhan to study; if there were unacceptable points, they could be discussed and changed. Karakhan refused to comment on the draft because he was not empowered to do so; he did state that it was his personal opinion that the matter could be resolved only by applying the British method.[8]

Two days later, on March 22, Yoshizawa transmitted to Karakhan the Japanese draft, together with a covering letter. The proposals were preceded by the statement that since many important questions between the two countries were still unresolved, Japan could not recognize the Soviet government at once without qualifications; she deemed it necessary first to come to a practical agreement concerning at least the most important of the unresolved questions. The last provision, item 8, was phrased as follows: "Upon conclusion of an agreement concerning the above points the Japanese government will immediately end the occupation of North Sakhalin and will officially recognize the Soviet government." The three prior conditions for holding negotiations, which Yoshizawa had posed on the 19th and then seemingly withdrawn the next day, reappeared in the written communication.[9]

Karakhan replied in the name of his government that while it had come forward against secret negotiations and desired to confer with Japan at an open conference, it was willing to go along with the first two prior conditions, namely that the talks be secret and be held in Peking without a particular label as to their status. But he "categorically rejected" the demand that the two alleged spies be freed, declaring that this issue had no direct bearing on the reestablishment of diplomatic relations between the two countries. After a lengthy exchange of views Yoshizawa gave in on this point, or so Karakhan understood.

After studying the eight point draft of the Japanese side, the Soviet government empowered Karakhan to enter into negotiations with Yoshizawa for the conclusion and signature of an agreement with the Japanese government. On April 8 Karakhan discovered, however, that Yoshizawa did not have full powers. The Japanese government planned to provide him with the letters patent at the conclusion rather than at the beginning of the negotiations as was customary. Karakhan told Yoshizawa that the Soviet government was prepared to forgo a public, official conference, but it could not agree that such serious negotiations be begun without the two representatives showing each other their full powers to enter into negotiations and to sign an agreement.[10]

On April 19 Yoshizawa informed Karakhan that the Japanese government did not deem it necessary for the plenipotentiaries to exchange letters patent at this time. "The Japanese government is ready to issue such full powers at any time and to sign an agreement as soon as both points of view will be in general concord and there will be hope for the possibility of reaching an agreement."

Karakhan rejected this. The Japanese government had strictly adhered to customary usage in the preceding negotiations at Dairen, Changchun and Tokyo. The exchange of full powers had always come before the commencement of negotiations. This had been true even in the case of the Ioffe-Kawakami talks, which both sides had agreed to regard as unofficial and not binding on either side. Karakhan insisted that letters patent be exchanged, particularly now that both sides had agreed to take important decisions leading to the immediate extablishment of official relations between the two governments.

When two weeks passed without a reply, Karakhan transmitted to Yoshizawa a note, dated May 5, in which he reviewed their contact since March 22 and repeated the request that Yoshizawa obtain due letters patent. Asking that the Japanese government answer as soon as possible, Karakhan expressed his government's expectation that the Japanese government would not allow this matter which had "all the prospects of yielding positive result" to come to naught even before negotiations had begun by violating international usage.[11]

The following day, on May 6, the Press Section of the Foreign Commissariat issued a release in which it objected strongly to allegations in the Japanese press that the delay in Russo-Japanese negotiations was due to the fact that Karakhan did not have full powers.[12]

On May 13 Yoshizawa acknowledged receipt of Karakhan's note of the 5th and promised to give a reply as soon as he heard from his government, to which he had duly relayed it. He felt "constrained", however, meanwhile to correct some of the Soviet assertions. Regarding the three prior conditions, which Karakhan had depicted as having been posed by the Japanese government, Yoshizawa asserted that he had explained to Karakhan orally during their meeting on the 5th that the first two of these "so-called prior conditions" had not been proposed by the Japanese government and had not been put forth by him as "conditions which must precede negotiations." As for the third condition, Yoshizawa wrote, the position of the Japanese government must be clear to Karakhan in view of the representations which he had made to him "so persistently on so many occasions." He took issue with the assertion made by Karakhan in the note that he had retracted the demand.

Yoshizawa stated that it was true that he had agreed that this problem be considered independently of the pending general negotiations, but he had done so with the important qualification that Karakhan himself, in his capacity as plenipotentiary of the Soviet government in the Far East, would make every effort to obtain the release of the Japanese subjects arrested in Vladivostok. The fact that these Japanese were still in jail aroused deep resentment among the Japanese people.

Yoshizawa also objected to the statement in Karakhan's note that Yoshizawa had agreed on April 8 to ask his government for full powers.

> That is not an exact statement of what actually took place at that meeting [Yoshizawa wrote with obvious annoyance]. There would seem to be a fundamental discrepancy of views between us on this question of full powers. As has been explained to you almost *ad nauseam* the Japanese Government feel it of extreme importance that any repetitions of the failures of previous negotiations should be guarded against as far as possible. My instructions are on that account none other than to enter into informal conversations with you and, through frank exchange of views on matters the settlement of which is the pre-requesite of the restoration on normal relationship, to inform my government whether there is any fair prospect for formal negotiations, if entered into, to be brought to a successful conclusion. It never was their intention to open negotiations irrespective of whether there was such prospect or not. The idea of investing me with full powers for carrying on conversations of the said character with you has never occurred to the Japanese Government.

All that he had agreed to do, Yoshizawa declared, was merely to relay Karakhan's demand for exchange of full powers. He expressed satisfaction, however, at Karakhan's assertion that the proposed negotiations had "all the prospects of yielding a positive result." Assuming this statement to mean that the Moscow government was willing to come to an agreement on the basis of the considerations advanced by Japan,

THE KARAKHAN-YOSHIZAWA TALKS 153

he was making every effort, he wrote, to induce his government to take a decision in the conciliatory spirit expressed by Karakhan.[13]

Thanking Yoshizawa for his letter, Karakhan wrote on May 15 that he understood that Yoshizawa merely wished to clarify and supplement some of the statements made in his note of May 5. But "to avoid misunderstandings," Karakhan declared it his duty to warn Yoshizawa that the statement that the negotiations had "all the prospects of yielding a positive result" must not be interpreted in the sense that the Soviet government regarded the Japanese conditions handed to him on March 22 as acceptable. "The thought which the phrase in question expresses means only the general conviction that there are no problems vital to the peoples of the Union of Soviet Socialist Republics and Japan on which the two countries could not reach agreement. This conviction is based on the fact that both countries have the intention of reestablishing normal relations on the basis of justice, equality and reciprocity."[14]

Meanwhile the Japanese cabinet had agreed to provide Yoshizawa with full powers, as demanded by the Soviet Union, and formal negotiations were begun at last on May 15. "Certainly, there is an enormous difference between the present parley and last year's at Tokyo," Karakhan declared in a press interview. "Here the negotiations have an official character, while in Tokyo they were not binding on either party. The Tokyo negotiations had as object only a preliminary preparation for the resumption of relations, while here, in Peking, the resumption of formal relations is a direct object of the conference."[15]

Karakhan handed Yoshizawa a Soviet draft agreement, drawn up "for convenience's sake" in an attempt to reconcile Japanese and Russian views. This draft was to be used as the basis for discussions for the next three weeks[16] and deserves to be quoted in full:

> The Government of the Union of Soviet Socialist Republics represented by ... and the Imperial Japanese Government represented by. . . .

d Yoshizawa's full powers were issued on May 13, 1924; a copy was transmitted to Karakhan only on May 29. (Japanese Archives, MT 251.106.19:2675-2676.

Desiring to re-establish good-neighbourly relations, tending to promote friendship and economic operation between the people of both countries, have agreed upon the following Articles:

I

The two Contracting Parties agree that simultaneously with the signing of the present Agreement normal diplomatic and consular relations shall be established between the U.S.S.R. and the Japanese Empire.

The Government of the U.S.S.R. shall adopt the necessary measures to transfer to the Imperial Japanese Government the Embassy, Consulates and other State property to be found in the territory of U.S.S.R. In its turn, the Imperial Japanese Government shall do the same with regard to the property to be found in the territory of the Japanese Empire.

II

Imperial Japanese Government shall withdraw its troops from and entirely cease occupation of territory of Northern Sakhalin. Imperial Japanese Government agrees to begin to free the territory of Northern Sakhalin from occupation immediately upon signing of present agreement and complete same within two weeks, during which period territory must be handed over to proper authorities.

III

Two Contracting Parties agree after re-establishment of diplomatic relations to conclude a commercial treaty, on strength of which nationals of one party shall enjoy full protection in territory of other subject to laws existing in respective territory, both personally and in regard to their properties, and shall be able to widely engage in trade and industries, as in accordance with the existing laws.

IV

In the interest of promoting economic relations, the Government of the U.S.S.R. is willing to meet halfway needs of the Japanese Empire in regard to natural resources existing in the territory of the U.S.S.R. With this end in view, it is willing to grant to Japanese subjects and juridical persons concessions for the exploitation of minerals, forests, etc., in the territory of the U.S.S.R. and, in particular, in Eastern Siberia and Northern Sakhalin.

V

The Government of the U.S.S.R. is willing, immediately upon the re-establishment of diplomatic relations between the two Contracting Parties, to conclude with the Imperial Japanese Government a fisheries convention on the conditions provided for by the Portsmouth Treaty and the Fisheries Convention of 1907.

VI

Both Contracting Parties agree to discuss the question of mutual state and private claims and debts, including the Japan's claim in reference to the Nikolaievsk affair and justly settle them at a future conference.

VII

Each of the Contracting Parties agrees to annul, upon the signing of the present agreement, all kinds of treaties or agreements that may have been concluded between itself and third parties, prejudicing sovereign or territorial rights of the other party, or constituting a menace to the safety of the latter.

VIII

Two contracting Parties mutually pledge themselves to respect national sovereignty of the other party and refrain from any interference with its internal affairs and in particular from agitations, propaganda and any kind of intervention and from supporting them. Two contracting parties pledge themselves not to create or support organizations whose aim is to carry on an armed struggle against the other party or prepare overthrow of violence.

In view of this, both contracting Parties pledge themselves not to allow such organizations, their agents or organs to stay in their territory.

IX

The present agreement shall come into effect from the date of signature.

In witness whereof, respective plenipotentiaries have signed the present agreement and have affixed thereto their seals.

Done at city of Peking this———————17

On May 21 Karakhan cabled a progress report to the People's Commissariat of Foreign Affairs. He summed up the results of the first five sessions in four points:

1. Yoshizawa now demanded merely an expression of regret regarding the Nikolsevsk incident, saying that he would make every effort to make the formula acceptable to the Russians. "I am rejecting [this]," Karakhan wired. They had decided to postpone this issue for the time being.

2. Karakhan had worded the article regarding the evacuation of Sakhalin. The Japanese would withdraw immediately upon signature of the agreement and would complete the evacuation within two weeks, during which the territory would be surrendered to the Russians. Yoshizawa had queried Tokyo by cable whether one could agree to a one month period or should stipulate simply to evacuate "immediately upon signing."

3. Karakhan had succeeded in obtaining Japanese renunciation of compensation in any form for the debts of the Tsarist and Provisional governments. Japan agreed to postpone the matter, provided she would not be put in a worse position than third powers; she had accepted the Soviet qualification "other conditions being equal." Yoshizawa himself had proposed the following formula the day before on May 20: "As regards

the debts to Japan, the Japanese government agrees to settle this question after further discussion on condition, however, that, other conditions being equal, the Japanese must in any case be treated on the part of the Soviet Government no less favorably than any third power." Karakhan had declined this formula; he had insisted on a reciprocal formulation and on adding state and private claims. This version frightened the Japanese with its intricacy. They objected to a reciprocal formula concerning debts, saying that they did not owe anything to the Russians. If absolutely necessary, Karakhan reported, he would be willing to accept their formulation about debts provided it would be followed by an article about state and private claims in the framework of the same formula.

4. Yoshizawa had objected to the general statement in Karakhan's draft that the Soviet Union was willing to grant concessions to the Japanese "in the territory of the U.S.S.R., particularly in Eastern Siberia and North Sakhalin." Yoshizawa wanted a more concrete commitment, specifying the regions and general conditions of the concessions. Karakhan suspected that the Japanese would want to indicate that oil region on Sakhalin, where they were now working. According to his information the Japanese had succeeded in discovering rich sources of oil, and he was sure that they would want to retain them.[18]

On May 23 Karakhan and Yoshizawa agreed on the statement prohibiting propaganda; they could not get together in regard to a treaty of commerce, however. Yoshizawa proposed that their treaties with third powers be taken into consideration when concluding one.

Karakhan reminded Yoshizawa that he had not received any answer from the Japanese government concerning the transfer of Soviet embassy, consular and other state property nor about the terms of evacuation of Sakhalin. Yoshizawa promised to try to obtain a reply, and the talks were recessed for a week.

Karakhan made good use of the interlude to conclude some Chinese affairs. On the morning of May 31 he signed an agreement with China whereby the Soviet Union regained Tsarist rights to the Chinese Eastern Railway in Manchuria. When the Soviet-Japanese negotiations were resumed on the afternoon of the 31st, Yoshizawa congratulated Karakhan "from the soul", but as Karakhan reported to Chicherin, it was obvious that Yoshizawa and many of his countrymen were distressed.[e]

In spite of the week's recess Yoshizawa had not received a reply concerning the transfer of Russian state property and the evacuation of Sakhalin. He requested from Karakhan clarification of the clause "all things being equal" in the article on debts, and sought to separate the debt question from the Nikolaevsk question. But Karakhan insisted that he wanted an answer to his questions before discussing anything else. They argued at length to little avail.

Karakhan and Yoshizawa did touch on the matter of concessions and Yoshizawa produced three maps showing the regions where the Japanese government wanted concessions. Try as he did, Karakhan could not find out whether the Japanese government wanted to get concessions for entire regions or for pieces of land in the regions. He made it clear, however, that the Soviet government could not grant concessions in specific areas, that such consideration would require the participation of specialists and would delay the proceedings too much. Karakhan reported that it could be seen from the maps, which Yoshizawa would not leave him on the ground that they were the only copies, that the Japanese wanted to get a concession on the narrow strip of eastern Sakhalin, where they had found oil. They desired the southwestern portion of North Sakhalin as a coal concession and the southern section of North Sakhalin as a lumber concession.

---

[e] On June 7, 1924, the Japanese government declared in a note from Yoshizawa to Karakhan that the rights and interests of Japan and her subjects would in no way be affected by the Soviet-Chinese agreement. The Soviet government replied through a note from Karakhan to Yoshizawa, dated July 10, that the question of the Chinese Eastern Railway concerned exclusively the U.S.S.R. and the Chinese Republic and that no other power nor the citizens of any other power could have any rights or interests in regard to the Chinese Eastern Railway. On October 4 Yoshizawa raised the question again in a note to Karakhan; Karakhan replied on October 25, reaffirming the Soviet position. (D.V.P., vol. VIII, pp. 396, 512)

It was Karakhan's belief that Yoshizawa did not wish to press exhorbitant Japanese concession demands, realizing that they would be rejected by the Russians, and had spent the week between the two meetings trying to persuade his government to modify its position. Karakhan reported to Chicherin that he had not yet agreed to the wording (to which Chicherin had already consented) granting to Japan "favorable" and "long-term" concessions. "In order to leave him with the impression of the absolute unacceptability of such a narrowing down to areas or [specifying] in any other respect," Karakhan reported, "I declined this proposal of his [when he showed the maps] in the most categorical manner." Yoshizawa promised to present a detailed, written statement of the demands of his government at the next meeting.[19]

Karakhan had insisted on written specifics from the Japanese side, because he suspected, as he told Yoshizawa, that the Japanese government did not evaluate the situation correctly and wished to create new difficulties. The Japanese draft agreement which Yoshizawa produced on June 4 and 7 and which hereafter replaced Karakhan's as basis for discussion did contain a number of new Japanese demands and in some instances reversed agreements already reached.[f]

Article 3 of the Japanese draft stated that the Japanese would evacuate North Sakhalin within three months from the moment that the agreement went into effect. Article 4 stipulated that oil, coal, forest and fishery concessions on North Sakhalin be granted for periods of 99 years from the moment the agreement went into effect at a lease fee of 5% of net income, with the Soviet government bearing all responsibility for compensating prior Russian interests that might exist in those places. Article 5 laid down some basic principles for commercial and navigational relations between the two countries to be in effect until the conclusion of a treaty of commerce and navigation, which would take them into

---

[f] On March 22 the Japanese had seemed satisfied with the retention of the Treaty of Portsmouth only and with the vague concession statement of Karakhan; on June 4 they demanded the review of other treaties as well and more detailed commitments concerning concessions.

consideration; it stressed reciprocal most-favored-nation treatment. Article 6 insisted on keeping the treaty of Portsmouth of 1905 in force and reviewing at a later conference other treaties and agreements between the two states to retain the rights and privileges which the governments and citizens of the two countries enjoyed thereby; agreements made by the two powers in conjunction with other states would not be reviewed until agreement was reached on an international level. Article 7 stated that upon the agreement going into effect the two contracting sides would begin the revision of the fishery convention of 1907.

A supplementary note, which accompanied the draft, stipulated that at the time of signing the basic convention both contracting sides would declare that neither had any treaty or agreement about a military alliance or any secret agreement, concluded with any third power in violation of the sovereign or territorial rights of the other side or threatening the security of the other side.[20]

During the session of June 7 Yoshizawa also produced a separate document with a draft of the Soviet note of regret for the Nikolaevsk incident.[21]

Karakhan refused to accept the new concession demands. He said that the Soviet government might perhaps agree to modify the phrasing in the article he had proposed to state that the concessions would be "favorable" and "long-term". If the Japanese government would be satisfied with this, he would take it upon himself to plead with Moscow. He pledged to exert every effort to have the Japanese wording accepted—all the while having Chicherin's permission for the modification.

The Japanese proposals seemed to usher in a new phase.

> There were two stages in the negotiations [Karakhan wrote Chicherin on June 16]. The first was until June, when the negotiations went rather smoothly and Yoshizawa during the discussion of questions showed great compliancy, and if on some of the questions in dispute he did not give final formulations, he at any rate expressed himself in such a way, that I obtained the impression that the negotiations would end favorably and even quickly. . . . But on June 4 they put forth their plan about the exchange of

THE KARAKHAN-YOSHIZAWA TALKS 161

instruments of ratification [and other new demands]. All this forces me to think, that after the report of Yoshizawa about the course of the negotiations during the first two weeks he received new instructions, which differed basically from those he had been given at first.

Karakhan wrote that Yoshizawa had exchanged many telegrams with his government during the week when they had interrupted the conference and that from what Yoshizawa's secretary had said Karakhan gathered that Yoshizawa was not satisfied with his new instructions and was trying to have them modified on the grounds that his discussions had already committed him to a certain degree.

Karakhan's impression was reinforced by Yoshizawa himself, who came to him on the 16th, the day Karakhan wrote the above letter, after another recess of over a week, and told him that he had received permission from his government to proceed to Tokyo to report in person. He expected to be away for two weeks, perhaps two or three days longer. He expressed the hope that Karakhan would be in Peking upon his return and that they could resume negotiations. Yoshizawa said that he had asked for permission to go to Tokyo because he had been unable to convey the true nature of the situation to his government. He asserted that he wanted to persuade his government not to insist on the wording which it had put forward regarding the concessions and to modify its stand on debts and other points on which the Soviets stood pat.

Karakhan was convinced from his conversation with Yoshizawa that Yoshizawa was in disagreement with the excessive demands of his government and wanted to go to Tokyo to use his connections there in direct talks with ministers and the Foreign Office to get the concessions necessary to conclude the agreement. As former director of the Foreign Affairs Bureau Yoshizawa had important connections in diplomatic and government circles; his father-in-law, Inukai Tsuyoshi 犬養毅, had just become minister of communications in the new Katō cabinet.[g]

---

[g] In his memoirs Yoshizawa merely states that the new cabinet wanted to hear*

Karakhan believed that the changes in Yoshizawa's instructions—and Japanese newspaper reports confirmed that new instructions had been sent toward the end of May—had been for domestic political reasons. At the time of assuming office in January of 1924, Premier Kiyoura Keigo had looked forward to the speedy conclusion of a Soviet-Japanese agreement during his administration. When he realized by the end of May that he would have to give up the premiership, Karakhan felt, Kiyoura decided to make it more difficult for his successor to obtain credit for such an agreement and introduced new demands in order to commit his successor to a tougher (and unsuccessful) policy. When Karakhan shared this speculation with Yoshizawa, "he laughed, but did not refute it."[22]

The new premier Count Katō Takaaki 加藤高明,[h] who assumed office on June 11, and his foreign minister, Baron Shidehara Kijūrō 幣原喜重郎, took a realistic look at the situation. Katō realized that with the withdrawal of Japanese troops from Siberia the opportunity for imposing a settlement on the Soviet Union had passed and that further delay might make a satisfactory agreement increasingly difficult. The demands of the preceding administration reflected public opinion—pressure from business circles and the military—but there was no sense in making demands that could not be realized. Thus Katō agreed with Yoshizawa to the modification of the Japanese position, notwithstanding the objections of some of the ministers.

The major subject of discussion between Yoshizawa and his superiors in Tokyo was the question of oil concessions on North Sakhalin, on which the navy insisted as a condition for the conclusion of an agreement. On July 12 Yoshizawa was sent with a group of seven experts to North

---

★the facts about the Japanese-Russian negotiations at Peking and ordered him to return home. (Yoshizawa, p. 74)

[h] Count Katō Takaaki had been foreign minister at the time of the conclusion of the Anglo-Japanese Alliance and at the time of the presentation of the Twenty-one Demands. He was premier from June 11, 1924 until January 28, 1926. Do not confuse with Admiral Katō Tomosaburō, who had been premier in 1922–23.

Sakhalin in order to make an on-the-spot study. On the basis of his findings it was determined to seek concessions for 60% of all explored oil fields.[23]

At a cabinet meeting on July 24 the Japanese government agreed to a modification of Japanese demands in line with Shidehara's general policy of conciliation. Yoshizawa was furnished with a new set of guiding principles. The Japanese government was willing to forego long-term concessions on North Sakhalin as compensation for the Nikolaevsk incident; it was willing to reduce the length of oil concessions that it wanted on North Sakhalin and to give Russia a share of the profits; a Soviet expression of regret would be sufficient to settle the Nikolaevsk affair. The Japanese government agreed to confine insistence on the retention of old treaties to the Treaty of Portsmouth and to revise other agreements such as the fishery convention; to leave the matter of Soviet repayment of the money owed by its predecessors to Japan (300 million yen to the Japanese government and 69 million yen to private companies and financiers) until international settlement of the debt questions; to postpone likewise the matter of public and private claims for damages; to leave the conclusion of a commercial treaty for future deliberation, securing meanwhile only a guaranty of freedom of trade and inviolability of private property. The Japanese government clung to the demand for mutual restraint from subversive propaganda and insisted on the withdrawal of Japanese forces from North Sakhalin within two months (rather than two weeks) after conclusion of an agreement.[24]

On July 26 Premier Katō gave a press interview while on a train, traveling to Ise. "Japan is ready to recognize Soviet Russia and settle questions in her favor, as for as possible, in case Russia should show herself as acting on the principle of international faith and in accordance with international duties," Katō declared. While Katō expressed confidence that the Russian question would be settled shortly in view of Yoshizawa's imminent return to Peking, he remarked: "What perplexes the government is that Russia is given to too much diplomacy."[25]

The patronizing tone of the statement elicited an angry response from Karakhan. In a statement to the press on July 30 (the day that Katō's interview had been carried in Peking newspapers), Karakhan declared that Katō's interview went far to explain why relations had not yet been restored between the U.S.S.R. and Japan. "Indeed Japan thinks she is making a big concession and putting the Soviet Union under an obligation by recognizing the Soviet Government," Karakhan stated and warned: "Until Japan realizes that both sides are equally interested in the restoration of mutual relations and that neither party is doing a favour in this matter, but that both are but fulfilling what is essentially their own interests, it is difficult to obtain a common end."[26]

On August 3 Yoshizawa left Tokyo and returned to Peking.[27] The following day, on August 4, he resumed his negotiations with Karakhan alternately at the Soviet and Japanese embassies. Yoshizawa had brought from Tokyo a new Japanese draft treaty, including attached protocols, and the proposed text of a Soviet note of regret about Nikolaevsk. These he now handed to Karakhan. Although the Japanese press asserted before Yoshizawa's return to Peking that the Japanese draft met the Soviet demands, a contention that Yoshizawa repeated, Karakhan disagreed. He felt that most of the modifications had been mainly editorial in comparison with the former Japanese draft. On the basic issue of the North Sakhalin concessions, for example, the Japanese still persisted in their demands. A special protocol B, attached to the draft agreement, stipulated the granting to Japan of concessions "free from all restricting conditions" for the exploitation of oil and coal resources on most of North Sakhalin; provision was made also for Japanese right to cut lumber, build port facilities and railways, lay oil pipelines and establish electric communication on North Sakhalin. Nor was the Soviet government to put any restrictions on the employment of labor and other personnel or to interfere in any way in the control or organization of labor in the Japanese concessions, nor levy any taxes on the Japanese enterprises. In return Japan was willing to reduce the original demand for 99 year leases to 55 years and to provide the Soviet government with 5% of the oil and coal production. Protocol A put off the debt question until its solution on an international level, yet it linked it with the occupation of North Sakhalin, stating that the troops would be withdrawn after this protocol went into effect. Japan insisted that the Treaty of Portsmouth remain in full force, the other Russo-Japanese treaties to be revised or abrogated in the light of changed conditions upon deliberation at a separate conference in the future. Article 4 of the draft treaty laid down conditions which were to form the basis of a later treaty of commerce and were to serve as interim rules until the conclusion of such a treaty of commerce. The article stipulated that citizens of both states, subject to the laws of the two countries, should enjoy freedom of entry, travel, and residence as well as full protection of person and property; wide and reciprocal rights of private property and freedom to engage in commerce, navigation, industry and other peaceful business in no respect inferior to rights and privileges extended to citizens of a third power. The article called for negotiation of a special treaty of commerce and navigation in order to promote economic relations between Japan and the Soviet Union.[28]

That day, in response to a proposal by Karakhan that each of the contracting parties agree to nullify any treaty or convention which constituted an infringement upon, or a menace to, the sovereignty, territorial rights or national safety of the other party and pledge not to enter into any such agreement thereafter, Yoshizawa brought a draft declaration to this effect. It was accepted by Karakhan and embodied in Protocol A.

For five sessions, lasting three to four hours each, beginning on Monday, August 4, and ending on Saturday, August 9, Yoshizawa and Karakhan argued about the new Japanese draft treaty. Yoshizawa kept underlining that it had been composed on the basis of Soviet objections and desires and—in Karakhan's words—"constantly tried to frighten" the Soviet plenipotentiary by asserting that this was the maximum and final Japanese proposal, that it had been confirmed by the Council of Ministers and that if the Soviet side rejected it, there would be created a very serious situation from which there might not be a way out. The entire week was devoted primarily to the discussion of the Japanese proposal as a whole without going into details. "I did not go into the substance of their proposals, refusing to discuss them," Karakhan reported to Chicherin on August 11; "we argued primarily whether it was necessary right now to determine merely a general formula, on the basis of which a concession treaty would be concluded in the future, or, as they insist, an agreement which will be signed right away and will constitute a final concession contract, on the basis of which the Japanese can get to work right away."

Unable to budge Karakhan on this issue, Yoshizawa announced that he had to seek instructions from Tokyo. Karakhan had his doubts. Judging Yoshizawa by himself, Karakhan wrote: "I suspect, that he has probably brought these new instructions with him and only makes believe that he is asking Tokyo." Karakhan was supported in this view by the assertions of American and Japanese journalists that Yoshizawa had instructions which permitted him to make further concessions.[29]

The crux of the problem was that the Soviets objected to extensive and specific concessions, lest they appear to be a condition of recognition or of evacuation and thereby violate the principle of equality and reciprocity on which they insisted. The Japanese, on the other hand, felt no less strongly that the concessions would be merely nominal unless definite arrangements were worked out in advance. For example, they believed that the exploitation of the mining concessions would be impossible if Soviet labor regulations were applied.[30]

Provoked by assertions in Japanese newspapers that he had not told the truth when he had declared in a press interview that Japanese demands were excessive, Karakhan threatened to publish the text of the Japanese drafts. When Yoshizawa reminded him that both sides had agreed to keep the negotiations secret, Karakhan retorted that he was sure the Japanese government had inspired the press articles which criticized the inflexibility of the Soviet negotiators and had provided the newspapers with at least partial information about the drafts and that therefore the Soviet side now was free to publish the text of the Japanese and Russian proposals. So vehement were Yoshizawa's objections, that Karakhan felt reassured in the belief that Yoshizawa had another draft and dreaded that publication of Protocol B would embarrass his government. Karakhan told Yoshizawa that he would honor his request and not make anything public in Peking, though he doubted that the government in Moscow would be moved by his considerations and expressed the thought that it might publish the Japanese demands and the Russian proposals.

Karakhan kept his word literally speaking in that he did not make the exchange public in Peking, but he did not try to dissuade his government from publishing the Japanese demands; on the contrary, he advised Moscow to do so.[31]

In the face of Soviet opposition to Protocol B, Yoshizawa brought a revised version thereof on September 28. It was proposed that the Soviet Union lease to Japan for 40 to 50 years oil concessions in an area totalling 4,000 square verst (over 2,600 square miles) and coal concessions, whose area was to be specified in contracts. Royalty for the oil leases was to amount to 20% of net yield or between 5 and 15% of shaft production; rental for the oil leases was to be 20 and 5% respectively.

On October 6 the Soviet delegation presented a counter-draft. In it the Soviet government agreed to lease to the Japanese 40% of the oil regions being worked. The lease areas were to be situated in chessboard fashion and must not be side-by-side. Japan would get the right, furthermore, to engage in oil exploration in a territory of 1,000 square verst (about 650 square miles) of the eastern shore of North Sakhalin for a period of five years. If, upon expiration of this period, oil was found in this region, the Japanese companies which would engage in this exploration could obtain concessions on the basis of 40% of each oil field. The coal regions would be determined by later contract negotiations. Payment for the exploitation of the resources would amount to between 10 and 15% of shaft production for oil and between 5 and 10% of shaft production for coal.[i]

The Soviets stated, furthermore, that until the conclusion of concession contracts with Japanese companies, during the transition period of six months after the conclusion of the general agreement, the Japanese would be allowed to continue work on existing enterprises on condition that they would not export from North Sakhalin all that they produced.

Yoshizawa and Karakhan discussed the Soviet proposal at some length.

---

[i] For the complete text of the Soviet counter-proposal see Japanese Archives, MT 251.106.19: 5061–5064.

When Yoshizawa stated that he could not accept it on the basis of his current instructions and must seek new instructions from Tokyo, the negotiations were recessed.[32]

Meanwhile, on October 8, Karakhan gave a press interview in which he stated that the Soviet-Japanese negotiations had entered a final and decisive stage. After reviewing the various issues still in dispute, he stated:

> At present the fate of the conference depends on the commercial calculations of Japan or of those persons to whom Japan intends to leave the exploitation of the Sakhalin concessions. We agree to these concessions only because we want an economic rapprochement with Japan and want to assist her in supplying her with oil and coal, although Japan has no right to demand concessions from us on any ground whatsoever. We have declared from the very beginning that the negotiations must not be complicated by secondary questions, but Japan herself has wanted this, and now we are drawn into endless details, which are beginning to threaten the favorable outcome of the conference.[33]

The following day, on October 9, Karakhan wrote to Chicherin: "One can consider that in all questions our points of view are in agreement with Japan. It is a matter of editorial changes, of editorial corrections. The basic question is about the concessions, where the major [problem] is the question of the areas of the oil concessions to be given. A very great deal of time has been spent with the Japanese on the discussion of this question."[34]

A memorandum, dated August 29, presented by Yoshizawa to the Soviets at their request, described the economic activity of the Japanese on North Sakhalin. Japanese companies were prospecting for oil and obtaining it in eight regions, with a total of 13,000 acres, and were working coal in two regions.[35]

The Japanese wished to lease all the eight regions, listed in the memorandum. As stated in the counter-draft of October 6, Karakhan wanted to limit the Japanese to some of the regions, but to no avail. He proposed 40%, but they wanted all. A break in negotiations ensued as a result of the deadlock. During the break Shimada, a diplomat who had participated in the negotiations, was sent by Yoshizawa to tell Karakhan that Yoshizawa had submitted his resignation; he had allegedly lost hope of reaching an agreement. Karakhan suspected that this was another stratagem to frighten him into further concessions or at least to learn whether or not he would be willing to make any. On the other hand, he thought, it was quite possible that the negotiations would come to naught over this issue, "since the policy of Japan was determined not only by the national interests of that state, political considerations, the need to get out of the isolated position and to strengthen its position in the Far East by means of friendship with us [the Soviet Union], but there are also the interests of the Mitsubishi Company, whose agents Katō and Shidehara are, and Mitsubishi is the firm which mainly works on Sakhalin and is interested in Sakhalin matters, and it is not impossible that, as it usually happens in all capitalist countries, the interests of an influential clique of capitalists may gain the upper hand over the overall national interests of the entire country, of all bourgeois-nationalist Japan." Shimada made the point that the Japanese had spent enormous sums on the Intervention and that no government could remain in office if it did not get favorable concessions which could justify all these great expenditures. Furthermore, Shimada argued, the firms which were exploiting the resources on Sakhalin had received a subsidy of 15 million yen from the Japanese government, money which had been used to drill wells. If the Japanese now received only some of the eight regions, the money invested in the others would be wasted, to which they could not agree.

Although Karakhan had no information on the basis of which he could conclude with certainty whether or not the Japanese would give in on this matter, he was inclined to think that they would, because great as the influence of Mitsubishi was, a break with the Soviet Union would seriously weaken the international position of Japan, particularly in China and in the Russian Far East. This would be the more damaging to Japanese interests now that Russia "sat also on the Chinese Eastern Railway."

But Karakhan expressed concern in his letter of October 9 to Chicherin that, even if he could come to an agreement with the Japanese in a week or two, the negotiations would fail because the Soviet Union had repeatedly insisted that there would be no agreement unless the Japanese evacuated North Sakhalin by winter. According to his information it would be physically impossible for them to do so after the end of October; the evacuation of the eastern shore ought to have been completed by the beginning of October and that date had passed already and there were still some 200 to 300 soldiers there. Noting that physical conditions might make it impossible to come to an agreement, Karakhan stressed that one must carefully weigh this matter. "Personally I am in favor of not signing an agreement if they cannot evacuate," Karakhan wrote, "because all the delay was their fault. They arranged for endless recesses between one meeting and another, waiting for instructions from Tokyo. But inasmuch as it may be desirable from an overall point of view to obtain Japanese recognition, the Soviet Union may find it possible to come to an agreement on the basis that the evacuation would be completed as soon as physically possible, in which case one might be able to state, that our [Russian] authority on North Sakhalin would be restored and that the Japanese forces would live there unarmed and not as a fighting unit but as Japanese citizens until a steamer could carry them away."[36]

On October 21 Karakhan wrote to Yoshizawa that two weeks had passed since the last session of the conference. He inquired when receipt of the new instructions concerning the Soviet counter-draft about the concessions could be expected from Tokyo. He reminded Yoshizawa of Japanese statements that the approach of winter would make the evacuation of North Sakhalin difficult and expressed the feeling that it would be a pity, now that they were so close to final agreement, if complications would arise because of such a technicality as delay in the arrival of instructions.

Karakhan asked once again that Yoshizawa reply to the query made by him in October when climatic conditions would permit the evacuation of North Sakhalin. "As I had the honor to state to you, Monsieur le Ministre, at the session of October 3, this question has the greatest significance for the Soviet-Japanese negotiations."[37]

The talks were duly resumed three days later, on October 24.[38] On October 27[j] Yoshizawa produced another Japanese draft of Protocol B. The Japanese government demanded 60% of the entire area of the discovered oil fields, as well as 60% of all oil fields which might be found by the Japanese in the future, 30% of coal deposits in the restricted area and all mines outside this area.[39] If the Soviet government within a period of three years did not begin exploitation of the remaining oil fields, it must lease them to the Japanese.[40]

On October 30 Karakhan handed to Yoshizawa the full text of the revised Soviet draft treaty, with all the protocols and notes. "I gave this a somewhat festive character and created an atmosphere, which had to convey to him, that this was our final decision, that either they must accept or else the negotiations will be broken off," Karakhan reported to Chicherin on November 1. "This was the easier to convey to him," he remarked, "since just on the eve [of the meeting] a telegram had been received about recognition of us by France...." In handing the treaty draft and documents to Yoshizawa, Karakhan stated that editorial changes of some of the articles were quite possible and that in the concessions article, which retained the 40% Soviet proposal, there was room for discussion about the percentage of the output the Russians were to receive, but in so far as the size of the concessions was concerned this was the final and definitive word: either they would accept it or the negotiations would be broken off.

"This made such a strong impression on Yoshizawa," Karakhan reported, "that the next day, the 31st, regardless of the fact that it was the Emperor's birthday and he had various receptions and congratulations, he came to me and stayed for two hours." In vain Yoshizawa sought some Soviet concessions or some supplementary material to help influence his government into coming to an agreement. Karakhan tightened the screws. In his words:

> To increase the seriousness of the situation, I told him, that the [Soviet] government is very dissatisfied with the endless interrup-

---

[j] On October 29 according to Tanaka (p. 92).

tions, which were allowed by the Japanese side systematically, that it is dissatisfied with the vagueness of the reply about the evacuation of Sakhalin, that it is thought in Moscow that I have shown weakness and that this has led to such a great delay in the negotiations, and that I, apparently, have acted without enough energy and determination and that, therefore, all there is left for me to do is to convey what I have received from Moscow. During the entire period of the negotiations we did not have such a critical moment.

Yoshizawa objected to Article 3 of the Soviet draft treaty.[k] The article stated that the two sides agreed to revise the fishery convention of 1907 in accordance with the new conditions and laws of the country and in conformity with the current system of leasing fishing grounds. Until the conclusion of the new convention the current system of leasing fishing grounds to Japanese subjects would be continued. Yoshizawa rejected the last clause, demanding that with the next fishing season leases be granted in accordance with the fishery convention of 1907, which the Japanese regarded as being still in force. Karakhan insisted that the article remain unchanged, adding that fishing grounds on North Sakhalin would not be leased, and that he wanted this spelled out in the protocol.

Article 4 of the Soviet draft concerned a trade agreement and was an edited version of article 5 of the Japanese draft of June 1924, except for adding the point of most-favored-nation treatment. It stipulated that the two countries would establish their trade relations in accordance with the laws of the two lands and would take no measures to discriminate against the other. Yoshizawa wanted the inclusion of a statement regarding reciprocity. Karakhan reported to Moscow that he thought that this could be accepted if Yoshizawa continued to insist on it, since it would not affect Russian interests seriously, if at all.

Article 2 of Protocol A left the question of the debt of previous Russian governments for later negotiation, promising that the matter would be

[k] An English translation of the entire draft was published in the *Tokyo Nichi-Nichi Shimbun* on November 4; see Japanese Archives, MT 251.106.19: 5430.

settled no less favorably for Japan than any other power; the matter of mutual claims also would be left for later consideration. Yoshizawa agreed to the protocol as a whole, but wished to break this article into two separate articles, to which Karakhan had no particular objections.

In connection with Soviet acceptance of the continued effectiveness of the Treaty of Portsmouth, the Soviet draft stated that such acceptance "does in no case mean that the Government of the [Soviet] Union takes on itself responsibility for the content of the said treaty, which responsibility rests entirely with the anti-people Tsarist Government." Although Yoshizawa vigorously objected to this clause, Karakhan reported that of all the objections that Yoshizawa had made concerning the draft treaty, the objections regarding this clause were the weakest.

The major dispute, as before, centered about the Sakhalin concessions. Not only did Yoshizawa continue to insist on 60% of the oil fields and on all kinds of "completely unacceptable" conditions, but strongly objected to the chess-board pattern of distribution. A note of sarcasm crept into Karakhan's report when he wrote that Yoshizawa "very touchingly" explained to him that the Japanese could not agree to it because the Russians might drill bore-wells next to theirs and pump out all their oil.[41]

Ioffe had procrastinated in order to improve Soviet Russia's bargaining position. Karakhan did not purposely delay the negotiations, yet his firm line was bolstered by the same conviction that time was on the side of Russia. In a letter to Dr. Sun Yat-sen in July of 1924 Karakhan had criticized the wavering attitude of the Japanese who on one hand were unwilling to "climb down" from their claims, while on the other they were "afraid of insisting on them resolutely," lest the talks collapse. Asserting that the Japanese preferred to drag on "ever deferring the decisive moment", Karakhan had observed: "A short-sighted policy indeed, for every day will accrue to our benefit, not to the Japanese."[42]

Japanese procrastination was not due to Yoshizawa's indecision. In the words of a Japanese historian: "Minister Yoshizawa's patience and prudence were beyond all praise, but Japanese diplomacy glaringly exhibited its drawbacks of indecision and instability."[43] The indecision was due to differences of opinion in the Japanese camp and these were brought to a head again by Karakhan's new threat to terminate the negotiations. Yoshizawa favored the acceptance of the last Soviet proposal; Katō and Shidehara held out for a larger percentage of oil fields for Japanese exploitation. Toward the end of November a member of the Mitsubishi combine, Sawada, arrived in Peking, apparently to keep an eye on Yoshizawa; this threatened to impair relations between Yoshizawa and Shidehara, and the former hastened to Tokyo to discuss the situation in person.[44]

On December 27, after an interruption of almost two months, negotiations were resumed in Peking. Japan agreed to scale down its demands on Sakhalin from 60% to 50% of the oil fields being worked or to be discovered in the designated area of 1,000 square verst; she gave up the demand that the remaining oil fields be leased to Japan if not exploited by the Soviet Union within three years. Japan did insist on equal opportunity to obtain leases on other fields, should the Soviet Union decide to make them available to other foreigners. Japan desired revision of the fishery convention of 1907 but agreed to application of the provisions of the temporary fishery agreement of 1924 and current practice until then.[1]

As foreseen by Karakhan, Yoshizawa declared that in view of the lateness of the season Japanese forces could not possibly be evacuated from Sakhalin immediately. Yoshizawa stated that the evacuation could be carried out in one month starting from mid-February, details of the withdrawal and of transfer of the administration to be resolved at Aleksandrovsk. Karakhan ensured as prompt an evacuation as possible by stipulating that the coveted concession contracts could be concluded only three months after the evacuation of the Japanese forces from North Sakhalin.[44]

On January 9 and 10, 1925, Karakhan presented counter-proposals in regard to Yoshizawa's draft treaty of December 27. Further debate ensued—Karakhan vainly tried to limit Japanese oil fields to at most

---

[1] See chapter on "Fishery Talks."

THE KARAKHAN-YOSHIZAWA TALKS 175

45%—but at last agreement was reached. The Soviet government was getting impatient and queried Karakhan for the cause of delay. On January 14 he replied by telegram that the Japanese were hurrying all they could and that they were expecting full powers from Tokyo by the end of the week, full powers that according to Yoshizawa could not have been given before. Karakhan reassured Chicherin that he did not hold things up with trifles.[45]

On January 16 Yoshizawa proposed and Karakhan agreed that the Japanese evacuation of Sakhalin be completed by May 15. Finally, on January 20, 1925, after five years of negotiation, the convention laying down the basic rules of relations between the U.S.S.R. and Japan was signed.

The official photograph of the signing of the convention shows Karakhan elegantly dressed, at a table, with part of the documents before him, while Yoshizawa, clad in a simple kimono, sits on a western bed and affixes his signature to papers resting on a pillow in his lap. One is reminded of the official photograph of the Ioffe-Kawakami talks, when the Soviet negotiator lay in bed in his nightshirt, while the Japanese representative stood formally attired. Dmitrii Akrikossow, the chargé d'affaires of the old Russian embassy, had expressed shock at Ioffe letting himself be photographed in such a pose: "All former Russian diplomats must have turned in their graves."[46] Yoshizawa did not take to bed to repay the slight imagined by Akrikossow. He had gone skating with the Italian Minister Vittorio Cerruti at the Peking Club on January 15th and in a fall had broken his hipbone.[47]

Vasilii Krupenskii, the last tsarist ambassador to Japan. (Courtesy of Professor Martin Ramming, Berlin, secretary-dragoman of the Russian embassy in Tokyo in 1917–23.)

Dmitrii Abrikossow, chargé d'affaires of the Provisional Government.
(Courtesy of Professor Martin Ramming)

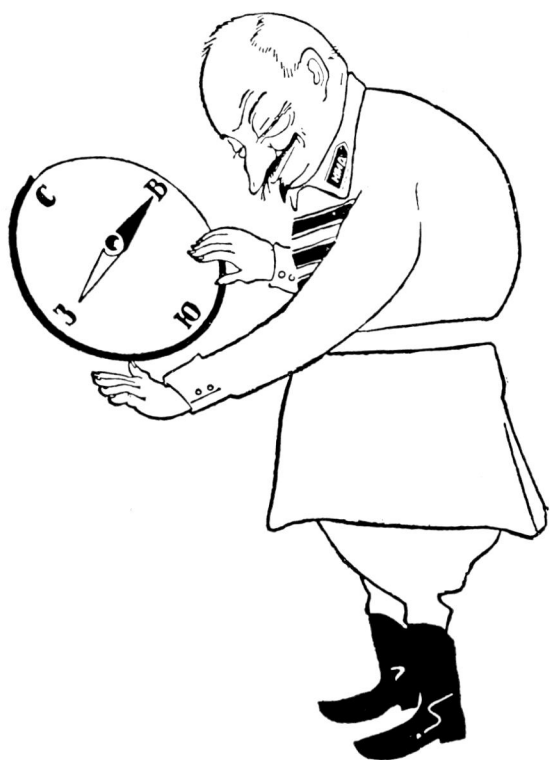

"The needle is turning east"
—*Pravda's* view of Commissar Chicherin's foreign policy.

The Ioffe-Kawakami dinner on August 1, 1923, the day after their last official meeting. From left to right: Ioffe, his private secretary Levin, Dr. Sakamoto, Mrs. Levin and Kawakami. (From *Nisso gaikō kankei shi*, the Japanese edition of L. N. Kutakov's history of Soviet-Japanese diplomatic relations, vol. I.)

Signature of the Basic Convention in Peking on January 20, 1925. The Japanese delegate, Yoshizawa Kenkichi, seated on his bed; the Soviet delegate, Lev Mikhailovich Karakhan, at the table. The gentleman with the bow-tie in back of Karakhan is Sawada, described by Leonid Kutakov as a member of the Mitsubishi combine, by the Japanese Foreign Office as Japanese secretary. (From *Shinsei Nihon gaikō hyakunen-shi*, p. 138.)

"Uncle Sam has remained alone"
—comment of *Izvestiia* on Japanese recognition of the U.S.S.R.

The arrival of Ambassador Tanaka in Moscow, on July 14, 1925. Tanaka stands hat in hand, Chargé d'Affaires Satō hands in pockets. (From *Nisso gaikō kankei shi*, vol. I.)

Signature of the North Sakhalin concession contracts on December 14, 1925, at the meeting of the Supreme Council of National Economy in Moscow. Seated (from left to right): Ambassador Tanaka, Deputy Commissar of Foreign Affairs Litvinov, Chairman of the Supreme Council of National Economy Derzhinskii, Admiral Nakasato, Director of the Foreign Section of the Supreme Council of National Economy Gurevich, and Foreign Office official Kawakami. (From *Shinsei Nihon gaikō hyakunen-shi* [History of a hundred years of rejuvenated Japan], published by the *Tōkyō Nichi Nichi Shimbun* under the editorial supervision of the Japanese Foreign Office in 1953, p. 138.)

CHAPTER SIX

The Basic Convention

THE Basic Convention, concluded by Karakhan and Yoshizawa, bore the lengthy title of "The Convention Embodying Basic Rules of the Relations Between Japan and the Union of Soviet Socialist Republics." Soviet historians generally refer to it as the "Peking Convention" (*Pekinskaia Konventsiia*) after the place of its signature; Japanese scholars use the term "Japanese-Soviet Basic Treaty" (*Nisso Kihon Jōyaku* 日ソ基本條約). We have adopted "Basic Convention" as brief and to the point.

The Basic Convention in its final form, as communicated to the League of Nations, consisted of the convention proper, two protocols, one declaration, an exchange of two notes, an annexed note, the protocol of signature, plus a memorandum. The full text of these documents, in their official English wording, was as follows:

THE CONVENTION EMBODYING BASIC RULES OF THE RELATIONS BETWEEN JAPAN AND THE UNION OF SOVIET SOCIALIST REPUBLICS.

JAPAN AND THE UNION OF SOVIET SOCIALIST, REPUBLICS, desiring to promote relations of good neighbourhood and economic co-operation between them, have resolved to conclude a Convention embodying basic rules in regulation of such relations and, to that end, have appointed as their Plenipotentiaries, that is to say:

HIS MAJESTY THE EMPEROR OF JAPAN:
Kenkichi YOSHIZAWA, Envoy Extraordinary and Minister Plenipotentiary to the Republic of China, Jushii, a member of the First Class of the Imperial Order of the Sacred Treasure;
THE CENTRAL EXECUTIVE COMMITTEE OF THE UNION OF SOVIET SOCIALIST REPUBLICS:
Lev Mikhailovitch KARAKHAN, Ambassador to the Republic of China;

Who having communicated to each other their respective full powers, found to be in good and due form, have agreed as follows:

ARTICLE I

The High Contracting Parties agree that, with the coming into force of the present Convention, diplomatic and consular relations shall be established between them.

ARTICLE II

The Union of Soviet Socialist Republics agrees that the Treaty of Portsmouth of September 5th, 1905, shall remain in full force.

It is agreed that the Treaties, Conventions and Agreements, other than the said Treaty of Portsmouth, which were concluded between Japan and Russia prior to November 7, 1917, shall be re-examined at a Conference to be subesquently held between the Governments of the High Contracting Parties and are liable to revision or annulment as altered circumstances may require.

ARTICLE III

The Governments of the High Contracting Parties agree that, upon the coming into force of the present Convention, they shall proceed to the revision of the Fishery Convention of 1907, taking into consideration such changes as may have taken place in the general conditions since the conclusion of the said Fishery Convention.

THE BASIC CONVENTION

Pending the conclusion of a convention so revised, the Government of the Union of Soviet Socialist Republics shall maintain the practices established in 1924 relating to the lease of fishery lots to Japanese subjects.

ARTICLE IV

The Governments of the High Contracting Parties agree that, upon the coming into force of the present Convention, they shall proceed to the conclusion of a treaty of commerce and navigation in conformity with the principles hereunder mentioned, and that, pending the conclusion of such a treaty, the general intercourse between the two countries shall be regulated by those principles.

1. The subjects or citizens of each of the High Contracting Parties shall, in accordance with the laws of the country: (a) have full liberty to enter, travel and reside in the territories of the other, and (b) enjoy constant and complete protection for the safety of their lives and property.
2. Each of the High Contracting Parties shall, in accordance with the laws of the country accord in its territories to the subjects or citizens of the other, to the widest possible extent and on condition of reciprocity, the right of private ownership and the liberty to engage in commerce, navigation, industries and other peaceful pursuits.
3. Without prejudice to the right of each Contracting Party to regulate by its own laws the system of international trade in that country, it is understood that neither Contracting Party shall apply in discrimination against the other Party any measures of prohibition, restriction or impost which may serve to hamper the growth of the intercourse, economic or otherwise, between the two countries, it being the intention of both Parties to place the commerce, navigation and industry of each country, as far as possible, on the footing of the most-favoured nation.

The Governments of the High Contracting Parties further agree that they shall enter into negotiations, from time to time as circumstances may require, for the conclusion of special arrangements relative to commerce and navigation to adjust and to promote economic relations between the two countries.

ARTICLE V

The High Contracting Parties solemnly affirm their desire and intention to live in peace and amity with each other, scrupulously to respect the undoubted right of a State to order its own life within its own jurisdiction in its own way, to refrain and restrain all persons in any governmental service for them, and all organisations in receipt of any financial assistance from them, from any act overt or covert liable in any way whatever to endanger the order and security in any part of the territories of Japan or the Union of Soviet Socialist Republics.

It is further agreed that neither Contracting Party shall permit the presence in the territories under its jurisdiction:

a. of organizations or groups pretending to be the Government for any part of the territories of the other Party, or
b. of alien subjects or citizens who may be found to be actually carrying on political activities for such organisations or groups.

ARTICLE VI

In the interest of promoting economic relations between the two countries, and taking into consideration the needs of Japan with regard to natural resources, the Government of the Union of Soviet Socialist Republics is willing to grant to Japanese subjects, companies and associations concessions for the exploitation of minerals, forests and other natural resources in all the territories of the Union of Soviet Socialist Republics.

ARTICLE VII

The present Convention shall be ratified.

Such ratification by each of the High Contracting Parties shall, with as little delay as possible, be communicated, through its diplomatic representative at Peking, to the Government of the other Party, and from the date of the later of such communications this Convention shall come into full force.

The formal exchange of the ratifications shall take place at Peking as soon as possible.

In witness whereof the respective Plenipotentiaries have signed the present Convention in duplicate in the English language, and have affixed thereto their seals.

Done at Peking, this twentieth Day of January, One Thousand Nine Hundred and Twenty-five.

(Signed) K. YOSHIZAWA
(Signed) L. KARAKHAN

PROTOCOL A

Japan and the Union of Soviet Socialist Republics, in proceeding this day to the signature of the Convention embodying Basic Rules of the relations between them, have deemed it adviseable to regulate certain questions in relation to the said Convention, and have, through their respective Plenipotentiaries, agreed upon the following stipulations:

ARTICLE I

Each of the High Contracting Parties undertakes to place in the possession of the Party the moveable and immovable property belonging to the Embassy and Consulates of such other Party and actually existing within its own territories.

In case it is found that the land occupied by the former Russian

Government at Tokyo is so situated as to cause difficulties to the town planning of Tokyo or to the service of the public purposes, the Government of the Union of Soviet Socialist Republics shall be willing to consider the proposals which may be made by the Japanese Government looking to the removal of such difficulties.

The Government of the Union of Soviet Socialist Republics shall accord to the Government of Japan all reasonable facilities in the selection of suitable sites and buildings for the Japanese Embassy and Consulates to be established in the territories of the Union of Soviet Socialist Republics.

ARTICLE II

It is agreed that all questions of the debts due to the Government or subjects of Japan on account of public loans and treasury bills issued by the former Russian Governments, to wit by the Imperial Government of Russia and the Provisional Government which succeeded it, are reserved for adjustment at subsequent negotiations between the Government of Japan and the Government of the Union of Soviet Socialist Republics.

Provided that in the adjustment of such questions the Government or subjects of Japan shall not, all other conditions being equal, be placed in any position less favourable than that which the Government of the Union of Soviet Socialist Republics may accord to the Government or nationals of any other country on similar questions.

It is also agreed that all questions relating to claims of the Government of either Party to the Government of the other, or of the nations of either Party to the Government of the other, are reserved for adjustment at subsequent negotiations between the Government of Japan and the Government of the Union of Soviet Socialist Republics.

ARTICLE III

In view of climatic conditions in Northern Saghalien preventing the immediate homeward transportation of Japanese troops now stationed there, these troops shall be completely withdrawn from the said region by May 15, 1925.

Such withdrawal shall be commenced as soon as climatic conditions will permit it and any and all districts in Northern Saghalien so evacuated by Japanese troops shall immediately thereupon be restored in full sovereignty to the proper authorities of the Union of Soviet Socialist Republics.

The details pertaining to the transfer of administration and to the termination of the occupation shall be arranged at Alexandrovsk between the Commander of the Japanese Occupation Army and the Representatives of the Union of Soviet Socialist Republics.

ARTICLE IV

The High Contracting Parties mutually declare that there actually exists no treaty or agreement of military alliance nor any other secret agreement which either of them has entered into with any third Party and which constitutes an infringement upon, or a menace to, the sovereignty, territorial rights or national safety of the other Contracting Party.

ARTICLE V

The present Protocol is to be considered as ratified with the ratification of the Convention embodying Basic Rules of the Relations between Japan and the Union of Soviet Socialist Republics, signed under the same date.

In witness whereof the respective Plenipotentiaries have signed the present Protocol in duplicate in the English language, and have affixed thereto their seals.

Done at Peking, this twentieth day of January, one thousand nine hundred twenty-five.

(Signed) K. YOSHIZAWA
(Signed) L. KARAKHAN

PROTOCOL B

The High Contracting Parties have agreed upon the following as the basis for the Concession Contracts to be concluded within five months from the date of the complete evacuation of Northern Saghalien by Japanese troops, as provided for in Article 3 of Protocol (A), signed this day between the Plenipotentiaries of Japan and of the Union of Soviet Socialist Republics.

1. The Government of the Union of Soviet Socialist Republics agrees to grant to Japanese concerns recommended by the Government of Japan the concession for the exploitation of 50%, in area, of each of the oilfields in Northern Saghalien which are mentioned in the Memorandum submitted to the Representative of the Union by the Japanese Representative on August 29, 1924. For the purpose of determining the area to be leased to the Japanese concerns for such exploitation, each of the said oilfields shall be divided into checker-board squares of from fifteen to forty dessiatines each, and a number of these squares, representing 50% of the whole area, shall be allotted to the Japanese, it being understood that the squares to be so leased to the Japanese are, as a rule, to be non-contiguous to one another, but shall include all the wells now being drilled or worked by the Japanese. With regard to the remaining unleased lots of the oilfields mentioned in the said Memorandum, it is agreed that, should the Government of the Union of Soviet Socialist Republics decide to offer such lots, wholly or in part, for foreign concession, Japanese concerns shall be afforded equal opportunity in the matter of such concession.

2. The Government of the Union of Soviet Socialist Republics also agrees to authorize Japanese concerns recommended by the Government of Japan to prospect oilfields, for a period of from five to ten years, on the Eastern coast of Northern

THE BASIC CONVENTION 185

Saghalien over an area of one thousand square versts to be selected within one year after the conclusion of the Concession Contracts, and in case oilfields shall have been established in consequence of such prospecting by the Japanese, the concession for the exploitation of 50%, in area, of the oilfields so established shall be granted to the Japanese.

3. The Government of the Union of Soviet Socialist Republics agrees to grant to Japanese concerns recommended by the Government of Japan the concession for the exploitation of coal fields on the western coast of Northern Saghalien over a specific area which shall be determined in the Concession Contracts. The Government of the Union of Soviet Socialist Republics further agrees to grant to such Japanese concerns the concession regarding coal fields in the Doue district over a specific area to be determined in the Concession Contracts. With regard to the coal fields outside the specific area mentioned in the preceding two paragraphs, it is also agreed that, should the Government of the Union of Soviet Socialist Republics decide to offer them for foreign concession, Japanese concerns shall be afforded equal opportunity in the matter of such concession.

4. The period of the concessions for the exploitation of oil and coal fields stipulated in the preceding paragraphs shall be from forty to fifty years.

5. As royalty for the said concessions, the Japanese concessionnaires shall make over annually to the Government of the Union of Soviet Socialist Republics, in case of coal fields, from 5 to 8% of their gross output, and, in case of oilfields, from 5 to 15% of their gross output: provided that in the case of a gusher, the royalty may be raised up to 45% of its gross output.

The percentage of output thus to be made over as royalty shall be definitively fixed in the Concession Contracts and it may be graduated according to the scale of annual output in a manner to be defined in such contracts.

6. The said Japanese concerns shall be permitted to fell trees needed for purpose of the enterprises and to set up various undertakings with a view to facilitating communication and transportation of materials and products. Details connected therewith shall be arranged in the Concession Contracts.

7. In consideration of the royalty above mentioned, and taking also into account the disadvantages under which the enterprises are to be placed by reason of the geographical position and other general conditions of the districts affected, it is agreed that the importation and exportation of any articles, materials or products needed for or obtained from such enterprises shall be permitted free of duty, and that the enterprises shall not be subjected to any such taxation or restriction as may in fact render their remunerative working impossible.

8. The Government of the Union of Soviet Socialist Republics shall accord all reasonable protection and facilities to the said enterprises.

9. Details connected with the foregoing articles shall be arranged in the Concession Contracts.

The present Protocol is to be considered as ratified with the ratification of the Convention embodying Basic Rules of the Relations between Japan and the Union of Soviet Socialist Republics, signed under the same date.

In witness whereof the respective Plenipotentiaries have signed the present Protocol in duplicate in the English language, and have affixed thereto their seals.

Done at Peking, this twentieth day of January, One thousand nine hundred and twenty-five.

(Signed) K. YOSHIZAWA
(Signed) L. KARAKHAN

DECLARATION

In proceeding this day to the signature of the Convention embodying the Basic Rules of the Relations between the Union of Soviet Socialist Republics and Japan, the undersigned Plenipotentiary of the Union of Soviet Socialist Republics has the honour to declare that the recognition by his Government of the validity of the Treaty of Portsmouth of September 5, 1905, does not in any way signify that the Government of the Union shares with the former Tsarist Government the political responsibility for the conclusion of the said Treaty.

(Signed) L. KARAKHAN

Peking, January 20, 1925

EXCHANGE OF NOTES

Peking, January 20th, 1925

MONSIEUR LE MINISTRE

I have the honour on behalf of my Government, to declare that the Government of the Union of Soviet Socialist Republics agrees that the work which is now being carried on by the Japanese in Northern Saghalien both in the oil and coal fields, as stated in the Memorandum handed to the Plenipotentiary of the Union of Soviet Socialist Republics by the Japanese Plenipotentiary on August 29th, 1924, be continued until the conclusion of the Concession Contracts to be effected within five months from the date of the complete evacuation of Northern Saghalien by the Japanese troops, provided the following conditions be abided by by the Japanese:

1. The work must be continued in strict accordance with the data of the said Memorandum of August 29th, 1924, as regards the area, the number of workers and experts employed, the machinery and other conditions provided in the Memorandum.
2. The produce, such as oil and coal, cannot be exported or sold and may only be applied to the use of the staff and equipment connected with the said work.
3. The permission granted by the Government of the Union of Soviet Socialist Republics for the continuation of the work shall in no way affect the stipulations of the future concession contract.
4. The question of operation of the Japanese wireless stations in Northern Saghalien is reserved for future arrangement, and will be adjusted in a manner consistent with the existing laws of the Union of Soviet Socialist Republics prohibiting private and foreign establishment of the wireless stations.

I avail myself of this opportunity to convey to you, Monsieur le Ministre, the assurances of my highest consideration.

(Signed) L. KARAKHAN

His Excellency
   Mr. Kenkichi YOSHIZAWA,
     Envoy Extraordinary and
     Minister Plenipotentiary of Japan.

Peking, January 20th, 1925

MONSIEUR L'AMBASSADEUR

I have the honour to acknowledge the receipt of the following Note from Your Excellency, under this date:

THE BASIC CONVENTION

"Monsieur le Ministre,

"I have the honour, on behalf of my Government, to declare that the Government of the Union of Soviet Socialist Republics agrees that the work which is now being carried on by the Japanese in Northern Saghalien both in the oil and the coal fields, as stated in the Memorandum handed to the Plenipotentiary of the Union of Soviet Socialist Republics by the Japanese Plenipotentiary on August 29th, 1924, be continued until the conclusion of the Concession Contracts to be effected within five months from the date of the complete evacuation of Northern Saghalien by the Japanese troops, provided the following conditions be abided by by the Japanese:

"1. The work must be continued in strict accordance with the data of the said Memorandum of August 29th, 1924, as regards the area, the number of workers and experts employed, the machinery and other conditions provided in the Memorandum.

"2. The produce, such as oil and coal, cannot be exported or sold and may only be applied to the use of the staff and equipment connected with the said work.

"3. The permission granted by the Government of the Union of Soviet Socialist Republics for the continuation of the work shall in no way affect the stipulations of the future Concession Contract.

"4. The question of operation of the Japanese wireless stations in Northern Saghalien is reserved for future arrangement, and will be adjusted in a manner consistent with the existing laws of the Union of Soviet Socialist Republics prohibiting private and foreign establishment of wireless stations."

On behalf of my Government, I have the honour to state that the Japanese Imperial Government agrees entirely with the said Note.

I avail myself of this opportunity to convey to you, Monsieur l'Ambassadeur, the assurances of my highest consideration.

(Signed) K. YOSHIZAWA

His Excellency
Mr. Lev Mikhailovitch KARAKHAN,
Ambassador of the Union of
Soviet Socialist Republics.

ANNEXED NOTE

In proceeding this day to the signature of the Convention embodying Basic Rules of the Relations between the Union of Soviet Socialist Republics and Japan, the undersigned Plenipotentiary of the Union of Soviet Socialist Republics has the honour to tender hereby to the Government of Japan an expression of sincere regrets for the Nikolaievsk incident of 1920.

(L.S.) L. KARAKHAN

Peking, January 20th, 1925

PROTOCOL OF SIGNATURE

Kenkichi YOSHIZAWA, His Imperial Japanese Majesty's Envoy Extraordinary and Minister Plenipotentiary to China, and Lev Mikhailovitch KARAKHAN, Ambassador of the Union of Soviet Socialist Republics to China, authorised under their respective full powers, found in due and good form, met this day at Peking and closely examined the following documents:

THE BASIC CONVENTION

1. A Convention embodying Basic Rules of the Relations between Japan and the Union of Soviet Socialist Republics.
2. Two Protocols.
3. One Declaration.
4. One set of Notes.
5. One annexed Note.

Having agreed upon every term and stipulation contained therein, the Plenipotentiaries have officially signed and sealed the respective documents.

The two Plenipotentiaries further agreed that there should be apposed to the present Protocol the Memorandum, handed by the Japanese Plenipotentiary to the Plenipotentiary of the Union of Soviet Socialist Republics on August 29th, 1924, and embodying a statement on the conditions of oil and coal fields worked by the Japanese in Northern Saghalien.

In faith whereof, the respective Plenipotentiaries of the two High Contracting Parties have signed the present Protocol in duplicate in the English language, and have affixed thereto their seals.

Done at Peking, this twentieth day of January, One thousand nine hundred and twenty-five.

(Signed) K. YOSHIZAWA
(Signed) L. KARAKHAN

MEMORANDUM SUBMITTED TO THE REPRESENTATIVE OF THE UNION BY THE JAPANESE REPRESENTATIVE ON AUGUST 29th, 1924.

OIL EXPLORATION OPERATIONS

I The exploration operations are being conducted by the Hokushinkai and Co. on behalf of the Government.

II Operations

Operations	Locations	Areas	Test boring Oil	Test boring No oil
Oha	Two and a-half miles west of Urkt Bay, in the valley of the River Oha.	2500 acres	4	7
Ehabi	One mile west of Ehabi Bay.	1600 acres	None	3
Pilutun	Six miles south-west of Kyakr Bay, along the River Pilutun.	1200 acres	None	3
Nutovo	Five miles west from the mouth of the River Nutovo.	2500 acres	1	2
Chaivo	Three miles west of Chaivo Bay along the Boatasin River.	1200 acres	1	1
Nuivo	Seven miles west of Nuivo Bay, in the valley of No-gric River (a branch of the Tuimi River).	1600 acres	1	1

THE BASIC CONVENTION 193

Vuigrektui	Three miles south of the mouth of the River Tuimi along the valley of that River.	800 acres	None	2
Katangli	On the shore of Lake Katangli north of Nabilisky Bay.	1600 acres	1	4

III Experts employed 20
    Workers 400 } in summer time.

IV Machinery:
    Hydraulic Rotary system 3
    Standard cable system 5 } for deep boring.

    Diamond Boring system 2 } for shallow
    Spring Boring system 10 } low boring.
    (worked by man-power

V Outfit.
    a. For communication: Telephone lines connecting the several operations, wireless stations at Oha and Chaivo.
    b. For transportation: One small steamer and several motor boats which are used in summer time for connecting the several operations, besides a dozen lighters and junks.
    c. Establishment:

	Oha	Ehabi	Pilutun	Nutovo	Chaivo
Houses for personnel and workers	30	1	2	7	8
Boring rigs.	11	3	3	3	1

Boiler houses.	6	0	0	1	0
Oil reservoir (earthen)	3	0	0	0	0
Fuel oil tank (steel)	4	0	0	0	0

	Nuivo	Vuigrektui	Katangli
Houses for personnel and workers	6	1	15
Boring rigs.	2	2	5
Boiler houses.	0	0	1
Oil reservoir (earthen)	0	0	0
Fuel oil tank (steel).	0	0	0

VI Light railway: none.

A trolley line extending for two and a-half miles between Urkt Bay and works at Oha, and another trolley line extending for about three miles between Katangli and Nabil.

VII Exportation of oil: none.

COLLIERY WORKS

I Exploiters.

Doue Mine: The Mitsubishi and Co. is working it on behalf of the occupation army.

Rogatui Mine is worked by the Staheeff and Co. and Mitsubishi as a joint enterprise.

THE BASIC CONVENTION 195

II Location of the mines.
Doue Mine: About six miles south of the harbour of Alexandrovsk, in the valley of Postvaya, close to the sea. There are two level pits now in operation, but no shaft. The output for 1923 was about 50,000 tons.
Rogatui Mine: About ten miles south of Alexandrovsk harbour toward the sea. Two pits now in operation. No shaft. The output for 1923 was about 30,000 tons.

III The number of experts and workers.

	Experts	Workers
Doue Mine	5	about 200
Rogatui Mine	3	about 150

(the numbers are those in summer time.)

IV Machinery.
At Doue mine small locomotives are used for the purpose of transportation of coal. In Rogatui mine no machinery is used, both digging and transportations being carried on by man-power and on horseback.

V Establishments.
No special establishments for colliery purpose except a little more than a mile of trolley line leading from the Doue Mine to the seashore, and another trolley line, less than a quarter-mile, at Rogatui.

VI Exportation.
The output of the Doue mine is consumed by the occupation army and the people residing within the occupation area, no part of it being taken out of the island.
About 30,000 tons of the output of the Rogatui mine is said to have been exported in 1923 by Mitsubishi and Staheeff.

(Signed) K. YOSHIZAWA[1]

The Basic Convention was ratified by the U.S.S.R. on February 20, 1925; by Japan five days later. The ratification of each contracting party was communicated to the government of the other party through their representatives at Peking on February 26, and the convention and its related documents went into effect that day. The formal exchange of ratifications was effected on April 15 at Peking.[2] The convention was registered with the League of Nations on May 20, 1925.

The conclusion of the Basic Convention was an event of utmost international importance. "Just as the materialization of the German-Russian treaty of Rapallo in 1922 aroused great attention among the other powers, so the fact that the conclusion of a treaty between Japan and the Soviet Union has been accomplished deserves the most careful consideration," the *Frankfurter Zeitung* wrote on January 24, 1925. The agreement with China in 1924 had already boosted Soviet prestige in Asia; the convention with Japan further strengthened the Russian position. Japan in turn profitted strategically. "In regard to the situation in East Asia and the Pacific Ocean the island empire has gained a great start over the United States," the *Frankfurter Zeitung* noted. Karakhan had implied as much when he had held out as one of the benefits accruing to Japan from recognition of the U.S.S.R.: "Japan can always count on the fact that Russia as a Communistic Soviet State will not conclude with any imperialistic power a military alliance directed against Japan. . . ."[3]

The Anglo-Japanese Alliance of 1902 had safeguarded Japan from the intervention of a third power in the approaching duel with Russia; now the convention with the U.S.S.R., which was widely regarded as the prelude to (and by some as the cover for) a Soviet-Japanese alliance, seemed to give Japan the same protection for war with the United States, D. Elias Hurwicz wrote in the *Hamburger Fremdenblatt* on February 2. "The immigration policy of the United States has provoked a deep resentment, against which all the amenities of diplomacy are likely to count for little," the *Statesman* of Calcutta remarked and, though seeing "no need to anticipate conflict," warned that there was "a fundamental clash of interests in the Pacific" on the part of the United States and Japan and that there were "hot heads and violent tongues in all countries."4 "It develops that the United States Navy Department has not been oblivious to the significance of the Japanese-Soviet treaty and its relationship to creating a reserve fuel supply of great proportions for the Japanese navy," Albert W. Fox reported.5 Sensational stories disseminated by *The World* earlier about the alleged conclusion of a secret treaty between Russia and Japan, whereby Japan was to supply Russia with heavy artillery and warships, including vessels which she was supposed to scrap under the Washington naval treaty, in return for "all rights to the oil fields of Sakhalin"6 no doubt had caused a stir in navy circles.

Edgar Ansel Mowrer reported from Berlin in July of 1925 that "the Japanese Government, alarmed by the increasing social unrest within Japan and the growth of Communist doctrines, promises to observe benevolent neutrality toward any Russian action in China and further to manufacture and deliver to Russia heavy artillery and submarines" in exchange for Soviet agreement to withdraw all Communist agents from Japan. Though he acknowledged the "mental reservations" with which both sides would have made such an agreement, Mowrer regarded it as "perhaps the most stupendous political event in the embittered fight for the control of Asia which has developed since the Washington Conference" and remarked that "the first country to feel the weight of it unquestionably will be the United States."7

"Because of its possibilities, the pact between Soviet Russia and Japan is one of the most dramatic political events in recent years," the *Oregon Journal* declared. Relating the convention to the agreement between Moscow and Peking, the paper, which regarded the three nations as "near kin by blood and birth," asserted with alarm that "the situation is tantamount to a league of the East facing an unleagued West across the Pacific, with the west coast of America as the first point of contact in case of conflict."8 Japanese publications foresaw the negative reaction of Great Britain and the United States to a Sino-Japanese-Russian alliance. "As the Nationalists of China advocate a federation among Japan, China and Russia, the ties of friendship among them will grow stronger," the *Chugai Shogyo* wrote on January 26. "This possibility will inevitably affect the British and American policy in the Far East, though we have no such intention. We must be watchful over the possible change of the situation in the Far East." Rooted in the fact that the Soviet Union had concluded agreements with both Peking and Tokyo, the rumors of a Russo-Chinese-Japanese coalition were given impetus by remarks made by Foreign Minister Shidehara in a speech to the prefectural governors of Japan that Russo-Chinese-Japanese cooperation was necessary for solving the diplomatic problems confronting these three states in East Asia.[9]

The *China Press* saw "slender foundation" for the hypothesis of a possible alliance between Japan, Russia and China, "if for no other reason than that China is not likely for a long time to be in a position to effect any alliance either with Russia, Japan or any other country in the world." "Obviously Japan would have been in a position of grave disadvantage were she to remain aloof from Moscow after an understanding had already been arrived at between China and Russia," the paper commented. The *China Press* actually thought that the convention might constrain Moscow, that it might prove "an impregnable bulwark against the bolshevization of China," for "formal restoration of relations with a well-ordered country like Japan is likely to impart to the Soviet a sense of responsibility which it has hitherto been sadly lacking."[10] Yet in April of 1925, as rumors of a secret treaty between the U.S.S.R. and Japan persisted, the *China Press* grew more alarmist: "The signature of an Agreement by the Soviet with a puppet Government in Peking has its dangers, in all conscience, but if to this is added the peril of a secret treaty between the Soviet and Tokio, we dread to contemplate the sinister possibilities of such a situation."[11]

The *North-China Daily News* expected an increase in Communist propaganda, now that the Soviet Union had received the right to open consulates in Japan:

In this respect the propaganda-prevention clause in the Russo-Japanese Treaty is, of course, not worth the paper it is written on . . . , especially as the Soviet Government refused to be responsible for the doings of the Third International. It may be technically true that the latter is not a Soviet Government organization; but, in fact it might as well be said that the sun has nothing to do with the maggots it breeds in a dead dog as to pretend that the two are not inseparably linked.[12]

The *North-China Daily News* expressed the view that the Soviet government had needed the agreement with Japan for internal reasons as well—"for the prestige which it gives the Soviet Government at home, where the necessity of withstanding the anti-communist feelings of the new bourgeoisie is increasingly felt."[13] The *Tokyo Nichi Nichi Shimbun* remarked that the convention would be used for domestic policy by both countries. It was in the international arena, however, that both Russians and Japanese now faced a crucial test: "They must show an excellent example to all the nations of Europe and of other continents, who pretend to be the champions of international morality, in their persistent advocacy of international peace and justice. Should Japan and Russia err in this, they will be the laughing-stock of the world."[14]

The *Yomiuri* was optimistic about economic relations between the Soviet Union and Japan. "It is our advice to the businessmen of this country to form a body of tourists so that they may inspect business conditions in Russia. They must notice that warm spring is coming back to Moscow."[15] Pointing to the desirability of combining Japanese skill and experience with Russian natural resources, the *Kokumin* proclaimed: "We dare advise the [Japanese] Government to send able businessmen to inspect the conditions existing in the fields of commerce, industry and economy of Russia that they may find an adequate market for our businessmen."[16]

The prospects of a Soviet-Japanese agreement on the heels of the Soviet-German agreement had alarmed Americans already in 1923. "Political seers often conjure up the mirage of a Japanese-Russo-German alliance extending from the North Sea to the Sea of Japan. It is a prospect that naturally gives us pause, and is not looked upon as a consummation Americans should devoutly wish for."[17] The potential implications of a Japanese-Russian-German alliance were dramatized in 1925 in the novel

The Red Camarilla. In return for the cession of Eastern Siberia to Japan, author E. J. Harrison envisaged, Japan would lend financial and perhaps military aid for the defeat of Poland and its repartition between Russia and Germany. The allies would rally to the defense of Poland and Japan would take advantage of the European war to attack the United States.[18]

While some speculated whether a Russo-German-Japanese or a Russo-Chinese-Japanese alliance would be more likely, others raised the quadruple threat of a Russo-German-Chinese-Japanese block. The newspaper *Progrès* rejected the hypothesis of such a four power alliance. "But the fact that the new treaty [between Japan and the U.S.S.R.] could give birth to such lively anxiety," it noted, "is a warning; and the question of the Far East, the question of the Pacific deserves to be followed with attention."[19]

In the United States disclosure of the Basic Convention triggered a debate as to whether or not Japan had violated the Open Door pledge made by Baron Shidehara at the Washington Conference. "In my opinion, it makes the open door proposition a mere matter of phrases," Senator William E. Borah, chairman of the Senate foreign relations committee declared. Former Secretary of State Robert Lansing concurred in this view.[20] A spokesman for the Siberian Veterans association, made up of men of the U.S. Army, warned: "Unless something is done to maintain America's position, we feel that all the suffering and sacrifices we went through in Siberia will have to be dedicated to Japanese exploitation rather than to our country and our flag and the great humanitarian work we undertook to do."[21] A *Public Ledger* story reported that the consummation of the Soviet-Japanese convention had been suspended for six months through representations of America, but that Japan went ahead with the agreement, "pleading that it was not possible longer to postpone it and that political circumstances would not countenance the explanation that it was being held in abeyance out of deference to the United States."[22]

Fuel had been added to the Open Door issue by Soviet cancellation of the Sinclair concession in North Sakhalin in view of American failure to recognize the Soviet regime. But the White House resisted pressure from the oil interests. In the words of David Lawrence, "the Washington Government refused to be swayed in its attitude toward Russia at this time by considerations of oil."[23] By April 10 the *New York Times* reported that President Calvin Coolidge and Secretary of State Frank B. Kellogg, after studying the text of the Soviet-Japanese agreement, had come to the conclusion that there had not been any violation of the Open Door principle on the part of Japan.

Japanese recognition of the U.S.S.R. revived agitation in the United States for American recognition. As a correspondent had predicted before the event, "a Russo-Japanese rapprochement is likely to advance the recognitionist cause in the United States, if for no other reason than that some authorities will think that we can no longer afford to stay out where Japan has seen fit to go in."[24] With the passing of Kellogg's predecessor, Charles Evans Hughes, the *bête noire* of the Bolsheviks, in the spring of 1925, the Baltimore *Evening Sun* had remarked:

> There are business men and bankers who think that recognition is inevitable; and not only inevitable but extremely desirable.
> They see that Japan has recognized Russia and that China has recognized Russia. That means that Japan will be on the ground floor when the inevitable development of Eastern Siberia begins. It also means that American business men, hat in hand, will be asking for crumbs that fall from the loaded table.

"As a matter of fact," the *San Francisco Examiner* added, "this recognition should have been accorded long ago, not as a matter of business, but of simple right and common sense."[25] In another column that day the *San Francisco Examiner* put it even more strongly: "This Government [of the United States] should keep track of Russia and Japan drawing together. And this Government should give up its idiotic claim of a right to tell Russia or any other country what kind of government it must have."

The San Francisco *Argonaut* took issue with the "professional 'viewers with alarm' and jingoes generally" for using the agreement concerning Sakhalin "as excuse to hoist again the bogey of the yellow peril."

All sort of deviltries have been discovered in the new treaty [the paper wrote]. We are solemnly warned that it is a sinister move to force the United States out of Asia; that it is a menace of sorts to Pacific Coast interests; that it is another move to compel the United States to reconsider its immigration policies; that Soviet Russia expects by this treaty to compel the recognition that Washington so long has withheld. These, and more, *ad nauseam*.

As a matter of fact, it is nothing of the sort, in any of these particulars. It does mark the healing of another sore spot in Asia, and sore spots in Asia are as dangerous as sore spots in Europe. The more of them that can be cured, the stronger the assurance for continued world peace and orderly progress in the development of the Orient.[26]

The well-known Japanese journalist and author K. K. Kawakami expressed doubt about the implementation of the Basic Convention. "Although the instrument is apparently most carefully drawn, one must not be too optimistic as to its practical operation," he warned. "More nations than one have been disappointed by Soviet promises and agreements." Yet should the convention prove workable, Kawakami admitted, "the name of Kenkichi Yoshizawa . . . will long be remembered by his countrymen."[27]

CHAPTER SEVEN

Exchange of Official Representatives

UPON the conclusion of the Basic Convention the imperial government notified the U.S.S.R. that it planned to send Satō Naotake 佐藤尚武, then Minister to Poland, to the Soviet Union as chargé d'affaires *ad interim* to make preparations for the establishment of a Japanese embassy. The Soviet government replied that while it had nothing against Satō, the appointment of a temporary chargé would be unbecoming of the new era. Yet once the Japanese approved of the appointment of a Soviet ambassador to Tokyo, the Soviet government did not persist in its objection and furnished Satō with an entrance visa. He arrived in Moscow on March 23, 1925, in the company of Second Secretary Sasaki Seigo 佐々木靜吾 and on the same day established a new Japanese embassy.[1]

The old Japanese embassy in the former capital (St. Petersburg, renamed Petrograd then Leningrad) had been closed in February of 1918. Optimistically the Japanese had renewed the lease for another three years and had left a counselor and a caretaker in the building until 1921. But from the middle of 1921 until the spring of 1925 the building was left forsaken. When Satō came to reclaim the furnishings he found only part of the contents. The silver, tableware, safe and records were missing. He asked the Foreign Commissariat to look into the matter, but it was evident that the objects could not be traced by this time.[2]

It was the Soviet government's hope that Yoshizawa Kenkichi, who had negotiated the Basic Convention, would become the first Japanese ambassador to the U.S.S.R.; the Japanese government deemed him suited for the task and issued informal orders.[3]

On April 20, 1925, Satō informed Foreign Commissar Chicherin that

Yoshizawa was too ill to assume the post of ambassador to the Soviet Union in the near future and that the Japanese government would like to send Tanaka Tokichi 田中都吉 in his stead.[a] Tanaka had never served in western Europe; his whole career had passed in the Pacific region, at first in consular positions in America, China, and the English colonies, then as counselor of the Japanese embassy in Washington. Later, Satō noted, Tanaka had been chief of the commercial section of the Ministry of Foreign Affairs and was well versed in Far Eastern economic relations. During Admiral Katō's administration Tanaka had been vice minister of foreign affairs; he was amicably disposed toward the U.S.S.R. and was a cool-headed and business-like person.

Satō raised some questions about the adequacy of Russian housing, a topic that must have been embarrassing to Chicherin considering the fact that it was Westerners who usually complained about Japanese housing. Satō was staying in the best suite at the Savoy, yet was not sure whether such accomodations would be good enough for the ambassador; he had seen a club and wondered if that building could be acquired.[4]

The Soviet Union agreed to the appointment of Tanaka, and the latter departed from Tokyo on June 30. He arrived in Moscow on July 14 and the following day, on July 15, presented his credentials to Mikhail Ivanovich Kalinin, chairman of the Central Executive Committee of the U.S.S.R.[5]

Tanaka expressed his pleasure at the resumption of diplomatic relations, but took the opportunity to state that the extent of economic and intellectual intercourse still left much to be desired. He warned that economic relations alone could not develop genuine friendship between the two peoples; mutual understanding of and respect for each other's civilization and ideals were essential. Tanaka promised to work for Russo-Japanese collaboration in order to obtain a better life for everyone,

---

[a] In his memoirs Yoshizawa writes that he had declined his government's offer to send him to Moscow on the grounds that his involvement in the negotiations with the Soviet Union had been accidental and that he wished to continue in his position as minister to China. (Yoshizawa, p. 79)

and looked forward to a "better era, in which the ideals of justice, equality and peace would govern." In accepting Tanaka's credentials, Kalinin echoed the hope that the normalization of relations between the two countries would contribute to peace not only between them but in the Far East in general.[6]

Soon afterwards a bizarre incident occurred. Some twenty Chinese were arrested in Moscow on the charge of plotting the Japanese ambassador's assassination. The alleged ringleaders of the conspiracy were three members of the Chinese embassy, who were subsequently recalled by the Chinese government. The latter circulated the rumor that there had been a different reason for the arrests: the Chinese in question had managed to obtain the figures of the Soviet Union's secret budget for Communist propaganda in the Far East. This was duly reported in the Japanese press, but as Tanaka Bunichirō wrote in his study for the Foreign Office, "in regard to this matter the explanations by both the Soviet Union and China are inaccurate and the truth is not clear."[7]

Tanaka Tokichi was to remain the Japanese ambassador to the U.S.S.R. for half a decade.[8] Although he departed in October of 1928, leaving the counselor as chargé d'affaires,[9] and although Premier Tanaka on April 25, 1929, informed the Soviet ambassador in Tokyo that Ambassador Tanaka would not return to Moscow because of ill health,[10] a month later, on May 24, Vice Minister of Foreign Affairs Yoshida announced that the Japanese government had failed in its search for a "more suitable" ambassador and that Tanaka would return to the Soviet capital shortly.[11] "The question of an ambassador is extremely important now in particular since the Japanese government strives to improve relations with the U.S.S.R.," Yoshida declared, adding: "Heretofore unfortunately the economic questions, and especially the fishery question, occupied the full attention of both governments, but there are actually much more important political questions which must be considered by the governments."[12]

The establishment of consulates was at least as important as the opening of an embassy, since Japanese fishery people and businessmen required visas and local protection. On March 2, 1925, before the arrival of Chargé d'Affaires Satō in Moscow, Ambassador Yoshizawa had notified Ambassador Karakhan in Peking that the Japanese government desired permission for its consulate general in Vladivostok to resume conducting business on an official basis; it also wished to open consulates general in Aleksandrovsk and Khabarovsk consulates in Petropavlovsk, Blagoveshchensk, Nikolaevsk and Odessa, and a branch office of the Aleksandrovsk consulate general in Okha. Karakhan had replied on March 20 that the Soviet Union planned to establish three consulates in Japan (in Tokyo, Tsuruga and Hakodate) and that it was agreeable therefore, for the Japanese to establish three consulates in the Soviet Union (in Moscow, Vladivostok and Harbin); as for consulates in additional cities, the Soviet government wished to defer the matter until its ambassador reached Tokyo and could discuss it further.

Satō, who arrived in Moscow later that month, reopened the issue. The Soviet Union insisted that the number of consulates to be opened be equal for both countries. Agreement was reached by the end of July, and on August 4 Ambassador Tanaka exchanged a verbal note with the Foreign Commissariat to the effect that the Soviet government had no objections to the establishment of nine Japanese consulates in the U.S.S.R. (in Moscow, Vladivostok, Aleksandrovsk, Khabarovsk Petropavlovsk, Blagoveshchensk, Nikolaevsk, Odessa and Okha) and that the Japanese government in turn allowed the Soviet Union to open nine consulates (in Tokyo, Tsuruga and Hakodate as well as Osaka, Kobe, Yokohama, Nagasaki, Seoul and Dairen) with the understanding that the places where the consulates were to be located could be changed at a later date by mutual agreement.

Meanwhile, on April 2, the Soviet government had informed Acting Consul General Watanabe Riye, who had been in Vladivostok since 1920, of the recognition of his official position (he was promoted to consul general later in the year). The action had come in exchange for the issuance of an exequatur to Soviet Visa Officer Aleksandr Nikolaevich Loginov in Hakodate as consul. On May 8, furthermore, the Soviet government had given notice to Satō that Japan could establish consulates in Aleksandrovsk and Okha following the completion of the evacuation of its forces from

North Sakhalin; within a fortnight, on May 19, the consulate general in Aleksandrovsk had been duly opened.

Following the exchange of the verbal note of August 4, a Japanese consulate general was established in Khabarovsk (September 3) and consulates in Petropavlovsk (August 18), Blagoveshchensk (November 1) and Odessa (January 4, 1926). No consulate was opened in Nikolaevsk; instead one was established in Novosibirsk (April 24, 1926).[13]

The establishment of Soviet diplomatic and consular offices in Japan was complicated by the fact that representatives of the Tsarist and Provisional governments had remained in possession of the old buildings; they had even continued their official functions. So long as Japan had not recognized the Soviet regime, the old embassy, albeit an embassy without a government, had continued to represent Russian interests in Japan and to minister to the needs of the many refugees who had fled east. Cut off from the revenues of the Russian state, the diplomatic corps in Japan and China had obtained the necessary operating funds from Peking, the Chinese government having agreed to continue making the Boxer indemnity payments to the Russo-Asian Bank, which in turn had supported the Russian diplomatic and consular officials in China and Japan.

The Soviet government had demanded, of course, that the old Russian embassy in Tokyo serve the new regime, but the ambassador and staff had refused. The Japanese government had continued to recognize Ambassador Vasilii Nikolaevich Krupenskii as *the* Russian representative; in fact for a while he had remained Dean of the Diplomatic Corps.[14, b]

---

[b] During the Siberian Intervention the embassy tried to support insofar as possible every local movement against the Bolsheviks. Yet at the same time it sought to preserve the territorial integrity of the Russian empire and had no illusions about any of Russia's allies. It worked against the sole intervention of Japan in Siberia, aware of the threat that this would pose to the Russian state. It also tried to stop Japanese support of Ataman Semenov and the splintering of Russian forces in the Far East. (George Alexander Lensen (ed.), *Revelations of a Russian Diplomat: The Memoirs of Dmitrii I. Abrikossow* (Seattle: University of Washington Press, 1964), pp. 258, 263–64, 269, 289).

In about 1921 the Japanese government had decided that Krupenskii could not retain his full position. Though it did not close the embassy, it had informed him that he could no longer serve as Dean of the Diplomatic Corps and would not be invited to court functions. Under the circumstances the ambassador had left for Europe and the embassy had passed into the hands of Dmitrii Ivanovich Abrikossow, first secretary and chargé d'affaires, who had continued to live in a "fool's paradise."[15]

Ioffe's arrival in Tokyo had alarmed Abrikossow, who had followed newspaper accounts of the Soviet-Japanese negotiations with understandable concern. "The behavior of Ioffe toward the Japanese was arrogant," Abrikossow asserted.[16] It had not been the bearing of another *"henna gaijin"* (strange foreigner), however, but the great earthquake of 1923 that had delayed Japanese recognition of the Soviet Union and the surrender of the old embassy to the Bolsheviks. Preoccupation with reconstruction had been one factor in the delay; there had been another. As Abrikossow realized: "Some of the Japanese statesmen probably understood the danger of admitting Soviet representatives with their inevitable propaganda at a time when the populace was still under the impression of the great disaster."[17]

Yet the destruction wrought by the earthquake had made Japanese access to the resources of the Russian Far East that much more urgent and the negotiations which had ensured between Karakhan and Yoshizawa in Peking had tolled the death knell for the old embassy. "This time the Japanese did not insist on an apology or compensation for the Nikolaevsk massacre, and the negotiations proceeded quickly," Abrikossow remembered. "Hence all the grand phrases pronounced after the murder of their subjects suffered the fate of all grand phrases—they remained empty words, and even the blindfolded figure of justice erected as a reminder of the tragedy was discreetly moved behind the temple of Kudan so as not to offend the eyes of the new friends."[18] The negotiations had been still in progress when the Foreign Office had invited Abrikossow to ask what he intended to do with the embassy and the rest of the property of the former Russian government upon the establishment of diplomatic relations between Japan and the U.S.S.R.

To this my answer had long been ready [Abrikossow reminisced]. I declared that I would never hand over the Embassy and the rest of the property to the Soviet government, because I did not consider it the rightful successor to the old government, adding, fond as we Russians are of grand phrases, "over my dead body." The Vice Minister looked astonished; surely I must realize, he said, that upon Japan's recognition of the Soviet government, the latter would be considered the legal Russian government and its representatives would have the right to occupy the old Embassy. I explained that I would be willing to surrender the Embassy to the Japanese government, providing I was permitted to declare in writing that I did not recognize the [new] Embassy and that the whole matter was so arranged as to avoid my being placed face to face with the Soviet representative. To my surprise the Vice Minister consented. He promised that I would be given advance notice when negotiations entered their final stage and that provision would be made for a time lapse of two weeks between my surrender of the Embassy to the Foreign Office and the arrival of Soviet officials. I thanked the Vice Minister for this arrangement; while it did not alter the fact that the Embassy would fall into Bolshevik hands, it at least saved me from the humiliation of a formal surrender.[19]

On January 25, 1925, five days after the signing of the Basic Convention, Foreign Commissar Chicherin cabled to Karakhan in Peking: "A ROSTA report has been received from Tokyo to the effect that local White guards are hastily cleaning out the building of our embassy in Tokyo, carrying away with them important documents, valuable things and property. If this is so, special measures must be taken to forbid the plundering."[20]

The information was more or less correct, but Karakhan was unable to do anything. Ratifications had not yet been exchanged and the convention was not in effect. Abrikossow recalled later how he had hastened back from the Foreign Office after the above-mentioned talk with the Vice Minister:

I returned to the Embassy and began to prepare myself for the final act in my diplomatic career. I instructed the Consulates to arrange with local authorities for the transfer to them of the property of the old Russian government. I added that I would not deem it possible for any of the officials to enter the Soviet service; if they wanted to leave Japan their passage to Europe or America would be paid. I must say that all of them remained loyal to the former Russian government and not a single one went over to the Soviets. Then I spent many days going through the archives, considering it my duty not to leave any letters or documents which could compromise those who had struggled against the Bolsheviks in Siberia and had not been able to escape. Many nights of hard work went on this, but had the Bolsheviks found their names in the Embassy files the position of many Russians could have become tragic.[21]

On February 16 Abrikossow surrendered the old embassy with its state property and archives to the office of the governor of Tokyo "for safekeeping until transfer to the legally constituted Russian authorities." A letter from Abrikossow to the governor, informing him of the transfer, notes that the contents of the archives were not examined at the time.[22] A Letter from Abrikossow to Foreign Minister Baron Shidehara, listing in general what was being transferred, remarked that the archives contained the note of November 22, 1917, signed by Foreign Minister Viscount Motono Ichirō 本野一郎, relative to the cession of the [railway] section connecting Kwanchengtze to the left bank of the Sungari and [relative to] the navigation of this river, a topic which the Soviets had refused to discuss.[23]

That day Foreign Minister Shidehara received Abrikossow in a farewell audience. In Abrikossow's words:

> He assured me that it was not love for the Bolsheviks that had induced Japan to recognize Soviet Russia, but Russia was her close neighbor and unless she recognized the Soviet government she had no one to whom to address her claims and protests and could

not avoid the constant violation of her interests. Now she could at least discuss the different questions which kept arising between the two neigboring states. When I expressed doubt that recognition would facilitate matters, because it would give the Soviets free entry into Japan and direct access to the Japanese public, the Minister acknowledged that the Japanese understood this very well and had obtained from the Bolsheviks the promise to abstain from spreading any propaganda in Japan, agreeing in turn not to allow any White activity in the country. It was obvious that Soviet-Japanese relations were not beginning in a particularly friendly atmosphere. . . .[24]

In a letter to Shidehara that day Abrikossow expressed his gratitude "for the kind and attentive treatment" which he had received in the difficult years when he had been chargé d'affaires of the embassy. He was thankful for the assurance of the Japanese government "that the Russian refugees who, not being able to acknowledge the soviet authority, found their home in Japan, shall enjoy due treatment and protection in accordance with the Japanese laws and regulations as well as the rules of International Law" and expressed confidence that they could safely continue living in Japan "outside the claims and regulations which the soviet representatives may deem necessary to apply to the soviet citizens in Japan."[25]

The ratifications of the Basic Convention were exchanged in Peking on February 26, 1925. On this occasion Ambassador Karakhan informed Ambassador Yoshizawa that the Soviet government wished to send Viktor Leont'evich Kopp, a member of the Council of the People's Commissariat of Foreign Affairs, as its first ambassador to Japan.[c] The im-

---

[c] Soviet documents usually used the term *"polpred,"* an abbreviation for *"polnomochnyi predstavitel"* (plenipotentiary representative) for Kopp and his early successors; they referred to their building as *"polpredstvo."* Occassionally, sometimes in the same document, they wrote *"posol"* (ambassador) and *"posol'stvo"* (embassy).

Grigorii Besedovskii, counselor of the Soviet embassy in Tokyo in 1926–27, wrote of Kopp: "Very intelligent, with a European education, [and] speaking foreign lan-★

perial government duly studied Kopp's personal history and on March 4 agreed to the appointment. Kopp was officially named ambassador on March 9 and a month later, on April 8, left Moscow with about a dozen subordinates. He reached Tokyo on April 24 and on May 5 presented his credentials. A shadow was cast on his arrival soon afterwards by an "unconfirmed" report that on his way to Japan he had told the Provincial Committee of the Communist Party at Harbin that the Soviet-Japanese convention was but a scrap of paper.[26, d]

On March 3, 1925, prior to Kopp's official appointment, the Soviet government had informed Japan that it would send Nikolai Kirillovich Kuznetsov, first secretary of the Soviet embassy in Peking, to take over the old embassy property and prepare for the arrival of the Soviet embassy to Japan. On March 16 the embassy property and documents, handed over by Abrikossow to the Japanese government, were transferred to Kuznetsov by Toki Chinjirō, representing the governor of Tokyo, and by Kawasumi Tadao 川角忠雄 representing the Foreign Office, in the presence of D. A. Tsiurp, attaché of the Soviet mission in China.[27, e]

Yet although Japanese sources state that Kuznetsov seemed to have been satisfied with the meticulous care taken by the Japanese government of the embassy property, Kopp upon his arrival missed more than the documents destroyed by Abrikossow. On June 8 he protested in a

*guages, Kopp has by nature little in common with revolutionary political activity. He is rather a political realist, seeking a compromise, very flexible, deep in his heart laughing ironically at experiments *à la Borodin*." (G. Z. Besedovskii, *Na putiakh k termidoru* [Iz vospominanii b. sovetsk. diplomata] [On the road to the Thermidor (From the recollections of a former Soviet diplomat)] [Paris, 1930], vol. I, p. 225.

d For the text of his speech, see the chapter on "Lingering Mistrust."

e The Japanese Foreign Office Archives contain inventory lists of the furniture, equipment and other belongings, surrendered by the Russian embassy and the various consulates, also correspondence related to the transfer. See MT 251.106.23: 211–213, 285–291, 322–324, 419–421, 538–540. For an architect's report on the damage suffered by the old embassy building in the great earthquake of 1923, see MT 251.106.23: 196–198.

note to Foreign Minister Shidehara that "a number of Japanese banks keep sums of money, deposited by former officials of the Tsarist government and representatives of various organizations and groups, which waged civil war on the territory of the U.S.S.R. against the Soviet Government." Kopp asserted that these sums had been designated originally for official purchases and expenses and had unquestionably constituted government funds; he insisted, therefore, that under article 1 of Protocol A of the Basic Convention these monies must be regarded as the property of the U.S.S.R. and must be made available to the Soviet embassy. He made special reference to the sums of the former Omsk government, deposited by Ataman Grigorii Semenov in the Tokyo branch of the Yokohama Specie Bank.

The Japanese government rejected the Soviet claim in a note, dated June 22, 1925. It interpreted the article as referring to the real estate of the embassy and the consulates. "Even if one were to admit that the deposits constituted the property of some government treasury," it added, "it would still be impossible to consider that they belonged to one of the embassies or consulates."[28]

By the end of 1926 Soviet consulates general had been opened in Tokyo, Kōbe and Seoul; consulates in Hakodate, Otaru, Tsuruga and Dairen.[29] The consulate general in Kobe had been formally opened on January 28, 1926. Anatolii Kolesnikov, the newly appointed consul, had proceeded to Kōbe from Tokyo several days later. The jurisdiction of the Kōbe consulate included Hyōgo, Okayama, Tottori, Hiroshima, Yamaguchi, Ehime, Kōchi and Tokushima prefectures and the islets of the Inland Sea. But there were few Soviet subjects whom the consulate had to serve. "In Chugoku district there are only about 60 Russians under the Soviet Government and about a dozen of the 400 local (Kobe) Russians are registered as Soviet subjects," the *Japan Chronicle* reported. "Regarding the registration of the remaining Russians the Prefectural Office, Far East Trading and Timber Office and Far Eastern Bank are now assisting, on the basis of the resolution passed at the Geneva Conference in 1922."[30]

Like the embassy in Tokyo the Soviet consulates experienced conflicts with anti-Communist emigrés. This was particularly true in Dairen, the former Russian possession in Manchuria, where many White Russians lived. In February of 1926 a group to White Russians invaded the consulate in Dairen and tore down the red flag. Although the local police arrested one of the emigrés, the Soviets felt that the case was not prosecuted with sufficient vigor and awareness of the seriousness of the crime. In a note to the Japanese government, dated March 8, 1926, they demanded that the Japanese government give satisfaction to the Soviet Union for the insult to its flag, that it see to it that appropriate punishment be meted out to the culprit and that measures be taken to prevent similar occurrences. The Japanese government on April 26 duly expressed its regrets, even though the culprit was not a Japanese subject.[31]

A more serious incident occurred on the afternoon of November 10, 1927. Secretary Cherkasov was walking down one of the streets in Dairen accompanied by his wife when suddenly the 18-year old son of a Russian priest in that city attacked him from the rear with a knife and inflicted over sixteen wounds on his head, neck and arms. Mrs. Cherkasov, who tried to ward off the blows from her husband was also injured slightly. Again the Soviet embassy protested and the Japanese Foreign Office expressed its regrets.[32]

By this time Kopp was no longer in Japan. He had been appointed Ambassador to Sweden at the beginning of the year, swapping posts with Comrade Valer'ian Dovgalevskii, who moved from Stockholm to Tokyo.[33]

The change in Soviet ambassadors coincided with a change in the Japanese cabinet, Baron Shidehara, who had been foreign minister from October 1926 until February 1927, being succeeded at this time by Baron Tanaka. Although Dovgalevskii received "an extremely friendly and hearty reception" on his arrival in Tokyo on March 25, his tenure was brief. Before the end of the year he was named ambassador to France. He was followed by Aleksandr Antonovich Troianovskii who stayed from 1928 until 1932.[34]

In the months between Kopp's departure and Dovgalevskii's arrival Grigorii Zinov'evich Besedovskii had acted as chargé d'affaires *ad interim*.

According to Besedovskii's memoirs there had been a deep rift in the Soviet embassy in Tokyo when he had arrived in the summer of 1926. The split had been caused not by any political differences but by a running feud between the wife of Military Attaché Iakov Ianel and Ambassador Kopp, who had treated her contumely. As supporters of the two accused each other of various wrongdoings and the charges were transmitted to the Central Committee of the Communist Party by the representative of the Security Police, Moscow recalled both Ianel and Kopp. Besedovskii's memoirs contain also reference to the nocturnal activities of Madame Dovgalevskii, the wife of Kopp's successor, in Paris and her recall to Moscow for interrogation by the Security Police.[35]

Unfortunately Besedovskii became the "self-acknowledged leader" of "the Besedovskii school" of private forgers of Soviet memoirs in the 1950's and, as a result, his own memoirs are suspect. The delightful tales of political and sexual intrigue in the Soviet embassy in Tokyo may be apocryphal, for Besedovskii boasted in connection with his other books that when he portrayed "Stalin or Molotov in pyjamas," when he told "the dirtiest possible stories about them—never mind whether they are true or invented," they would be read by intellectuals and capitalist statesmen alike. "Allah has given money to the stupid in order that the intelligent can live easily," he sneered in justification of his falsification of history.[36] On the other hand, various statements made by Besedovskii in his own memoirs are corroborated by Japanese sources. His recollections thus cannot be dismissed, even if they must be used with mental reservations.

According to Besedovskii the two first secretaries Nikolai Kirillovich Kuznetsov and Georgii Aleksandrovich Astakhov knew Japan well and spoke Japanese and English. The second secretaries Lev Il'ich Vol'f and Alfred Austrin were excellent chancery workers with "really German accuracy." The wife of Professor Evgenii Genrikhovich Spal'vin, the noted Japanologist who served as interpreter of the embassy, was "a sympathetic Japanese, a widow, whose first husband was knifed to death on a street in Tokyo after the Russo-Japanese War because he was somehow accused in the Japanese press of a suspicious acquaintance with the Russian military attaché then in Tokyo."[37] Besedovskii himself took a liking to Japanese culture. He settled in Kamakura, where he wandered about in kimono and geta. Like many students of Japanese he was spellbound by the language.

> Having begun the study of the Japanese language I found, when pronouncing Japanese phrases, that I not only expressed some idea or other, but got a deep enjoyment from the sounds, from the combination of words. This was not merely satisfaction from the study of a foreign tongue. I know several languages, which I learned easily, yet I got no pleasure in studying them. But Japanese phrases gave me the sort of pleasure that a man gets who finally remembers a word he has forgotten.[38]

Besedovskii spoke highly of the work of Aleksandr Nikolaevich Loginov, the Soviet consul in Hakodate. Able and tactful, Loginov was one of the best consuls he had ever met. Besedovskii had a very different opinion of Iurii Vladimirovich Mal'tsev, the Soviet consul general in Kobe, an old member of the Communist Party and a personal friend of Molotov, who spent much of his time playing cards and drinking with foreigners. Besedovskii found the consulates in Nagasaki and Otaru torn by dissension and personal feuds. He attributed this to the lack of work on one hand and the isolation of the Soviet personnel from their country and the European and Japanese community on the other hand.

Besedovskii was deeply impressed by the Japanese Vice Minister of Foreign Affairs Debuchi.

> I shall not hide [the fact] that I was under the strong influence of the intelligence, erudition and talent of Mr. Debuchi, and it was frequently very difficult for me not to agree with him on some questions, which I had orders from the People's Commissariat of Foreign Affairs to discuss with him. The strength of the logical deductions of Mr. Debuchi was truly wonderful and I was sometimes literally delighted by the bright brilliance of his argumentation.[39]

Besedovskii had to return to the Soviet Union because of the deteriorating health of his entire family, particularly of his wife, who had frequent fainting spells. He was able to leave only after acquainting the new ambassador, Dovgalevskii, with the state of affairs in Japan, a lengthy process because Dovgalevskii spent the summer months in his country home instead of getting down to work in Tokyo. Besedovskii departed for Paris via Moscow in September of 1927.[40]

The exchange of official representatives between the Soviet Union and Japan was not confined to diplomatic and consular officials. In view of the fact that foreign trade was a state monopoly in the U.S.S.R. the Soviet Union demanded official status for its trade representatives abroad. The issue gave substance to Japanese misgivings that the development of trade with the Soviet Union would be beset by difficulties because of the difference in economic systems.

The Soviet Union appointed as its first trade representative to Japan Iakov Davidovich Ianson, the former foreign minister of the Far Eastern Republic who had assisted Ioffe in the negotiations at Changchun in 1922. Upon his appointment as trade representative, Ianson went to the Japanese embassy in Moscow and applied for a visa.

Chargé d'Affaires Satō did not issue the visa at once. On April 20, 1925, he asked Foreign Minister Chicherin for a specific written description of the functions and rights of the trade delegation (*torgpredstvo*) and an indication of the size of its staff and the number of members with diplomatic privileges. Satō wanted to know whether the trade delegation would be a completely separate agency. When Chicherin alluded to the existence of commercial attachés in other countries, Satō said that there would, of course, be no objection to the inclusion of a commercial attaché in the staff of the embassy. Chicherin explained that in countries where foreign trade was in private hands the functions of the commercial attaché were quite limited and essentially informative in nature, because business deals were concluded by the merchants; the Soviet trade representative, on the other hand, by whatever title he might go, conducted trade, since in the Soviet Union trade was a state enterprise. Satō rejoined that he recognized the difference but could not issue a visa unless the functions and rights of the trade delegation were defined in writing. He pointed out that Ianson was a member of the collegium of the People's Commissariat for Foreign Trade and therefore equal in rank with Ambassador Kopp; how could he be a simple attaché in Kopp's embassy? If, on the other hand, his position was parallel to that of Kopp, agreement must be reached prior to his departure regarding the functions and rights of his office.

Satō reminded Chicherin that Yoshizawa had stated during the negotiation of the basic convention that it would be desirable to send "not too many" officials following the re-establishment of relations. The Japanese government had heard that the Soviet Union dispatched everywhere a large number of personnel and was afraid of this. Kopp had already brought some 16 or 17 collaborators and Ianson, according to his information, wanted to take along 15. Chicherin countered that the trade delegation and the economic organizations (*khozorgany*) had to perform the same tasks as those carried out by the large private firms of other countries. He was sure that the Mitsubishi Company of Japan had a large number of offices with many employees in America. Trade with the Soviet Union was impossible unless a well-staffed trade delegation be allowed to function. Chicherin said that at first a relatively small trade delegation would do, but that with the development of economic relations between the two countries a larger delegation and representation from various economic organizations would be necessary.

When Satō reiterated that he needed a written formulation of the functions and rights of the trace delegation and of the number of its collaborators and of the officials with diplomatic privileges, Chicherin replied that he would send such a statement in a number of days; he had to discuss it with the People's Commissariat for Foreign Trade.[41]

On May 5 B. N. Mel'nikov, director of the Far Eastern section of the Foreign Commissariat, handed to Satō the desired memorandum. It described the functions of the trade delegation as assistance in the development of commercial and economic relations between the U.S.S.R. and Japan, the regulation of foreign trade between the U.S.S.R. and Japan, and the carrying out of commercial transactions in Japan in the name of the U.S.S.R. It did not specify the size of the delegation, stating that this would be determined after the opening of the trade delegation and its branches. It stipulated that the trade representative, the deputy trade representative and the members of the soviet (council) of the trade delegation would have diplomatic privileges; the remaining collaborators would be on a par with the technical employees of the embassy. The building of the trade delegation would enjoy extraterritoriality. The Soviet government would be responsible for commitments made by the trade delegation. Disputes that might arise concerning commercial transactions made between the trade delegation and Japanese subjects would be settled on the basis of Japanese laws.[42]

On June 3 Satō informed the Foreign Commissariat that his government doubted the possibility of allowing the trade delegation to function as a state agency with diplomatic privileges. Not only would this be contrary to Japanese law, but it would violate the right to equal treatment of foreign merchants resident in Japan; indeed, the Japanese did not have such privileges in the Soviet Union. The Japanese government did not reject the Soviet proposal outright, but asked that a final decision be deferred until the conclusion of a treaty of commerce in which the problem could be worked out by mutual agreement. As a temporary compromise Satō suggested that the trade representative and two or three collaborators be regarded as equivalent to the commercial attachés and secretaries of other embassies; this would give them extraterritorial rights and diplomatic immunity but their functions would be limited to licensing imports and exports and to assisting in the development of economic relations; they would not be allowed to make trade deals. Such deals would have to be concluded by third persons or by a specially formed agency without extraterritorial or diplomatic privileges.[43]

On July 15 Kopp discussed the question with Shidehara in Tokyo. The Soviet ambassador argued that diplomatic privileges had been extended to Soviet trade representatives by Germany and other countries; it would be difficult to make an exception in the case of Japan. Foreign trade, furthermore, was an important function of the Soviet government and in many instances, such as in the ordering of military supplies, required secrecy; it was necessary, therefore, to grant to trade representatives the same sort of privileges and protection as to other state representatives. The compromise proposed by Satō, Kopp added, conflicted with Soviet law.

The Japanese foreign minister retorted that although Soviet trade representatives enjoyed diplomatic privileges in some European countries, this was not a universal practice. Japan had struggled long and hard to rid herself of the extraterritorial rights of foreign commercial enterprises in Japan; to allow them again, even as an exception, would be a step backwards. Government management of foreign trade was not a ground for extending diplomatic privileges to trade representatives; in Japan the export, import and sale of tobacco were a state monopoly yet no need had been felt to obtain diplomatic privileges for officials in charge of the transactions. The secrecy of commerce was duly protected in Japan, except in cases involving the public good; the Japanese government could not agree to absolute secrecy at the possible expense of national welfare. Japan herself frequently purchased military supplies abroad without finding it necessary to garb the officials involved in diplomatic privileges. Japan did not object to trade representatives being part of the diplomatic establishment in so far as internal Soviet organization was concerned; there was no need to extend to them diplomatic privileges in Japan. Shidehara made it clear that he was not objecting to the establishment of a trade mission—in fact would welcome one—so long as it conformed to Japanese laws.[44]

The fact that the privileges demanded by the U.S.S.R. would have put the Soviet trade representative in a position of advantage that might have antagonized the foreign business community was a consideration that was voiced publicly. Privately, the Japanese government was concerned lest the extraterritorial position of the Soviet trade mission make it a base for Communist propaganda and permit it to evade the payment of taxes.[45, f]

Ianson reputedly doubled as Comintern agent in Japan. (Eudin and North, pp. 459–60)

The Japanese had been first to raise the issue of putting the functions and rights of the Soviet trade delegation in writing. As the Soviet side persisted in its demand for diplomatic and extraterritorial privileges, however, the Japanese sought to defer the matter. Eager for trade with the Soviet Union and particularly for economic concessions on Soviet territory, they invited the U.S.S.R. to open the trade delegation without prior agreement on its exact status. On July 26 Chicherin telegraphed Kopp that the Soviet Union was willing to do so only if the Japanese government would engage in a written note to extend extraterritoriality to the trade delegation and to take whatever measures might be necessary to permit its unhindered operation. "Under extraterritoriality is understood the extraterritoriality of the trade delegate and his assistants, and of the building of the trade delegation but not of its warehouses." Chicherin put pressure on the Japanese by adding that a speedy decision was necessary not only to work out the schedule of imports and exports for the following year but also to prepare a plan for the concessions which Japan wanted. Without a trade delegation it was impossible to determine either the import and export possibilities or the contractors for the respective concessions.[46]

On September 18 Kopp handed to Shidehara a "final" compromise proposal according to which the Soviet Union would send to Japan a trade delegate and three deputies as members of the diplomatic mission, with the trade delegate having the right to conclude commercial deals. The transactions were to be subject to Japanese law, but the property of the trade delegation was to be protected by extraterritoriality.[47]

In repeated talks between Kopp and Shidehara, the Japanese foreign minister argued that diplomats did not trade and that traders could not be diplomats; yet at the same time he did not wish to close the door to economic relations between the two countries. In November it was agreed to let Ianson proceed to Tokyo as commercial attaché in order to assist Kopp in resolving the issue; his role as trade representative would not be recognized for the time being and he would not be allowed to engage in commercial transactions. On December 12 Ianson set out for Japan, where he arrived by the end of the year.

Negotiations continued in 1926. The Soviet side eventually bowed to the Japanese conditions, but did not want this to be made public, lest her bargaining position on this issue be undermined elsewhere. When Shidehara pointed out that he could not guarantee the secrecy of a regular agreement, which was subject to approval by the Privy Council and the Diet, it was decided not to conclude a formal agreement on this subject, but to draw up a confidential "exchange of views" between Shidehara and Kopp for deposit in the archives. Not only would such a document be leak-proof, but it would make it possible for the Soviet Union to assure Germany, Italy, France, and Turkey, which had extended diplomatic privileges to her trade representatives, that it had made no agreement to the contrary with Japan.[48]

On June 23, 1926, after ten months of negotiations, the "exchange of views" was approved at an "interview" between Kopp and Shidehara. The provisions were regarded as tentative, the informal nature of the document being underlined by the fact that it was not signed by Shidehara or Kopp but merely by the two interpreters, T. Yamaguchi and Evgenii Genrikhovich Spal'vin. It read as follows:

RECORD FOR ARCHIVES

Confidential

The following is the result of the exchange of views between the Japanese Minister for Foreign Affairs and the Ambassador of the U.S.S.R. in their recent interviews on the subject of the status of the U.S.S.R. Trade Delegation:

1. The functions of the Trade Delegation which is to be established by the Government of the U.S.S.R. in Japan shall be:
    (a) to encourage and facilitate trade and other commercial intercourse between the U.S.S.R. and Japan,
    (b) to control exportation from the U.S.S.R. to Japan and
    (c) to conduct commercial transactions on behalf of the U.S.S.R.

EXCHANGE OF OFFICIAL REPRESENTATIVES 223

2. The Government of the U.S.S.R. may designate the head of the Trade Delegation and his assistants, respectively, as Commercial Counsellor and Commercial Secretaries of the Embassy of the U.S.S.R., who, in such supplementary capacity, shall be authorized to exercise the same official functions and to enjoy the same diplomatic immunities as similar officials of other foreign Embassies at Tokyo. The Commercial Counsellor shall be one in number and the Commercial Secretaries not more than three.
3. The head of the Trade Delegation, recognized as Commercial Counsellor of the Embassy of the U.S.S.R., shall be authorized inter alia to issue licenses for export from and import into the U.S.S.R., thereby controlling exportation from the U.S.S.R. to Japan and importation into the U.S.S.R. from Japan.
4. The Trade Delegation, as well as its officials (i.e. head and members), except those recognised as Commercial Counsellor or Commercial Secretaries to the Embassy of the U.S.S.R., shall act in Japan subject to the laws and jurisdiction of the country, and shall in all cases confine their activities within the limits of the specified functions for which the Delegation is to be established.
5. All commercial transactions, which may be conducted in Japan by the Trade Delegation as well as the properties of the U.S.S.R. situated in Japan and connected with the business of the Trade Delegation shall likewise be subject to the laws and jurisdiction of the country.
6. The Trade Delegation shall carry on its business in an office outside the premises of the Embassy of the U.S.S.R.; provided, however, that the officials of the Trade Delegation, recognised as Commercial Counsellor or Commercial Secretaries to the Embassy of the U.S.S.R. may exercise their functions, due to such supplementary capacity, in the office of the Embassy.
7. Whenever it is intended to establish any agency or branch office of the Trade Delegation in Japan, the consent of the

Japanese Government to such establishment shall be previously obtained.

8. All passports for officials of the Trade Delegation proceeding to Japan shall be viséed at the Japanese Embassy at Moscow. In special circumstances, they may be viséed at the Japanese Consulate at Vladivostock or Habarovsk, and in that event the Government of the U.S.S.R. shall previously communicate to the Japanese Embassy at Moscow the names of the Officials whose passports are to be viséed at such Consulate.

9. (i) The Embassy of the U.S.S.R. in Tokyo shall notify the Japanese Government
    (a) of the names of the officials of the Trade Delegation who shall be authorized to conduct commercial transactions on behalf of the Trade Delegation, and to sign contracts, bills and other commercial documents, based on such transactions,
    (b) of the extent of powers invested in each of such officials, and
    (c) of any subsequent change in such personnel or in the extent of such powers.
  (ii) Upon receipt of notification as aforesaid the Japanese Government shall in due course publish the terms of the notification in the Japanese Official Gazette.
  (iii) Upon such publication in the Japanese Official Gazette, the designated officials of the Trade Delegation may exercise their respective functions in accordance with the terms contained in the notification.

The above shall be regarded as provisional subject to further alterations which may hereafter be agreed upon.

/s/ T. YAMAGUCHI
/s/ SPALVIN

Tokyo, June 23d 1926[49]

On the same day Ianson called on Vice Minister of Foreign Affairs Debuchi and made arrangements with him regarding the number of his staff and the names of the traders.[50] The last obstacle seemed to have been removed for the development of normal commercial and diplomatic relations.

CHAPTER EIGHT

Concession Contracts

AS soon as the exchange of representatives had been effected in the spring of 1925, work was begun on carrying out the provisions of the Basic Convention. A commission, headed by Comrade Aboltin, was sent to North Sakhalin to accept the territory from the Japanese as they evacuated on May 15, 1925.[1]

Article IV of the Basic Convention provided for the granting "to Japanese subjects, companies and associations concessions for the exploitation of minerals, forests and other natural resources in all the territories of the Union of the Soviet Socialist Republics." Protocol B, appended to the convention, laid down the basis for the concession contracts. It stipulated that the contracts be concluded "within five months from the date of the complete evacuation of Northern Saghalien by Japanese troops, as provided for in Article 3 of Protocol A." Article III pledged completion of the withdrawal by May 15, 1925. Full Russian sovereignty over North Sakhalin was duly restored on May 14,[2] and the concession contracts were to be concluded, therefore, by October 15 of the same year.

In mid-July 1925 two Japanese delegations arrived in Moscow: an oil delegation, headed by Admiral Nakasato Shigetsugu 中里重次, representing the Kita Sagaren Sekiyu Kigyō Kumiai 北サガレン石油企業組合 (Association of North Sakhalin Oil Enterprises), and a coal delegation under Okumura Masao, representing the Sakai Kumiai 坂井組合 and the Kita Sagaren Sekitan Kigyō Kumiai 北サガレン石炭企業組合 (Association of North Sakhalin Coal Enterprises). With them came Kawakami Toshitsune, the Foreign Service officer, in the capacity of an advisor. The Soviet Union formed a special commission of the Main Concession Committee (*Glavkontsesskom*) to confer with them. Ioffe, who had negotiated with Kawakami in Tokyo in 1923, was appointed chairman of the concession committee.[3]

In a letter to Ioffe, dated Moscow, August 1, 1925, Okumura expressed the expectation that the concession contracts would be concluded "quite smoothly and promptly." Noting that the language of the conference was to be Russian, with the contracts and all other documents formulated in English, as had been done at Peking, Okumura conveyed a nine point list of important items to be determined at the concession contract conference, and asked Ioffe to set the date and place for their first meeting.[4]

A general meeting on August 14 inaugurated the conference, during which Japanese concession demands were matched against a 47-article oil contract draft and a 40-article coal contract draft, submitted by the Soviet side.[5]

In regard to the oil concessions the Soviet Union asserted that the buildings, machines and tools connected with the oil enterprises and located on the site of the concessions were Soviet property. The Japanese could use them for an annual rental of 10% of the appraised value; they could install and use new equipment, but within two months after the expiration of the concession contracts all property connected with the concessions had to be returned to the Soviets. The Japanese objected. Firstly, they argued, the enterprise property had been installed by Japanese and thus was clearly Japanese and not Russian; secondly, if it were regarded as Russian, Japanese firms would have insufficient security to operate the concessions. The question could not be resolved and was left for future determination; the Soviet side gave in to the extent of lowering the rental from 10% to 4%.

Protocol B, appended to the basic convention, had stated that the period of the concessions should be from 40 to 50 years. The Soviet draft offered concessions for 40 years; the Japanese wanted concessions for 50 years. The negotiators split the difference and agreed on 45 year terms, i.e. until 1970.

In the matter of determining the area of the oil fields already in operation a compromise was reached that was generally favorable to the Japanese side; although the Soviets had wished to postpone a decision on the ground that surveys had not been completed, they gave in to the Japanese demand that the location, size and method of partition be worked out on a map and attached to the contracts. The selection of oil fields for future exploitation, on the other hand, was left for later; once an area of exploration had been designated, the concessionaries would be free to conduct surveys and tests to determine whether or not to engage in exploitation; if they decided to go ahead the area of exploitation was to be split between both sides.

There was much debate about the rate of compensation for the use of the oil fields. The Japanese proposed to pay a royalty of 5% for the first 100,000 tons of oil obtained in a year, with an increase of $\frac{1}{4}$% for each additional 10,000 tons, up to 15% for 500,000 tons. The Soviets insisted that the 5% royalty be limited to the first 20,000 tons with the 15% rate reached already at 420,000 tons. A Japanese compromise offer of 5% up to the first 65,000 tons was rejected and the Soviet terms prevailed. It was agreed that all compensation for the concessions be made in cash, prices to be based on California oil quotations in the case of 25° Baumé or under and on Gulf of Mexico oil in the case of over 25° Baumé.

Both sides began with different figures for royalty payments on gushers. They compromised on a pay rate for gushers up to a daily yield of 10 tons equal to that for ordinary wells, beyond that on 15% for gushers yielding between 10 and 50 tons, 20% for between 50 and 60 tons, 25% for 60–70 tons, 30% for 70–80 tons, 35% for 80–90 tons, 40% for 90–100 tons, and 45% for over 100 tons. As for gasoline plants, it was agreed that on the basis of 1,000 cubic feet, compensation be 10% for up to 2 gallons, 15% for up to 3 gallons, 20% for up to 4 gallons, 25% for up to 5 gallons, and 35% for up to 6 gallons.

There was considerable debate also about taxation, social security payments, Soviet priority in the purchase of oil, the employment of foreigners and the application of the Soviet labor code, and incidental rights of the concessionaires.[6]

In regard to the coal concessions there was lengthy discussion of the question of proprietary rights. It was agreed that at the time of the expiration of the contract the concessionaires surrender to the Soviet government without compensation property, installed by them, on which depreciation had been completed; property which had not yet been fully depreciated was to be sold to the Soviet side. Rental for existing property was to be 5%, with the cost of major repairs to be deducted from the assessed value.

There was considerable controversy about the location of the colliery works. During the military occupation, as listed in the memorandum appended to the basic convention, the Japanese had operated the Due and Rogatui coal mines. They now wanted to work the same mines plus some others. The Russians replied that the Rogatui mine was to be a Soviet state enterprise; they agreed to part but not all of the Due mining field; and they rejected the other areas proposed by the Japanese. It was finally agreed that the Japanese syndicate be allowed to mine at Due (except for one area already granted to a Soviet enterprise) at Vladimirskii and at Machi; additional coal fields were to be provided to the Sakai Association at Agnevo and later to the Tsukahara Association at the upper reaches of the Kosuchina River.

The Japanese syndicate proposed a royalty payment of 5% for the first 500,000 tons of coal, with a $\frac{1}{4}$% increase for each additional 10,000 tons up to 8% for 1,700,000 tons; the Soviets demanded 5% for the first 25,000 tons, with 8% already for 320,000 tons. The two sides compromised eventually, the syndicate to pay in kind F.O.B. 5% for up to 100,000 tons with a $\frac{1}{4}$% increase for each additional 50,000 tons up to a total of 8% for 650,000 tons and over; the Sakai Association was to pay 5% for up to 50,000 tons, with a $\frac{1}{4}$% increase for each additional 10,000 tons up to 8% for 160,000 tons and above.

The Soviet Union demanded the prior right to purchase up to half of the annual output by giving notice six months before the start of work in a given operating year. The Japanese consented with the proviso that the Soviet side would exercise this option for the purpose of purchasing coal for its own consumption only.

The Japanese desired exemption for their coal operations of all taxes and imports other than the above-mentioned royalties; the Russian negotiators felt that Japanese enterprises should be treated on a par with Soviet state enterprises. In the end the two sides compromised on a tax of 3.3% on F.O.B. sales.

The Japanese did not quarrel with Soviet insistence that they comply with the Soviet labor code. They objected, however, to the demand that over half of their work force be recruited from among Soviet nationals, breaking the percentage down by degree of skill.

As in the case of the oil concessions, the Japanese strove for a 50 year term, the Soviets for 40 years; again agreement was reached eventually on 45 years.

The Soviet draft stipulated a social insurance deduction of 13% from the total annual wages; the Japanese negotiated a 3.5% deduction in view of the fact that they planned to use their own medical facilities.[7]

The process of hammering out the oil and coal agreements took longer than anticipated and the original deadline of October 15 had to be extended. Although the contracts were negotiated between private Japanese companies and Soviet state enterprises, Ambassador Tanaka smoothed the way in talks with Deputy Foreign Commissar Aralov. On November 30 agreement was reached regarding the oil concessions and two days later, on December 1, regarding the coal concessions. A fortnight was needed to whip the provisions into shape and to formalize them in a resolution of the Council of People's Commissars.[8]

The coal agreement was signed on the afternoon of Friday, December 11, by Okumura, the Japanese coal delegate, who had to leave for Germany that evening. He did so in the presence of Kawakami and the legal adviser to the Supreme Council of National Economy (VONKH), Etefovich. The formal signature of the concession agreements took place after the weekend, on Monday, December 14, at the meeting of the Supreme Council of National Economy. Nakasato put his name to the oil agreement for the Japanese side;[9] F.E. Derzhinskii, chairman of the Supreme Council of National Economy, signed both agreements for the Soviet Union. Deputy Foreign Commissar Litvinov fastened them together. Present at the signing and photographed with the delegates were also

Kawakami, the adviser of the delegation, and Ambassador Tanaka and the secretaries of the Japanese embassy, as well as the members of the Soviet commission for the conclusion of the agreements. Minkin, a member of the Main Concession Committee, Gurevich, director of the foreign section of the Supreme Council of National Economy, and Musatov, Stepukhovich, and Iampol'skii.[a]

The coal agreement was between the Soviet government on one hand and Sakai Kumiai and Kita Sagaren Sekitan Kigyō Kumiai on the other hand; the oil agreement was between the Soviet government and Kita Sagaren Sekiyu Kigyō Kumiai. Neither the Japanese nor the Soviet collections of diplomatic documents nor the British or League of Nations treaty series contain the text of these "private" agreements. But the following summary appeared in *Izvestiia:*

> An oil concession is granted on the eastern shore of North Sakhalin; it is composed of 8 oil deposits—Okha [Oha], Nutovo, Piltun [Pilutun], Ekhabi [Ehabi], Chaivo, Nyivo [Nuivo], Uiglekuty [Vuigrektui], and Katangli—with a general area of 4,800 dessiatines [13,000 acres according to the memorandum on oil exploration appended to the basic convention]. 50% of these fields to be exploited are to be given to the government of the U.S.S.R. in chess-board fashion. The concessionaire is granted the exclusive right for a period of 11 years to explore for oil, *kira* [?] and inflammable gas in an area of 1,000 square versts, with the understanding that in the process of exploration he will narrow down his activity, exploring as a preliminary in areas of 960 dessiatines [about 2,600 acres], then single out from these areas over a period of three years

---

[a] On the same day that the concession contracts were signed (December 14, 1925) the Soviet delegation to the international railway conference gave a return banquet to the Japanese delegation. In addition to the Japanese railway delegation there were present Ambassador Tanaka and the staff of his embassy as well as the Soviet railway delegation and members of the collegium of the People's Commissariat of Transportation and the People's Commissariat of Foreign Affairs and their collaborators. (*Izvestiia*, December 15, 1925, p. 2)

lots to be exploited. The concessionaire makes detailed topographical surveys of the entire area and compiles corresponding maps.

The coal concessions are situated on the western shore of North Sakhalin: in the district of Due 18 square versts [12 square miles] in size, in the region of the Vladimirskii mine $14\frac{1}{2}$ square versts [about 10 square miles in size] and in the region of Machi River 24 square versts [16 square miles in size]. As in the case of the oil treaty agreement the concessionaire is granted the exclusive right to explore and mine coal in the agreed upon localities.

The share to be deducted in the case of the coal concession is set at 5% in the event of an annual shaft production of up to 100,000 metric tons, with an additional 0.25% for every additional 50,000 metric tons, paid by the concessionaire in kind. In the case of the oil concession the share to be deducted is pegged at 5% for nongusher oil in the event of a well production of 30,000 metric tons, with an additional 0.25% for every [additional] 10,000 metric tons up to 15%. As for gusher oil, the share to be deducted is set at 15% in the event of a daily well production from 10,000 to 50,000 metric tons, with an addition of 5% for every 10,000 metric tons up to 45%, which are paid by the concessionaire in cash.

Besides paying all state and local taxes, the concessionaires also make a lease payment of 4% of the value of the property being handed over.

For the coal concession enterprise the concessionaires are given the right to use within the territory of the concession forest and minerals in general use. Outside this territory [wood] cutting areas are set aside according to the tariff of 1912; the export of lumber abroad can take place only on a universal basis; the extraction of minerals in general use is done by the concessionaire on the general basis of the mining legislation of the U.S.S.R.

The [Soviet] government has also granted to the associations the right to form and exploit all kinds of subsidiary enterprises necessary for operating the oil concession.

The coal concession contracts stipulate the right of the concessionaire to build a port provided he clears its location and building plan with the People's Commissariat of Transportation [NKPS] The constructed port comes under the jurisdiction of the commisariat, which sets aside for the concessionaire a specific part of this port on conditions agreed upon with him. The oil contract stipulates also the right of the concessionaire to lay oil pipelines, provided he clears with the [Soviet] government all technical conditions of their construction and assumes also the obligation to let the [Soviet] government make use of the pipelines at cost to pump through oil which it owns.

In giving to the concessionaires the right to lay new telephone lines and to make use of those already in existence, the [Soviet] government stipulated that this be done in concord with the plans of the People's Commissariat of Post and Telegraph [Narkompochtel] and under the control of its local organs; provision is also made for the right of the government organs on Sakhalin to use the above-mentioned telephone lines freely.

The importation of all kinds of machines, parts for them, and technical articles and materials for the supplying and outfitting of concession enterprises as well as of consumer goods and of provisions for supplying the workers and employees of the concessions is carried out by the concessionaires duty free and without payment of license fees. The concessionaires must supply the workers and employees with these articles at prices specially approved by the commander of the mining district of North Sakhalin; imported consumer goods and provisions cannot be sold on the domestic market without the special permission of local government organs. The export by the concessionaires of the production of the concession enterprises is also done duty-free, without payment of license fees. The coal concession contracts stipulate the right of the concessionaires to sell coal on the domestic market, the amount of the sale for every operational year being agreed upon in advance with the Far Eastern organs of the [Soviet] government. The government has retained the preferential right to purchase from the concessionaires coal necessary for domestic use in the amount of up to 50% of the production of the concession enterprises for every preceding year.

The concessionaires insure all the property of the concession enterprises in insurance institutions of the U.S.S.R. at their expense and in the name of the [Soviet] government.

Working conditions in the concession enterprises are regulated by the existing laws in the U.S.S.R. and by appropriate corresponding collective contracts. All workers and employees of the concession enterprises must be furnished with living quarters, meeting sanitary-living norms established in the U.S.S.R.

Besides Russian workers, the concession contracts stipulate also the employment of a foreign labor force in the amount of up to 50% for administrative-technical personnel and highly skilled workers and up to 25% for foreign workers of medium skill and lower qualification and unskilled workmen. The above-mentioned ratio of foreign and Russian workers is readjusted every three years downward [i.e. the proportion of foreign workers is to be reduced].

The Soviet government retains the right to cancel the concession contracts in effect in the event that the concessionaire will be declared an insolvent debtor, if he violates the law and allows the predatory exploitation of ores, if he does not pay his share of taxes, and if he oversells consumer goods and provisions imported for the coal enterprise on the domestic market without appropriate permission. Disputes and disagreements which might arise both in regard to the interpretation as well as the execution of the concession treaties are considered by the Supreme Court of the U.S.S.R.

The period of the coal and oil concessions is fixed by contract for 45 years. Upon the expiration of the terms of the contract, as well as in the event of their premature cancellation, the concession enterprises are transferred to the Soviet government without compensation.[10]

According to Article 9 of the concession agreement the oil concessionaires were to consolidate their activity on North Sakhalin in a joint-stock company. In June of 1926 the Kita Karafuto Sekiyu Kabushiki Kaisha 北樺太石油株式會社 was formed. Its stockholders included the biggest oil producing concerns in Japan: Kuhara Kogyo, Mitsubishi Goshi, Okura Gumi, Nakano Kogyo and Mitsui Kozan. On February 21, 1927, the new company concluded the supplementary agreement setting aside for exploration 1,000 square versts [about 650 square miles] of oil fields on the eastern shore of North Sakhalin, as stipulated in 1925.[11]

The operations of the North Sakhalin coal syndicate Kita Sagaren Sekitan Kigyō Kumiai also were consolidated in a joint-stock company, the Kita Karafuto Kōgyō Kabushiki Kaisha 北樺太鉱業株式會社 (the North Sakhalin Mining Company, Ltd.) in August of 1926.[12] Meanwhile another coal company, the Tsukahara Association (Tsukahara Kumiai), on February 19, 1926 concluded a separate agreement as an ordinary concessionaire (i.e. not on the basis of the Basic Convention) for coal mining in the valley of the Kosuchina River.

The Soviet government also granted two alluvial gold mining concessions near the city of Okhotsk—one for the Rizhinskii (Lishinskii?) mine to Tanaka Yotarō 田中與太郎 in the fall of 1925 and one for the Vladimirskii, Pravyi (Right) and Levyi (Left) mines to the Shōwa Kinkō Kabushiki Kaisha 昭和金鉱株式會社 in 1927.

In addition to the mining concessions the Japanese obtained also lumber concessions. In the early 1920's a number of Japanese firms exploited the rich forest regions of the Russian Far East. In 1924, on the eve of Japanese recognition of the Soviet Union, the following were active: the Kyokutō Shinrin Kōgyō Kabushiki Kaisha 極東森林興業株式會社 (Far Eastern Forestry Industry Company). the Enkaishū Ringyō Dan 沿海州林業団 (Maritime Province Forestry Company), the Karafuto Kōgyō 樺太工業 (Karafuto Industry), Fukushima Shoten 福島商店 (Fukushima Shop) and the Azhia Ringyō Kabushiki Kaisha 亜細亜林業株式會社 (Asian Forestry Company, Ltd.)

In January of 1925 the Soviet authorities at Khaborovsk offered to

Narita 成田, who had been conferring with them in the name of the Japanese forestry interests since the preceding October, to grant forestry concessions up to a period of twenty years. The Japanese forestry companies thereupon formed the Roryō Ringyō Kumiai 露領林業組合 (Russian Territory Forestry Association) and through Narita and Takiguchi 瀧口 entered into negotiations with a Soviet Far Eastern Concessions Committee, headed by Far Eastern Agricultural Representative Mamonov, with the chief of the Vladivostok Forestry Affairs Bureau Lebedev as his deputy. Preliminary talks were held at Khabarovsk from September 25, 1925, until mid-November, with a brief interruption during which Narita returned to Tokyo for consultation.

Toward the end of January 1926 the Roryō Ringyō Kumiai sent Umeura Kenkichi 梅浦健吉 to Moscow for formal negotiations. For almost a year—from the beginning of February until December—the two sides conferred on the basis of a 78 article draft contract submitted by the Soviet Union. In July an impasse was reached and the negotiations were saved from collapse only by the intervention of Ambassador Tanaka, who appealed to Foreign Commisar Chicherin.

On December 4, 1926, a contract was initialled. The Japanese received forest concessions, totalling over 1 million hectares, in three regions (Shurukumu [?], Hajiya [?], and Murashiki [?]) for a period of six years, with the right to fell 7½ million cubic feet [?] (over 560,000 koku) of lumber a year.

Disagreement developed after the initialling of the contract in regard to payment for the concessions. In an attempt to control the financial transactions so as to prevent the fall of the value of the ruble in the Far Eastern Region, the Soviet side tried to change the provision that the remittance and conversion of business funds could be made either through the Soviet State Bank or through the branch of a foreign bank (i.e. the Vladivostok branch of the Bank of Korea) and limit all transactions to the Soviet State Bank. The Japanese regarded this as discrimination against the concessionaires and accused the Russians of bad faith. Eventually a compromise was reached: the body of the contract was modified in accordance with the Soviet demand, but a memorandum was attached in which the Concessions Bureau stated that the concessionaires could make use of the Bank of Korea so long as it continued the remittance and exchange of rubles (a right that the Soviet government could revoke if it felt the value of the currency threatened).

The forestry concession contract was finally signed on February 18, 1927, and in November of the same year the Roryō Ringyō Kumiai was succeeded by the incorporated Roryō Ringyō Kabushiki Kaisha 露領林業株式會社 (Russian Territory Forestry Company, Ltd.). Kadono Jukurō 門野重九郎, head of the former association became president of the new joint-stock company.[13]

Various other concessions were discussed. Viscount Gotō envisioned the development of rice paddy fields by Japanese peasants in the Lake Khanka region of the Maritime province. In November of 1925 he proposed to his own government the founding of the Kyokutō Takushoku Kabushiki Kaisha 極東拓植株式會社 (Far East Exploitation Co. Ltd.) and in May of 1927 handed to Ambassador Dovgalevskii a project for founding the Enkaishū Kaikon Kaisha 沿海州開墾會社 (Maritime Province Development of New Land Company).

On January 6, 1926, Ambassador Tanaka had told Foreign Commissar Chicherin that Japan was in need of more rice and strongly desired to see the development of rice cultivation in neighboring countries. Japanese enterprisers, he had said, were prepared to teach the technique of rice cultivation to Russian peasants so that Russian peasants themselves eventually could develop rice cultivation in Soviet territory. He proposed the development of mixed companies, and cited as an example the learning of rice cultivation by American farmers from the Japanese. Chicherin replied that the memory of the Japanese occupation and of the partisan struggles against the Japanese forces might hinder the harmonious cohabitation of Japanese agricultural workers with the native population in the Maritime Province. He wondered whether agricultural concessions might not fare better in Western Siberia, near Tomsk and Irkutsk, where there were no bitter feelings. Tanaka did not think so because of the great distance of the region from Japan.[14]

Gotō's proposal of May 1927 entailed a 75 year concession for over

860,000 hectares (over 2 million acres) of land. Counselor Besedovskii replied in August of the same year that the matter might be considered favorably if the term were reduced to 30 years and the area to under 10,000 hectares (under 25,000 acres) and if application were made to the Central Concessions Committee in Moscow through the Soviet Trade Mission in Tokyo, but the project never materialized.[15]

The conclusion of the oil and coal concession agreements evoked various comments in the Japanese press.

> In view of the wide difference existing between Russia and this country in respect of their national conditions, all negotiations that have been opened up to the present have been attended with peculiar difficulties [the *Japan Weekly Mail* observed, and reflected:] Similar difficulties are experienced by all countries more or less in their dealings with Russia. Indeed, very few countries have ever succeeded in concluding detailed agreements with that country.... When these facts are taken into due consideration, the conclusion of the concession agreements between Japan and Russia may well be counted a great success for the negotiators on both sides.[16]

It was clear that there would be many problems ahead and that not all of them would be due to the "wide differences" between the two countries. "Many of the Japanese semi-official concerns have done very badly in the past, partly because of their party connections and partly owing to the arbitrary management of their affairs by a few leaders," the *Japan Weekly Chronicle* paraphrased an *Asahi* editorial. "There are already sordied rumors afloat about the flotation of shares for the new companies, and the Tokyo journal hopes that those concerned will use special care to see that all matters are transacted squarely...."[17]

The *Yorodzu* warned Japanese businessmen "against the illusion into which they are apt to fall that there is every opportunity of making money in Northern Saghalien."

> They must know that the only profitable way is to carry on all

undertakings in that territory on a sound and solid basis, ever mindful of promoting Russo-Japanese economic *rapprochement*. Another important thing for the cultivation of close economic relations is that both peoples should learn to know each other. Some Russians are apt to look upon Japan as a protagonist of militarism, while, on the other hand, some Japanese regard Russia as if she were some devil conspiring to destroy Japan's national constitution. Neither view is correct. A better understanding of each other's national characteristics will greatly help their economic co-operation. The closer the economic relations between Japan and Russia, the better assured will be the permanent peace of the Far East. . . .[18]

CHAPTER NINE

Fishery Talks

THE fishery convention of 1907 had been signed for a period of twelve years; it expired in September of 1919. The Japanese, who at that time occupied Siberia, sought to extend the convention by agreements with local regimes. When local authorities in 1921 and 1922 rejected Japanese demands, Japanese fishermen resorted to unrestricted fishing as a means of protecting, if not expanding, their interests. In 1923, after the withdrawal of Japanese forces from Siberia and the inundation of the Pacific coast by the Bolsheviks, Japanese enterprisers negotiated a one year contract for the lease of fishery lots with the Soviet authorities at Vladivostok.[1]

On the eve of the fishing season of 1924 the Japanese press clamored for the resumption of unrestricted Japanese fishing in Soviet waters under the protection of Japanese warships if the Soviet Union did not accept Japanese demands and conclude the basic treaty. The Soviet Union responded by holding the auction of fishing lots without the Japanese. The strong Soviet position forced the Japanese government to make concessions. After it agreed to abide by Soviet conditions, a supplementary auction was held in which Japanese fishermen obtained 229 fishing lots and one crabbing lot. That day, on April 6, 1924, a temporary fishery agreement was signed for a period of three years. In the agreement the Japanese fishery people accepted the Soviet claim that they owed 2,750,000 yen for the use of fishery lots since the Russian revolution and committed themselves to pay 1,550,000 yen in a lump sum and the remainder over a period of three years with 8% interest, payment being guaranteed by the Bank of Chosen.[2]

The Basic Convention stipulated that the procedure established by the fishery agreement of 1924 be followed until the conclusion of a new fishery convention.³ The first plenary session of the Soviet-Japanese Conference for the Revision of the Fishery Convention of 1907 was held in Moscow on December 22, 1925. It was chaired by S. I. Aralov, delegate of the U.S.S.R. and member of the Collegium of the People's Commissariat for Foreign Affairs. Martin Ivanovich Latsis was Deputy Delegate of the U.S.S.R.; he was a member of the Collegium of the People's Commissariat for Agriculture. Ambassador Tanaka was the delegate of Japan. The delegates were assisted by seventeen experts—eight Russians and nine Japanese.ᵃ

A large part of the two hour conference was devoted to an exchange of greetings and the expression of hope that the question of the exploitation of the fishery resources of the U.S.S.R. could be settled to the mutual benefit of the peoples of both countries. Latsis stated that the fishery convention of 1907 would be used as the basis for discussion. At his suggestion the conference agreed to form a preparatory commission to determine the order of business of the conference and to prepare materials necessary for the sessions.⁴, ᵇ

Ambassador Tanaka presided over the second plenary session on January 4, 1926. The following order of business was adopted: (1) The sessions of the conference would be chaired alternately by the Japanese and Russian delegates or the deputy delegates. (2) The negotiations would be conducted in Japanese and Russian. (3) In addition to the delegates, experts and secretaries, only persons assisting in the conference in a technical capacity, such as interpreters, stenographers, etc. could be present at the sessions; the experts could speak only after

---

ᵃ G. N. Lashkevich, F. I. Andrianov, I. P. Babkin, N. A. Ergamyshev, M. A. Kozakov, G. A. Kryshov, N. G. Chernobaev, I. A. Chichaev, Yamazaki Jirō, Sako Shuichi, Nishi Haruhino, Shimada Masaharu, Miyakawa Funao, Matsumura Shinichirō, Koshida Tokujirō, Ide Masataka, Nakatani Sadayori.

ᵇ The preparatory commission consisted of Lashkevich, Chichaev, Andrianov, Kozakov, Babkin, Eragamyshev, Kryshov and Chernobaev for the Soviet side and Sako, Koshida, Shimada and Miyakawa for the Japanese side.

preliminary notice had been given to the other side. (4) Minutes of the sessions would be kept in Russian and Japanese; upon joint agreement they could be translated into English. (5) The minutes would be prepared by the general secretariat of the conference, consisting of two secretaries, one appointed by each side (Iagrin and Miyakawa). (6) The preparation of materials necessary for the sessions, the drawing up of the agenda and the preliminary examination of questions selected by the conference were left to the preparatory commission. (7) The preparatory commission was to present to the conference signed written reports of questions it had examined. (8) Press releases about the content and course of conference proceedings could be made only after joint agreement by the two delegates regarding the content and form of the releases. (9) Upon the signature by the two delegates of the new fishery convention, both delegations would sign the final protocol, certifying that article 3 of the basic treaty had been executed and that the convention of 1907 would be null and void the moment that the new fishery convention went into force.

At the second plenary session Latsis announced also the principles by which the Soviet delegates would be guided in the revision of the convention: (1) Japanese workers and Japanese employers of Russian workers must be subject to the Soviet labor code; furthermore, in order to provide gainful employment to local inhabitants, a definite number of Russian workers must be used in convention water fishery. (2) The fishing activity of the coastal population must not be hindered, because fishery was vital to their livelihood; the local inhabitants should enjoy special privileges and advantages. (3) Japanese enterprises could obtain fishery rights equal only to those of private citizens of the U.S.S.R.; by Soviet law the U.S.S.R.'s state enterprises and fishery cooperative had special rights. (4) Fishery must be set up on a rational basis to preserve the aquatic resources, which were basic to the economic development of the Russian Far East; the Soviet government reserved the right to impose any restrictions for the sake of conservation, the restrictions to be applied equally to all fishery enterprises.[5]

The aims of the imperial government in conducting the negotiations were: (1) to revise the provisions in the old treaty, which were burdensome or unfavorable to Japanese fishery people; (2) to supplement or revise provisions which were unclear; and (3) to modify provisions which had become dated in view of technical progress.[6]

At the third plenary session, on March 17, the Japanese replied to the principles communicated by Latsis. (1) They reserved judgment on the matter of extending the labor code to fishery until it was clear what effect this would have on fishery; as for the employment of a definite number of Russian citizens in convention water fishery, they felt that the enterprisers should be free to hire the most suitable persons, regardless of nationality. (2) While the Japanese agreed in principle that the local population enjoy privileges and advantages, they insisted that the latter be limited so as not to violate the rights and interests of the Japanese fishery people. (3) The Japanese objected to the special position of Soviet state fishery enterprises and the fishery cooperative, saying that it left the Japanese fishery enterprises in a most unfavorable and unstable position in regards to the obtaining of fishery ground leases, the paying of taxes, etc.; they wanted regulations that would apply fairly to all fishery enterprises, regardless of type and relationship to Soviet law. (4) The Japanese agreed that rational measures must be taken for the conservation of fishery resources, but insisted that they be determined jointly by both countries; they demanded also that the sea fishing enterprises be left free to determine the most appropriate measures, as sea fishing differed greatly in character from river and lake fishing.

Latis replied point by point: (1) It was doubtful that the application of the Soviet labor code to fishery would give course to serious disagreement; the Soviet delegation concurred that the special character of fishery in the Far Eastern region required special regulations in the regulation of labor. Provision for exceptions existed in the Soviet labor code and the Russians would be willing to consider all Japanese suggestions, particularly since the national customs of employees hired abroad must be taken into consideration. But Latsis reiterated the demand that a certain percentage of Soviet workers be employed in the Japanese enterprises; this was important in view of the unemployment which then existed in the U.S.S.R.; furthermore it was a condition required of all foreign enterprises admitted to the Soviet Union. It was not a matter of supplying the Japanese with unsuitable labor; they would always have the right to dismiss those who were not fit for such work. (2) Latsis accepted the Japanese demand that the privileges and advantages of the local population and settlers be limited so as not to violate Japanese rights; the question had been dealt with in the protocol attached to the convention of 1907. One would have to find a formula that would protect the rights of Japanese enterprisers, particularly their right to retain convention fishery lots. Latsis asserted that there was no danger of the local population eventually gaining the best fishery lots by virtue of their privileges, because this would be contrary to the fiscal interests of the U.S.S.R.; Soviet finances depended in part on the sums realized from the auction of the fishery lots. (3) The Soviet delegation felt that the matter of the rights of private and state enterprises must be studied by a commission of experts. While the state enterprises had certain privileges they also had certain obligations which the Japanese probably would not wish to assume. For example, the state enterprises in question paid to the People's Commissariat of Finances a tax of up to 80% of their income. The Soviet delegation felt that once a commission of experts had clarified the situation it would not be difficult to regulate the matter. (4) Latsis stated that the Soviet side was pleased to learn of Japanese willingness to cooperate in conservation measures and expressed the expectation that joint scientific work in this field would be of great benefit in the future. Yet the Soviet delegation felt that certain restrictions concerning fishing methods must exist for both Soviet and Japanese enterprises, and that the matter should be studied by a commission of experts; quite possibily the conditions put forth by the Soviet delegation would prove to be not burdensome for the Japanese enterprisers.

Tanaka expressed satisfaction with the Soviet reply and remarked that the views of both sides were drawing closer. The Japanese were delighted with the idea of setting up commissions of experts to study points 3 and 4 and felt that the two commissions should be joined into one. Tanaka named six Japanese experts to the commission, Latsis five

Russians; both delegates reserved the right to call in specialists on questions of a special character.[7]

Deputy Delegate Latsis was present at the fourth plenary session, which was held in Moscow on May 25, but Delegate Aralov had gone on leave and had been replaced by B. S. Stomoniakov, another member of the Collegium of the Foreign Secretariat. Stomoniakov expressed pleasure at being able to participate in the conclusion of a fishery convention, which was of enormous importance in the economic relations of the two countries. The two delegations had exchanged drafts of a new convention.[8] Stomoniakov stated that he hoped that the differences in the Soviet and Japanese drafts would not be insurmountable. Tanaka acknowledged that the two versions were far apart; it was necessary, he said, to seek a general line of agreement. At Tanaka's suggestion it was agreed that the commission of experts study the two drafts and try to find a common basis for discussion by the conference plenum. Should this prove impossible, the commission was to present the divergent views of the two sides to the plenum. Both delegates declared that they had instructed their experts to increase the tempo of the deliberations.[9]

At the fifth plenary session, on September 7, Stomoniakov, who chaired the session, announced that the commission of experts had partly harmonized the Soviet and Japanese convention drafts and protocols and had prepared a report to the plenum. The report was presented by Sako, the chief Japanese member of the commission.

Sako stated that the commission had deemed it necessary to amplify the drafts by preparing a number of declarations to be appended to the final protocol of the plenary session. The stipulations concerning the labor of Japanese workers on Japanese fishing lots had been formulated in a separate protocol, Protocol B, since they might be changed before the expiration of the convention. The commission had prepared a total of four documents for the plenum; a draft of the fishery convention itself; drafts of Protocols A and B, to be attached to the convention; and a draft of the final protocol of the conference.[10]

Sako pointed out that there had been agreement on over half of the articles. The Soviet Union would not levy duties on fish or aquatic products caught in its Far Eastern waters when destined for export to Japan (Article 5) nor impose on Japanese lease holders any restrictions on the methods for the preparation of fish and aquatic products from which Soviet citizens were exempt (Article 7). Both sides had concurred also on the issuance of navigation and health certificates to Japanese subjects by Soviet consular officers and Japanese authorities respectively for direct navigation from Japan to the fishery grounds (Article 8); they had agreed that Japanese subjects required no licenses for the export of fish or the import of fishing equipment (Article 9) and that they be placed on a footing of equality as respected the laws, regulations and ordinances concerning pisciculture (Article 10). Japan engaged not to levy any import duties on fish caught in Soviet Far Eastern waters (Article 12). The Soviet Union agreed to take into consideration Japanese habits and characteristics in the application of its laws and regulations regarding the protection and regulation of labor and to allow Japanese employees free passage between Japan and the fishery grounds as well as a share of catches in addition to regular wages and free medical aid (Article 13); she granted to Japanese subjects the same treatment as to Soviet citizens in the fishing industry (Article 14). Both sides had agreed that the convention be ratified and ratifications exchanged in Tokyo (Article 16). Sako stated that the above articles were being submitted to the plenum for approval, except that the question whether they should apply only to fish or to all aquatic products remained open for the present.

Sako declared that the article dealing with taxes, imports and fees levied in connection with the fishing industry (Article 4) was only tentative and needed further study and elaboration. The preamble of the convention as well as the articles dealing with the lease of fishery lots (Article 2), the right to make free use of the littoral within the limits of the fishery lots (Article 3), and the period of the convention had been harmonized by and large but could not be regarded as accepted, because of disagreement on individual points. No agreement had been reached on the first article, stipulating the regions where Japanese subjects could catch and prepare fish, and on the articles requiring the employment of a certain percentage of Soviet workmen (Article 6) and giving the Japanese the right to prepare fish and aquatic products in the landed lots set aside for them (Article 11). These articles were being submitted to the plenum in parallel formulation.

Sako announced that complete accord had been reached on the preliminary part and most of the articles of Protocol A, elaborating on the provisions of the fishery convention, and on the entire text of Protocol B, regarding the protection and regulation of Japanese labor. Protocol B and articles of Protocol A which had been fully accepted by the commission of experts were submitted to the plenum for approval; the others were presented for further discussion. Sako remarked that there had been almost complete agreement on the draft of the final protocol of the conference by the plenum, and that it too was being submitted for approval. Only the declaration regarding the buildings erected by Japanese subjects on fishery lots was still in dispute. Statements concerning taxes also had been adopted tentatively in private wording; the commission regarded them as merely the basis for further negotiation.

The following disagreements remained:

1. The Japanese experts deemed it necessary to make reference in the preamble of the convention to the revision of the fishery convention of 1907; the Soviet experts disagreed.
2. The Japanese experts deemed it necessary to stipulate the right of Japanese subjects to take aquatic products and to catch sea animals except fur-seals and sea-otters; the Soviet experts disagreed. (Article 1 of convention and Article 20 of Protocol A).
3. The Japanese experts deemed it necessary to stipulate the right of Japanese subjects to engage in fishery in the basin of the Amur river; the Soviet experts disagreed. (Article 1 of convention, Articles 1 and 3 of Protocol A)
4. The Soviet experts wished to mention that the fishing rights of Japanese subjects were limited to the mainland coastline of the U.S.S.R.; the Japanese experts opposed this.

(Article 1 of convention, Article 1 of Protocol A)
5. The Soviet experts wished to mention that the convention applied merely to those regions, in which the Japanese had until the present time actually engaged in fishery; the Japanese disagreed. (Article 1 of convention, Article 1 of Protocol A)
6. The Soviet experts wished to establish that Japanese subjects required concessions (i.e. special contracts) for canning fish; the Japanese experts objected to this. (Article 1 of convention, Article 21 of Protocol A)
7. The Soviet experts wished to state that the Soviet government had the right to give up to 35% of the existing fishery lots without auction to its state enterprises, cooperatives and the local population; the Japanese disagreed. (Article 2 of convention, Article 4 of Protocol A)
8. The Japanese experts wished to mention in Article 3 of the convention that Japanese subjects had the right to obtain littoral lots for the preparing and preserving of the fish, caught on ships; the Soviet experts felt that the Japanese could have such rights only in conformity with Article 11 of the convention.
9. The Soviet experts wanted to stipulate the obligation of Japanese subjects to hire a certain percentage of Soviet workers; the Japanese experts were against this. (Article 6 of convention, Article 10 of Protocol A)
10. The Japanese experts favored stating that the convention would remain in force for 12 years; the Soviet experts considered that the convention should be concluded for four years. (Article 15 of convention)
11. The Soviet experts desired to mention that the bay of the city of Okhotsk was not open to Japanese fishermen; the Japanese experts were against this. (Article 1 of Protocol A)
12. The Japanese wanted to state that the Soviet Union would not close lots once they were opened; the Soviet experts

objected, though they were willing to state that the U.S.S.R. would not decrease the total area of fishery. (Article 8 of Protocol A)

13. The Soviet experts wished to indicate that the fishery lots would be leased the first time after the conclusion of the convention for a period of one year, thereafter every time for periods of three years. The Japanese experts felt that those lots which would be worked for the first time should be leased for one year; all other lots should be leased for five years. The commission believed that this matter could easily be resolved once agreement had been reached on the length of the duration of the convention. (Article 6 of Protocol A)

14. The commission did not give final consideration to Article 18 of Protocol A, feeling that the question it had raised regarding the rights of Japanese subjects should be decided after a decision had been made about articles 2, 4, and 11 of the convention. It presented Article 18 in the variant versions, proposed by the experts of both sides.[11]

The conference approved the report presented by Sako and confirmed the text of articles 5, 7–10, 12–14, and 16 of the convention, the preliminaries and articles 2, 5, 7, 9, 11–17, 19, and 22 of Protocol A, all of Protocol B, and the entire Final Protocol. No decision was reached concerning aquatic products. Tanaka and Stomoniakov agreed to negotiate further regarding the variant versions of the convention and protocol articles which had been submitted in parallel construction, referring them back to the commission of experts as the need might arise.

The convention article about taxes (Article 4) and a corresponding statement in the Final Protocol were returned to the commission of experts for further study as was the draft regarding the activity of Japanese canneries, presented by the delegates of both countries.

Kolchanovskii, the chief Soviet member of the commission of experts, reported on the text of a press release about the state of the negotiations;

the committee approved it as the official communiqué of the delegates of both countries.[12]

On January 15, 1927, Vice Minister Debuchi told Chargé d'Affaires Besedovskii that there remained only one point beyond the possibility of agreement, namely the desire of Soviet state enterprises, which were to receive 20% of the fishery lots, to participate also in the auctions of the remaining fishery lots, something to which the Japanese government could never agree. The other issues, Debuchi felt, could be worked out.[13]

On January 18 Karakhan instructed Besedovskii to tell Debuchi in his own name that he must not be well informed of the course of the negotiations if he thought that there was only one point of serious disagreement left between them. Besedovskii was to state to Debuchi that according to information he had received from Moscow there were serious disagreements also concerning the Amur Basin, taxes, canneries, the period of the convention, etc. Besedovskii was to assert that while the Soviet side was constantly making concessions in the lengthy meetings that took place almost every day, the Japanese kept presenting increasingly steep demands and to go back on concessions already made. The Commissariat of Foreign Affairs was prepared to ask the government for some sort of compromise regarding the participation of state enterprises in the auctions, but could not present this issue to the government without an account of the state of the negotiations as a whole. The decisions of the government would depend to a large extent on the balance of the negotiations. It was essential, therefore, to reduce the areas of disagreement. The Japanese government could facilitate this, Besedovskii was to point out, by instructing its delegation to make some concessions.[14]

Half a year passed between the fifth and sixth plenary sessions of the fishery conference; the sixth plenary session was held in Moscow on February 19, 1927. The commission of experts had been busy in the interim and the delegates had conferred on various problems. Tanaka, who chaired the sixth session, announced that full agreement had been reached on a number of articles; on some there had been partial agreement, but some remained completely unresolved. Tanaka proposed that the conference confirm the balance of the negotiations, instructions to be sought from Tokyo and Moscow regarding the articles on which agreement had not been reached. They decided to use the parallel texts as basis for negotiation after receipt of instructions.[15]

The variant versions presented at the sixth conference were as follows:

ARTICLE I

(Japan)

The Union of Soviet Socialist Republics grants to Japanese subjects, in conformity with the stipulations of the present Convention, the right to catch, to take and to prepare all kinds of fish and aquatic products, except fur-seals and sea-otters, along the Union coasts of the Japan Sea, the Okhotsk Sea and the Behring Sea, with the exception of rivers and inlets. The inlets comprised in this exception are enumerated in Article 1 of the Protocol (A) attached to the present Convention.

(U.S.S.R.)

The Union of Soviet Socialist Republics concedes to the subjects of Japan the right to catch and to prepare fish, along the mainland coast-line of the seas of Japan, Okhotsk and Behring, extending from the southern entrance of the Anadyr Liman (Cape Geta) to the Cape Povorotny, with the exception of the Amur Liman, and rivers and bays. The bays subject to the said exception are enumerated in Article 1 of the Protocol (A) hereby annexed.

ARTICLE 2

(Japan)

Japanese subjects are at liberty to engage in catching, taking and preparing fish and aquatic products in the fishery lots lying both in the sea and on shores which are specially designated for the purpose of catching, taking and preparing fish and aquatic products. The lease of the said fishery lots shall be granted by public auction, without any discrimination being made between Japanese subjects and citizens of the Union of Soviet Socialist Republics.

It is understood, however, that the lease of the said fishery lots may also be granted not by auction, but by special arrangements under agreement to be arrived at between the Japanese Government and the Government of the Union of Soviet Socialist Republics.

(U.S.S.R.)

Japanese subjects are at liberty to engage in catching and preparing fish in the fishery lots lying both in the sea and on shores which are specially designated for the purpose of catching and preparing fish.

The lease of the said fishery lots, with the exception of those lots to be transmitted by the measure specially provided for in the Convention and the instruments attached thereto, shall be granted by public auction, without any discrimination being made between citizens of the U.S.S.R. and Japanese subjects.

The U.S.S.R., however, reserves the right to transmit without auction separate fishery lots situated within the regions comprised under the stipulations of the Convention, for exploitation by the state enterprises of the Union, one hundred per cent of whose capital belong to the Government, provided, that fishery lots, leased in accordance with the foregoing paragraph, may be transmitted only after the expiration of their lease-term.

(Joint)

The aforesaid auctions shall take place at Vladivostok in February every year, and the dates and localities designated for this purpose, as well as the necessary details relating to the lease of various fishery lots to be sold, shall be officially notified to the

Japanese Consular officer at Vladivostok at least two months before the auctions.

With regard to fishery lots for which there shall have been no successful bidder, they shall again be put to auction within fifteen days, but not earlier than five days, after the preceding auction.

Catching of (whales) and codfish, as well as of all fish (and aquatic products) which cannot be caught in special lots is permitted to Japanese subjects on board sea-going vessels furnished with a special licence.

ARTICLE 3

(Japan)

Japanese subjects who have obtained fishery lots in conformity with the provisions of Article 2 of the present Convention shall have, within the limits of those fishery lots, the right to make free use of the littoral. They may there carry out necessary repairs to their vessels and nets, haul them ashore, and land, prepare and preserve their catches (and collections). For these purposes they shall be at liberty to erect there buildings, warehouses, huts and drying-sheds or to remove the same.

(U.S.S.R.)

In case the fishing industry by vessels furnished with a special licence calls for the use of shores for its exercise, necessary landed lots shall, upon application therefore, be let to Japanese subjects engaged in the said industry.

ARTICLE 6

(Japan)

No restriction shall be established with regard to the nationality of the employees of Japanese subjects engaged in catching, (taking) and preparing fish (and aquatic products) in the districts specified in Article 1 of the present Convention.

(U.S.S.R.)

However, the number of the workmen-citizens of the U.S.S.R. engaged in the fisheries shall not be under a certain ratio to the whole number of the workmen engaged, as defined in the Art. 22 of the Protocol (A) hereby annexed.

ARTICLE 11

(Japan)

Japanese subjects are at liberty to engage in the preparation of fish (and aquatic products) in the landed lots let to them outside of the limits of the districts specified in Article 1 of the present Convention, always complying with the laws, regulations and ordinances which are or may be in force and applicable to all foreigners in the Union of Soviet Socialist Republics.

ARTICLE 15

(Japan)

The present Convention shall remain in force for ten years and shall be renewed or revised at the end of every twelve years.

(U.S.S.R.)

The present Convention shall remain in force for six years and shall be renewed or revised at the end of every six years.

(Joint)

Either of the High Contracting Parties may give notice to the other of its desire to revise the present Convention, twelve months before the expiration of the period abovementioned. Negotiations for the revision shall be concluded within the said twelve months.

(Japan)

Should neither of the High Contracting Parties give notice for such revision, the present Convention shall remain in force for the period of another twelve years.

(U.S.S.R.)

Should neither of the High Contracting Parties give notice for such revision, the present Convention shall remain in force for the period of another six years.[16]

Stomoniakov stated that the note appended to Article 21 of Protocol A made it possible for Japanese subjects to open small canneries without concession procedure. The Soviet government did not change its position that the fishery convention did not give Japanese subjects the right to build and operate canning factories; it merely tried to help meet the needs of small Japanese enterprisers, not wishing to put Japanese subjects into conditions less favorable than private persons in the Soviet Union.

Tanaka retorted that his government felt that the right to prepare fish entailed the right to can it and to operate factories for this purpose; it considered canning one of the ways of preparing fish. He would be willing to recommend to his government acceptance of a text that could be worked out jointly for the practical solution of this question. A compromise was approved by the plenum in the form of a statement made in connection with the confirmation of Article 5 of Protocol C which laid down the basic conditions of concession contracts with Japanese fishing enterprisers concerning the right of operating canning factories. The statement declared that while the Soviet delegate assumed that interested Japanese subjects must ask the main Concession Committee of the Council of People's Commissars of the U.S.S.R. before the concession treaty expired to open negotiations regarding the renewal of existing treaties or the conclusion of new treaties and that these negotiations would lay the foundations for further operation of the canning factories, the Japanese delegate felt that the matter must be considered following the expiration of the concession treaty as a revision of the fishery convention. In view of the fact that this difference of opinion had no practical meaning at the moment and since the delegates did not wish to delay the conclusion of the fishery convention, the statement concluded, the delegates had agreed to leave the question open for further negotiations, as provided in paragraph 2 of Article 5 of Protocol C.

The conference appointed an editorial commission (Kolchanovskii, Kozakov, Ergameshev, Sako, Koshida, Nishi, and Miyakawa). Tanaka remarked that the most important phase of the conference's work had passed, and that remaining differences would soon be resolved. Stomoniakov added the hope that Tanaka and he would do everything in their power to sign the convention before the beginning of the approaching auction of fishery lots. Tanaka agreed.[17]

On March 17 Stomoniakov cabled to the Soviet chargé d'affaires *ad interim* in Tokyo, that agreement had been reached on the question of the Amur basin by giving to the Soviet Union the unrestricted right to grant fishery lots to its state and cooperative enterprises as well as to the local population without auction; the question of employing Soviet workers had been resolved by means of a joint declaration and the willingness to conclude an agreement concerning the percentage of such workers, who until then were to be hired on an equal basis with Japanese workers. Agreement had been reached also on the question of the protection of labor in canneries; the Japanese had accepted the Soviet conditions. In the matter of state enterprises, the Japanese had consented to a series of Soviet demands concerning the method of selecting lots, the period of negotiations, the reservation of new fishery lots and the obligations of the state enterprises toward private enterprisers.

Disagreement remained regarding enterprises with a minority of state capital. The Japanese proposed that the Soviet government consult with the Japanese government concerning the method by which such enterprises could obtain fishery lots; the Soviet side insisted on the right of these enterprises to participate in the auctions. As for the cooperative, Tanaka proposed on his own that it nominally be given the right to take part in the auctions, with the Soviet government pledging, however, to consult with the Japanese government in the event of need regarding other methods by which the cooperative would obtain fishery lots. Tanaka pointed out that if the cooperative did not present a threat to the Japanese at the auction, its participation in the auctions would not be cancelled. The Soviets on the other hand continued to insist that the cooperative have an unlimited right to participate in auctions.

The question of new canneries remained unsettled, but Tanka promised to make a new proposal. The Soviet Union refused to allow unlimited establishment of canneries; Stomoniakov wrote that the Soviet proposal of 20 canning factories was fully sufficient. In view of Tanaka's stubborness, the Soviet side had proposed to leave the question of new canning factories open, agreeing to regulate it by the fishing season of 1928 while permitting the construction of two or three factories as concessions in 1927; Tanaka had not given a final reply.

No definite agreement had been reached on the question of that year's auction. "We categorically rejected any idea of a make-believe auction, proposed by Tanaka, and feel the practice of 1924 and especially of 1925 to have been the most normal auction with the state enterprises participating," Stomoniakov cabled. "The Japanese object strenuously, believing that there had been collusion [against them] in those years and that in 1927 they should receive all their former fishery lots. I proposed either to schedule a normal auction immediately or to await the signing of the convention, pointing out that I was doing so privately, since the fixing of auctions was the internal business of the U.S.S.R."

"The question of new canning factories is the most difficult," Stomoniakov concluded, "since the Japanese demand boils down to placing the Japanese in a more privileged position than our citizens, who according to our basic laws do not have the right to build and operate factories. We are waiting for a compromise proposal of Tanaka."[18]

On March 22 the Foreign Commissariat informed the Japanese Embassy in Moscow that the Soviet Union, in response to a request submitted by the Japanese Ambassador that the auction of fishery lots for the catching of herring and crabs be fixed as soon as possible, was willing to announce immediately the auction of such fishery lots. It expressed confidence that the fishery convention would be signed soon, a statement echoed by the Japanese embassy on the 26th, when it thanked the Commissariat for having met its request.[19]

Yet on March 22, the day after writing the note to the Japanese embassy and before dispatch of the Japanese reply, Chicherin telegraphed to the Soviet chargé in Tokyo: "We are getting the impression that Ambassador Tanaka is not inclined to hurry with the fishery convention. Indicate to Debuchi that he carry out his promise about concessions regarding the convention and put pressure on Tanaka so that we sign it as soon as possible. Point out during the talks that the fixing of auction for [fishery lots for] humpbacked salmon [*gorbusha*] and Siberian salmon [*keta*] must take place in two to three weeks and that it would be desirable to sign the convention by that time."[20]

On June 30 Stomoniakov communicated to Tanaka the decision of the Soviet government: (1) The Soviet Union agreed to give [to the Japanese] the right to build and operate an unlimited number of factories for the period of the lease of the respective fishery lots, going further than the Japanese demand that such permission be granted for 25 factories. (2) The Soviet Union agreed to exclude the point about labor from Protocol 3 and to delete the demand about the relief of workers in factories; it did not agree, on the other hand, to give to the factories in case of obstruction of fish conventional rights and to fix the pay for overtime work at not more than 50% of the base salary. It had been pointed out to Tanaka that both these conditions applied to the catching of fish, since it was not possible in the catching of fish to operate on an eight hour day; but in factories, if there were ice boxes, the working day could be normal, and overtime work and its compensation must be regulated by agremeent between the enterprisers and the Labor Commissariat (Narkomtrud) in Khabarovsk. (3) The Soviet Union was lowering considerably the amount deducted per crate of canned goods and was prepared to decrease the total sum of duties on fishery to 30% of the lease fee. (4) As for the cooperative, the Soviet government wished to leave in the convention the stipulation that it would receive lots by auction; it would, however, commit itself in a separate note to enter into negotiations about a different method of obtaining lots, if the Japanese would find in practice that the cooperative was in a privileged position. (5) Similarly the Soviet Union wanted to leave in the convention the right of enterprises with a minority of state capital to take part in auctions, while agreeing in an exchange of notes that in the event of the appearance of such enterprises before the fixing of a means of their obtaining lots the Soviet Union would consult with the Japanese government whether to give them lots with or without auction. (6) The Soviet government was prepared to declare in the protocol of the plenum that the Tsentrosoiuz (the central union of consumers' cooperatives) did not intend to engage in fishery in the convention region during the period that the convention was in effect.

Reporting the above decision of the Soviet government to Ambassador Dovgalevskii in Tokyo on June 30, Chicherin commented that Tanaka had received this information "quite indifferently" and declined to discuss it. Nor had he deemed the time ripe to listen to the smaller decisions of the Soviet government concerning other outstanding issues. "The general impression," Karakhan cabled, "is [of] an unwillingness to conclude the convention now. The negotiations will be renewed upon receipt by Tanaka of the opinion of the Japanese government regarding the above-mentioned proposals."

> See the premier [Karakhan instructed Dovgalevskii], and announce to him that having made the stated significant concessions on the most important questions in dispute, we expect that the Japanese government, if it at all wants to conclude the convention, will make a concession to us concerning the cooperative. Point out that our proposals concerning the cooperative and mixed companies concur with the proposals made by Tanaka in the preceding phase of the negotiations but later retracted. To deprive the cooperative of the right to participate in the auctions would embitter the local population and would turn it against the Japanese. The right of the cooperative to participate in the

auctions is important for us from the point of view of internal politics and is dictated also by the long-term interests of Japan. Insist on as quick as possible a decision: one must either conclude the convention or postpone the negotiations. The question is so important that you must specially see Premier Tanaka.[21]

On October 10, 1927, the fishery convention and the attached documents were initialled by Karakhan and Tanaka. "In view of the fact that the above-mentioned texts received the prior approval of the Japanese government, the receipt by Mr. Tanaka of the formal plenary powers for the conclusion of the convention is expected within the next few days, when its signature will follow," *Izvestiia* announced on October 11 optimistically.[22] Karakhan wrote to Ambassador Dovgalevskii on the same day that Tanaka merely awaited the plenary powers to sign the convention. As Tanaka had told him figuratively: "You and I can take off on a vacation, leaving here only our right hands for the signature." Karakhan added that Tanaka had raised the question of fishery grounds not as an official demand of the Japanese government, but as an unofficial desire. "After the initialling our position has become stronger," Karakhan informed Dovgalevskii, "and gives you the necessary strength to decline all new proposals and to declare that the Japanese government is responsible for the delay in signing [the convention.]"[23]

Unperturbed, the Japanese advanced new demands. They felt that later difficulties could be avoided if agreement were reached before the signature of the convention on its enforcement in regard to the fishery areas of the state enterprises and fishery lots connected with the existing canneries; the Soviets believed that the matter raised by the Japanese was a needless complication.[24] Eager to break the deadlock, Premier Tanaka asked Viscount Gotō to approach the Russian government.

Old and feeble though he was after a stroke, Gotō had been planning a private visit to the U.S.S.R. ostensibly to look at the new Russia and observe the results of the New Economic Policy. The underlying reasons for his one month visit to Moscow (from December 22, 1927, to January

21, 1928) were to confer with Soviet leaders about China and about economic concessions in the Russian Far East.

At Tanaka's request Gotō called on Deputy Foreign Commissar Karakhan on January 8, 1928, in order to ask what was holding up signature of the fishery convention. Karakhan replied that the Soviet government could not accept any conditions for the signing of the protocol; he insisted on its signature without any conditions. He added that no additional safeguards for Japanese fishery people were necessary, because the convention itself stated that the Soviet government would consult with the Japanese government before taking back any fishery lots.

Gotō replied that the Japanese government insisted that fishery grounds then being worked by the Japanese remain in their hands; he himself realized that such a demand complicated matters, yet he reported this since the Japanese government had so decided and wanted to know the opinion of the Soviet government directly. He underlined that the Soviet position was officially correct, and that the Japanese government acted in the present case under the duress of pressure from fishery enterprisers and from Minister of Agriculture Yamamoto Teijirō. It was essential for the Japanese government from the point of purely internal political considerations to satisfy the fishery people.

Karakhan responded that he had an idea, but did not know whether it would be acceptable to his own government, namely to declare orally at the time of signature that in allocating lots for the state economy the Soviet government would keep in mind the interests of the Japanese fishery enterprisers within the limits of the convention being signed. Gotō stated that he merely wanted to inform himself about the state of the fishery convention and to assist in bringing the matter to a conclusion by bringing influence to bear on Tanaka and the Japanese government. He said that he would talk to Tanaka and if he found it convenient and purposeful he would undertake some steps to bring about the signature of the convention.[25, c]

---

[c] Japanese sources corroborate that Gotō "interceded with the authorities of both countries in an individual capacity." (Tanaka, p. 139)

On January 11 Gotō brought to Karakhan the draft of the following declaration: "The Government of the Union of Soviet Socialist Republics, recognizing the economic status obtained by Japanese subjects in the fishing industry in the regions stipulated by the Fishery Convention, is prepared to see to it that the existing interests of the Japanese subjects will not be harmed and will not propose in general to reserve for exploitation by state enterprises any fishery lot, being worked by Japanese subjects in the year 1927."

The Soviet Union felt that it could not agree to leave all the fishery lots formerly exploited by the Japanese in Japanese hands. At the same time, in order not to delay further the signature of the convention, the Soviet government on January 14 confirmed the text of a modified formula, which Karakhan on January 16 handed to Professor Yasugi [Sadatoshi of Tokyo University?] for transmittal to Gotō. The Soviet version read: "The Government of the Union of Soviet Socialist Republics, recognizing the great economic importance of fishery, in which Japanese subjects engage in regions stipulated by the fishery convention, is prepared to take into consideration that in conformity with the said convention no harm be done to the reasonable and legal interests of Japanese subjects." In handing the statement to Yasugi, Karakhan asked that he convey to Gotō that the formula had been accepted by the Soviet government after prolonged discussion and that it deemed it unnecessary to supplement the convention, which had already been initialled.

Gotō hastened to the Foreign Commissariat the same day to declare that the Soviet formula was unacceptable and that his formula of January 11 must be used instead. Tanaka called on Karakhan later in the day, on January 16, and handed him a new, even more specific formula, in which the Soviet government pledged "in so far as possible" with few exceptions not to offer to reserve for exploitation by state enterprises fishery lots worked by Japanese subjects in 1927 and declared itself ready "in addition to the stipulations in the said Convention (in so far as possible) to see to it that the area of fishery activity of Japanese subjects would not be decreased."[26]

On January 19 Karakhan asked Tanaka to come to his office. He informed Tanaka that the Japanese formula conveyed through Gotō was unacceptable and that the Soviet government stuck to its own formula, presented to Gotō on the 16th. If the Soviet formula were accepted, the convention could be signed immediately. Karakhan explained that the Soviet government had gone as far as it could in the convention and could make no further concessions. Tanaka made no effort to persuade Karakhan; he merely stated that he tried to find a way out of the impasse regardless of which side was right or wrong. The Japanese government had granted full powers to Gotō and had thus drawn him into the matter. It had consented to the signature of the convention, leaving it up to him and Gotō to agree on an acceptable formula in Moscow. Tanaka said that the formula he himself had presented could be modified so as to make it acceptable to the Soviet side. He argued that the Japanese formula did not exceed the convention and if the Soviets thought it did, it could be revised accordingly. Indeed he tried to alter his formula so as to approximate it to the Soviet version. He feared that the simple rejection of the Japanese formula might make a "bad impression" and have an adverse effect on the chances of concluding the convention and on Soviet-Japanese relations in general. Tanaka stated that he did not insist that the formula be part of the convention or be official in character; an informal letter addressed to him would be sufficient. But however much Tanaka asked that the Soviet government reconsider its rejection of the Japanese proposal, Karakhan replied that there were no new facts to justify this.[27]

The following day, on January 20, Tanaka called on Foreign Commissar Chicherin to ask if he had anything to add about the formula concerning fishery lots. Chicherin replied no; the Soviet government regarded its own formulation as binding and final.

Tanaka declared that he had come to point out the seriousness of the present moment in Soviet-Japanese relations. Just now there was an attempt to bring about a rapprochement with the Soviet Union. But should this extremely important and favorable moment be lost, the opposite tendency would be strengthened again, and these tendencies would grow increasingly; it was not merely a matter of the fishery convention but of Russo-Japanese relations in general.

It was extremely dangerous in politics to miss the [right] moment, Tanaka asserted. In given periods some tendency begins to develop, but if this tendency leads to failure the opposite tendency is strengthened again and in view of the missed moment such opposite tendencies can dominate for a long time. Sometimes an issue that seems of secondary importance may play a determining role when it comes to the question as to whether the right moment has been missed or not. Gotō's visit to the Soviet Union was one of these favorable moments, that could have unfavorable consequences if it were missed. It was as if Japan stood at the crossroads, and the voyage of Gotō was of the greatest importance for directing Japan to the road friendly toward the Soviet Union. Gotō's voyage was of decisive significance for the development of good relations between the two countries. He was leaving the next day. He had striven most energetically to reach an agreement with the Soviet Union. He was extremely worried about this question, since if the matter intrusted to him would end in the rupture of the negotiations, it would be a blow to his entire mission and have opposite effects. He was very well known in Japan and all of Japan was watching the outcome of his visit.

Tanaka asserted that both Gotō and he himself were deeply disappointed that Gotō's friendly efforts had not led to success. Both had stated that their formulas were subject to change. Karakhan had refused to discuss the formulas in detail. Could Chicherin not state what was objectionable in them so that they could be modified accordingly?

Chicherin replied that there were three objections to the Japanese formulas: (1) the assigning of specific fishery lots to state enterprises; (2) the specific assigning of the present lots to Japanese fishery enterprisers; and (3) the fact that change was proposed after the convention had been concluded and initialled. Chicherin added that he was not empowered to negotiate concerning these points, but had listed them because he felt that he could not leave Tanaka's question unanswered.

Tanaka denied that Japan wished to do any of the above, and suggested that Chicherin make any necessary changes and add a statement to the effect that neither side would get any new rights not stated in the convention. Chicherin retorted that Tanaka himself had advised them before Gotō's arrival not to give ground. Tanaka jumped up in surprise and said that that was a mistake; that he had not and could not have said any such thing. How would a Japanese ambassador tell another government that it should not make concessions to the Japanese government? What he had said was that when Chicherin would talk to Gotō, he should give him a clear answer—yes or no—rather than to evade the issue or delay an answer. He had urged a clear answer not a negative one.

When Chicherin asked why the Japanese had not proposed inclusion of the provisions while the treaty was being negotiated, Tanaka replied that such questions were useless, for they did not alter the situation which had arisen since and made the addition necessary.

> I take the liberty of pointing out to the Ambassador [Chicherin stated impatiently], that the whole course of negotiations with Japan has left a strong aftertaste. Japan made proposals and then took them back. Japan came to an agreement with us on some points and the next day advanced new demands, which altered everything. It is not so with us, our word is a firm word. If we make a promise, we keep it. . . . Now the ambassador says that one must take another little step, and everything will be alright. It was the same thing all the time. We made concessions and the ambassador thereafter came and said that we must take another little step. Finally after so many efforts the treaty was concluded. It contains a mass of concessions on our part. The population of the [Russian] Far East is outraged by our concessions. All local authorities protest against our having made so many concessions, and after all this has been brought to an end, the ambassador appears and demands yet another step. This means that everything has to be brought to an end and that we then must begin all over again from the beginning. Let the ambassador

think for himself how this reflects on the attitude of our political leaders toward these questions.

Tanaka refused to get into an argument about this with Chicherin; as he said, he could not criticize his own government. He returned to the significance of Gotō's trip; it was a symbol, a turning point in Soviet-Japanese relations, designed to bring about a turn in Japanese policy favorable toward Russia. He likened it to the voyage of Marquis Itō Hirobumi to St. Petersburg in 1901 and warned that the failure of the mission would give hostile forces in Japan a new impetus.[d] Tanaka accused the Soviet Union of ruining everything by refusing to come to an agreement with Gotō. "The price is very high. I deeply fear the consequences."[e]

Chicherin reiterated that he could not ask his government to reconsider; its decision was final.

"Is it possible that you do not want to help me?" Tanaka asked in desperation.

"General Tanaka, your premier, can help you," Chicherin replied unmoved.

"Truly only General Tanaka?"

"Of course, only General Tanaka, as it is up to him to preserve what we have agreed upon."

Tanaka asked Chicherin how he could be so strict and stonehearted, and went over the same arguments again and again until Chicherin told him that it was like being on a merry-go-round. Tanaka replied

---

[d] Russian unwillingness to negotiate with Itō seriously, contributed to the formation of the Anglo-Japanese alliance and eventually to the outbreak of the Russo-Japanese War.

[e] On his return to Japan Gotō had some criticism of the Japanese side. Speaking of the need to conclude a commercial agreement with the U.S.S.R. and to solve various outstanding issues and above all to develop the natural resources of Siberia, Gotō complained that the Japanese people showed "more zeal over political squabbles than on the question of bread and butter." (*Japan Weekly Chronicle*, February 16, 1928)

gloomily that Chicherin's observation was very funny but of little consolation.

Chicherin told Tanaka that when the question was being discussed by the Soviet government he had stated that the Japanese side was willing to declare that this formula did not go beyond the convention. The other members of the government then had asked him for what purpose the Japanese needed the formula, if it contained nothing that went beyond the treaty.

"You are too logical," Tanaka retorted. "In politics not everything is that logical. If we need some formula for internal political reasons that does not mean that the formula must go beyond the treaty. If one is to reason as you are, in such a case your formula of January 14 [transmitted on the 16th] is also superfluous. By agreeing to it you have broken the steel front of your logic."

"The purpose of our formula of January 14 was to convey our good will," Chicherin answered. "This is a specific purpose."

Chicherin agreed to see Gotō the following day, but warned that he would tell him the same thing. Tanaka departed with the comment that he was leaving deeply shaken and full of despair.[28]

The next day, on January 21, Tanaka informed Karakhan that the Japanese government had agreed to the Soviet formula and that he was prepared to sign the convention. They decided that the signing take place on Monday, January 23, at 9 A.M. In cabling this to Ambassador Troianovskii in Tokyo, Karakhan commented that although the efforts of Gotō had played a certain part in hastening the signature, the major impetus had been given apparently by internal political developments in Japan—the dissolution of the Diet and the calling of general elections for February 20.[29]

The final, seventh plenary session was held in Moscow on January 23, 1928. It was the culmination of two years of negotiation, including over 160 meetings—5 gatherings of the preparatory committee, seven plenary sessions, about 81 meetings between the two plenipotentiaries and some 71 meetings of the technical experts.[30] Stomoniakov had been replaced as chief delegate and plenipotentiary by Karakhan, who had signed the basic treaty of 1925. Latsis, who had co-signed the basic treaty, had participated from the very beginning. Present also on the Russian side were People's Commissar for Foreign Affairs Chicherin; Aralov, who had been the chief Soviet delegate at the outset of the conference and had become a member of the Presidium of the Higher Soviet of the People's [Popular] Economy; A.V. Sabanin, chief of the economic-legal section of the People's Commissariat for Foreign Affairs; B. N. Mel'nikov, Chief of the Far Eastern Section of the People's Commisariat for Foreign Affairs, as well as five experts and a secretary (I. Iu. Tsalem-chuk). Tanaka and seven experts represented the Japanese side. The delegates together examined the definitive texts of the fishery convention, three protocols (A, B, and C), one Final Protocol with two annexes and four exchanges of notes. After agreeing on all texts and the contents therein, the plenipotentiaries signed the documents and affixed their seals.[31]

CHAPTER TEN

The Fishery Convention

THE official English text of the Fishery Convention between Japan and the U.S.S.R., in the wording communicated by the director of the Imperial Japanese Office accredited to the League of Nations, was as follows:

His Majesty the Emperor of Japan and the Central Executive Committee of the Union of Soviet Socialist Republics,[a] for the purpose of concluding a Fishery Convention in conformity with the provisions of Article 3 of the Convention embodying Basic Rules of the Relations between Japan and the Union of Soviet Socialist Republics concluded at Peking on January 20th, 1925, have named their respective Plenipotentiaries, that is to say:

His Majesty the Emperor of Japan:

Tokichi Tanaka, Ambassador Extraordinary and Plenipotentiary to the Union of Soviet Socialist Republics, Jushii, a member of the First Class of the Imperial Order of the Sacred Treasure;

The Central Executive Committee of the Union of Soviet Socialist Republics:

Lev Mikhailovich Karakhan, People's Deputy Commissary for

---

[a] The preamble of the Soviet text reverses the order in the first sentence. It begins: "The Central Executive Committee of the Union of Soviet Socialist Republics and His Majesty the Emperor of Japan. . . ." (Japanese Archives, Russo-Japanese Treaties, p. 32/56)

Foreign Affairs of the Union of Soviet Socialist Republics, and

Martin Ivanovitch Lacis [Latsis] a member of the Collegium of the People's Commissariat for Agriculture of the Russian Socialist Federative Soviet Republic;

Who, after having communicated to each other their respective Full Powers, found to be in good and due form, have agreed upon the following Articles:

ARTICLE I

The Union of Soviet Socialist Republics grants to Japanese subjects, in conformity with the stipulations of the present Convention, the right to catch, to take and to prepare all kinds of fish and aquatic products, except fur-seals and sea-otters, along the coasts of the possessions of the Union of Soviet Socialist Republics in the Japan, Okhotsk and Behring Seas, with the exception of rivers and inlets. The inlets comprised in this exception are enumerated in Article I of the Protocol (A) attached to the present Convention.

ARTICLE II

Japanese subjects are at liberty to engage in catching, taking and preparing fish and aquatic products in the fishery lots, lying both in the sea and on shore, which are specially designated for that purpose. The lease of the said fishery lots shall be granted by public auction, without any discrimination being made between Japanese subjects and citizens of the Union of Soviet Socialist Republics.

It is understood, however, that, as an exception to the foregoing, those fishery lots for which the Governments of the two High Contracting Parties have so agreed may be leased without auction.

The auction of fishery lots shall take place at Vladivostok in February every year, and the date and locality designated for this

THE FISHERY CONVENTION 273

purpose, as well as the necessary details relating to the lease of various fishery lots to be sold, shall be officially notified to the Japanese Consular officer at Vladivostok at least two months before the auction.

With regard to fishery lots for which there shall have been no successful bidder, they shall again be put up to auction within fifteen days, but not earlier than five days, after the preceding auction.

The catching of whales and codfish, as well as of all the fish and aquatic products which cannot be caught or taken in special lots is permitted to Japanese subjects on board sea-going vessels furnished with a special licence.

ARTICLE III

The Japanese subjects who have obtained the lease of fishery lots in conformity with the provisions of Article II of the present Convention shall have, within the limits of those fishery lots, the right to make free use of the littoral. They may there carry out necessary repairs to their boats and nets, haul them ashore, and land, prepare and preserve their catches and collections. For these purposes they shall be at liberty to erect there buildings, warehouses, huts and drying-sheds or to remove the same.

ARTICLE IV

With regard to taxes, imposts and fees to be levied in connection with the fishing industry, Japanese subjects shall be subject to the following conditions and shall under no circumstances be subject to any treatment less favourable than that accorded to citizens of the Union of Soviet Socialist Republics.

1. The amount of the business tax chargeable to Japanese subjects having fishery rights shall not exceed three per cent of the price on the fishery grounds of fish and aquatic products caught, taken or prepared by them.

2. The said Japanese subjects shall be exempted from all kinds of taxes, imposts and fees, except the business tax and the taxes, imposts and fees mentioned in Article 9 of the Protocol (A) attached to the present Convention.

3. The payment of the business tax and other taxes, imposts and fees may be arranged by a special agreement between the two Governments.

4. No taxes or imposts shall be levied on the income of Japanese employees having their domicile in Japan and engaged in seasonal labour on fishery grounds leased to Japanese subjects.

ARTICLE V

The Union of Soviet Socialist Republics shall levy no duties on fish and aquatic products caught or taken in the Far Eastern waters of the Union of Soviet Socialist Republics, whether such fish and aquatic products have or have not undergone a process of manufacture, when they are destined for export from the Union of Soviet Socialist Republics to Japan.

ARTICLE VI

No restriction shall be established with regard to the nationality of the employees of Japanese subjects engaged in catching, taking and preparing fish and aquatic products in the districts specified in Article I of the present Convention.

ARTICLE VII

So far as concerns methods of preparation of fish and aquatic products, the Union of Soviet Socialist Republics engages not to impose upon the Japanese subjects who have obtained fishery rights in the districts specified in Article I of the present Convention any restriction from which the citizens of the Union of Soviet Socialist Republics who have obtained fishery rights in the said districts are exempt.

ARTICLE VIII

The Japanese subjects who have obtained fishery rights may make use of sea-going vessels furnished with a navigation certificate issued in Japan by the competent Consular officer of the Union of Soviet Socialist Republics, as also with a health certificate issued by the Japanese authorities, for the direct navigation from Japan to their fishery grounds, from one of their fishery grounds to another as well as from their fishery grounds to Japan; the said vessels may also proceed from the fishery grounds direct to a third state, provided they conform to the formalities required for the exportation to the said state of the fish and aquatic products on board, caught or taken in the Far Eastern waters of the Union of Soviet Socialist Republics.

The above-mentioned vessels shall be at liberty to transport, free of imposts and taxation, the persons and things necessary for the fishing industry, as also catches and collections.

The Japanese subjects who have obtained fishery rights may, free of imposts and taxation, transport by land, along shore or by sea, on board fishing boats the above-mentioned persons, things, catches and collections between their own fishery lots or vessels furnished with the licence mentioned in the last paragraph of Article II of the present Convention.

The provisions of the present Article shall equally apply to the case when the respective holders of separate fishery lots or licences make use of a vessel or a boat jointly.

The provisions of the present Article shall apply to the removal of remaining properties in the fishery lots, the lease-term of which has expired, to the other fishery lots or to Japan.

The above-mentioned vessels and boats must in all other respects comply with the laws of the Union of Soviet Socialist Republics which are or may be enacted respecting the coasting trade.

ARTICLE IX

The Japanese subjects who have obtained fishery rights may freely export to Japan fish and aquatic products caught or taken by Japanese subjects, without any export-licence, they may also export such fish and aquatic products to a third state, conforming to the formalities required for the exportation thereof.

For the exportation of fish and aquatic products bought from the state or other enterprises or citizens of the Union of Soviet Socialist Republics, the said Japanese subjects shall conform to the formalities required for the exportation thereof.

The said Japanese subjects are at liberty to import the necessaries solely intended for use for their fishing industry, as well as for themselves or their employees, without any import-licence.

No duties or imposts shall be levied on the importation of the goods above mentioned; the said goods as well as their quantity will be defined in the list, which shall be formulated every year in due time by the competent local authorities subject to the approval of the central authorities of the Union of Soviet Socialist Republics.

ARTICLE X

With regard to the entry, stay, removal and departure of the Japanese subjects who have obtained fishery rights, as well as of their employees who are not citizens of the Union of Soviet Socialist Republics, the summary regulations which are or may be enacted by the authorities of the Union of Soviet Socialist Republics shall be applied in the districts specified in Article I of the present Convention; in all other cases, Japanese subjects shall conform to the laws and regulations which are or may be enacted concerning the entry and stay in, and departure from, the Union of Soviet Socialist Republics, of foreigners.

The Japanese subjects and the citizens of the Union of Soviet Socialist Republics who have obtained fishery rights in the districts above-mentioned shall be placed on a footing of equality as regards the laws, regulations and ordinances which are or may be enacted concerning pisciculture and the protection of fish and aquatic products, the control of industry germane thereto and all other matters relating to fisheries.

Information of newly enacted laws and regulations, applicable to the fishing industry in the Far Eastern waters of the Union of Soviet Socialist Republics, shall be furnished to the Japanese Government at least three months before they are put in force; information of ordinances of the same nature newly issued by the local authorities of the Union of Soviet Socialist Republics shall be furnished to the Japanese Consular officer at Khabarovsk at least two months before they are put in force.

ARTICLE XI

Japanese subjects are at liberty to engage in the preparation of fish and aquatic products in the landed lots leased to them outside the limits of the districts specified in Article I of the present Convention, always complying with the laws, regulations and ordinances which are or may be enacted and applicable to all foreigners in the Union of Soviet Socialist Republics.

ARTICLE XII

The Japanese Government, in consideration of fishery rights accorded by the Union of Soviet Socialist Republics to Japanese subjects in virtue of the present Convention, engages not to impose any import duties on fish and aquatic products caught or taken in the Far Eastern waters of the Union of Soviet Socialist Republics, whether such fish and aquatic products have or have not undergone any process of manufacture.

ARTICLE XIII

Recognizing that Japanese employees, with their place of habitation in Japan, are engaged there and return thereto after carrying on labour in the seasonal industry of fishery; that their habits and customs are characteristic of Japanese nationality; that free passage between Japan and fishery grounds and free rations during the whole term of engagement are granted; that a share of catches and collections is given them in addition to regular wages, and that medical aid and other means of relief are provided for free of charge.

The Union of Soviet Socialist Republics agrees to conform to the above-mentioned facts in the application of its laws and regulations regarding the protection and regulation of labour, which are or may be enacted, to the labour of Japanese employees in the fishery grounds leased to Japanese subjects in accordance with the provisions of the present Convention.

ARTICLE XIV

So far as concerns matters not specially dealt with in the present Convention, but yet relating to the fishing industry in the districts specified in Article I of the present Convention, Japanese subjects shall be entitled to the same treatment as accorded to the citizens of the Union of Soviet Socialist Republics who have obtained fishery rights in the said districts.

ARTICLE XV

The present Convention shall remain in force for eight years and shall be revised or renewed at the end of the said period; thenceforth the Convention shall be revised or renewed at the end of every twelve years.

Either of the High Contracting Parties may give notice to the other of its desire to revise the present Convention, twelve months before the termination of the Convention. Negotiations for the revision shall be concluded within the said twelve months.

Should neither of the High Contracting Parties give notice for such revision, the present Convention shall remain in force for a further period of twelve years.

ARTICLE XVI

The present Convention shall be ratified, and the ratifications thereof shall be exchanged at Tokyo at as early a date as possible and in any case not later than four months after its signature.

The Convention shall come into force on the fifth day following the date of the exchange of its ratifications.

In witness whereof the respective Plenipotentiaries have signed the present Convention in duplicate in the English language and have affixed thereto their seals.

Done in the City of Moscow, this 23rd day of January, 1928.

(Signed) L. KARAKHAN
(Signed) M. LACIS
(Signed) T. TANAKA

PROTOCOL A

In proceeding this day to the signature of the Fishery Convention between Japan and the Union of Soviet Socialist Republics, the Plenipotentiaries of the two High Contracting Parties have agreed as follows:

ARTICLE I

The inlets which are the object of the exception contained in Article I of the Fishery Convention are as follows:

1. St. Lawrence Bay, up to a straight line drawn from Cape Pnaugun to Cape Khargilakh.
2. Mechigme Bay.
3. Konyam Bay (Penkegunei Bay), up to a straight line drawn from Cape Netchkhonone to Grab Peak.
4. Abolechef Bay (Kalagan Bay).
5. Roumilet Bay.

6. Providence Bay, up to a straight line drawn from Cape Lissovsky to Lysaya Golova.
7. Holy Cross Gulf, up to the parallel of Cape Meetchken.
8. Anadyr Bay, up to a straight line drawn from Cape St. Basilius to Cape Geka.
9. St. Pavla Bay.
10. Shliupochnaya Harbour.
11. Tuilen Lake.
12. Six Feet Lake.
13. Northern portion of Baron Korfa Gulf.
14. Kraga Harbour.
15. Bechevinska Bay.
16. Avatcha Bay, up to a straight line drawn from Cape Bezimyanni to Cape Dalni.
17. Gulf of Penjinsk, up to the parallel of Cape Mamet.
18. Milkachinsky Bay.
19. Iamskaia Bay.
20. Aian Bay.
21. Grand Duke Constantine Bay.
22. St. Nicholas Gulf, up to a straight line drawn from Cape Lamsdorf to Cape Groto.
23. Schastiya Gulf.
24. Baikal Gulf, up to a straight line drawn from Cape Tshauno to Cape Vitovta.
25. Nuiskii Gulf.
26. Nabilskii Gulf.
27. Krestovaya Bay.
28. Starka Bay.
29. Vanina Bay, up to a straight line drawn from Cape Vesseli to Cape Burni.
30. Port Soviet, up to a straight line drawn from Cape Milyutina to Cape Putyatina.
31. Terne Bay, up to the meridian of Cape Strashni.

32. St. Vladimir Bay, up to a straight line drawn from Cape Balusek to Cape Vatovskago.
33. Small inlet situated in the north-eastern portion of Preobrazheniya Bay, as far as the meridian of Cape Matveeva.

It goes without saying that the exception in question shall not apply to high seas.

As regards the northern coast of the Okhotsk Sea, from the estuary of the Podkagernaya to Aian Bay, with the exception of Penjinsky Gulf (see No. 17), Milkachinsky Bay (see No. 18), Iamskaia Bay (see No. 19) and Aian Bay (see No. 20), the inlets which are to come within the exception above referred to shall be determined according to the following definition:

Such bays as shall penetrate into the mainland for a distance (measured along the deepest channel) which shall be more than three times the width of the entrance.

Fishing shall, moreover, be barred to Japanese subjects, as to other foreigners, within the following bays not, as a matter of course, including high seas:

1. De Castries Bay with Fredericks Bay, up to a straight line drawn from Castries to Cape Kloster Kamp and up to a similar line from Cape Kloster Kamp to Cape Ostri.
2. St. Olga Bay, up to a straight line drawn from Cape Manevskago to Cape Shkota.
3. Peter the Great Bay, from Cape Povorotni to Cape Gamova, including the islands situated in that bay.
4. Posiette Bay, from Cape Gamova to Cape Butakov.

ARTICLE 2

In matters concerning the boundaries of rivers in relation to the sea, the two Governments shall follow the principles and usages of the law of nations.

ARTICLE 3

The fishery rights accorded to Japanese subjects in the Liman of the Amur in virtue of the Fishery Convention are subject to the special provisions which follow:
1. Japanese subjects may obtain in this district fishery lots by public auction on the same footing as citizens of the Union of Soviet Socialist Republics.
2. Japanese subjects who have obtained fishery lots are placed in all respects, so far as the fishing industry is concerned, under the same laws, regulations and ordinances which are or may be enacted respecting river fisheries in the basins of the Amur, as citizens of the Union of Soviet Socialist Republics who are successful bidders for fishery lots, and in particular the provisions which forbid the lessees of the fishery lots in this district to employ foreign workmen.

ARTICLE 4

Japanese subjects may upon making application therefore obtain in accordance with the provisions of Article II of the Fishery Convention the lease of fishery lots in any part of the districts specified in Article I of the said Convention, submitting to the laws, regulations and ordinances which are or may be enacted in the Union of Soviet Socialist Republics, for the culture and protection of fish, for the control of the industry germane thereto, and for all other matters regarding fisheries in the above-mentioned districts.

In case the species of fish to be caught are not defined in the contract for the lease of fishery lots, the Union of Soviet Socialist Republics shall not impose any restrictions on the species of fish to be caught, unless they are rendered necessary for the protection of fish of the salmon tribe.

ARTICLE 5

As regards the transfer of fishery rights between Japanese subjects as well as between Japanese subjects and citizens of the Union of Soviet Socialist Republics, permission shall be given upon application therefore, in conformity with the formalities prescribed by the laws of the Union of Soviet Socialist Republics.

ARTICLE 6

The duration of the lease of fishery lots shall be determined as follows:
  One year, in the case of lots which have been already opened, but not yet worked, before the coming into force of the Fishery Convention, or of lots opened for the first time since then;
  Three years, in the case of lots which have been worked for not less than one year;
  Five years, in the case of lots which have been worked for not less than three years.

It is understood that the above-mentioned terms may be modified in the case of fishery lots which may be granted for special lease by virtue of the provisions of the second paragraph of Article II of the Fishery Convention and the instruments attached thereto.

ARTICLE 7

The fishery rights, the terms of which shall not have come to an end at the date of the expiration of the term of the Fishery Convention, shall continue to be valid for the whole duration of their terms, whatever may be the decision come to by the two High Contracting Parties concerning the Fishery Convention itself.

ARTICLE 8

The fishery lots already existing in the districts specified in Article I of the Fishery Convention shall remain open for exploitation for the whole duration of the Fishery Convention.

ARTICLE 9

With regard to the provisions of Paragraph 2 of Article IV of the Fishery Convention, Japanese subjects are liable to the following taxes, imposts and fees:

1. The local imposts on means of conveyance (horses, automobiles, bicycles, motor-cycles, and motor-boats not provided with a navigation certificate).
2. The fee for inspection certificate for boilers, apparatus worked by pressure, lifts and elevating machines.
3. The local imposts on building, now in practice in towns, when such imposts are to be applied to localities where there are fishery grounds.
4. The stamp-duties, notarial fees, judicial fees and other similar taxes, imposts and fees, instituted by the central authorities of the Union of Soviet Socialist Republics and having indirect bearing on fishery lots and the equipments of fishery grounds, as well as the local taxes instituted by the local authorities on transactions carried out or registered at an exchange.
5. The consular fee and the registration fee concerning entry into, stay in, and departure from, the Union of Soviet Socialist Republics.
6. The consular and other official fees for the issue or certification of documents.
7. The registration fee for lease contract of fishery lot.
8. The imposts on timber sold out from forests.
9. The income-tax on profit accruing from sale of fish and aquatic

products for consumption in the Union of Soviet Socialist Republics, as also the transportation tax concerned there with.

ARTICLE 10

The Government of the Union of Soviet Socialist Republics engages to maintain, for the duration of the Fishery Convention, its present ruling exempting from duties fish and aquatic products exported from the Far Eastern District of the Union of Soviet Socialist Republics, except in the case when with regard to a particular third state or states, the duties applicable to goods in general exported thereto are to be altered.

So far as concerns fish and aquatic products reimported into the Union of Soviet Socialist Republics without having been worked upon in Japan, the Government of the Union of Soviet Socialist Republics engages likewise to maintain, for the duration of the Fishery Convention, its present regulation exempting from duties reimported goods, the produce or manufacture of the Union of Soviet Socialist Republics.

ARTICLE 11

The Government of the Union of Soviet Socialist Republics has no objection to the making of manure by Japanese subjects from herrings and other species of fish which are of minor value, as well as from refuse produced in the preparation of fish and aquatic products. Nor has the Government of the Union of Soviet Socialist Republics any objection to Japanese subjects preparing and curing fish of the salmon tribe according to Japanese methods.

ARTICLE 12

The navigation certificate mentioned in the first paragraph of Article VIII of the Fishery Convention is to be issued by the Consular officer of the Union of Soviet Socialist Republics on the presentation of:

1. Documents certifying the lease of the fishery lot or lots to which the vessel desires to resort.
2. A certified list of the persons on board with documents of their identification.
3. Documents certifying that the cargo of the vessel consists solely of goods mentioned in the third paragraph of Article IX of the Fishery Convention; in such documents amount of the cargo is also to be indicated.

The following shall be indicated in the navigation certificate:

1. The name of the vessel and her port of registry.
2. The name of the lease-holder or lease-holders of the fishery lot or lots.
3. A precise indication of the fishery lot or lots, to which the vessel desires to resort.
4. The nature and amount of the cargo.
5. The names of the crew.

Vessels furnished with the above-mentioned certificate and a health certificate are authorized to enter and remain at only those points of the coast of the Union of Soviet Socialist Republics which are mentioned in the navigation certificate. It goes without saying that ports where there is a custom-house are always open to such vessels.

Japanese vessels resorting to the Far Eastern waters of the Union of Soviet Socialist Republics in virtue of the last paragraph of Article II of the Fishery Convention must first put into one of the ports of the Union of Soviet Socialist Republics specially designated, where the competent authorities of the Union of Soviet Socialist Republics shall issue to them a special licence for catching, taking and preparing fish and aquatic products, the said licence shall at the same time take the place of a navigation certificate. The licence may also be obtained through a Consular officer of the Union of Soviet Socialist Republics in Japan; in this case the said vessels shall not be required to proceed to any of the above-mentioned ports.

ARTICLE 13

The Government of the Union of Soviet Socialist Republics has no objection to the individual voyage in Japanese fishing boats (rybolovnye lodki) between fishery grounds leased to various Japanese subjects; in the case of the voyage, with or without boats tugged, of fishing boats provided with motors, permission shall be obtained from the local authorities of the Union of Soviet Socialist Republics.

ARTICLE 14

Japanese steamers engaged in the fishing industry or in its auxiliary services, within the waters of the Union of Soviet Socialist Republics, shall be provided with a Russian or English translation of the log-book; Japanese sea-going motor or sailing vessels shall conform to the said stipulation so far as it is possible.

ARTICLE 15

The Government of the Union of Soviet Socialist Republics guarantees that on formulating and approving the list mentioned in Article IX of the Fishery Convention, the actual requirements of the fishing industry of Japanese subjects shall receive fullest consideration.

ARTICLE 16

Japanese subjects fitted for the work of any branches of fishing industry and not exceeding one hundred persons in all, shall have the right to winter in the fishery lots leased to Japanese subjects, provided they conform to laws and regulations relating to the entry and residence in the Union of Soviet Socialist Republics. Watchmen required for wintering in the said fishery lots shall be employed from among citizens of the Union of Soviet Socialist Republics.

ARTICLE 17

For catching and taking the fish and aquatic products which may call for protective measures for their propagation, a standard by which the amount of such catching and taking may be limited shall be determined by the authorities of the Union of Soviet Socialist Republics, by taking as a basis of consideration the actual tendency of their propagation both in the rivers and seas of the Union of Soviet Socialist Republics in the Far East.

The employment of "tateami" shall be authorized in all fishery lots leased to Japanese subjects, except in those lots which are situated in the closest proximity to estuaries; it is also agreed that in the case of the fishery lots last mentioned, the employment of "tateami" shall be authorized in case fishing with movable nets prove impraticable there. Moreover, in no fishery lots shall any restriction be imposed on the use of winches, escalators, conveyers, capstans, blocks or other instruments, machines and equipments which facilitate the working of fishing industry.

ARTICLE 18

It is understood that the terms "Japanese subjects" and "citizens of the Union of Soviet Socialist Republics" employed in the Fishery Convention and in the instruments attached thereto include public and private enterprises of Japan and the Union of Soviet Socialist Republics respectively, and that the term "citizens of the Union of Soviet Socialist Republics" does not imply local peasants and fishermen enjoying special treatment. It is further understood that, with regard to the matters particularly dealt with in Article IV of the Fishery Convention as well as in Article 9 of the present Protocol, the state enterprises and co-operative societies of the Union of Soviet Socialist Republics are accorded special status.

ARTICLE 19

At any time after the auction of the fishery lots in the first year of the duration of the Fishery Convention shall have been conducted, the Government of the Union of Soviet Socialist Republics may grant without auction the lease of fishery lots situated in any part of the districts specified in Article I of the Fishery Convention to the local peasants and fishermen who are now established or may happen to establish themselves there; such grant may be given only in respect of those districts where no application mentioned in Article 4 of the present Protocol shall have been made for two successive years in the duration of the Fishery Convention, or of those fishery lots for which there shall have been no bidder at auction for more than three successive years prior to such grant. The Government of the Union of Soviet Socialist Republics shall take necessary measures in order not to contract by such grant the sphere of fishing activities in the Far Eastern waters open for Japanese subjects, and in order to cause the competent authorities to conform to the desire of Japanese subjects for the opening of new fishery lots.

The Government of the Union of Soviet Socialist Republics engages to put up to auction the fishery lots thus leased to the local peasants and fishermen, in case they shall not have been operated for two years in succession, as also to forbid sub-lease or transfer of such lots to anybody other than local peasants or fishermen.

The local peasants and fishermen are at liberty to obtain the lease of fishery lots by auction in accordance with the provisions of Article II of the Fishery Convention, but those who have so obtained the lease of fishery lots shall not at the same time be in possession of fishery lots granted, sub-leased or transferred in virtue of the present Article.

It is agreed that the status of the said local peasants or fishermen is accorded only to the persons and their families who engage personally in the fishery for their livelihood without having recourse to the employment of workmen.

ARTICLE 20

It is understood that the term "fish and aquatic products" employed in the Fishery Convention and in the instruments attached thereto is to mean all kinds of fish, animals, plants and other aquatic products, except fur-seals and sea-otters.

ARTICLE 21

The present Protocol is to be considered as ratified with the ratification of the Fishery Convention signed this day and shall have the same duration as that Convention.

In witness whereof the respective Plenipotentiaries have signed the present Protocol in duplicate in the English language and have affixed thereto their seals.

Done in the City of Moscow, this 23rd day of January, 1928.

                                (Signed) L. KARAKHAN

(Signed) T. TANAKA   (Signed) M. LACIS [Latsis]

PROTOCOL B

In proceeding this day to the signature of the Fishery Convention between Japan and the Union of Soviet Socialist Republics, the Plenipotentiaries of the two High Contracting Parties have agreed as follows:

In consideration of the provisions of Article XIII of the Fishery Convention, the application of laws and regulations regarding the protection and regulation of labour to Japanese subjects having fishery rights and to their Japanese employees, shall be conditioned as follows:

1. With regard to the supply by the employer to his employees of the clothing and other articles necessary for their work, as well as of dwellings, the national habits and customs of the employees shall receive due consideration.

2. A basic amount of wages may be arranged in the Japanese currency and for a whole fishing season, according to the usage in the fishing industry of the Far Eastern District; if the employee so desires, part of the said basic wages shall be paid to him in advance. The said basic wages for the whole season shall, however, not be less than the amount corresponding to fifteen yen a month, even when the employer is responsible by the contract of engagement for the expenses of the employees' transportation and rations, and even when the employer allows his employees an extra pay corresponding to a certain proportion of catches and collections in virtue of the so-called "kuichi" or similar practice.

The above stipulation having been adopted by taking into consideration the law of the Union of Soviet Socialist Republics concerning minimum wages on one hand and the actual economic and social conditions in Japan on the other, it is agreed that, when the stipulation shall have become inadequate, a necessary readjustment may be made by agreement between the two Governments, with the view to suit new circumstances.

3. Working hours in the fishery grounds shall as a rule be eight hours a day; however, in view of the special features of the fishing industry and in accordance with the laws of the Union of Soviet Socialist Republics providing for the conditions of working in seasonal labours, the employer may by agreement with his employees put them to work more than eight hours a day, provided he makes an arrangement with the competent local organs of the People's Commissariat of Labour relating to the working hours as well as the wages, even for a whole fishing season.

So far, however, as labour in fishing operations is concerned, at any time of the season, on occasions of an abundance of fish coming in shoals, the employees may, when they so agree, be put to work outside regular hours, on holidays and at night-time, for which no arrangement with the above-mentioned organs of the People's Commissariat of Labour is to be required.

As regards labour in canning operations, the above paragraph is applicable only in the case when, owing to excessive accumulation of catches on occasions of an abundance of fish coming in shoals, extra work is necessitated in order to prevent the quality of the products from being deteriorated, subject to the condition that the employers concerned shall inform the local labour organs, as soon as possible and in any case before the closing of the fishing season of the corresponding year, of the conditions of the agreement made between the employers and employees regarding the extra work.

4. (a) In case the employer owes the obligation to pay the social insurance premium in accordance with the laws of the Union of Soviet Socialist Republics, his employees, even after their return to Japan, or their families in Japan shall enjoy the same rights as citizens of the Union of Soviet Socialist Republics or their families residing in the Union of Soviet Socialist Republics.

(b) In case the social insurance is due to Japanese subjects or their families residing in Japan, it shall be paid to them by the Government of the Union of Soviet Socialist Republics through its Consular officers in Japan, within four months after social insurance premium for the season shall have been paid.

(c) In all calculations and payments pertaining to the social insurance, the respective mint value of the currencies of Japan and the Union of Soviet Socialist Republics shall be taken into account instead of the current rates of exchange.

(d) The employer's obligation for social insurance shall be limited to the following three categories:

  I. When the employee is temporarily incapacitated for work;

II. When the employee is invalided or dies because of an accident;

III. When the employee needs medical treatment.

(e) The employer shall be exempt from the payment of the premium for the case III of the section (d), in case he undertakes in agreement with the sanitary authorities of the Union of Soviet Socialist Republics the supply of medical aid.

The employer shall be exempt from the payment of the premium for the cases I and II of the section (d), in the case when in accordance with the regulations approved by the Japanese authorities, such measures of relief shall be undertaken by a group of employers of other organizations as shall prove equally or more favourable to the employees compared with those provided for in the social insurance of the Union of Soviet Socialist Republics.

5. It may be stipulated in the contract of engagement that, when the employer shall have cancelled the contract of his own volition, he shall bear the expenses of passage from the fishery ground to Japan, it being understood that the employer shall be responsible for the employee's embarkation for Japan.

When the employer shall have dismissed his employee on his fishery ground, the employer shall pay the expenses of the latter's return to Japan.

As a matter of course, a stipulation may be included in the said contract of engagement for payment of an indemnity in the case when the employer or employee shall not, without due cause, carry out the contract before the employee's departure from Japan.

The provisions of the present Protocol shall be subject to change or supplement by a mutual agreement which may be arranged between the two Governments.

The present Protocol is to be considered as ratified with the ratification of the Fishery Convention signed this day and shall have the same duration as that Convention.

In witness whereof the respective Plenipotentiaries have signed the present Protocol in duplicate in the English language and have affixed thereto their seals.

Done in the City of Moscow, this 23rd day of January, 1928.

(Signed) L. KARAKHAN
(Signed) T. TANAKA (Signed) M. LACIS [Latsis]

PROTOCOL C

In proceeding this day to the signature of the Fishery Convention between Japan and the Union of Soviet Socialist Republics, the Plenipotentiaries of the two High Contracting Parties have agreed as follows:

The establishment and operation of canning factories by Japanese subjects having fishery rights, in the districts specified in Article I of the Fishery Convention, shall be conditioned as follows, provided that, in all that concerns the canning industry, Japanese subjects shall not be placed in a position less favourable than that accorded to private persons or enterprises of the Union of Soviet Socialist Republics.

(A) In the fishery lots leased by auction to Japanese subjects they may establish and operate canning factories during fishing seasons of their lease-term, by giving notice in advance to the competent authorities of the Union of Soviet Socialist Republics, and subject to the application of the provisions of Sections (1), (2), (6), (7), and (9) of Paragraph (B) of the present Protocol.

(B) For the operation of the canning factories owned by Japanese subjects and actually existing at the time of conclusion of the Fishery Convention, special contracts shall be concluded between the competent authorities of the Union of

THE FISHERY CONVENTION 295

Soviet Socialist Republics and the Japanese subjects concerned in conformity with the following conditions:

(1)

Japanese subjects are at liberty to make alterations in the scope and equipments of their canning factories, provided that, when such alterations are made, they shall make notification thereof to the competent authorities of the Union of Soviet Socialist Republics, in accordance with the formalities prescribed by the regulation of the Union of Soviet Socialist Republics. Moreover, they shall not be prohibited or restricted to transport fish and aquatic products from fishery lots granted to other lessees to the said canning factories, or to prepare them.

(2)

All the properties not belonging to the Government or citizens of the Union of Soviet Socialist Republics in the fishery lots where canning factories are found may, after the expiration of the term of special contracts, either be transported by the Japanese subjects concerned to other fishery lots or outside the Union of Soviet Socialist Republics, or, with the permission of the Government of the Union of Soviet Socialist Republics, be sold off within the territory of the Union of Soviet Socialist Republics, in case the said properties shall not have been disposed of as above mentioned, within one year after the expiration of the said contracts, they shall come into the possession of the Government of the Union of Soviet Socialist Republics without compensation.

(3)

For the operation of the canning factories now in existence, each canning factory shall be provided with the fishery lot where the factory is situated and also with another fishery lot lying in the neighbourhood, both of which are to be leased without auction in accordance with the provisions of the second paragraph of Article II of the Fishery Convention.

In case Japanese subjects make application to the competent authorities of the Union of Soviet Socialist Republics for the lease of fishery lots for the purpose of establishing therein canning factories, in accordance with the provisions of the second paragraph of Article II of the Fishery Convention, the Government of the Union of Soviet Socialist Republics will agree to enter into negotiations with the Japanese Government, with a view to granting such lease so far as the circumstances permit.

(4)

The term of special contracts concerning the canning factories mentioned in Section (3) shall be ten years.

As regards measures to be taken with respect to the canning factories after the expiration of the term of the said special contracts, the two Governments shall enter into negotiations on this question either on occasion of the negotiations for the revision of the Fishery Convention, or one year before the said expiration.

(5)

Japanese subjects who desire to conclude the special contracts mentioned in Section (4) shall be recommended by the Japanese Government to the competent authorities of the Union of Soviet Socialist Republics.

(6)

The special royalty (dolevoe otchislenie) for the operation of canning factories shall be calculated in the gold currency of the Union of Soviet Socialist Republics at the following rates for the actual amount of the fish and aquatic products prepared in the canning factories concerned:

1. For red salmon, 20 copecks per case.

2. For silver salmon, king salmon and dog salmon, 16 copecks per case.
3. For humpback salmon, 9 copecks per case.
4. For crabs, 40 copecks per case.

It is understood in this connection that one case of canned goods contains forty-eight cans of one pound each, or ninety-six cans of half a pound each.

The said special royalty, together with the taxes, imposts and fees chargeable thereon, shall be paid in December every year.

The above-mentioned rates of the special royalty may be altered by mutual agreement, in case the market price of the respective merchandise now obtaining has considerably changed.

(7)

As regards taxes, imposts and fees, the provisions of Article IV of the Fishery Convention as well as those of the instruments attached thereto shall be applicable, it being understood in this connection that the term "royalty" employed in the said instruments shall be held to include the royalty for the lease of fishery lots and the special royalty (dolevoe otchislenie) for the operation of canning factories provided for in Section (6).

(8)

For the purpose of determining the amount of ordinary royalty for the fishery lots leased in accordance with the provisions of Section (3), the following method shall be adopted:

Every three years shall be taken, as a standard, fishery lots amounting so far as practicable to four in all, which are leased by auction and lie in the closest proximity to the fishery lots appertaining to canning factories and where the same kinds of fish are caught as in the latter, and the quotient obtained through dividing the sum total of the royalty for their lease by the sum total of their standard amounts of catch shall be considered as basic unit; the royalty in question shall be computed expressed in the gold currency of the Union of Soviet Socialist Republics by multiplying the said basic unit by the standard amount of catch assigned to the fishery lots concerned.

(9)

In all that concerns the operation of canning factories and fishery lots and which is not specifically dealt with in the present Protocol, the provisions of the Fishery Convention and the instruments attached thereto shall be applicable.

(10)

For the purpose of concluding special contracts concerning the canning factories now in existence, the Japanese subjects concerned shall as soon as possible apply to the competent authorities of the Union of Soviet Socialist Republics for the opening of negotiations with a clear indication of the fishery lots which they propose to obtain without auction according to the present Protocol.

The negotiations shall be concluded within two months after the coming into force of the Fishery Convention.

(11)

In case the said negotiations fail to be concluded within the stipulated time, the Japanese subjects concerned may continue the operation of the canning factories in the fishery lots concerned, in conformity with the arrangement that shall be agreed upon between the two Governments on the basis of the provisions of Paragraph (B) of the present Protocol. The above-mentioned negotiations shall, as far as possible, be concluded within six months thereafter.

Should for any reason any special contract concerning the canning factories owned by Japanese subjects and actually existing at the time of conclusion of the Fishery Convention fail to be concluded, or any special contract so concluded become void, the fishery lots assigned to the canning factory or factories in question shall, as a matter of course, be put up to auction with a view to ensuring the continuance of their exploitation.

The present Protocol is to be considered as ratified with the ratification of the Fishery Convention signed this day and shall have the same duration as that Convention.

In witness whereof the respective Plenipotentiaries have signed the present Protocol in duplicate in the English language and have affixed thereto their seals.

Done in the City of Moscow, this 23rd day of January, 1928.

(Signed) T. TANAKA   (Signed) L. KARAKHAN
(Signed) M. LACIS

FINAL PROTOCOL

In proceeding this day to the signature of the Fishery Convention between Japan and the Union of Soviet Socialist Republics as well as of the Protocol A and the Protocol B attached thereto, the Plenipotentiaries of Japan and the Union of Soviet Socialist Republics have made the following declarations:

PART I

1. re *Article II of the Fishery Convention*

A. With regard to the provisions of the first paragraph of Article II of the Fishery Convention, the Plenipotentiaries of the Union of Soviet Socialist Republics declare as follows:

1. Under normal conditions, the upset price at auction of a fishery lot which has already been operated is to be determined by taking as standard its upset price at the last auction, it being understood that, should there be any change in the economic value of the said fishery lot after the last auction, its upset price may be correspondingly adjusted; in the case of a fishery lot which is newly opened

for exploitation, its upset price is to be determined by taking as standard the proportion between the royalty paid on, and the standard amount of catch assigned to, the neighbouring fishery lots.

2. As regards a fishery lot for which there has been no successful bidder at auction, its upset price is to be published immediately after the auction, and in putting it up to the following auction, due consideration will be paid in the determination of its upset price with a view to affording a better chance of success to bidders.

The Plenipotentiary of Japan declares that he has no objection thereto.

B. With regard to the provisions of the second paragraph of Article II of the Fishery Convention, the Plenipotentiaries of Japan and the Union of Soviet Socialist Republics declare that they have agreed to the following:

1. The Government of the Union of Soviet Socialist Republics will grant, without auction and for the lease-terms provided for in the first paragraph of Article 6 of the Protocol A attached to the Fishery Convention for the duration of the said Convention, the lease of fishery lots lying in the districts specified in Article 1 of the said Convention to its state enterprises for their own exploitation. It is understood that in the case of fishery lots dedicated to catching fish of the salmon tribe, the grant of such lease shall be limited to those lots, of which the standard amount of catch does not exceed 2,000,000 poods in aggregate, corresponding to about twenty per cent of the total standard amount of catch obtaining at the time of coming into force of the said Convention. In the case of fishery lots dedicated to catching or taking the other fish and aquatic products, the said grant shall be limited to those lots, of which catches and collections in aggregate correspond to twenty per cent of

the total amount of catches and collections of respective fish and aquatic products.

2. When the state enterprises have wholly and completely operated for themselves all the fishery lots within the above-mentioned limit, the two Governments shall, if the Government of the Union of Soviet Socialist Republics so propose, enter into further negotiations on the increase of the standard amount and the number of fishery lots to be granted to the said enterprises.

3. In determining the fishery lots to be leased to the state enterprises, the Government of the Union of Soviet Socialist Republics will be guided, as far as practicable, by the principle of apportioning the percentage mentioned in the foregoing Paragraph 1 to each of the groups into which the fishery lots may be classified according to the kind and amount of catches and collections, and having due regard to the reasonable desire which may be entertained by the Japanese subjects interested, and also to the fact that in the year 1927, i.e. at the time of the negotiations for the conclusion of the Fishery Convention, the fishery lots operated by the state enterprises did not amount to twenty per cent, while those operated by Japanese subjects exceeded eighty per cent, of all the fishery lots then leased for exploitation, the Government of the Union of Soviet Socialist Republics will confer with the Japanese Government before coming to final decision as to the said determination.

4. The fishery lots, destined for lease without auction to the state enterprises, but not actually operated by them, shall either be put up to auction in due course of time before the fishing season of the corresponding year, for lease for one year or more, or be leased to local peasants and fishermen without auction. It is understood, as a matter of course,

that the fishery lots so leased shall not be considered as operated by the state enterprises.

5. So far as concerns the Fishery Convention and the instruments attached thereto, the term "state enterprises" shall be held to imply all kinds of enterprises more than one half of whose capital is invested by the organs of the Union of Soviet Socialist Republics, or of its component Republic or Republics, or more than one half of whose directing officials are appointed by the said organs. So far as concerns any enterprises which do not belong to the said category, and in which the said organs participate in some form or other, or any enterprises in which some organs of the various local administrative organizations in the Union of Soviet Socialist Republics participate wholly or partly in whatever form or manner it may be, the Government of the Union of Soviet Socialist Republics shall confer with the Japanese Government for deciding whether, for the purpose of obtaining fishery lots, the enterprises in question shall be enabled to participate in auctions or be included in the category of the state enterprises prescribed in the present Protocol. Provided, however, that any enterprises which may have, in the course of ordinary commercial transactions with the organs of the Union of Soviet Socialist Republics, or of its component Republic or Republics, or of local organizations, placed themselves in a position of debtor in relation to the latter, or a minority of whose shares may have come into temporary possession of the latter, shall be considered as outside the scope of the foregoing provisions.

6. Notwithstanding the provisions of the Fishery Convention and the foregoing paragraphs, the Government of the Union of Soviet Socialist Republics may lease without auction the fishery lots, irrespective of their number, which are or may be opened in the Liman of the Amur, to the state enter-

prises and various cooperative societies, as well as to local peasants and fishermen.

It is further agreed, however, that when fish in the Liman of the Amur have conspicuously increased, the present stipulation may be modified by agreement between the two Governments.

C. With regard to the provisions of the last paragraph of Article II of the Fishery Convention, the Plenipotentiaries of the Union of Soviet Socialist Republics declare:

1. The Government of the Union of Soviet Socialist Republics has in view the issue in a near future of a regulation, in conformity with which Japanese subjects may obtain the licence mentioned in the last paragraph of Article II of the Fishery Convention.

2. The Government of the Union of Soviet Socialist Republics is ready to lease to Japanese subjects engaged in the fishing industry landed lots as basis for whaling, up to a number not more than five.

The Plenipotentiary of Japan declares that he has no objection thereto.

2. *re Article III of the Fishery Convention*

Regarding the provisions of Article III of the Fishery Convention, the Plenipotentiaries of the Union of Soviet Socialist Republics declare:

1. In case the landed area of a fishery lot proves to be too steep or swampy, or too small, for providing equipments necessary for the fishing industry, application may be made for the lease of a littoral in the neighbourhood; the authorities of the Union of Soviet Socialist Republics shall take the application into due consideration and, when it is found reasonable, shall grant the said application.

2. The refuse produced in the operation of fisheries may be thrown away in the offing.
3. The authorities of the Union of Soviet Socialist Republics shall have no objection to granting the application for obtaining timber, fuel as well as water from outside fishery lots, when necessary for the fishing industry; it goes without saying that the charges and dues which may be required in this respect shall be paid by the persons interested.
4. Buildings, warehouses, huts and drying sheds erected in accordance with the provisions of Article III of the Fishery Convention shall be removed within one year after the expiration of the lease-term of the fishery lots concerned, or transferred to the new lessee thereof.

The Plenipotentiary of Japan declares that he has no objection thereto.

3. re *Articles IV and X of the Fishery Convention and Article 9 of the Protocol A*

The Plenipotentiaries of the Union of Soviet Socialist Republics declare:

1. The determination of "the price on the fishery grounds" of fish and aquatic products shall be made by deducting freight and other charges connected with transportation from the average price of respective kinds of such merchandise obtaining in their principal market in Japan or in any third state.

    However, the business tax on dealings in fish and aquatic products carried out between individual fishery lots shall be levied on the basis of the price actually paid.
2. The consular fee concerning entry into, and departure from, the Union of Soviet Socialist Republics of Japanese subjects mentioned in the first part of the first paragraph of Article X of the Fishery Convention shall be, when

included in a list presented for collective visé, fixed at the rate of fifty-five copecks per capita, and the registration fee for their stay in the Union of Soviet Socialist Republics shall be ten copecks per capita.
3. The consular fee and the registration fee for Japanese subjects excluding those mentioned in the foregoing paragraph and including those mentioned in Article 16 of the Protocol A shall be charged in conformity with general regulations applicable to foreigners proceeding to the territory of the Union of Soviet Socialist Republics.
4. The registration fee on lease contract of fishery lot shall not exceed three per cent of the royalty for the lot concerned.
5. The question concerning the inheritance of fishery lots, as well as the equipments and personal belongings which may be left there shall be, in so far as the deceased are Japanese subjects, an object of special arrangement with the Japanese Government.
6. The provisions of Article 9 of the Protocol A shall not be construed to prevent the change of terminology of any of the taxes, imposts and fees mentioned therein, provided the taxes, imposts and fees so affected shall retain the same character as before.
7. So far as the burden shall not fall exclusively on Japanese subjects, consumption tax and import duty on things purchased in the Union of Soviet Socialist Republics, as well as taxes and imposts to be levied concerning acts, done outside the fishery grounds, shall be regarded to be outside the scope of Article IV of the Fishery Convention and chargeable to Japanese subjects in accordance with general regulations.

The Plenipotentiary of Japan declares that he has no objection thereto.

4. re *Article VI of the Fishery Convention*

1. The Plenipotentiaries of the Union of Soviet Socialist Republics declare that the term "nationality" employed in Article VI of the Fishery Convention shall be understood to correspond to "grajdanstvo [grazhdanstvo]" and "poddanstvo" of the Russian language.

    The Plenipotentiary of Japan declares that he has no objection thereto.

2. The Plenipotentiaries of Japan and the Union of Soviet Socialist Republics declare that they have agreed as follows:

    Taking into consideration that the Japanese subjects having fishery rights have employed and are always ready to employ citizen-workers of the Union of Soviet Socialist Republics, so far as it is practicable and on equal conditions to those applying to Japanese labourers, the question of employing a certain number of such citizen-workers by the said Japanese subjects shall, when circumstances warrant, be negotiated between the two Governments.

5. re *Article VIII of the Fishery Convention*

In answer to the inquiry of the Plenipotentiary of Japan, the Plenipotentiaries of the Union of Soviet Socialist Republics declare that, as a matter of course, Japanese vessels and boats shall, in case of stress at sea, enjoy the right of refuge at any point of the coast of the Union of Soviet Socialist Republics.

6. re *Article IX of the Fishery Convention*

The Plenipotentiaries of the Union of Soviet Socialist Republics declare:

1. The formalities other than export licence, which may be required concerning the exportation to Japan of fish and

aquatic products caught or taken by Japanese subjects in the waters of the Union of Soviet Socialist Republics, shall not be of any prohibitive or restrictive character against such exportation.

2. The formalities other than import licence, which may be required concerning the importation into the Union of Soviet Socialist Republics of goods mentioned in the third paragraph of the above mentioned Article, shall not be of any prohibitive or restrictive character against such importation, so far as these goods are included in the list mentioned in the said Article.

3. The formalities which may be required concerning the exportation, other than that mentioned in Paragraph 1, by Japanese subjects of fish and aquatic products shall be of summary order.

4. Japanese subjects having fishery rights are at liberty to buy or sell fish and aquatic products, to or from other Japanese subjects having fishery rights, or citizens or various enterprises of the Union of Soviet Socialist Republics, so far as such fish and aquatic products are destined for export from the Union of Soviet Socialist Republics.

5. When Japanese subjects having fishery rights desire to sell their fish and aquatic products in mass transactions for the home market of the Union of Soviet Socialist Republics, they shall enter into an arrangement regarding the said sale and its amount in each business year, with the competent local authorities of the Union of Soviet Socialist Republics; such an arrangement shall not be required with regard to the transactions of small amount carried out individually by the said Japanese subjects, as when selling such fish and aquatic products to the local population.

The Plenipotentiary of Japan declares that he has no objection thereto.

7. re *Articles IX and X of the Fishery Convention*

The Plenipotentiaries of the Union of Soviet Socialist Republics declare that the provisions of Articles IX and X of the Fishery Convention do not, as a matter of course, in any degree exempt Japanese subjects from the application of proper measures for the prevention of smuggling.

The Plenipotentiary of Japan declares that he shares the same opinion.

8. re *Article XIII of the Fishery Convention and the Protocol B*

The Plenipotentiaries of Japan and the Union of Soviet Socialist Republics agree that the provisions of Article XIII of the Fishery Convention and those of the Protocol B attached thereto have no application of the persons, mentioned in Article 16 of the Protocol A, with regard to whom the laws and regulations which are or may be enacted regarding the protection and regulation of labour shall be wholly applied.

9. re *Article I of the Protocol A*

The Plenipotentiaries of Japan and the Union of Soviet Socialist Republics declare that, in order to prevent future misunderstandings regarding certain inlets mentioned in Article I of the Protocol A, they have agreed to annex to the present Final Protocol the maps showing the precise boundaries of the said inlets.

10 re *Article 3 of the Protocol A*

The Plenipotentiaries of Japan and the Union of Soviet Socialist Republics declare that they have agreed as follows:
1. The term "the Liman of the Amur" indicates the extent of waters contained in the following boundaries:
In the North—a straight line drawn from Petrovskoe Spit to Cape Tshauno.

In the South—a straight line drawn from Cape Lazarev to Cape Pogobi;

In the West—the coast-line of the Far Eastern District of the Union of Soviet Socialist Republics;

In the East—the coast-line of Northern Saghalien.

2. (a) It goes withoutsaying that the restrictions regarding nationality mentioned in Paragraph (2) of Article 3 of the Protocol A are not to be applied to persons who do not come within the category of workmen, such as managers, overseers, etc.

(b) The Japanese subjects who have obtained the lease of fishery lots for more than one year may obtain for a period of less than one year the lease of landed areas to be used for the preparation of fish, in the localities situated over one half verst from these fishery lots. In these landed areas and in fishery lots leased for less than one year, no restrictions shall be imposed as to the nationality of workmen employed there and not engaged in the actual fishing.

11. *re Article* 8 *of the Protocol A*

The Plenipotentiaries of the Union of Soviet Socialist Republics declare that, as a matter of course, the provisions of Article 8 of the Protocol A shall not apply to cases of closing fishery lots, caused by elemental forces.

The Plenipotentiary of Japan declares that he has no objection thereto.

12. *re Article* 11 *of the Protocol A*

The Plenipotentiaries of Japan and the Union of Soviet Socialist Republics agree that of the total amount of fish of the salmon tribe caught by Japanese subjects, no more than sixty per cent may be prepared in the "bara" method, and that manure from herrings may be made in ten fishery lots to be leased to Japanese subjects.

13. *re Article 13 of the Protocol A*

The Plenipotentiaries of Japan and the Union of Soviet Socialist Republics agree that fishing boats provided with motors up to three horse power belong to the category of the fishing boats (rybolovnye lodki) mentioned in the first part of Article 13 of the Protocol A.

14. *re Article 17 of the Protocol A*
   1. The Plenipotentiaries of the Union of Soviet Socialist Republics declare:
      (a) The standard amount of catch, which will be established with regard to each fishery lot, is determined first of all by taking into consideration the actual amount of fish caught in the past either in the fishery lot (in case it has already been operated) or in the lot lying in the nearest proximity thereto (in case the lot in question has been newly opened) when, therefore, Japanese subjects shall have made an application, with a detailed statement of reasons, for the alteration of the standard amount thus determined, the authorities of the Union of Soviet Socialist Republics shall give due consideration to the application and, when it is found reasonable, take necessary steps to alter the said amount.
      (b) In case the total amount of catch in a given fishery lot proves, as a result of the last netting before the assgined standard amount is reached, to be in excess of the latter amount, the excess amount shall be regarded as lawful catch.
   2. Concerning the "tateami" mentioned in the second paragraph of Article 17 of the Protocol A, the Plenipotentiary of Japan maintains that the term "tateami" indicates not only the ordinary "tateami" and "nakanukiami", but also the so-called "kairyoami", while the Plenipontentiaries of

the Union of Soviet Socialist Republics, not objecting in principle to the contention of the Plenipotentiary of Japan declare that the employment of "kairyoami" by Japanese subjects shall be automatically authorized when the employment thereof shall be authorized to any of the state, cooperative or private fishing enterprises of the Union of Soviet Socialist Republics.

15. *re Article 19 of the Protocol A*

1. The Plenipotentiaries of Japan and the Union of Soviet Socialist Republics agree that the periods of time provided by the first paragraph of Article 19 of the Protocol A have no application to those fishery lots which were granted without auction to local peasants and fishermen before the coming into force of the Fishery Convention.
2. Regarding the provisions of the first paragraph of Article 19 of the Protocol A, the Plenipotentiaries of the Union of Soviet Socialist Republics declare:

    According to the first paragraph of Article 19 of the Protocol A, the fishery lots for which there shall have been no bidder at auction for more than three successive years, may be granted without auction on lease to local peasants and fishermen; however, considering that the appraisement by the competent authorities of the Union of Soviet Socialist Republics of a fishery lot at auction is to be determined by taking into account the economic value of the lot and the existing royalty either of the said lot (in case it has already been operated) or of neighbouring lots (in case the lot in question has newly been opened) and also considering that bidders in determining their bidding price take into account the same factors, the Government of the Union of Soviet Socialist Republics reserve the right to hold a lot or lots as open to lease without auction to local peasants and fishermen, even when there shall have been actual bidders, provided their bidding price shall have been notably at variance with the appraisement determined by the competent authorities of the Union of Soviet Socialist Republics on the aforementioned bases.

It goes without saying that the present declaration shall not be held to restrict in any degree the right of the competent authorities of the Union of Soviet Socialist Republics to determine the equitable appraisement of individual fishery lots.

The Plenipotentiary of Japan declares that he has no objection thereto.

3. The Plenipotentiaries of the Union of Soviet Socialist Republics declare that the provisions of Article 19 of the Protocol A shall not prevent the local peasants or fishermen mentioned in the last paragraph of the said Article from employing workmen up to two persons when engaged in fishery by themselves individually or with their own family.

The Plenipotentiary of Japan declares that he has no objection thereto.

16. *re Paragraph 2 of the Protocol B*

The Plenipotentiaries of the Union of Soviet Socialist Republics declare that if the employee so desires, the employer may of course pay in Japan the wages of all kinds as well as the extra pay due to the employee.

The Plenipotentiary of Japan declares that he has no objection thereto.

17. *re Paragraph 3 of the Protocol B*

The Plenipotentiaries of the Union of Soviet Socialist Republics declare:

1. There shall be no objection to the view that the wages for additional work on Japanese fishery grounds shall, under

normal conditions of the industry, correspond in general to fifty per cent of the basic wages for a whole fishing season.

2. The term "the local organs of the people's Commissariat of Labour" mentioned in the said Paragraph, indicates the organs stationed at Khabarovsk, and the Government of the Union of Soviet Socialist Republics shall issue necessary instructions directing these organs to make the arrangement referred to in the said Paragraph, with Japanese fishing enterprises on terms most favourable to the latter.

The Plenipotentiary of Japan declares that he has no objection thereto.

18. re Paragraph 4 of the Protocol B

The Plenipotentiaries of the Union of Soviet Socialist Republics declare that the insurance premium for all the three categories of insurance, mentioned in the section (d) of the said Paragraph, constitutes 8.3 per cent of the wages due to the employees, and may be subject to changes in future.

The Plenipotentiary of Japan declares that he has no objection thereto.

19. re Protocol B

The Plenipotentiaries of the Union of Soviet Socialist Republics declare that the Japanese fishing enterprises in the districts specified in Article I of the Fishery Convention may adopt for the rules of internal order the Specimen Rules for these enterprises, attached to the present Final Protocol.

The Plenipotentiary of Japan declares that he has no objection thereto.

PART II

The Plenipotentiaries of Japan and the Union of Soviet Socialist

Republics have agreed that with the coming into force of the Fishery Convention signed this day, the provisions of the first paragraph of Article 3 of the Convention of Peking concluded on January 20th, 1925, shall be considered as completely executed, and the Fishery Convention of 1907 as of no further force of effect.

Signed in the City of Moscow, in duplicate in the English Language, this 23rd day of January 1928.

(Signed) T. TANAKA   (Signed) L. KARAKHAN
(Signed) M. LACIS

Two annexes and eight notes completed the Fishery Convention.[b] Prior to signing the various documents the Japanese and Soviet Plenipotentiaries made the following clarification:

(1)

With regard to the provisions of Article XV of the Fishery Convention, the Plenipotentiary of Japan expressed the following view:

Should occasion present itself when the negotiations for the revision of the Fishery Convention do not end within the period prescribed in the said Article, it is a matter of course that a modus vivendi shall be agreed upon between the two Governments.

The Plenipotentiaries of the Union of Soviet Socialist Republics states that they shared the same view.

(2)

With regard to the provisions of Article 10 of the Protocol A attached to the Fishery Convention, the Plenipotentiaries of the Union of Soviet Socialist Republics gave the following reply to the Japanese Plenipotentiary's inquiry:

---

[b] See Appendix.

The phrase "except in the case when, with regard to a particular third state or states, the duties applicable to goods in general exported thereto are to be altered" in the first paragraph of the said Article is meant to refer to such extraordinary cases in which the Government of the Union of Soviet Socialist Republics is compelled to make any alteration in the export tariff, as when the Government of the Union of Soviet Socialist Republics may enter into a tariff war against a particular third state or states.

(3)

The Plenipotentiaries of the Union of Soviet Socialist Republics stated that, should any fishery lots opened for exploitation in accordance with the provisions of the Fishery Convention be granted for lease to local peasants and fishermen without auction by virtue of the provisions of Article 19 of the Protocol A, the duration of the lease of fishery lots provided for in the first paragraph of Article 6 of the Protocol A shall, as a matter of course, be applicable to the above-mentioned lease.

The Plenipotentiary of Japan concurred.

(4)

The Plenipotentiaries of Japan and the Union of Soviet Socialist Republics concurred that the first part of the declaration of Section (2) of Paragraph 15 in Part I of the Final Protocol has in view the prevention of unfair bidding at the auction of fishery lots, and shall not be held to affect in any way the provisions of Division (I) in Section A of Paragraph 1 in Part I of the Final Protocol.

(5)

The Plenipotentiaries of Japan and the Union of Soviet Socialist Republics declared that each of the two Governments holds itself ready to render necessary facilities to the experts of the other, desiring to make officially or privately technical or scientific investigations into matters relating to fishery, and, whenever in future either of the two Governments deems desirable, it will invite the experts of the other to cooperate in such investigations.

(6)

The Plenipotentiaries of the Union of Soviet Socialist Republics declares that the Government of the Union of Soviet Socialist Republics, recognizing the great economic significance of the fishing industry of the Japanese subjects in the Districts under the purview of the Fishery Convention, is prepared to pay due regard to the effect that in accordance with the said Convention the reasonable and lawful interests of the Japanese subjects may not be impaired.[2]

The signature of the convention did not spell an end to the fishery negotiations. The agreement could not take effect until ratified, and ratification was delayed by Japan for five months. Soviet sources suggest that the Japanese delayed ratification in an attempt to retain all the fishery lots in their hands in 1927.[3] Meanwhile another fishing season approached and agreement had to be reached on what procedure to follow. The Soviets felt that the spirit of the new convention should be applied forthwith; the Japanese preferred to adhere to the practice of the preceding year. The Russians gave in, and at last on May 23, 1928, ratifications were exchanged in Tokyo. The convention went into effect five days later, on May 28, 1928.

CHAPTER ELEVEN

Expanding Contacts

THE Basic Convention and related agreements laid down the ground rules for Soviet-Japanese relations. In a telegram dated February 25, 1925, Foreign Minister Shidehara expressed satisfaction with the ratification of the convention that day. "Nothing could give me greater pleasure than the thought that the friendly good-neighborly relations between our two peoples have been reestablished anew officially and are now firmly secured." Chicherin, his Soviet counterpart, cabled back the same day that Shidehara's feelings were shared in Moscow.[1]

With the conclusion of the Basic Convention sincere efforts were made by individuals and organizations on both sides to improve Soviet-Japanese relations by personal and cultural contacts. Exchange visits were paid by performing artists, industrial representatives and fliers. The Russo-Japanese (later Soviet-Japanese) Society in Tokyo, which was under the patronage of Prince Kan-in and included among its membership, besides its president Viscount (from 1928 Count) Gotō, prominent Japanese bureaucrats and businessmen, worked for the development of mutual understanding and the strengthening of cultural ties and friendly feelings. It promoted cultural exchange and closer economic relations. "Just now it is the fashion in Japan to emphasize things Russian," the *Honolulu Star-Bulletin* reported on April 8, 1925. "Recent news articles from Tokio have told how hundreds of Japanese are studying Russian, and thousands are hoping to enter Siberia and exploit that rich and undeveloped country."

In order to expedite Russo-Japanese trade the Russo-Japanese Society fostered a Russo-Japanese commercial and industrial exhibition at the

Daimaru department store in Osaka in January of 1926. As the *Japan Weekly Chronicle* reported in advance: "All the exhibits consist of those having export probabilities to Japan, and among samples to be shipped from the Habarovsk Government are timbers, ores, skins, medicinal plants, rice, cereals, etc., those from the Siberian district include butter and other produce, and from European Russia tobacco, kerosene oil, and many other specimens."[2]

On the death of Emperor Taishō (Yoshihito), the Soviet government was faced with the question of whether its representative should lay a wreath on the grave of the emperor, participate in the religious ceremonies and generally conform to a court etiquette which it disdained. The Politbureau decided in the affirmative, because Moscow "extremely valued good relations with the Japanese at the moment of the development of the Chinese revolution." Besedovskii was instructed to lay a wreath which bore the Soviet state emblem but tactfully omitted the motto "Proletarians of all countries unite!"

In October of 1926 a delegation from the Academy of Sciences of the U.S.S.R. attended the third Pan-Pacific Congress in Tokyo in response to a Japanese invitation. According to Besedovskii's memoirs the Politbureau had at first decided against Soviet participation under the misapprehension that it was to be a meeting of pacifists rather than of Pacific scholars.[3]

In 1927 a group of agricultural, industrial and financial experts from the Russian Far East and a group of Soviet university professors, heads of scientific and research institutes and museum directors toured Japan. The works of Soviet painters were exhibited in Tokyo and in Osaka in May of 1927 under the auspices of the All-Union Society for Cultural Relations with Foreign Countries (VOKS) on the Soviet side and the Japan-Soviet Society and the newspaper *Asahi* on the Japanese side.

In return, Japan sent the prominent industrialist Kuhara Fusanosuke 久原房之助, accompanied by Baron Itō Fumikichi 伊藤文吉 and Consul General Saitō Hiroshi 齋藤博, to inspect economic conditions in the U.S.S.R. and in Germany; Kuhara met with the Soviet leader Joseph Stalin and with Anastas Ivanovich Mikoian, commissar for foreign and domestic trade. Gotō, president of the Soviet-Japanese Society, himself visited Moscow for some three weeks in December of 1927 and, as has been seen, used his influence to further the signature of the fishery convention.

A specialist in rice cultivation was delegated by the Soviet-Japanese Society to study the possibility of establishing rice plantations in the Russian Far East. The maritime region bordering Korea had already attracted a rapidly growing number of agriculturists, Korean by nationality, Japanese by citizenship. According to Russian statistics there had been about 54,000 Koreans in the Maritime Province in 1917; six years later there were almost 95,000. (This was an increase of over 76% and compared with an increase of only 10%—from 285,000 to 315,000—in the population of Europeans and a decrease of 5%—from about 5,500 to about 5,200—in the population of Chinese in this area.)[4] Thus there was reason for the Japanese to hope that they could turn the Maritime Province into a source of rice for themselves as well as for the local inhabitants—an interesting twist, if one recalls that eighteenth and early nineteenth century Russian attempts to open Japan and establish commercial relations with her had been motivated to a large extent by the desire to obtain Japanese food for the Russian Far East.

In July and August of 1928 Ichikawa Sadanji 市川左團次 and his Kabuki troupe thrilled audiences in Moscow and Leningrad. "Take into consideration that there are coming to us celebrated artists who enjoy enormous fame in Japan," Ambassador Troianovskii had cabled to Foreign Commissar Chicherin; "their impressions from the trip, particularly in the present situation, will have great significance."[5]

The Soviet-Japanese Society and the newspaper *Asahi shimbun* also took an active part in organizing a welcome reception for the Soviet fliers who visited Tokyo in September of 1925 in return for a visit of Japanese aviators to Moscow. The two Japanese Breguets, sponsored by the *Asahi*, had left Yoyogi, Tokyo, on July 25 at 9:07 a.m.; they had reached Moscow on August 23 at 5 p.m. after a total flying time of 503 hours and 53 minutes. (As part of the promotion of the flight the *Asahi* offered a prize of a residence covering 15 *tsubo* (about 534 feet) to the reader guessing most closely the actual time taken; it also gave prizes for the successful completion of a cross word puzzle, made up of the names of the places passed by the Japanese planes.)[6]

The Soviet pilots were members of two flying associations; theirs was the extension of a good will visit to China. On September 1 they set out in two planes from Taiku, Korea. As in the case of some of the other goodwill missions, unexpected complications threatened to dispell the friendly atmosphere in which they had been undertaken. In this instance heavy fog over the Japan Sea separated the two machines. While one duly landed on the eastern parade ground of Hiroshima, the other made an emergency landing at Hikoshima, an island in the fortified zone of Shimonoseki, flight over which without prior permission of the commander of the fort was forbidden by law under penalty of imprisonment for a term not exceeding a year, or detention for over eleven days, or a fine not exceeding 50 yen.

By order of the minister of war the machine that had landed on Hikoshima was taken apart and moved by the troops outside the fortified zone. Although Volkoveiov, the pilot, was urged to continue his flight from here, he refused to do so without instructions from Ambassador Kopp. He dismantled the plane and proceeded to Tokyo by rail. Both sides issued statements to the effect that the respective actions had been unavoidable and did not adversely affect their friendship, yet the very fact that such statements were deemed necessary showed how sensitive relations were between the two countries. Still, there was genuine enthusiasm when the other plane arrived at Tokorozawa airport near Tokyo on the afternoon of September 2. Since morning the town had festively waited for the Russian aviators.

> Every house hoisted flags, and school children, girl pupils, ex-soldiers, and young men assembled in the aerodrome with the *hinomaru* [rising sun] and red flags in their hands in the afternoon [the *Japan Weekly Chronicle* reported]. The aerodrome was decorated gorgeously with festoons, flags, etc.
>
> In motor-cars, Mr. Kopp, the Soviet Envoy and his staff, about

fifty Russian residents, General Sugiyama, proxy of the Aviation Headquarters, Mr. Hatano, Director of Aviation Bureau, Lieut.-Col. Kodama, many other army and navy generals, admirals, and officers reached the scene, and joined the crowds of spectators.

Shortly after 2 p.m. a telegram was received stating that the Soviet machine passed above Osaka at 1.58 p.m. and later over Shizuoka at 3.55 pm.. At 3.40 p.m. two military aeroplanes started from Tokorozawa to meet the oncoming Soviet machine. About an hour later the Russian aeroplane was sighted to the southwest of the aerodrome. Deafening cheers rose from the crowds below. After a circuit over the ground the Russian flying machine descended with admirable dexterity amid a tremendous ovation at 4.42 p.m. . . .[7]

Another Soviet goodwill flight took place two years later, in August of 1927, when Pilot S. A. Shestakov and Mechanic D. V. Fufaev flew from Moscow to Tokyo in eleven days, a noteworthy achievement in those days. "The difference in the political structure of the U.S.S.R. and Japan does not hinder the development of mutual friendship between both peoples, the *Asahi* remarked and asserted: "We believe that the development of air communication between Japan and the U.S.S.R. will contribute to the deepening friendship between both countries, and we therefore warmly welcome the Soviet pilots."[8]

Japan offered technical assistance to the Soviet Union. In February of 1927 a group of Japanese railway experts proceeded to Russia at the invitation of the Soviet government to assist in the assembly and repair of locomotives and of passenger coaches for the Kazan line. Working primarily at the Murom railway plant the Japanese so impressed the Soviets, that the latter wished to apply Japanese methods to all the Soviet railways; they frankly called it "Japanization" of the lines. In February of 1931 the *Japan Weekly Chronicle* reported optimistically:

> The use of Japanese methods of repairing locomotives in the Murom railway shops have given favourable results. The [a]mount of labour has been decreased and locomotives have been

capitally repaired in three days. Japanese methods are also being introduced to maritime and river transport repair shops. In 1931 Japanese methods are expected to enable a saving in expenditure of 29,000,000 roubles.

The Commissariate of Ways and Communications is sending to Japan thirty railwaysmen to make a further study of Japanese methods. The Japanese repair system has been introduced into transport colleges and schools as the regular discipline.[9]

But by the end of the year a reorganization of the People's Commissariat for Communication and a shake-up in its leadership led to a shift in policy, and the employment of Japanese technicians was discontinued. Conceivably the retention of Japanese technicians appeared dangerous in view of mounting Soviet-Japanese friction. The idea of Soviet employment of Japanese hydroelectric engineers to supervise the construction of Russian hydroelectric power stations, broached to Foreign Minister Shidehara by Ambassador Troianovskii was dropped in 1931. Negotiations for Japanese technical assistance in the development of Soviet sericulture similarly were discontinued. Experts in the manufacture of cans, employed through the Hakodate office of the Soviet Trade Mission in the spring of 1930 as instructors at the cannery of the Sakhalin Development Company, on the other hand, were reemployed for some time.[10] Japanese industrial know-how continued to arouse respect; Soviet economists pointed to the need of studying the Japanese technical school system and the practical factory training received by Japanese students.[11]

The prospects for trade between Japan and the Soviet Union appeared bright as the 1920's drew to a close. During the First World War, when the closing of the Black Sea and Baltic ports had cut Russia off from her traditional markets and sources of supply, Russia had become Japan's No. 1 customer.[12] Throughout the civil war and the Japanese intervention in Siberia, Russo-Japanese trade had continued on a large scale, with consumer goods being the major category of Russian import. Following the Japanese evacuation and the consolidation of Communist power in the Russian Far East, the volume of trade had declined sharply, but the feasibility of large-scale commerce between the two countries had been demonstrated. While the situation at the time of World War I and the civil war had been abnormal, "abnormal" conditions were becoming increasingly normal; the perennial shortage of foreign exchange experienced by the Soviet Union left open the door for large-scale barter transactions between Japan and the U.S.S.R.

Early Soviet-Japanese trade differed in nature as well as scale from Tsarist-Japanese trade, as the U.S.S.R. tried to industrialize her Far Eastern regions. The motivation was not merely economic, but also political and ideological. The Soviet Union wanted to industrialize Asiatic Russia as a showplace of socialist building to impress and win over the neighboring colonial and "semi-colonial" peoples. The Soviet Union continued to purchase some foodstuffs, notably tea and seafood, but 30 per cent of her imports in 1926–27 consisted of spun materials such as nets and ropes for the fishing industry in the Okhotsk-Kamchatka region and the Amur estuary. She also bought ores, metals, metal products, lumber and chemical products (mainly iodine and camphor). Russian exports consisted primarily of lumber and fish products as well as agricultural produce and oil-cakes.[13]

With the growing industrialization of the U.S.S.R. a further change in the character of trade occurred. Shipments of fish, lumber and agricultural produce from Russia declined while industrial exports rose. Oil, charcoal, manganese, asbestos, fertilizers, ferrous metal and chemical and pharmaceutical goods which had once been imported from Japan, now were sold to Japan. By 1930 industrial exports accounted for almost 73 per cent of Soviet sales to Japan.[14] In 1929 the total volume of trade between the two countries had increased by 25% over 1928. It amounted to 15 million yen each for export to Japan and import from Japan. Large Japanese firms were beginning to participate in the exchange, among them Mitsui, Mitsubishi and Akura Gumi.[15]

Protocol C of the Fishery Convention had provided for the conclusion of special contracts for the establishment and operation of canning factories. In July of 1928 Shindō Shintarō 眞藤愼太郎 proceeded to Moscow as representative of the Nichi-Ro Gyogyō Kaisha and three other corporations, recommended by the Japanese government, to negotiate concerning this matter. On November 3, 1928, he concluded a ten year contract. It provided that there should be two fishing grounds for everyone of the 22 canneries in operation by the Japanese at the time of the conclusion of the convention.[16]

There were difficulties in the application of the Fishery Convention. It had been agreed in the Final Protocol (part I, B 1) that the Soviet government could grant without auction to its own state enterprises fishery lots corresponding to about twenty per cent of the total catch. Late in 1928 the Soviet government accordingly set aside 84 fishery lots for the Kamchatka Company, Inc. (Ako), a state enterprise established in 1926 for the purpose of developing fishery, agriculture, forestry, mining and transportation on Kamchatka. But the 84 fishery lots included 30 which had been operated by the Japanese for many years. Japan protested against the requisitioning of these lots and demanded that the action be revoked or that other lots be given to Japan in compensation without auction. The Japanese objected, furthermore, that the Russians had inflated the number of fishery lots reserved by underestimating the yearly catch of these fishery lots. The Soviets agreed to let the Japanese have 12 of the disputed fishery lots; the Japanese continued to demand the remainder, keeping alive the "18 fishery lot issue." The Russians finally gave to the Japanese some other fishery grounds in compensation for the 18 in dispute, but in January of 1931 included some of these in a group reserved for their own state enterprise, and the argument continued.[17]

The auctioning of fishery lots also was accompanied by controversy. In protest against the above-mentioned Soviet reservation of fishery lots for its state enterprises Japanese fishery concerns boycotted the auctions on February 28 and on March 15, 1929. When they participated on April 5, 1929, they were outbidden by one of their own countrymen, Uda Kanichirō 宇田貫一郎, who was not a member of the association of Japanese fishery in Soviet waters. Uda, backed by Shima Tokuzo 島德藏, acquired 78 fishery lots heretofore exploited by the Nichi-Ro Gyogyō Kaisha.[18]

A great hue-and-cry went up in the Japanese press that the Japanese fishery people were being deprived of their legal rights. Troianovskii protested. He told Premier Tanaka on April 25, 1929, that the convention of 1928 had given the Japanese more rights than the convention of 1907. The share of Soviet state enterprises had been limited to 20% of the total catch and in fact did not amount to 20%; Soviet; small private enterprisers had less than 10%. Over 200 new fishery lots had been opened in 1929 and more were operated by the Japanese in 1929 than the preceding year. It was the Soviet Union which had cause for alarm.

> The fishery convention stipulates that Japanese subjects obtain fishery lots by competition at auction, which in accordance with the fishery convention must be held not later than February [Troianovskii declared]. An auction is an auction, i.e. it presupposes free competition of the participants in the auction, including the Japanese fishery enterprisers. Auctions are stipulated by the convention of 1907; auctions are stipulated by the convention of 1928. An exception is made for lots set aside for canneries. Reports have reached us that the Japanese fishery enterprisers of the [Roryo Suisan] Kumiai association of fishery enterprisers have conspired concerning the distribution of the lots among themselves and concerning the prices on them. But we did not know anything about them, at least officially, and could not know. But now, to my surprise, the Minister of Agriculture Yamamoto [Teijirō 山本悌二郎], a member of the cabinet, declares that he is an opponent of free competition of the Japanese among themselves at the auctions and that he sees in this free competition, even though it is stipulated by the convention, a violation of Japanese rights. In point of fact a compart before the auction annuls the auction and is contrary to the laws of the U.S.S.R. as well as of Japan. I do not understand how a member of the cabinet can in such a way call for the violation of the fishery convention and for intolerable actions.[19]

Ignoring the irony of Communist insistence on free competition (so long as it involved others, whom such competition hurt), Tanaka replied that Yamamoto had been misquoted. The Japanese were concerned that Uda had paid too much for the lots, but, he agreed, the action had been legal and gave no cause for government intervention.[20]

Uda and the Nichi-Ro Gyogyō Kaisha eventually reached an agreement and Uda gave up the acquired lease on the ground that it was unprofitable at the high price which he had bid, yet his action cost the Japanese fishery industry dearly, for the rent at which the Nichi-Ro Gyogyō Kaisha was able to regain the fishery lots was much higher than before. In 1928 the average rent for a fishery lot had been about 7,500 rubles; in 1929 it rose to almost 18,000 and by 1931 exceeded 20,000 rubles.

At the auction in 1930 the Japanese bade successfully for only 86 out of 241 fishing lots, the others going to Soviet bidders at what seemed to the Japanese as unreasonably high prices. Alarmed lest Japanese fishery rights become merely nominal, the Japanese exerted strong diplomatic pressure. Another auction was held at which the Japanese acquired 61 out of 85 fishery lots. Adding other fishing grounds exploited by the Japanese, the latter held a total of 318 fishery lots in Soviet waters in 1930. Although this represented an increase of only 15 lots over the preceding year as compared with an increase of 110 lots for the Russians, the Russians still operated only 272 fishery lots, i.e. less than the Japanese in Soviet territory.[21]

The increase in rental for fishery lots was aggravated by the decline in the value of the ruble and by Soviet insistence in September of 1930 that the rent be paid at the official rate of exchange as quoted by the Vladivostok branch office of the Bank of Korea (called also the Bank of Chosen), the chief credit organ of the Japanese fishery interests. There was a difference of between 5 and 6 million yen between the cost of the ruble on the open market and the official rate of exchange, and the Japanese felt their enterprise drained of profit. Japanese objections that they used to purchase rubles at a lower rate first fell on deaf ears, the Russians replying that the matter was beyond the scope of the fishery convention. But the continuance of amicable economic relations with

Japan was in the Soviet interest and a compromise was finally worked out. Since it was difficult to fix a separate rate of exchange for Japan, it was decided that the Soviet state enterprise Ako issue bonds and sell them to Japan at a discount for use as payment for fishery lots rental and other charges. Dispute continued over the percentage of discount to be allowed. On April 26, 1931, a provisional agreement was signed, providing for the purchase of the Ako bonds by Japanese fishery interests at the rate of 1 ruble for 0.325 yen.

In spite of the settlement of the ruble issue the Japanese remained uneasy about the future of their fishery concessions. They felt that the increasing agressiveness with which the Soviet Union began to exploit her own fishery resources threatened Japanese interests. In 1930 pressure by fishery concerns had prompted both houses of the Diet to pass resolutions calling for the security of Japanese fishery rights in the northern waters.[22] In the spring of 1931 Japanese politicians once again urged their government to pursue a stronger policy toward the U.S.S.R.

On March 16, 1931, prior to the conclusion of the provisional agreement, Marquis Sasaki Yukitada 佐々木行忠 and twelve other peers introduced a resolution in the House of Peers urging the defense of Japan's fishery rights and interests in the northern seas. Viscount Nomura Masuzo asserted that the Soviets brought pressure to bear upon Japanese fishery interests, imposed heavy levies, sought to transfer many Japanese fishery grounds to Russian state management, defied the custom of a three-mile territorial limit and even committed "savage acts" against the Japanese; yet Japanese negotiations with Russia were at a standstill. Admiral Baron Sakamoto Toshiatsu 坂本俊篤 accused the Soviet Union of violating the rights granted to Japan by the Treaty of Portsmouth and by the Basic Convention.[a] Sakamoto declared that the only way to save the Japanese fishing interests was for the government to make Russia

---

[a] Sakamoto was quoted as having referred to the treaty signed between Japan and the Soviet Union in 1928 by Yoshizawa and Karakhan. The Fishery Convention of 1928 was signed between Karakhan and Tanaka; the Yoshizawa and Karakhan agreement was the Basic Convention of 1925.

desist from her current attitude of defying the treaty. The resolution, which was regarded as a "sharp reminder" to the government, passed almost unanimously.[23]

The Koseikai, an influential faction in the House of Peers, which had spearheaded the sponsoring of the resolution continued its agitation for a stronger policy after the conclusion of the provisional agreement. At a meeting at the Shōwa Kaikan on May 2, 1931, the political inquiry committee of the Koseikai condemned the Foreign Office for its conclusion of the agreement on terms decidedly unfavorable to Japan. It threatened to impeach the Foreign Office officials if they continued their weak policy.

On May 6 Mr. Sasaki, Vice President of the Russian Waters Fishery Union, and Mr. Endo, a director of the Nichi-Ro Fisheries Company, addressed a plenary session of the Shōwa Club, which included not only members of the Koseikai but of other factions in the House of Peers (the Doseikai, Dowakai, Kayokai and Koyu Club) on the subject of the Russo-Japanese fishery problem. On May 13 the Kenkyūkai, the biggest faction in the House of Peers, and the Koseikai held separate meetings to discuss the same issue. "There is general discontent among the members of all factions with the weak attitude of Baron Shidehara, the Foreign Minister, towards Russia," the *Japan Weekly Chronicle* reported on May 14. "Much regret is expressed at the fact that after two years' negotiations, no settlement is yet reached of many disputes outstanding between the two countries."[24]

Responsible Foreign Office officials realized, however, that the Soviet Union would not agree to amending the fishery convention prior to the time stipulated for revision. The Japanese government, therefore, suggested to the U.S.S.R. that an attempt be made to smooth Japanese-Soviet relations by ironing out remaining problems without making any changes in the existing convention. To this Moscow consented.

On November 26, 1931, Ambassador Hirota Kōki 廣田弘毅 proposed to Deputy Commissar of Foreign Affairs Karakhan that they discuss differences in the interpretation and application of the fishery convention and appended protocols and consider concrete measures for the improvement of Japanese-Soviet relations. Hirota had instructions to focus on specifics, lest a debate about principles lead nowhere. He stressed, therefore, the need to stabilize the fishing grounds of both sides and proposed that the fishery lots already allocated be retained in the same hands for five years (excepting the lots attached to the crab-packing plants where 10 year leases were in effect); fishery lots not yet leased were to be divided equally between both sides.

Karakhan replied on December 7 that Hirota's position was contrary to the auction system, which was a basic tenet of the convention. While he refused, therefore, to go along with the automatic retention of all the fishery lots by both sides, he offered a compromise: the Japanese were to keep 70 (he later went as high as 75) per cent of their fishery lots without auction, the rest to be put up for public tender again. At the same time the Soviet state enterprises were to be exempt from the auction process or from prior agreement with Japan in acquiring fishery lots so long as Russian fishery was less developed than that of Japan. (It was specified later that the total number of fishery lots reserved for Soviet state enterprises could not exceed 40% of the total standard catch in the northern water.) Karakhan further demanded as condition for the Soviet concession that Japan sign an agreement recognizing a 12 nautical mile limit for territorial waters and drop the objections she had raised to the assignment of a number of fishery lots to the Soviet state enterprise (the 18 and 7 lots, etc.)

While Karakhan's proposal was tossed back and forth, the 1932 auction was held. It turned out very favorable for the Japanese. Japanese bidders obtained 13 out of 15 lots which they had leased in 1931 for one year, 14 lots which had been exploited by the Soviets in 1931, as well as a number of additional lots. This gave the Japanese a total of 392 fishery lots in 1932 as compared with 309 in 1931; of these 52 were "stabilized" (44 were under special contracts, 8 on five-year leases). Consequently the Japanese shifted their position. Instead of demanding the stabilization of the fishery lots which they had held in 1931, they proposed on May 14, 1932, that 41 fishery lots—half of the 82 which they had obtained at the auction that year—be subject to re-auction; the rest were to remain automatically in Japanese hands. The Soviets countered on May 18 that 60 fishery lots should be auctioned off; the remaining grounds—280 out of 340 or 80% would remain unchallenged in Japanese hands until the expiration of the convention. They did not insist on the 12 mile limit for territorial waters, advanced as a condition earlier.

The Japanese agreed to put 60 of their lots up for auction, provided they could determine which ones. They dropped their objections to Soviet reservation of lots for their state enterprises, cooperatives and local inhabitants, and agreed that the number of salmon fishing grounds reserved for state enterprises could be increased to a certain extent until 1936. Negotiations continued about the degree to which the number of lots set aside for Soviet state enterprises could be increased, the way in which this degree could be calculated, and whether this required prior consultation with the Japanese. The matter was complicated by the many shades of meaning of the Japanese word "*kyōgi*" 協議; it was not clear whether the convention had provided for Soviet consultation of the Japanese, or for discussion, deliberation, the formation of a council or the holding of a conference in connection with the reservation of fishery lots for Soviet state enterprises.

On August 13, 1932, Ambassador Hirota and Deputy Foreign Commissar Karakhan signed an agreement. It provided for the auctioning of the abovementioned 60 Japanese fishery lots as well as of fishing grounds which the Japanese wished to exploit newly and of other grounds. As for the question of consultation or discussion, the two sides agreed in a secret document that in the case of reserved fishing grounds selected from among those that had been in Soviet hands in 1932, discussion or consultation was to be regarded as having been completed; all the Soviet Union had to do was to provide Japan with information about the number, location and standard catch of the particular grounds. In other instances discussion with the Japanese would be necessary; mere notification by the Soviet side would not meet the provisions of the treaty.

The Hirota-Karakhan agreement did not settle all outstanding problems. Many issues were left for direct discussion between the Japanese enterprisers and local Soviet authorities.[25]

The dispute over the extent of Soviet territorial waters, mentioned above, was not confined to words. In the years between the conclusion of the basic convention and the signature of the Hirota-Karakhan agreement Japanese crab and fish packing vessels were repeatedly seized by Soviet naval vessels. Although Chargé d'Affaires Besedovskii informed Vice Minister of Foreign Affairs Debuchi in fall of 1926 that Japanese vessels which violated Soviet waters would not be seized so long as they stayed more than two miles from shore, they were taken into custody sometimes within the undisputed three mile limit, sometimes within the twelve mile limit proclaimed by the U.S.S.R. and occasionally even farther out on the high seas. One need not reconstruct all the incidents, catalogued in the Japanese Foreign Office archives, or seek to determine which side was legally right in a given situation to understand the danger with which these confrontations were fraught. The arrest, trial and temporary detention or fining of Japanese for poaching was less serious than the very act of seizure, which was often accompanied by gun fire. Repeatedly Japanese were injured and killed. Eventually the Japanese began to return fire. In one instance, in June of 1930, Japanese fishermen captured and held captive Soviet officials until a Japanese destroyer ordered their release; in another instance the following month Japanese gun fire injured a Soviet official. The success of the fishery talks in the summer of 1932 prompted the Soviet side to desist from its insistence on the twelve mile limit and the incidents which had entailed the risk of an accidental collision between regular naval forces dwindled.[26]

While Japanese sources contend that the Soviet side did not live up to the obligations of the fishery convention, Russian sources accuse the Japanese of wrongdoings. "The agreement was testimony of the goodwill of the Soviet state, of its striving to help the Japanese solve serious economic problems. But the good-neighborly and benevolent policy of the Soviet Union did not meet with understanding on the part of the Japanese ruling circles," Dr. Leonid Kutakov asserts. Soviet officials registered hundreds of infractions of the convention by the Japanese. Not satisfied with the wide economic advantages which they had gained, the Japanese, according to Kutakov, tried to turn Kamchatka and several other regions into their spheres of interest. Japanese consular officials who visited Kamchatka sought to meddle in the dealings of the Soviet authorities with local Japanese fishery people. The Soviet Union thereupon restricted their travel, but the Vladivostok branch of the Bank of Korea, which handled the transactions between the Japanese fishery enterprises and Soviet organizations continued to undermine Soviet authority and, according to Russian sources, to disorganize the Soviet money market.

The threat of Japanese economic domination in the Soviet Far East prodded Moscow to strengthen the Soviet enterprises by recruiting and training suitable labor and by supplying greater funds in the form of credit to state, cooperative and private fishery enterprises. It was this assistance that permitted Soviet enterprises to participate in the auctions more vigorously and to garner a mounting percentage of fishery lots. In 1928 the Japanese obtained 86% of the fishery lots, in 1929 65% and in 1931 only 51%.[27]

The exploitation of the Japanese concessions also was beset with difficulties. Protocol B of the Basic Convention had provided for the prospecting of oil fields by Japanese concerns on the east coast of North Sakhalin over an area of one thousand square versts (650 square miles) "to be selected within one year after the conclusion of the concession contracts." In April of 1925, prior to the conclusion of the concession contracts, the Japanese government asked Soviet permission to send a geological survey party; precise knowledge of the area seemed necessary before the boring region could be selected. The Russians turned down the Japanese request on the ground that such an investigation would take a year or a year and a half and thus would exceed the time limit of the protocol; they also felt that since the Japanese government had not yet named the companies that were to exploit the concessions all matters connected with the choosing of the boring area should be left until the conclusion of the concession contract.

During the negotiation of the contract, dispute arose as to which side should select the said area. It was finally agreed that the Soviet side do so within a year after the contract went into effect. Applications by Japanese concerns to send geological survey parties to the unexplored regions of the east coast of North Sakhalin and diplomatic representations in their support were again turned down by the Soviet side. In November of 1926 a series of discussions was begun in Moscow between the appropriate Soviet authorities and representatives of the Japanese oil companies, granted the concessions. Both sides proposed different areas and it was not until three months later—after the expiration of the original deadline—that agreement was reached. The following eleven areas were set aside for oil exploration by the agreement, signed on February 18, 1927: Severnaia Okha; Ekhabi; Kydylan'i; Poromai (Paromai); Severnyi Boatasin; Iuzhnyi Boatasin: Chemerin-Dagi; Katanoki-Noglin (Katanga-Nogliki?); Myngi-Kongi; Chakre-Kampi Changu; and Vengri-Bol'shaia Khuzi (Daifuji).[28]

Another source of dispute was the question of the ownership of the old concession property and royalty payments for its use, a matter that had not been settled in the concession contracts but left for later deliberation. The Soviet side argued that the buildings, machines and tools connected with the old oil enterprises—first the Hokushin-kai 北辰会, Mitsubishi 三菱, and the Oriental Syndicate and later by their successors, the Kita Karafuto Sekiyu Kabushiki Kaisha, Kita Karafuto Kōgyō Kabushiki Kaisha, and the Sakai Kumiai during the Japanese Occupation of North Sakhalin had all become Soviet property under the provisions of the mining enterprises nationalization law. The Japanese countered that they had purchased some of the property from Russian enterprisers (Stakheev and Kuznetsov) and had contracts stipulating joint ownership of other property. The Soviets replied at first that arrangements made before the revolution and during the Japanese occupation were null and void, but later modified their stand and offered to recognize Japanese ownership of property which had been the fruit of purely Japanese investment, independent of any Russian enterprisers. No agreement was reached and a running dispute continued in consequence about royalties, the Soviet authorities demanding payment and the Japanese concessionaries refusing it.[29]

There was controversy in this connection also about the insurance of concession property. The Soviet authorities on North Sakhalin demanded in the spring of 1927 that the Japanese concessionaries draw up a list of all the property and insure it at their expense, listing the Soviet government as the beneficiary. This the Japanese refused to do lest their claims to ownership of the property be compromised.

The periodic revision of collective labor contracts in the oil and coal concessions, Soviet extension to the Japanese concessions of extra pay allowances to Soviet workers to induce them to move to Sakhalin, the attempted Soviet levy of a surtax on social insurance premiums, and controversy over the proper division of land for boring areas complicated the resolution of Japanese-Soviet differences. Japanese efforts to make substitutions in the allocated mining areas were unsuccessful. On the positive side, contracts were signed in 1928 and in subsequent years for Japanese purchase of Okha crude oil.

With the inauguration of the first five-year plan in 1928 the Soviet government openly clamped down on foreign concessions; all but those of Japan were forced to suspend operations. Increasingly from the closing days of 1930, pressures mounted on the Japanese coal concessions. New domestic labor legislation provided for a seven hour work day, and fines were imposed on the Japanese for violating this or other provisions of the labor laws or of collective contracts. The Japanese were forced to reduce the prices of goods which they furnished to their Soviet employees. At the same time Russian wage demands soared with every labor contract renewal. The difficulties posed for Japan by the steady rise in operating costs were compounded by political harassment, such as the arrest of Soviet employees loyal to the Japanese company and repeated demands for the revocation of various leases.[30]

As noted before, the maintenance of a branch office of one of their own banks in the Soviet Union was regarded as vital by the Japanese. The Bank of Korea was a Japanese bank. It had opened a branch office in Vladivostok in Tsarist times. Refusing the demand of Soviet officials who had come to power in Vladivostok following the withdrawal of Japanese occupation troops in 1922 that the Vladivostok branch of the Bank of Korea apply for a license as a Soviet commercial bank, the Japanese succeeded in November of 1923 in obtaining the Maritime Province's recognition of their branch office as the branch office of a foreign bank, and the following year, in 1924, received permission to engage in the business of foreign exchange. After the conclusion of the basic convention the Soviet People's Commissariat of Finance in September of 1926 formally confirmed the right of the Bank of Korea to operate the branch in Vladivostok. In February of 1928 the branch office registered with the Department of Commerce of the Vladivostok district; it renewed the registration annually. Soviet finance officers inspected the bank records and found nothing amiss.[31]

The Soviet Union was as sensitive about reciprocity and equality of treatment as Japan. She insisted on the establishment of a branch office of her Far Eastern State Trade Bank in Kobe. Japan granted permission in September of 1925 lest the operation of the Bank of Korea be endangered. She refused to give a 25 year business licence requested by the Soviet Union, however, and insisted on annual renewals until a comprehensive Japanese-Soviet commercial agreement was worked out.[32]

In the fall of 1930 inspectors from Khabarovsk suddenly descended upon the Vladivostok branch of the Bank of Korea and after a long and careful inspection forbade it to remit money abroad and to trade in Soviet currency except at the official Soviet rate of exchange. The Japanese government protested against the manner of the inspection and against the prohibition. It argued that the order was contrary to the historical function of the bank and would make its continued operation difficult. Deaf to the representations of the Japanese government and to the plea that the branch played a key role in the development of economic relations between the two countries, the People's Commissariat of Finance ordered on December 7 that the office be closed, a fine be paid and three of the bank officers be put on trial. Although the Japanese government failed in its efforts to keep the Vladivostok branch of the Bank of Korea open, it arrived at a face-saving arrangement with the Soviet government whereby Japan "voluntarily" closed the bank office and the Soviets dropped the matter of a fine and the trial of the Japanese bank officers.[33]

"The official explanation from Moscow of the reasons for closing the

Vladivostok branch of the Bank of Korea is not altogether satisfactory," the *Japan Weekly Chronicle* declared on January 8, 1931. "If the bank's transaction in paper roubles disturbed the Soviet's financial programme— which it is difficult to believe—that is mainly the fault of the Soviet Government which tries to maintain a fiction regarding the value of its currency. It is evident that the ordinary operation of a foreign banking house is, in such circumstances, impossible."[34]

The closing of the Vladivostok branch of the Bank of Korea led to the departure of some 400 Japanese residents from Vladivostok by mid-July 1931. The Japanese primary school in that city and the Japanese newspaper *Vladivostok Nippō* (Vladivostok Daily News) were closed. The Japanese consulate general and the agencies of the Osaka Shosen Kaisha and the Kawasaki Steamship Company remained the only Japanese interests in that region.[35]

During their occupation of North Sakhalin the Japanese had communicated with their homeland by radio-telegraph from Aleksandrovsk via Toyohara 豊原 on South Sakhalin. There had been contact also between Aleksandrovsk, Japan proper, Korea and Khabarovsk, and wireless stations had been set up by the Japanese navy at Okha and Chaivo for communication via Otomari (South Sakhalin) and Soya (Hokkaido). Since the Japanese received concessions for the exploitation of North Sakhalin's natural resources as they withdrew, it was agreed that they continue operation of their radio stations under Soviet supervision. This was confirmed in a protocol concerning the Okha and Chaivo stations, signed by the commander of the Japanese army of occupation on North Sakhalin and the Soviet committee which officially accepted the territory from him on May 1, 1925.

Difficulties arose almost at once. The U.S.S.R. protested to the Japanese government on October 17, 1925, that the Japanese authorities had carried away a large part of the equipment of the radio-telegraph station at Aleksandrovsk, that the Japanese consul at Aleksandrovsk denied access to the Japanese stations to Soviet telegraphers who had come to establish communication with the rest of the U.S.S.R. and, above all, that the Japanese stations continued to send messages from private

Japanese in code without revealing the code to the Soviet authorities. The Japanese replied on October 29 that they would look into the matter of the alleged removal of radio-telegraph equipment from Aleksandrovsk, but that no changes in the operation of the stations should be made until an agreement was worked out; they argued that the use of code "could not call forth objections."[36]

The Soviet government responded on November 13 that the U.S.S.R. had regained full sovereignty over North Sakhalin. Soviet laws prohibited the use of code by private individuals and associations; to allow it to the Japanese would be tantamount to granting them extraterritoriality. Hence the practice must cease forthwith.[37]

On November 24 the Japanese Ministry of Foreign Affairs reported that investigation showed no evidence that all the items listed in the Soviet inventory had been at the radio stations when the Japanese had first taken the over. All that they had removed was some new equipment installed by themselves. As a matter of fact, the Japanese Ministry of Foreign Affairs declared, they had left some Japanese equipment behind to assure the continuance of communication.[38]

In December of 1925 operation of the Okha and Chaivo wireless stations was assumed by the Kita Karafuto Sekiyu Kaisha.[39] On May 5, 1926, the Foreign Commissariat of the U.S.S.R. informed the Japanese embassy in Moscow of its desire to set a date for the commencement of negotiations to draw up regulations for the operation of the Japanese wireless stations at Okha and Chaivo. Upon consultation with Tokyo the Japanese embassy on August 19 agreed to hold discussions.[40] On September 11 the Soviet Foreign Commissariat proposed that negotiations begin on October 15. The Japanese embassy on October 8 accepted the date, and negotiations were duly opened a week later. Accord was reached on such matters as allocation of time for the operation of the wireless stations and the use of the Japanese telegraph code and the international code. But the Japanese were reluctant to accept the Soviet proposal that Japanese telegraph operators be replaced by Soviet nationals if the latter became fully qualified in the use of the Japanese telegraphic code, and the talks were recessed temporarily—until the summer of 1928 as it turned out.[41]

Communication by mail also was the subject of prolonged discussion. Service had been resumed following the conclusion of the basic convention. The Japanese side forwarded mail to the post offices at Vladivostok and Moscow; the Soviets delivered mail to Tsuruga. In regard to North Sakhalin it was decided that mail to and from the Aleksandrovsk district be carried by coal ships of the concession company during the summer; in winter mail would be exchanged at Handazawa 半田澤 on the Japanese-Soviet border on the island. Mail to and from Okha and other places on the east coast of North Sakhalin would be carried by oil concession vessels in the summer months. Mail to and from the Petropavlovsk district of the Kamchatka peninsula was conveyed by regular Japanese liners in summer; in winter it was forwarded by way of Vladivostok.

In February of 1931 the Soviet government proposed the conclusion of a treaty for the exchange of mail at the Japanese-Soviet frontier in winter. Japan replied in August that it preferred an agreement between the postal authorities of both countries. Although no comprehensive agreement was concluded at this time, it was decided by the end of the year that as of mid-January 1932 mail between Aleksandrovsk and Onor be exchanged twice a week in winter.

The above arrangement did not extend to parcel post. The U.S.S.R. seemed less eager for such an exchange and Japan had to make repeated overtures before Moscow agreed to a round of conferences. Negotiations dragged on from October of 1928 until November of 1931 as the Japanese vainly tried to lower Soviet postal rates and to extend delivery to countries which had not concluded a postal agreement with the U.S.S.R. The parcel post agreement was signed on November 23, 1931; it went into effect almost a year later, on August 23, 1932.[42, b]

A series of conferences was held also in regard to railway communication. The location of Russia left overland transportation between Japan and Western Europe at her mercy, and Japan was eager to regulate the matter. On May 11, 1925, the Japanese embassy in a *note verbale* proposed

---

[b] For the French text of the parcel post agreement, see Japanese Archives, Russo-Japanese Treaties, 34/1–34/28.

discussion in Moscow of the restoration of railway traffic between Japan, Manchuria and the U.S.S.R.

Before the [First] World War the above-mentioned communication took place by way of three routes, namely via Vladivostok, Korea and Dairen [the Japanese note stated]. The main purpose of this direct communication was the facilitation of passenger and freight transport between the major cities of Japan proper, Korea, Manchuria, as well as Siberia and European Russia. The following railway and steamship companies participated in the transportation: the Japanese government railways, the railways of the Korean governor-generalship, the South Manchurian railway, the Osaka Shosen Kaisha, the Russian Volunteer Fleet, the Ussuri and other Russian railways, interested in communication.

The Ministry of Railways wishes subsequently to exchange opinions regarding the question of the restoration of direct passenger and freight communication between Japan and Western Europe via the U.S.S.R., primarily of direct passenger and freight communication between Tokyo and Berlin or Paris via Moscow, as well as direct conveyance of silk from Japan to Moscow via Vladivostok.[43]

The Japanese planned to send representatives of the Railway Bureau of the Korean governor-generalship of the South Manchurian railway and of the Osaka Shosen Kaisha along with their delegation.

The Foreign Commissariat replied on June 16 in a *note verbale* that it did not object to a conference for the improvement of communications between Japan and the U.S.S.R., but inasmuch as the negotiations were bound to touch upon the interests of the Chinese Eastern Railway (which was under joint Russian-Chinese management), it deemed it essential that representatives of this company participate.[44]

The Japanese embassy responded on July 13 that it agreed fully that representatives of the Chinese Eastern railway must participate in the conference and that their exclusion had been inadvertent.[45] On August

18 the Japanese Foreign Office informed the Soviet embassy in Tokyo that representatives of the Soviet merchant marine were invited too, and proposed that the conference begin in the first ten days of October. They reiterated that they wished to discuss communication with Western Europe after transportation between Japan and the Soviet Union had been settled.[46]

Ambassador Kopp replied on September 2 that his government agreed to the opening of discussions regarding Japanese-Soviet railway transportation in early October. As for the matter of transit through the U.S.S.R. to Western Europe, he reported that a railway conference between his country, Estonia and Latvia had already been set for November 2, and invited Japan to participate.[47]

A Japanese delegation consisting of the Ministry of Railway's Traffic Bureau Director Taneda 種田, Section Chief Usami 宇佐美 of the South Manchurian Railway, and of representatives of the Korean railway and the O.S.K. (Osaka Shosen Kaisha) shipping company duly proceeded to Moscow. On October 19 negotiations were begun, with the Soviet delegate Rudyi acting as chairman of the conference, Taneda and the representative of the Chinese National Railways as vice-chairmen.[48]

On August 25 the Soviet Ministry of Communications had cabled an invitation to the management of the Chinese Eastern Railway to attend the conference. When the Chinese Foreign Office, informed of this by the Chinese Eastern Railway authorities, on September 25 requested from the Soviet embassy detailed information about the make-up and agenda of the conference, the embassy in its reply on October 3 invited the Chinese government to send a plenipotentiary representative of its own. The Soviet note stated that representatives of the Soviet railways, the Japanese railways, the South Manchurian Railway and the Korean railways as well as of Sovtorgflot (the Soviet merchant marine) and the Osaka Shosen Kaisha steamship company would participate in the Soviet-Japanese railway conference to deal with a draft convention between the governments of the U.S.S.R., China and Japan concerning direct passenger and freight communication, draft regulations for the transport of passengers and freight, regulations for sea transport, the question of passenger routing, rates, currency, classification, the regulation of mutual compensation, and the calculation of through handling of rolling stock in direct communication via the Chinese Eastern railway.

The Chinese embassy in Moscow replied on October 10 that representatives would be sent from the Chinese Ministry of Communications as well as from the Chinese Eastern Railway. On October 15 the Chinese Foreign Ministry notified the Soviet embassy that it was sending the director of international direct transport as its representative; he would come together with the representative of the Chinese Eastern Railway. But inasmuch as no detailed data on the points to be discussed had as yet been furnished and the invitation to send a plenipotentiary representative had only just been received while the conference was about to begin, it could not grant to the representatives plenipotentiary powers since they were not prepared for this. "Therefore," the Chinese note continued, "the representatives both of the Ministry of Communications and of the Chinese Eastern Railway can participate only in the examination of questions concerning the exploitation of the Chinese Eastern Railway; concerning all questions of territorial sovereignty, political authority and others pertaining both to the Chinese Eastern Railway and the national railways of China, however, the Ministry must, of course, make the qualification that such questions will not be valid without confirmation by the government [of the republic of China].[49]

The tripartite conference began on October 19 but broke down a month later, on November 24, at the third session, because the Chinese delegation did not have the powers to conclude an agreement about freight transport and because it had received instructions while the negotiations were in progress not to sign the agreement about through passenger service between the U.S.S.R., China and Japan. (China objected to through train service via the Chinese Eastern Railway without changing trains.) Japan and the Soviet Union continued their discussions at an international railway conference in Moscow on December 7–16. In addition to Estonia and Latvia, with whom the U.S.S.R. and Japan had already negotiated, Poland, Germany and France joined the talks. An agreement was duly worked out for direct European-Asian passenger and freight communication via Siberia. Passengers were to be served by an international train of eight cars. Through traffic west of Moscow was to proceed via Riga; in the Far East there were four routes: Vladivostok-Khabarovsk, Vladivostok-Harbin, Harbin-Pusan, and Harbin-Dairen. The conferees reserved the right for China to join in the agreement at a later date.[50]

CHAPTER TWELVE

Lingering Mistrust

NOTWITHSTANDING honest efforts on both sides to improve Japanese-Soviet relations, neither party lowered its guard. The U.S.S.R. arrested a number of Japanese. In April of 1925 four Japanese working in Vladivostok were taken into custody on suspicion of trying to bribe a Soviet official. In June of the same year Major Shibuya 澁谷 and a civilian companion, Mr. Nakai 中井, en route from Germany to Japan by way of Siberia, were detained as military spies. Two other Japanese, Shirahama Fuku 白浜フク and Kiyokaze Fukumatsu 清風福松, were jailed in July on the double-barrelled charge of spying and illicit transportation of liquor. Other Japanese were arrested on the suspicion of spying, for violating the Soviet frontier, and for failure to pay the wages of some of their employees. In the spring of 1930, on the eve of the sudden inspection of the Vladivostok branch of the Bank of Korea, several Japanese and Russian money changers in Vladivostok were seized for trading in rubles at other than the official rate.[1]

Soviet vigilance was nourished by lingering mistrust of Japanese intentions. As Foreign Commissar Chicherin wrote to Ambassador Kopp in Tokyo on June 23, 1925:

> Not one state, after recognizing our government, was so friendly in its expressions toward us as the Japanese one. Satō in his meetings with me is the very embodiment of friendliness. Your reports about the receptions at the crown prince, the empress dowager and the like also point to a strikingly, even exceptionally strikingly underlined friendliness. What is the meaning of this?

That is what one must decipher. What do they expect? Do they want territory for immigration, do they want concessions, or do they want a safe rear for the coming war with the United States? There is a clash between us and the Japanese first of all on the approaches to the Chinese Eastern Railway. This question is most serious. If the Japanese have further designs on Eastern Siberia, there can be further friction with them and they will be beset by disappointment. As for our future trade with Japan, Japan is, of course, in great need of our fish, raw materials and lumber, but there is skepticism in our country about what we can import from there. . . .[2]

The Japanese trusted the Soviets as little as the Soviets trusted them. The Communist Party of Japan was a blood relative, if not the offspring, of Moscow. The program of the Japanese Communist Party had been drafted by Nikolai Bukharin at the fourth congress of the Third International in Moscow in November 1922. The platform of the Japanese Communist Party, formulated at its first convention in Ichikawa, Chiba Prefecture, in February of 1923, had been based on the Moscow program and had included demands for the abolition of the Japanese monarchy, the army and police, Japanese withdrawal from Russian territory and recognition of the Soviet government.[3] A police round-up in 1923 had seriously curtailed the Communist Party of Japan, yet the following year it had been reorganized and had recruited a sizeable membership.[4] The Japanese authorities, therefore, did not have faith in the Soviet pledge, made in the Basic Convention, not to subvert the Japanese government or to spread propaganda.

Japanese misgivings were justified. Not only had Foreign Commissar Chicherin publicly stated on May 14, 1925, at the third session of the Soviets of the U.S.S.R. that the Soviet Union would continue its propaganda at home, for "to say that all propaganda in general must be stopped in the Soviet Union that is to demand that the Communist Party cease to be the Communist Party,"[5] but Ambassador Kopp had made all too plain his disdain for the Basic Convention.

Mention has been made of the "unconfirmed" report which swept Japan shortly after Kopp's arrival that he had dismissed the Basic Convention as a scrap of paper. The report was not "unconfirmed" as far as the Japanese government was concerned, for a copy of the stenographic transcript of Kopp's speech before the Politbureau of the Harbin Provincial Committee of the Communist Party, dated April 17, 1925, recorded by Ershova and testified to be true by Secretary Anokhin, was obtained by the Foreign Office. It was stamped "top secret" in Japanese, however, and not released to the press since its publication would have been at least as embarrassing to the imperial government as to the Foreign Commissariat.

In the Far East, in foreign policy, I shall adhere to the theses laid down by the Central Committee [of the Communist Party], and make use of Japan as an enemy [Kopp had confided to his countrymen]; prior to the official recognition of Soviet Russia by America, our close alliance with Japan constitutes a threat to American society, which will react to our surrender of the mineral resources in the Far East to exploitation by Japanese capital by putting pressure on its government to hasten official relations with Soviet Russia. As for the alliance with Japan, as [an alliance] with a country with an imperialist system, it is not particularly solid; it will be a mythical treaty, binding us to nothing in the event of good relations with America, merely giving us the possibility for the legal existence in the territory of Japan of the leading organ of the vanguard of the revolution.

In regard to the question put to me in the note about my political work in Japan—I look upon it completely differently, on the basis of the above-mentioned theses of foreign policy, i.e. I leave the conduct of the political work in Japan entirely in the hands of the Japanese socialists, giving them only moral support in getting rid of defects, permitted by Japanese workers in party building, again I repeat, making use of Japan as a threat to America in the Far East.

My outlook on party building, approved by the Ministry of Foreign Affairs and the Central Committee, is as follows: to use our mission in Japan in regards to the party in so far as possible in the preparation of future workers without attaching to them the label of party-membership, but to limit ourselves to the founding of associations [*zemliachestva*] (socialist circles), to which all those elements with a bent for socialism will be drawn spontaneously and will contribute to the strengthening of the general work, which particularly has the special purpose of disseminating among the workers and peasant masses appropriate literature, which the Comintern Z[emliachestvo] soon plans to publish locally. At the same time new and especially valuable groups of workers who know village work more intimately are picked out as village [political] workers; this branching off will be done at the expense of the union of workers, who will without question belong to us when the struggle of the working class will enter the phase of direct struggle for socialism and will follow our party, to which the future belongs.[6]

The Japanese police kept Soviet visitors under close surveillance. When four delegates of the All-Union Soviet of Trade Unions stayed in Japan in the fall of 1925, Japanese policemen in Tokyo, Osaka and Kobe invaded their private buildings and refused to leave when asked to do so. They kept most private Japanese individuals from visiting the Soviet delegates. When a few individuals, notably some newspapermen, after prolonged interrogation about the specific purpose of their visit, were admitted, the police remained in the room during the discussions and recorded what was said. Policemen accompanied the visiting delegates when they went out and if they took a car climbed in without invitation. When a large crowd gathered at the time of the departure of the delegates, the police assaulted and battered persons who tried to approach them. Among the Japanese who were thus beaten up was a Japanese employee of the Soviet Embassy who was helping the delegates with their baggage. Ambassador Kopp protested in a note to Foreign Minister

Shidehara, dated September 29, 1925, that the restrictions imposed on the Soviet trade union delegates were "contrary to the elementary rules of international courtesy" and a violation of the Soviet-Japanese agreement.

Kopp asserted that the treatment of the delegates was not an exception—Japanese policemen treated all Soviet citizens in this fashion. First Secretary Nikolai Kirillovich Kuznetsov had already made an oral representation to Vice Minister Debuchi about a number of cases of the illegal actions of the Japanese police in regard to Soviet student trainees. Although Debuchi had promised that the illegal restrictions would be lifted, they had in fact become more severe. "The students who are here are subject not only to the most troublesome police surveillance—numerous police agents do not confine themselves to following on their heels watching their every movement—but quite frequently these agents enter an apartment, where, in their opinion, a given person has stopped too long and invite him to depart for home. When the students ride in an automobile the police agents take a seat in the automobile and refuse to get out, in spite of the most persistent invitations [to do so]."

Kopp complained that other Soviet citizens, particularly those working in Soviet offices in Japan, were treated in the same fashion. Employees of the Far Eastern Bank and of the Far Eastern State Trade Bank in Kobe, the director of the telegraph agency of the U.S.S.R. and his family, and the technical employees of the Embassy in Tokyo all were under similar police surveillance. In every instance the surveillance was expressed "in the following of police agents after the employees and members of their family, in attempts to penetrate into their private apartments by the most diverse contrivances, directed toward carrying out a search without having any legal right to do so." When Soviet citizens who were being shadowed told the policemen who followed them that they would appeal to the embassy for protection, the policemen made "inappropriate and sometimes downright insulting" remarks directed at the person of the ambassador.

The most serious violations of international law are committed by the Japanese police in regard to the embassy of the U.S.S.R. itself and its members, who enjoy extraterritoriality [Kopp protested to Shidahara]. In recent days I have repeatedly noticed instances of police agents being on watch at the very gates of the Embassy. These agents looked into the automobiles which were driving out from the courtyard of the Embassy. The private apartments of the Embassy secretaries, Messrs. [Georgii] Astakhov [First Secretary] and [Lev] Vol'f [Second Secretary], who live outside the embassy, are persistently besieged by the police, who make all sorts of attempts to penetrate into the building. The members of the families of the said persons are so terrorized thereby that they declare it impossible to continue living in Japan unless the illegal actions of the Tokyo police will be terminated.

Kopp expressed the "liveliest concern" for the future development of relations between the U.S.S.R. and Japan" if the police harassment of Soviet citizens would not be halted; he warned that if the measures were not cancelled the Soviet Union would retaliate in kind. The measures would not remain "one-sided", as he put it diplomatically.[7]

In a conversation with Kopp on October 5 Shidehara expressed regret at the conduct of the Japanese police. He asserted that although he had not had the opportunity to familiarize himself with Kopp's letter, the the Japanese government definitely did not condone police actions which might adversely affect relations between the two countries.[8]

Yet within a fortnight, on October 18, another incident occurred. Professor Evgenii Genrikhovich Spal'vin, who served as Japanese Secretary of the Soviet embassy, was to read a paper on "The Pedagocial Principles in the U.S.S.R." at a general meeting of the Literary-Artistic Japanese-Russian Society (Literaturno-artisticheskoe iaponorusskoe obshchestvo), a group dedicated to the study of various aspects of the intellectual life of the Soviet Union. Professor Spal'vin was the fifth speaker. He was preceded by four Japanese, who gave papers on Russian art, drama, and music. Spal'vin got up and after a few introductory remarks turned to the meat of his talk. No sooner did he utter "Communist doctrine constitutes the underlying principle in the Soviet Union," however, than a plainclothes police officer interrupted him and forbade him to continue. When Spal'vin asked what was the matter, the officer beckoned to several uniformed policemen who approached and grabbed Spal'vin. Only with difficulty did he dissuade them from arresting him and taking him to the station house, pointing out that he had diplomatic immunity.

In a note to Foreign Minister Shidehara Ambassador Kopp expressed his "deep surprise" at the action of the police. It was obvious, he wrote, that the Japanese police were well informed about the papers to be read and the persons who were to present them. They knew that Professor Spal'vin was associated with the embassy and enjoyed diplomatic immunity. To lay hands on him and to order his arrest (even though the order was not carried out) was, therefore, not a misunderstanding but a crime under article 91 of the criminal code of Japan. For the sake of the friendly relations existing between the two countries Spal'vin refrained from bringing charges—for the time being—provided the Japanese themselves thoroughly investigated the matter at once and informed the ambassador of the punishment meted out to the policemen concerned.[9]

Yet fear of subversion remained alive in both countries. The Japanese government was disconcerted that the crews of Japanese merchant ships were propagandized at the International Seamen's Club in Vladivostok, and on January 14, 1927, Vice Minister of Foreign Affairs Debuchi complained to Chargé d'Affairs Besedovskii that Japanese fishermen were subjected to Communist propaganda in concessions along the Soviet coast. The propaganda was disseminated by pistol-packing Japanese and Korean Communists, who came to the Japanese fishing sheds allegedly under the protection of the Soviet secret police, made speeches and distributed printed material. Besedovskii promised to telegraph his government and ask that such activity be stopped.[10]

In his memoirs Besedovskii elaborated on Soviet propagandization of Japanese fishery workers and remarked:

Nominally, it was difficult for the Japanese to protest: the propaganda took place on Soviet territory. But the Khabarovsk authorities did everything to irritate the Japanese government as much as possible. The Japanese workers on the concessions were literally coralled into the clubs and there forced to listen to speeches by Korean agitators of the Comintern. Agents of the G.P.U. [Security Police] with revolvers were stationed at the doors of the club and did not let the workers out until the end of the meeting. If anyone of the workers, among whom there were sometimes Socialists, spoke up in protest, he was immediately arrested and after a beating at the G.P.U. [office] was deported to Japan.[10]

In August of 1926, on instructions from the Soviet government, Besedovskii proposed to Vice Minister of Foreign Affairs Debuchi the conclusion of a Soviet-Japanese non-aggression pact, analogous to the Soviet-German pact, concluded in Berlin in April of that year between Ambassador Nikolai Nikolaevich Krestinskii and Foreign Minister Dr. Gustav Stresemann.[a] It was the hope of Moscow, Besedovskii later noted in his memoirs, that a Soviet-Japanese non-aggression pact would drive a wedge between England and Japan and prevent them from coordinating their policy versus the U.S.S.R. and forestall their intervention in the Chinese revolution, which Borodin sought to Sovietize.

On September 17 Debuchi informed Besedovskii that he would receive him shortly to discuss Soviet-Japanese relations in general and the non-aggression pact in particular. The meeting took place on September 30. Debuchi declined the Soviet proposal without rejecting it. He shelved the issue for a number of years by saying that the fishery convention and the treaty of commerce, envisioned in the Basic Convention of 1925, must be concluded before a new agreement, embodying pro-

---

[a] The Treaty of Berlin was a treaty of "friendship and neutrality." The Soviet Union and Germany agreed to consult with each other on all major political and economic questions and to remain neutral if the other was attacked by a third power or subjected to an economic boycott.

visions of non-aggression and arbitration, could supercede the Basic Convention. He feared that a new treaty at this time might be misunderstood by the Japanese public as an attempt on the part of Moscow to replace the Basic Convention before all of its provisions had been carried out.

Although Besedovskii sympathized with Debuchi's position, he deemed it his duty to state that the Soviet-German treaty confirmed the obligations of the Treaty of Rapallo and that the non-aggression pact with Japan could similarly reconfirm the Basic Convention, so that there could be no question about the Soviet Union's intention to live up to the obligations which she had assumed, but Debuchi did not change his mind. In his memoirs Besedovskii asserts that he exchanged oral assurances with Debuchi that neither side planned to attack the other. This was a "gentlemen's agreement," not a secret oral non-aggression pact, rumored in the press.[11]

In a lengthy speech before the lower house of the Diet, Foreign Minister Shidehara stated on January 18, 1927, that in the two years since the signature of the basic convention Japanese-Soviet relations had been steadily strengthened and held out great possibilities for the future.[12]

The question of a non-aggression pact was raised again by Ambassador Dovgalevskii in a conversation with Premier Tanaka on May 24. Referring to the objections voiced by Debuchi, Dovgalevskii asserted that the Soviet government had carried out the economic points stipulated in the basic convention; it was not its fault that the conclusion of a fishery convention was being delayed. He declared that the Soviet government was prepared to negotiate with Japan concerning a treaty of commerce and to be favorably disposed toward granting to Japanese new concessions in the Soviet Far East. He noted that no complaints had been received by the Japanese government in connection with the Soviet pledge not to intervene in the internal affairs of Japan and expressed confidence that no cause for complaint would be given in the future also.

Tanaka replied on June 16. He expressed satisfaction that the Soviet government would be favorably disposed toward granting new concessions to Japanese and that it loyally adhered to its promise not to engage in propaganda or meddle in the internal affairs of Japan. But although he assured Dovgalevskii that the Japanese government was not involved in any negotiations with England about the renewal of the Anglo-Japanese alliance and had received no official proposals regarding this, the tenseness of the international situation made the signing of a political pact—i.e. a non-aggression pact—between the Soviet Union and Japan inopportune and expressed the belief that it would be possible to return to this question after the strengthening of economic relations between the two countries.

Dovgalevskii replied on July 1 that the Soviet government would assist the Japanese through the Far Eastern authorities when granting them new concessions. It expected that the Japanese government would give to its ambassador in Moscow the necessary instructions to bring the fishery negotiations to a successful conclusion. The Soviet government felt that the commercial relations were hindered primarily by the absence of a treaty of commerce and it was prepared to begin negotiations for its conclusion; naturally during the negotiations consideration would be given to Japanese desires to facilitate the development of economic relations between the two countries. Dovgalevskii expressed regret that the Japanese government deemed it inopportune to conclude a non-aggression pact since just such a pact could contribute to the lessening of international tension and normalize the general situation in the Far East.[b]

Tanaka declared that negotiations concerning a treaty of commerce would be begun following the conclusion of a fishery convention.[13]

[b] On October 19, 1928, Deputy Foreign Commissar Litvinov telegraphed to Troianovskii that Ambassador Tanaka during his farewell visit had inquired "for some reason" whether the Soviet Union was still interested in a non-aggression pact. "I replied affirmatively," Litvinov cabled, "since the pacts proposed by us include neutrality, which is not in the Kellogg pact, whose fate, furthermore, is not known, while bilateral pacts can be realized more easily and quickly. I also mentioned that bilateral pacts about non-aggression symbolize friendship more clearly than does a multilateral pact. Am reporting this for your information, just in case." (D.V.P., vol. XI, p. 543)

On March 8, 1928 a most interesting two-hour tête-à-tête took place in the Soviet embassy between Ambassador Troianovskii and General Tanaka Giichi, who was concurrently Premier and Foreign Minister. One of the army's top experts on Russian affairs and chairman of the Siberian War Planning Committee of the General Staff at the time of the Japanese intervention, Tanaka was an economic rationalist identified with a "positive" policy on the continent. Troianovskii had asked for an appointment with Tanaka to discuss the general state of Soviet-Japanese relations; he had arrived in the midst of Tanaka's election campaign and there had been no opportunity for leisurely discussion until now. Tanaka had replied that he would prefer to visit Troianovskii—to come to the Soviet embassy informally on foot, so as not to arouse the jealousy of the ambassadors of the other powers; too frequent (public) meetings with Troianovskii could lead to unnecessary talk. Troianovskii agreed and on March 8 Tanaka strolled unobtrusively into the embassy, accompanied only by the interpreter Sawada. Troianovskii and Tanaka conferred as they ate *bliny* (Russian pancakes). Tanaka spoke mostly in Japanese, Troianovskii in French. Sawada did all the interpreting. A remarkable exchange took place in this informal atmosphere.

Tanaka declared that he wanted to have an unofficial, completely private and absolutely frank talk with the ambassador. He asked Troianovskii to tell him everything that he thought in regard to Russo-Japanese relations, both pleasant and unpleasant, openly, not as one diplomat to another but as a private person who desired to remove all misunderstandings and to lay the groundwork for the strengthening of friendship between Japan and the U.S.S.R. Not being a diplomat by profession he preferred such talks, feeling that they would contribute more to a rapprochement than negotiations accompanied by all kinds of formalities. Besides, as a military man he found matters of protocol very difficult. He wanted to hear Troianovskii's frank views, give an immediate answer to some and think the others over to give an answer later, if necessary.

Troianovskii agreed that unofficial talks paved the way for official talks and facilitated ascertaining the position of both sides in order to find a common language and basis for official negotiations. He said that he too liked such frank discussions and had frequently resorted to them in his former commercial activity in order to find the possibility of reconciling the true desires and interests of the negotiating parties; such method of talking gave good results most of the time. Troianovskii stated that such a private frank conversation was particularly appropriate in the present case, since he had no instructions from his government concerning quite a number of questions about which he was going to talk. He felt that his obligations as ambassador were not limited to carrying out instructions but included taking the initiative for finding and paving the way for the improvement and development of Soviet-Japanese relations and to make appropriate recommendations to his government.

Tanaka asserted that he had confidence in Troianovskii and expressed the hope that Troianovskii had similar confidence in him. He asked that Troianovskii take as broad a view as possible of current Japanese-Soviet relations since this was a private conversation. He would listen with attention and, he repeated, wanted to hear unpleasant as well as pleasant things. Troianovskii agreed, asking that Tanaka not take offense if he said something that the latter did not like.

Troianovskii declared that Soviet-Japanese relations were developing satisfactorily and that friendship between the two countries was growing, since it no doubt corresponded to the interest of the two great neighboring countries. But the unpleasant aftertaste of recent history had remained in the Soviet Union and there were some misgivings of the true plans of Japan toward the Soviet Union. Statements made by Tanaka himself to Valeriian Dovgalevskii (Troianovskii's predecessor) on June 16, 1927 that the open door policy should be applied to Siberia as well as various hints made by such people as Kuhara Fusanosuke, the Minister of Transport, made Russians suspect that Japan harbored some grand designs toward Siberia.

Tanaka asserted that this was purely a misunderstanding and formally assured Troianovskii that the Japanese government had not the remotests thought of seizing Soviet territory, attacking the U.S.S.R., intervening or doing anything of the sort. Japanese policy toward the Soviet Union was being formulated in terms of economic relations. Economic dealings could and should be developed considerably but, he insisted, by peaceful means.

Troianovskii agreed that there must have been a misunderstanding. The Japanese government could not harbor any aggressive desings toward the Soviet Union, for such designs—their mere existence—would be as harmful to Japan as to the Soviet Union. Yet Troianovskii deemed it necessary to add that any attempt to realize such plans would lead to a struggle unto death, for in spite of all the might of the Japanese people and its army, the Soviets knew how to stand up for themselves.

Tanaka retorted somewhat irritatedly that the matter was not worth discussing, because as he had just said Japan had no aggressive plans whatever. He wanted Troianovskii to address himself to the questions which he regarded as most important in Soviet-Japanese relations.

Troianovskii replied that the fishery question had not been concluded yet; the convention had been signed but not yet ratified. Meanwhile the new fishing season was upon them. He suggested that the spirit of the new convention be applied in the interim.

Tanaka agreed that a temporary arrangement was necessary. He said that ratification would not occur soon. The Privy Council included old diplomats, scholars and lawyers who studied every letter, every paragraph at length; ratification could take several months longer. He suggested, therefore, that the practice of the preceding year be continued. He had duly instructed Ambassador Tanaka in Moscow and hoped he would come to an agreement with Karakhan.

Troianovskii then turned the conversation to the question of a commercial treaty and proposed that discussions be held in Moscow, because the Soviet Union was currently negotiating commercial treaties with a number of countries and could not send delegations everywhere. The Japanese representatives in Moscow were experienced men who had successfully concluded the fishery convention; he himself had only recently come to Japan and should concentrate on becoming acquainted with Japan; he would not like to begin his service as ambassador with negotiations concerning a commercial treaty.

Tanaka stated that he would make the necessary preparations for the commencement of negotiations and would further communicate on this subject with Troianovskii later. "During the negotiations about a commercial treaty there will be many difficulties," Tanaka stated. "I see the basic difficulty in the difference of economic systems. In your country the government is in charge of trade, in our country private persons. And your government has a somewhat one-sided approach toward commercial transactions. Your goods must be sold in our country always for cash and even with an advance payment, while our goods must be exported and bought for credit of 3, 6 and even 9 months. This creates great difficulties. If a manufacturer can wait for the payment of money, a banker cannot do so. Furthermore the sale for credit leads to an increase in the price. Credit is rather expensive in our country. The matter would be much simpler if there were no difference in economic system."

"I do not think that the basic difficulty lies in the difference of the economic systems," Troianovskii countered. "Thanks to the fact that trade in our country lies in the hands of the government, you can solve all the most important questions more firmly and solidly. For example, the question that you have raised about credits. Of course, without credits trade will develop meagerly. According to our commercial custom transactions in foreign trade in the area of purchasing foreign goods have been made on credit since olden times, still before the war (i.e. under the Tsarist regime), and in the very same way our goods were sold for cash and even with an advance. There are many reasons for this, which it is impossible to change now no matter what we could like to do. It seems to me that the Japanese commercial-industrial world must comprehend the fact, which has already been grasped by all the other states—Germany, England, and America—that the Soviet Union constitutes even in the case of purchases on credit the most solid and reliable buyer and payer. You must understand that we cannot fail to pay for transactions concluded by our commercial delegation, we cannot go bankrupt, and consequently all transactions with our commercial agencies are better secured than all transactions with private persons."

When Tanaka mentioned that Japanese bankers were not accustomed to such credit transactions, Troianovskii replied that the matter of credit was not the most basic problem, for even if credit were available, the question remained what goods Japan had to sell that were suitable for the Russian market and that were priced competitively. Troianovskii noted that the United States was able to supply various items from the Philippines cheaper than Japan, and Tanaka agreed that American competition was a serious factor that had to be considered.

Troianovskii expressed the belief that the Japanese government would have to help out with extending credit and lowering Japanese prices. He reiterated that the problem lay not in the differences of the economic systems but in conditions within Japan—in Japan's industry, her goods and prices. "I suppose that during the commercial negotiations it will be necessary to decide a whole series of concrete questions, and I take the liberty of giving some advice," Troianovskii stated; "don't touch on economic systems, talk as little as possible about principles and as much as possible about business." Noting that he spoke so from his previous experience in the commercial field, Troianovskii added frankly: "We cannot change our economic system, and it is not worth touching on anything that is connected with it, [such as] for example the organization of our foreign trade."

Troianovskii then broached the subject of the relationship of the Chinese Eastern Railway and the South Manchurian Railway; he had found rather strained relations between them during his trip through Manchuria. Tanaka replied that the China question as a whole interested Japan very much and that Troianovskii and he ought to talk about it. Troianovskii replied that he did not quite know what Tanaka meant by "the China question," but that they could not settle Chinese affairs without China being represented. But, he asked, had the time not come to speak of a non-aggression pact between Japan and the Soviet Union. There was talk now of a non-aggression pact between America and France and between America and Japan. "The time has not yet come for this," Tanaka replied. "Events must develop gradually. We still have in our country various tendencies and various attitudes. One must go step by step. I feel that the question of a commercial treaty must come first. If we conclude it, it will be a great achievement; after that we shall see." Troianovskii replied: "To be sure, fruits can be eaten only when they are ripe. The whole question is whether they have become ripe or not. If Japan will have pacts with a whole row of other states and will not have a pact with the U.S.S.R., the necessary balance will not be preserved. The international situations is such that one can perhaps talk of a pact already." "Let us not hasten," Tanaka warned. "If one climbs too high at once, one can fall."[14]

As Japan moved steadily to the right, she became increasingly concerned about subversion from the left. A round-up of Communists and other radicals was begun in March of 1928 and in June the death penalty was instituted for violation of the Peace Preservation Law. The Executive Committee of the Communist International in turn exhorted the Communist Party of Japan to strengthen and improve its illegal apparatus, so as to counteract the measures of the Japanese government.[15]

In the spring of 1928 stories appeared in the Japanese press that the Japanese government wondered where the proletarian parties of Japan had obtained the funds for the elections. In his confidential conversation with Tanaka on March 8, 1928, Troianovskii took exception to assertions in the Japanese press that the Soviet government and the Soviet embassy in Tokyo had contributed money to the proletarian parties of Japan. He insisted that the Soviet Union was faithfully abiding by the basic convention and was not interfering in the internal affairs of Japan. He asked Tanaka to absolve the U.S.S.R. in a public statement to the press lest the development of friendly relations between the two countries be endangered.[16]

But anti-Soviet agitation mounted. On the evening of March 23 at 8 p.m. several paper balls filled with explosives were thrown at the main entrance of the Soviet embassy and exploded. When the Russians came out of the building they found a silk kerchief attached to a tree with a dagger. The kerchief bore a Japanese message which accused the Soviet ambassador of transmitting money to the Communist Party of Japan and of distributing pamphlets against the Japanese polity while in Russia

[sic]; it called on the ambassador to go home. The message was signed "Kenkokukai [The State Foundation Society]—Order of the League of Blood." Proclamations were scattered on the street around the embassy with the heading: "Drive out the Russian ambassador—the leader of Bolshevik propaganda!" Like the message knifed to the tree, the proclamations, signed by the Kenkokukai, accused the ambassador of supplying the Japanese Communist Party with funds; they called for the expulsion of the ambassador and the breaking off of diplomatic relations with the Soviet Union. The Japanese government promptly expressed its regret, but Troianovskii believed that there were men in the cabinet itself, specifically Home Minister Suzuki Kisaburō 鈴木喜三郎, who supported the campaign against him and the Soviet Union. He attributed the incident to the attacks of the Japanese press against himself and the embassy and to the soft attitude of the authorities toward such acts as the attack on Cherkasov in Dairen.[17]

On June 25 Ambassador Troianovskii cabled to Deputy Commissar of Foreign Affairs Karakhan:

> The activity of fascist organizations against the embassy recently has increased. Aside from articles in the rightist press I receive threatening and warning letters. Some two weeks ago fascists appeared at the embassy to hand in a communication in which there was a polite request [for the ambassador] to leave Japan. Today some 15 fascists gathered at the gates and asked me to receive them for a discussion of an ideological character. I replied that their previous statements made it impossible to have a discussion. Thereupon they transmitted a communication: the council points to the violation by the U.S.S.R. of international confidence, to the work "regarding the bolshevization of Japan," to the agitation against Japan in Manchuria and to the failure to carry out the fishery treaties and asks me to take appropriate measures. They promised to come once more to talk. Since morning the embassy was guarded by a reinforced detail of police. When the fascists dispersed, the police too left at

once, having all the while chatted amicably with the fascists.[18]

Karakhan replied the following day, on June 26, that no steps should be taken concerning the above for the time being.[19] Troianovskii agreed in a telegram of the same day:

> We must not give reason to think that one can put pressure on us by such a method. Today in a conversation with Debuchi I stressed primarily the agitation of the fascists against the voyage of the Kabuki [troupe] to Moscow, pointing out that the Japanese government would be disgraced in Europe if it gave the blessing to such actors as [Ichikawa] Sadanji for the trip, and a group of hooligans would prove stronger. Debuchi agreed and promised to take [some] steps. Tomorrow Count Ogasawara is giving a dinner for Tanaka, Sadanji and me. This will cool down the fascists and police somewhat.[20]

Widespread arrests of Communists were renewed in 1929 and the Communist Party of Japan was decimated in spite of the return of Japanese students from Moscow. The Comintern instructed the Japanese Communists not to try to establish a legal Communist Party at this time, but to infiltrate workers' and peasants' organizations and combining illegal and legal work to fight against "the government of White terror and the capitalist offensive."[21]

Comrade Ichikawa at his trial in Tokyo boasted that the Communist Party of Japan had never ceased to exist since its founding in Moscow under the auspices of the Comintern:

> The bourgeoisie says that the Japanese Communist Party reappeared many times in different, changeable forms.... But this is a lie from beginning to end. The Japanese Communist Party suffered many blows under bourgeois repression; and it was even forced to resort to dissolution. Yet the Japanese Communist Party as such continued to exist together with the Comintern and grew and developed as one of its sections.[22]

Desirable as the communization of Japan would have been for Moscow, however, it remained a long-term and thus secondary objective. In the late 1920's the Russian leaders took pains not to endanger Soviet-Japanese relations by overt subversion, and the above-mentioned instructions to Japanese Communists to infiltrate workers' and peasants' organizations were dispatched in the form of a resolution from the West European Bureau of the Comintern.[23]

Repression of Communists in Japan was expected by the Soviet Government; it did not preclude peaceful, even amicable, relations between the two states. The event which turned lingering Russian mistrust into dire apprehension and abruptly ended the chapter of relatively good relations was the Japanese invasion of Manchuria, for it brought Japanese armies back within striking distance of Siberia and thus constituted a direct threat to the national security of the U.S.S.R.

Epilogue

THE Russo-Japanese War of 1904–1905 had not left a legacy of hatred. Within two years of its termination Russia and Japan had drawn together in an entente and by 1916 had become full-fledged allies. Although Premier Stalin was to allege years later that men of his generation had been waiting for four decades to avenge themselves, at the time of the Russo-Japanese War he and other Bolsheviks had welcomed the defeat of their country for the revolutionary opportunity that it offered. The Japanese intervention in Siberia during the Civil War had been anti-Communist and thus became the object of more consistent condemnation by Soviet writers. Yet its historical residue of hostility formed no more of a barrier to the resumption of Russo-Japanese cooperation than had the Russo-Japanese War. In 1925 as in 1907 statesmen in both countries realized that Japan and Russia had more to gain by working together than at cross-purposes.

The normalization of relations between Japan and the Soviet Union after World War II has taken longer than after the Russo-Japanese War or the Siberian Intervention, even though the confrontation in 1945 had been less prolonged and less bloody. In part, this has been due to Japan's reluctance to reconcile herself to having lost more territory by defeat than she had gained by victory. But for a number of years the major obstacle to the full-scale resumption of Russo-Japanese relations was Japan's temporary loss of independence. So long as the essentially American Occupation lasted, Japan could not resume normal relations with the U.S.S.R., with whom the United States was engaged in a "cold war."

Involvement in Russo-American rivalry was not a new experience for Japan. In the 1850's, when the United States and Russia had competed in the opening of Japan, she had elicited promises from the commanders of the rival fleets that they would protect her from each other. In 1904–1905 Japan had obtained the support of American bankers for her war effort against Russia; in 1907 she had joined hands with her recent foe to block American penetration of Manchuria. When the Communist coup d'état of 1917 and the Civil War which ensued had left Russia more weakened than had the Russo-Japanese War and the United States had taken Russia's place (as Russia two decades earlier had taken China's place) as the major opponent of Japanese expansion, many Soviet leaders, including Lenin himself, had given thought to a Soviet-American rapprochement as a means of defense against Japan, which Lenin regarded as the most dangerous state to the Soviet Union. Even before the transfer of the capital to Moscow in 1918, Karl Radek and Iurii Larin advocated the surrender of Kamchatka to the United States in order to drive a wedge between the United States and Japan.[1]

American insistence on Japanese withdrawal from Siberia and North Sakhalin had contributed to the deterioration of Japanese-American relations, but this had not signified a change in American feeling toward the Soviet regime. Washington had not been "duped" by the Communists. American opposition to the carving up of the Russian empire had been in line with traditional U.S. policy in defense of the Open Door and territorial integrity. There was uneasiness in the United States that the frustration of Japan's attempt to gain control of Siberia by force might lead to a complete turnabout in Japanese policy and the drive to secure Japanese interests in that region by diplomatic means. A Soviet-Japanese alliance was deemed possible because of Russian and Japanese dissatisfaction with the attitude of Great Britain and the United States. Soviet Russia had been excluded from the Paris Peace Conference after the First World War and from the Washington Conference; Japan had participated, but had come away disgruntled.[2]

As noted, it had been partly for the purpose of frightening the United States into adopting a less hostile attitude toward the U.S.S.R., that Moscow had concluded the Basic Convention with Tokyo. Although a Soviet cartoonist had sneered upon the signature of the Basic Convention that *"diadia Sem ostal'sia sam"* (Uncle Sam has remained alone),[3] most Russians would have preferred an agreement with the United States to an agreement with Japan. As a writer in the Far Eastern Republic had put it in 1922: "Japanese capital is more political than American [capital]. Japanese capital is followed by the Japanese gendarme, and that makes it less acceptable to us than American capital."[4] But in the face of continued American non-recognition what could the Soviet Union do but join hands with those willing to work with her?

Although Soviet leaders, in what Louis Fischer described shortly afterwards as "their somewhat schematic approach to American foreign policy and... their ignorance of American psychology and conditions,"[5] were mistaken in their belief that the United States could be scared into abandoning the policy of principle which it believed to be pursuing, they were realistic enough to perceive that Japan's shift in policy was as opportunistic as their own. They understood that it was partly the economic crisis that had engulfed Japan in the 1920's and particularly after the great earthquake of 1923, partly Japanese hostility toward the United States (due not only to American pressure for Japanese withdrawal from the Russian Far East but to her immigration policy and her economic and political competition in East Asia) and not sudden Japanese sympathy toward Bolshevism that had made possible the renewed Russo-Japanese rapprochement. Soviet writers remarked that it was Japan's need to secure her back in the coming struggle with the United States that had brought about the Russo-Japanese agreement. The basis of the convention was economic—the joint exploitation of Russia's natural resources—yet even here, Japanese-American rivalry was a factor as the Japanese navy pressed for the acquisition of oil reserves.[6]

The Soviet view of American reaction to the Basic Convention was expressed by Boris Evseevich Skvirskii, formerly of the Ministry of Foreign Affairs of the Far Eastern Republic, in a telegram from Washington, where he was stationed as the unofficial representative of the U.S.S.R.:

> The American military circles are worried by the signature of the Russo-Japanese agreement. There is particular discussion of the

question of oil. It is pointed out that the Japanese are engaged in fortifying the southern shores of Korea and the nearby region of the southern islands of Japan. These fortifications complete the closing of the Japan Sea, and the treaty with Russia provides the Japanese to a considerable degree with the sources of supply of raw materials. In military as well as in other circles the question is considered what effect the agreement will have on American trade interests in the Far East. There is talk in this connection of the necessity of changing the [American] policy toward the U.S.S.R.[7]

In Soviet eyes Japanese recognition of the U.S.S.R. brought about an immediate change in the Far Eastern situation, "which must give pause to many imperialists." Commenting on the observation of the *New York Times* that it was too early to tell what the political significance of the Soviet-Japanese convention would be, B. Semenov declared: "but this is only written; in actuality, however, America undoubtedly experiences great alarm over it."[8] He expressed the conviction that Japanese recognition of the U.S.S.R. at once transformed the latter into a first class power in the Far East and, since Far Eastern problems had become of world significance, this boosted the standing of the Soviet Union in world affairs. Ridiculing the expectation of the *New York Times* that the gift of 4 million yen by [John D.] Rockefeller to the library of Tokyo Imperial University to replace books lost in the great earthquake and the 3 million yen donation of the American Red Cross for the reconstruction of Japanese hospitals would somehow weaken the anti-American feeling, then current in Japan, Semenov sneered: "However many new books Rockefeller will buy for Japan and [however many] hospitals the Red Cross will rebuild, the fact will remain that Japan has recognized the U.S.S.R. and America already fancies to see the specter of the "Red menace" in the Pacific Ocean."[9]

The Basic Convention not only restored Russian sovereignty in North Sakhalin; it strengthened the Soviet position in China and curbed (or so it seemed) unilateral Japanese action in Manchuria and Mongolia.

Last but not least, it assured Russian access to the Pacific Ocean. "Thereby," one Soviet writer boasted, "the Soviet state system and economic construction are putting a road through to the new center of the world capitalist economy, and here, in connection with the successes in friendly and equal China, there is laid the firm foundation of the [Soviet] Union, which will step forth as the grave-digger of the titans of capitalism in their inevitable coming collision and will carry out the historical role of the proletariat, the mission of the liberation of the colonial and semi-colonial peoples."[10]

Underneath the Bolshevik rhetoric was a cool realism. As Foreign Commissar Chicherin cabled to Soviet representatives abroad in September of 1926 in reference to Japanese machinations in Manchuria: "The Japanese government speaks friendship, but actually Japanese agents unofficially instigate our enemies. We must preserve with Japan friendly relations, which serve as some curb on the militarists."[11] The Soviet leaders remained well aware of the importance of the Japanese people, with their high level of education and industrial skill, in the power struggle for Asia. "An alliance between the Japanese and Soviet peoples would mark a decisive moment in the task of liberating the East," Joseph Stalin, then Secretary General of the Communist Party, told a Japanese newspaperman in the summer of 1925. "Such a union would mark the beginning of the end for the great colonial powers, for world imperialism; and it would be invincible."[12] (The military possibilities of a Soviet-Japanese alliance were to be held out again twenty years later by one-time premier and ambassador to the U.S.S.R. Hirota Kōki in a vain effort to pull the Soviet Union from the American side, when he told Ambassador Iakov Aleksandrovich Malik that the Japanese navy together with the Soviet army would form an unbeatable combination.)[13]

Fanciful as the ideas of Stalin and Hirota may have been, it was common sense for Japan to seek a *modus vivendi* with the Soviet Union. As the French paper *l'Asie Française* had said in May of 1923: "The policy of economic concessions, the war horse of Moscow, whets the appetite of the whole world. It is inevitable that Japan come to an understanding with Russia in the Far East. They have so many interests in common!" Even such a fierce critic of the Communist regime as the emigré historian Boris Ivanovich Nikolaevskii wrote in regard to the convention of 1925 that it had been natural for Japan to seek an agreement with the Russian bear, though it had been painted red. "Essentially, Japan has no other policy that makes sense from the Japanese point of view than to live in peace and harmony with Russia."[14] At the same time the Basic Convention constituted a revolutionary change in Soviet foreign policy. In 1922 the Soviet leaders had tried to break with the most basic elements of Tsarist Far Eastern policy; in 1925 they had returned to them at least partially.[15] There was one important difference between Soviet and Tsarist policy, however. While Tsarist Russia had sought to expand her national boundaries, the U.S.S.R. strove for power on a global scale by attempting to foster world revolution. Now and again the ideal of world revolution was shelved temporarily for more limited immediate gains, but it was never discarded.

Within a decade and a half after the conclusion of the Basic Convention between Tokyo and Moscow, Japan was to vacillate again between the United States and Russia, pondering which way to strike and how to avoid simultaneous engagement with both. What was new about Japan's position on the chessboard of Russo-American rivalry after the Pacific War was that she was to be a pawn rather than a knight in the game. Yet not for long. Like a century before, she was to garb her weak body politic in diplomatic armor and use the United States as a shield against the Soviet Union, whose military power had increased greatly. But the war of 1945 between the U.S.S.R. and Japan had destroyed the Basic Convention of 1925, and the territorial and economic questions that had been settled after five years of negotiations became issues again. The United States could neither facilitate nor prevent a resolution of the age-old Russo-Japanese controversy; direct negotiations between Japan and the Soviet Union were necessary.

At the dawn of the 1970's the Sakhalin question is no longer an issue. Japan gave up her concessions in North Sakhalin during the Pacific War in a futile attempt to avoid Soviet intervention. As the result of her defeat Japan also lost South Sakhalin, but this was "fair and square" because the territory had been seized from Russia after Japan's victory in the Russo-Japanese War. The dispute is over the Kuril Islands, specifically the southern Kuril Islands, and the Habomai Islands, which the Soviet Union also annexed, though they had been "always" Japanese. Yet there may be a parallel in the Japanese occupation of North Sakhalin in the 1920's and the Soviet occupation of the Habomai Islands. Both were ostensibly temporary; both seemed to become permanent; both were eventually liquidated. There is no parallel between the Japanese occupation of North Sakhalin and the Soviet occupation of the southern Kuril Islands, however. The former was repeatedly proclaimed to be temporary and was denounced by the United States from the very outset; the latter was repeatedly proclaimed to be permanent and, in spite of belated second thoughts by the State Department, was sanctioned by the United States and Great Britain at the Yalta Conference.

In seeking to justify her occupation of North Sakhalin Japan had groped for historical precedents. The nearest case that her advisers had been able to find had been U.S. occupation of portions of Florida! Florida had been Spanish territory when American troops under General Andrew Jackson had been operating against "savage and predatory" Indians in the neighborhood. When Spain had failed to restrain the Indians, Jackson had seized the forts of St. Marks and of Pensacola, destroying much Spanish property in the process. The United States had retained the Spanish towns and forts until 1818, Secretary of State John Quincy Adams justifying Jackson's action as having been done "not in a spirit of hostility to Spain, but as a necessary measure of self-defense; giving notice that they should be restored whenever Spain should place commanders and a force there able and willing to fulfill the engagements of Spain towards the U.S. or of restraining by force the Florida Indians from hostilities against their citizens."[16]

In attempting to secure Soviet withdrawal from the southern Kuril Islands the Japanese Foreign Office argues that the Yalta agreement, in which the United States and Great Britain had concurred with Soviet annexation of the islands, is not binding for Japan, since it had been a secret agreement to which Japan had not been a party, and that the San Francisco Peace Conference of 1951, though it divested Japan of the Kuril Islands, did not specify to whom they were to be given.

While the Japanese occupation of North Sakhalin and the Soviet occupation of the southern Kuril Islands are basically different, there is a lesson that is clear from the negotiations concerning the liquidation of the former, namely that neither side will be swayed by legalistic arguments but by political and economic considerations. American pressure to withdraw and her own original pledge to do so had contributed to Japan's evacuation of North Sakhalin; but broad Soviet economic concessions to Japan in the Russian Far East as well as on the island were an overriding factor. Should the Soviet Union ever agree to return some of the southern Kuril Islands, it would be for political and economic reasons—perhaps at a crucial moment of history, if she thought that such action would swing Japanese public opinion in her favor, or in exchange for large scale Japanese economic aid in the development of Siberia and of Russian industry in general.

It is, of course, in the area of economic cooperation that the experiences of the 1920's are most applicable. While Americans have become accustomed to the flooding of the domestic market by quality Japanese products, the tendency still is to think in terms of American companies engaging in joint ventures in Japan. To be sure, there is knowledge of the activity of Japanese enterprises in prewar China, but the longstanding ambition of Japanese industrialists to participate in the development of the Russian economy is not appreciated. The many concessions extended by Tsarist Russia to Japan during the First World War would have left much of the development of Siberia in Japanese hands. The Japanese intervention following the Russian revolution was in part a desperate attempt to save Japanese investments. The concessions that the Soviets granted to the Japanese while they cancelled the concessions of other powers were not of benefit to Japan alone. Leaving aside the political implications of the concessions, they profitted the Russian economy as well. As it developed, the concessions eventually became a burden for Japan—one of the justifications for their surrender during the Pacific War.

The concession agreements, as will be recalled, had been concluded between Soviet authorities and private Japanese companies. They did not work out well for a number of reasons: the Japanese companies received insufficient financial backing from the Japanese government, the laws and *modus operandi* of Communist Russia were frequently in conflict with the methods of capitalist Japanese corporations, and political factors were allowed to intrude as Soviet-Japanese diplomatic relations deteriorated, the Soviet government interfering in the running of the concessions to put pressure on the Japanese government.

The unprecedented economic growth of Japan in the 1950's and 1960's has revived hopes in Tokyo and Moscow for Japanese participation in the development of Siberia. Premier Nikita Khrushchev specifically invited Japanese assistance in this endeavor. Delegations of Japanese businessmen frequent Irkutsk and other Siberian cities, while Soviet commercial and industrial experts come to Japan.

As before, Japan and the Soviet Union both have foreign exchange problems. Trade continues to be conducted essentially on a barter basis, the two sides agreeing to specific goods to be exchanged. The planned economy of the U.S.S.R. is a mixed blessing, offering stability on one hand and inflexibility on the other hand. The two major obstacles to significant Soviet-Japanese economic cooperation still are the lack of a profit-sharing system that would allow private Japanese companies (in the field of electronics, for example) to participate in the Soviet economy effectively and Soviet insistence that Japan furnish not only the know-how but a large part of the capital for the development of Siberia. The old argument as to what constitues a fair ratio of investment on the part of the two sides in the exploitation of a given concession continues.

While it seems obvious that the deterioration of Soviet relations with China makes the speedy economic development of Siberia a strategic "must," Soviet diplomats assert that it is of no particular interest to them. If Japanese businessmen want to develop Siberia in order to make a profit, that is alright with the U.S.S.R., they say, but Japan will have to lend her the money to provide the necessary services (build railway lines, move workers, etc.). The retort that Japan lends money only to underdeveloped countries ends the discussion, for the Soviet Union cannot ask for funds on this basis. To the query whether it is not humiliating for the U.S.S.R. to request loans from Japan and whether it might not be in the Soviet interest even to sustain an economic loss for the sake of the strategic advantage that the prompt development of Siberia would entail and the political dividends that would accrue to the U.S.S.R. within Japan from large-scale contacts, Soviet diplomats confide in frustration that the various projects are not in the current five-year plan.

Soviet inflexibility on the territorial issue, on profit-sharing, and on the financing of Siberian projects has left the Japanese business community luke-warm to doing business with the Russians. But as our study has shown, the Soviet government can be flexible and opportunistic, particularly if the international balance of power is at stake. A change in Soviet attitude, which would make Japanese economic participation attractive either financially or politically (by offering the return of some of the southern Kuril Islands, for example) would meet with a favorable response in Japan.

There are two other factors, which could drive the Japanese into economic cooperation with the Soviet Union *without* the latter changing her stand, and it is possible that Soviet intransigence has been due to expectation of either or both of these developments. The first is a depression or a recession in the United States and the consequent exclusion of Japanese products. Cut off from the American market to any significant extent, Japan would have to turn elsewhere as a matter of self-preservation, and the U.S.S.R. would be the most logical alternative. The second factor is the resurgence of anti-American feeling due partly to the Vietnam War but primarily to the continued presence of American bases in Japan. The bases which protected a prostrate Japan from possible Russian or Chinese encroachment have become anathema to large segments of the Japanese public and may in the long run do more to help than to hinder the Soviet cause if they are not withdrawn or drastically curtailed.

Thus in the foreseeable future, as in the past, we discern an inexorable link between Japan, the Soviet Union and the United States. And as before, the specter of a Russo-Chinese alliance hovers in the shadows.

A Soviet-Japanese understanding need not be a threat to the United States or to China. It could contribute to the economic development and stability of Northeast Asia. It would certainly be a natural development. As the *New York Herald Tribune* put it in August of 1924:

> They simply have got to come together, Russia and Japan. There is no room for argument whatsoever. If Mr. Abe does not like Mr. Baba, his neighbor, he can take his worldly possessions and go his way. A nation differs from an individual in this. Japan cannot fold her tent and steel away like an Arab simply because she does not like the way her "Red" neighbor is carrying on at the other side of the Nippon Sea.[17]

Appendix

ANNEXES AND NOTES APPENDED TO THE FISHERY CONVENTION

Annex No. 1

SPECIMEN RULES OF INTERNAL ORDER FOR THE FISHING ENTERPRISES OF JAPANESE SUBJECTS IN THE DISTRICTS SPECIFIED IN ARTICLE I OF THE FISHERY CONVENTION BETWEEN JAPAN AND THE UNION OF SOVIET SOCIALIST REPUBLICS

ART. 1. The beginning and the end of the normal working day as well as of the special working day in each fishery ground shall be fixed by agreement between the lessee of the fishery ground and the competent local organs of the People's Commissariat of Labour.

ART. 2. The above-mentioned beginning and end of the working day is signalled to the employees by means of a bell, a whistle or in some other similar way.

ART. 3. With regard to those absent from work after the expiration of 15 minutes after the signal, and to those who leave work before the end of the working day, in so far as no good reasons can be adduced for such absence, the wages as well as "kuichi" and other forms of remuneration can be curtailed for the time of absence.

ART. 4. The employees, who wish to be absent or late at work, or leave work before the working day is over, on account of justifiable causes, must inform their immediate superior and obtain his consent.

ART. 5. Employees are allowed intervals for meals and rest.

ART. 6. Employees must carry out all the orders of the administration and the officials concerning their duties.

ART. 7. The administration distributes work among the employees.

ART. 8. The employees, who owing to the nature of their work have to handle machines, tools and appliances for work, must take proper care of them.

ART. 9. The administration must see to it that no machines, tools or appliances for work cause any danger to the life and health, and must provide them with necessary precautionary equipments. Moreover, the administration must train the employees, who for the first time enter into work or receive tools, instruments, etc., to the use of the latter, and particularly warn them of the dangerous parts of such tools, instruments, etc., as well as of the dangerous or harmful features of the industry.

ART. 10. The employees handling machines, tools and appliances for work must take measures of precaution, and handle them with the utmost care.

ART. 11. In case any tools, machines and appliances for work as well as the means safe-guarding the work thereof, become deteriorated or are rendered unfit, the employees must immediately inform of it their superior official.

ART. 12. In case of any accident to an employee in the course of his work, he must immediately inform of it his immediate superior and render himself to the ambulance for medical assistance. If the injured man is unable to do so himself, his fellow-workers must immediately inform the administration, which shall send him to the ambulance at once and at the same time adopt all possible measures of precaution with regard to the particular work, where the accident took place.

ART. 13. Employees in those branches of work which are foreseen by special regulations of the People's Commissariat of Labour, must be given special attire and footwear as well as precautionary appliances. Such branches of work in the fisheries of the Far Eastern District, where these special objects shall be given out, as well as the kind and amount of such objects, are to be determined by the lessee of fishery grounds, subject to approval by the competent local organs of the People's Commissariat of Labour.

ART. 14. It is forbidden to employees:

(a) to smoke in a place where there is a notice prohibiting smoking.
(b) to change one kind of work for another, when there is no necessity to do so.

APPENDIX 377

(c) to use aribitrarily machines, tools and appliances for work contrary to established rules.
(d) to play cards while working, to swear, and to quarrel.
(e) to work while in a state of drunkenness.
(f) to prepare fish for their own consumption both in working hours and at other times, as well as to use prepared fish for their own necessity, without a corresponding permission from the administration.

ART. 15. At necessary places of the enterprise, the administration must set up wash-stands provided with soap for washing hands.

ART. 16. A sufficient number of wash basins must be provided with near the dwellings and at other convenient places, which must be kept clean and in proper order.

ART. 17. At working places as well as at the dwellings of employees, the administration must set up a sufficient number of lavatories which must be kept in good order and clean. It is forbidden to use any other places not intended for this purpose.

ART. 18. The administration must see to it that the fishery grounds be kept clean and take all necessary measures of sanitation. Employees are likewise responsible for the cleanliness of the premises where they work.

ART. 19. For the sake of their own health, the employees must observe all sanitary rules and all labour protection rules, which are to be posted in a conspicuous place.

ART. 20. The work connected with elemental calamities is obligatory on all the employees of the enterprise and must be carried out at the first demand of the administration, irrespective of the time when it has to be fulfilled.

ART. 21. The present rules may be complemented or amended by agreements between employees on one hand and the administration on the other, subject to approval by the competent organs of the People's Commissariat of Labour.

ART. 22. The rules of internal order must be posted both in Japanese and in Russian in a conspicuous place for general information.

MAPS SHOWING THE BOUNDARIES OF

(1) Mechigme Bay.
(2) Konyam Bay, Abolechef Bay (Kalagan Bay) and Roumilet Bay.
(3) St. Pavla Bay.
(4) Karaga Harbour.
(5) Northern portion of Baron Korfa Gulf.
(6) Bechevinska Bay.
(7) Milkachinsky Bay and Iamskaia Bay.
(8) Aian Bay.
(9) Grand Duke Constantine Bay.
(10) Krestovaya Bay.

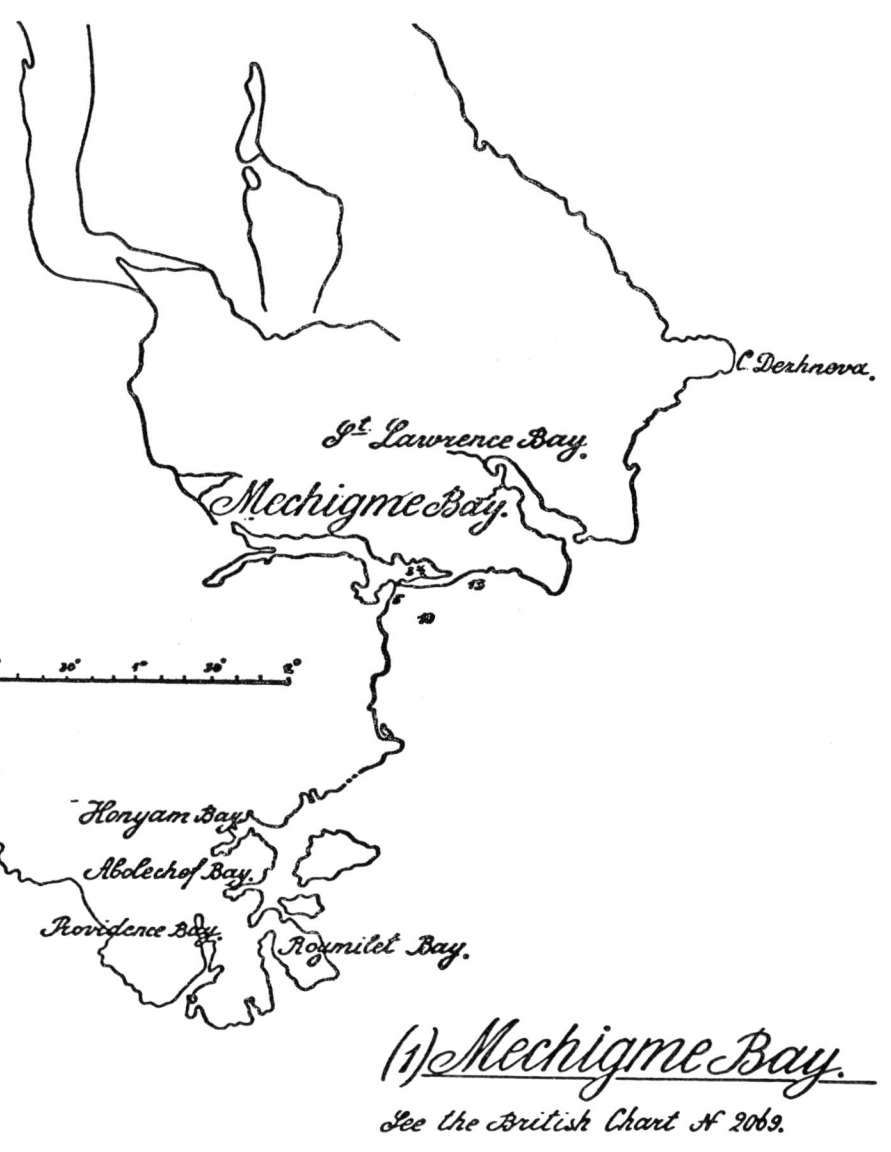

Plate 1: Mechigme Bay.

Plate 2: Konyam Bay. Abolechef Bay. Roumilet Bay.

Plate 3: St. Pavla Bay.

Plate 4: Karaga Harbour.

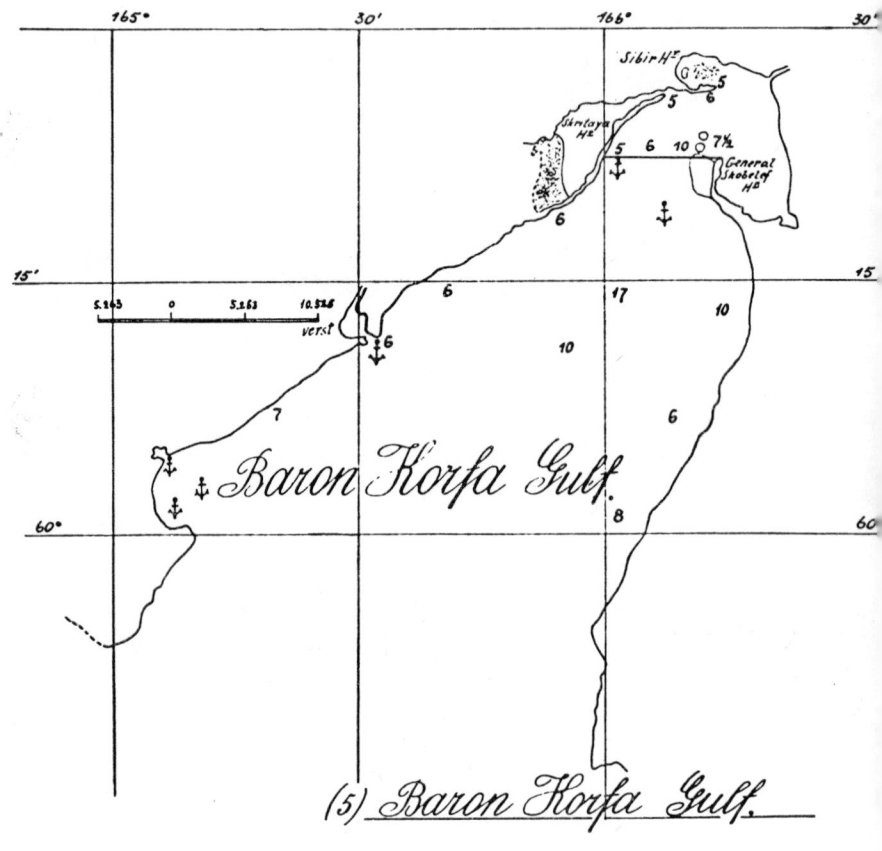

Plate 5: Baron Korfa Gulf.

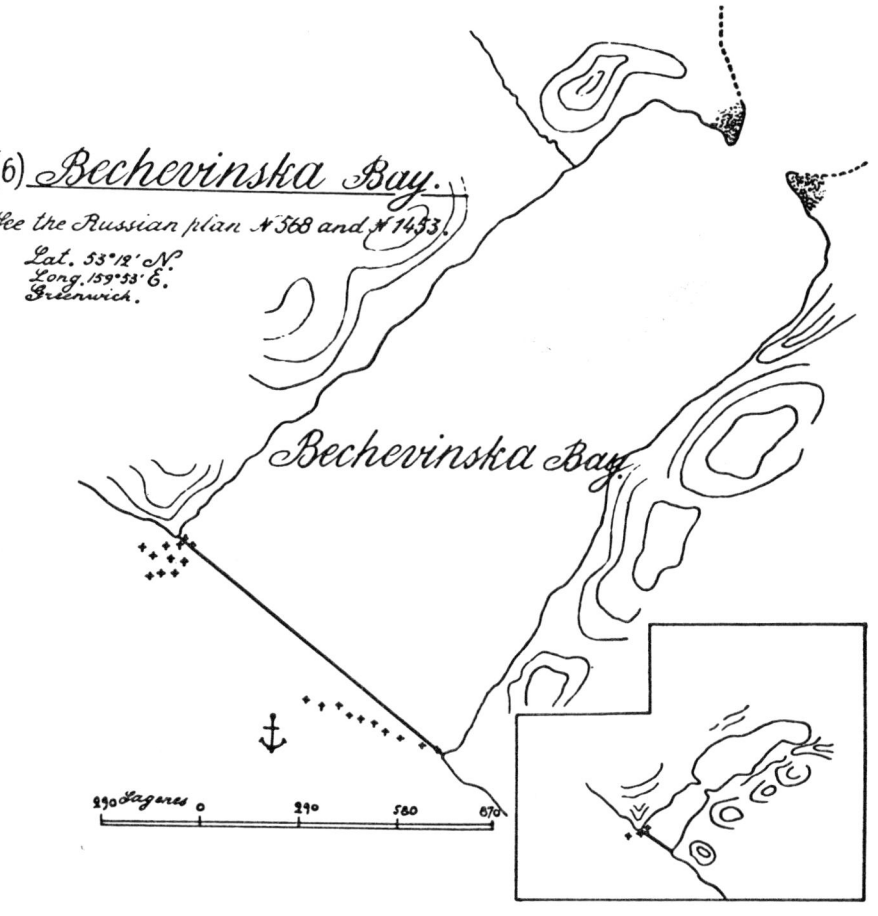

Plate 6: Bechevinska Bay.

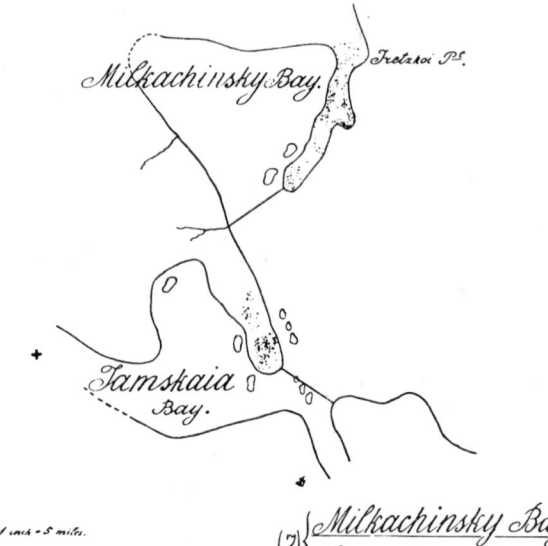

Plate 7: Milkachinsky Bay. Iamskaia Bay.

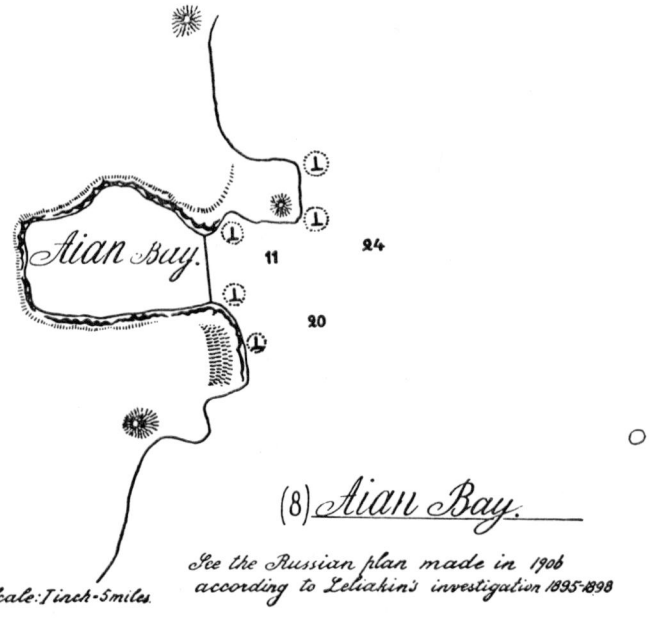

Plate 8: Aian Bay.

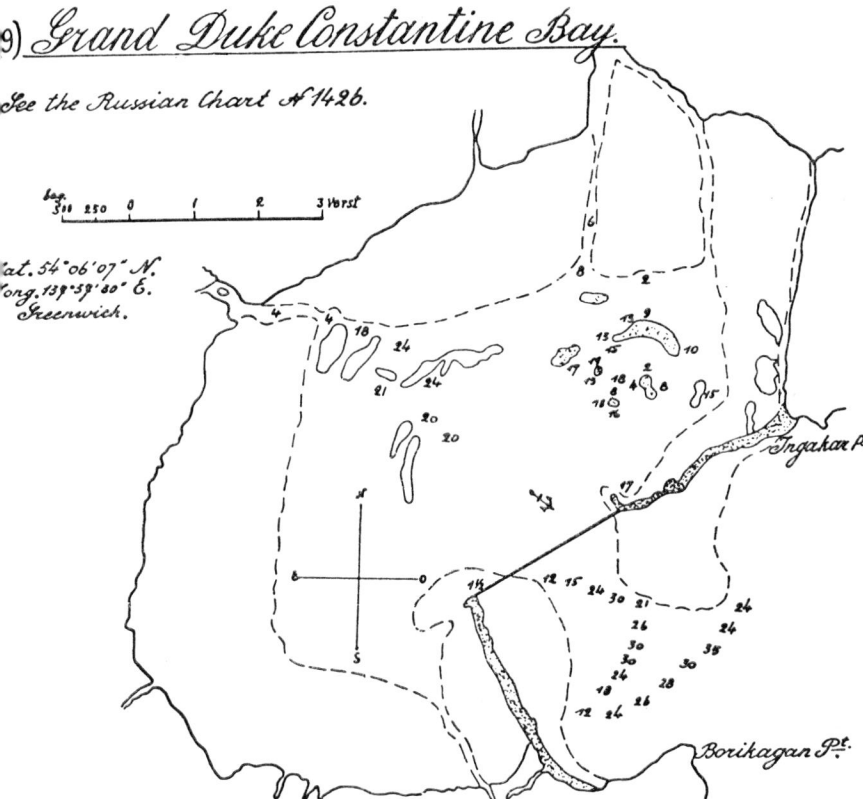

Plate 9: Grand Duke Constantine Bay.

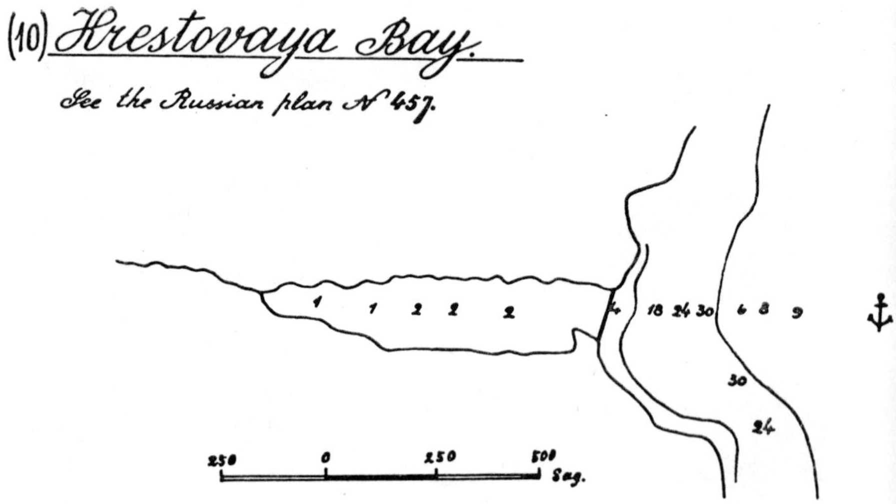

(10) *Krestovaya Bay.*
See the Russian plan N° 457.

Plate 10:   Krestovaya Bay.

APPENDIX 379

NOTES

No. 1

Moscow, 23 January 1928

Monsieur le Plénipotentiaire,
With regard to the provisions of Article IV of the Fishery Convention between the Union of Soviet Socialist Republics and Japan signed this day as well as those of Article 9 of the Protocol A attached thereto, I have the honour on behalf of my Government to declare as follows:
In view of the special features of the fishing industry of Japanese subjects in the Far Eastern waters of the Union of Soviet Socialist Republics, the Government of the Union of Soviet Socialist Republics agrees that the business tax, together with the taxes and fees mentioned in Paragraphs (7) and (9) of Article 9 of the Protocol A, chargeable to Japanese subjects, shall be paid in the form of a commutation tax amounting to 28 per cent of the royalty for the lease of their respective fishery lots, which payment shall be made at the same time and in the same manner as the said royalty.
I avail myself of this opportunity to convey to you, Monsieur le Plénipotentiaire, the assurances of my highest consideration.

(Signed) L. KARAKHAN

Monsieur Tokichi Tanaka,
Plenipotentiary of Japan, etc., etc.

No. 1

Moscow, 23 January 1928

Monsieur le Plénipotentiaire,
I have the honour to acknowledge the receipt of the following Note from you, under this date:

Monsieur le Plénipotentiaire,

With regard to the provisions of Article IV of the Fishery Convention between the Union of Soviet Socialist Republics and Japan signed this day as well as those of Article 9 of the Protocol A attached thereto, I have the honour on behalf of my Government to declare as follows:

In view of the special features of the fishing industry of Japanese subjects in the Far Eastern waters of the Union of Soviet Socialist Republics, the Government of the Union of Soviet Socialist Republics agrees that the business tax, together with the taxes and fees mentioned in Paragraphs (7) and (9) of Article 9 of the Protocol A, chargeable to Japanese subjects, shall be paid in the form of a commutation tax amounting to 28 per cent of the rayalty for the lease of their respective fishery lots, which payment shall be made at the same time and in the same manner as the said royalty.

On behalf of my Government, I have the honour to state that the Japanese Government agrees entirely with the said Note.

I avail myself of this opportunity to convey to you, Monsieur le Plénipotentiaire, the assurances of my highest consideration.

(Signed) T. TANAKA

Monsieur Lev Karakhan,
Plenipotentiary of the Union
of Soviet Socialist Republics
etc., etc.

No. 2

Moscow, 23 January 1928

Monsieur le Plénipotentiaire,

With regard to the provisions of Section (B) of Paragraph 1 in Part 1 of the Final Protocol attached to the Fishery Convention between the Union of Soviet Socialist Republics and Japan signed this day, I have the honour to notify you on behalf of my Government that, in view of the said provisions ensuring the state enterprises of the Union of Soviet Socialist Republics necessary fishery lots for the duration of the Fishery Convention, the said enterprises shall, for the duration of the Fishery Convention, abstain not only from participating directly or indirectly in the auction of fishery lots, but also from operating fishery lots leased by auction to private persons or enterprises.

I avail myself of this opportunity to convey to you, Monsieur le Plénipotentiaire, the assurances of my highest consideration.

(Signed) L. KARAKHAN

Monsieur Tokichi Tanaka,
Plenipotentiary of Japan, etc., etc.

No. 2.

Moscow, 23 January 1928

Monsieur le Plénipotentiaire,
I have the honour to acknowledge the receipt of the following Note from you, under this date:

Monsieur le Plénipotentiaire,
With regard to the provisions of Section (B) of Paragraph 1 in Part I of the Final Protocol attached to the Fishery Convention between the Union of Soviet Socialist Republics and Japan signed this day, I have the honour to notify you on behalf of my Government that, in view of the said provisions ensuring the state enterprises of the Union of Soviet Socialist Republics necessary fishery lots for the duration of the Fishery Convention, the said enterprises shall, for the duration of the Fishery Convention, abstain not only from participating directly or indirectly in the auction of fishery lots, but also from operating fishery lots leased by auction to private persons or enterprises.

In reply, I beg to state that I take note of your communication above mentioned.

I avail myself of this opportunity to convey to you, Monsieur le Plénipotentiaire, the assurances of my highest consideration.

(Signed) T. TANAKA

Monsieur Lev Karakhan,
Plenipotentiary of the Union
of Soviet Socialist Republics,
etc., etc.

No. 3

Moscow, 23 January 1928

Monsieur le Plénipotentiaire,
I have the honour to declare on behalf of my Government that for the duration of the Fishery Convention, the Centrosoyuz of the Union of Soviet Socialist Republics has no intention of engaging in the fishing industry in the districts specified in Article I of the said Convention.

I avail myself of this opportunity to convey to you, Monsieur le Plénipotentiaire, the assurances of my highest consideration.

(Signed) L. KARAKHAN

Monsieur Tokichi Tanaka,
Plenipotentiary of Japan, etc., etc.

No. 3

Moscow, 23 January 1928

Monsieur le Plénipotentiaire,
I have the honour to acknowledge the receipt of the following Note from you, under this date:

Monsieur le Plénipotentiaire,
I have the honour to declare on behalf of my Government

APPENDIX 383

that, for the duration of the Fishery Convention, the Centrosoyuz of the Union of Soviet Socialist Republics has no intention of engaging in the fishing industry in the districts specified in Article I of the said Convention.

In reply, I beg to state that I take note of your communication above mentioned.

I avail myself of this opportunity to convey to you, Monsieur le Plénipotentiaire, the assurances of my highest consideration.

(Signed) T. TANAKA

Monsieur Lev Karakhan,
Plenipotentiary of the Union
of Soviet Socialist Republics, etc., etc.

No. 4

Moscow, 23 January 1928

Monsieur le Plénipotentiaire,

I have the honour to notify you on behalf of my Government that the Government of the Union of Soviet Socialist Republics agrees to arrange that when either of the two Governments so proposes at any time after the auctions of the year 1928, the mode of obtaining the lease of fishery lots by various cooperative societies of the Union of Soviet Socialist Republics shall be an object of negotiations between the two Governments and thenceforward shall be subject to the decision of such negotiations. As to the measures to be taken in case the negotiations fail to be concluded in due course of time before the forthcoming auctions, a modus vivendi shall be arranged between the two Governments.

I avail myself of this opportunity to covey to you, Monsieur le Plénipotentiaire, the assurances of my highest consideration.

(Signed) L. KARAKHAN

Monsieur Tokichi Tanaka,
Plenipotentiary of Japan, etc., etc.

No. 4

Moscow, 23 January 1928

Monsieur le Plénipotentiaire,

I have the honour to acknowledge the receipt of the following Note from you, under this dare:

> Monsieur le Plénipotentiaire,
>
> I have the honour to notify you on behalf of my Government that the Government of the Union of Soviet Socialist Republics agrees to arrange that when either of the two Governments so proposes at any time after the auctions of the year 1928, the mode of obtaining the lease of fishery lots by various cooperative societies of the Union of Soviet Socialist Republics shall be an object of negotiations between the two Governments, and thenceforward shall be subject to the decision of such negotiations. As to the measures to be taken in case the negotiations fail to be concluded in due course of time before the forthcoming auctions, a modus vivendi shall be arranged between the two Governments.

On behalf of my Government, I have the honour to state that the Japanese Government agrees entirely with the said Note.

I avail myself of this opportunity to convey to you, Monsieur le Plénipotentiaire, the assurances of my highest consideration.

(Signed) T. TANAKA

Monsieur Lev Karakhan,
Plenipotentiary of the Union
of Soviet Socialist Republics, etc., etc.

Source Notes

CHAPTER ONE: The Dairen Conference

[1] Tanaka Bunichirō 田中文一郎, *Nisso Kōshō-shi* 日ソ交渉史 (History of negotiations between Japan and the Soviet Union) (Tokyo: Foreign Office, Political Affairs Bureau, 1942), "Secret," Vol. IIIA, pp. 41–42; Leonid Nikolaevich Kutakov, *Istoriia sovetsko-iaponskikh diplomaticheskikh otnoshenii* (History of Soviet-Japanese diplomatic relations) (Moscow: Izdatel'stvo Instituta mezhdunarodnykh otnoshenii, 1962), pp. 7–8.

[2] Kajima Morinosuke 鹿島守之助, *Teikoku gaikō no kihon seisaku* 帝國外交の基本政策 (Basic policy of the [Japanese] empire's diplomacy) (Tokyo, 1940), p. 399.

[3] Commissar Chicherin to Foreign Minister Uchida Kōsai, February 24, 1920, in Ministry of Foreign Affairs of the U.S.S.R., *Dokumenty vneshnei politiki SSSR* (Documents of the foreign policy of the U.S.S.R.), hereafter cited as "D.V.P.," Vol. II (Moscow, 1958), pp. 388–89; Kutakov, *Istoriia*, p. 8; Tanaka, pp. 41–42.

[4] G.Z. Besedovskii, *Na putiakh k termidoru (Iz vospominanii b. sovetsk. diplomata)* (On the road to the Thermidor [From the recollections of a former Soviet diplomat]) (Paris: Izdatel'stvo "Mishen'," 1930) vol. I, pp. 211–16; Tanaka, pp. 41–42.

[5] Xenia Joukoff Eudin and Robert C. North (comp.), *Soviet Russia and the East 1920–1927, A Documentary Survey* (Stanford: Stanford University Press, 1957), p. 209.

[6] Tanaka, pp. 41–42.

[7] D.C.H. d'Avigdor, "The Siberian Situation," *The Contemporary Review*, No. 676 (April 1922), pp. 482–90.

[8] Tanaka, p. 42; D.V.P., vol. II, pp. 414–15 and note 77 on pp. 754–55; George Alexander Lensen (ed.), *Revelations of a Russian Diplomat: The Memoirs of Dmitrii I. Abrikossow* (Seattle: University of Washington Press, 1964), p. 296; George M. Beckmann, *The Modernization of China and Japan* (New York: Harper and Row, 1962), p. 375.

[9] Tanaka, p. 42.

[10] Academy of Sciences of the U.S.S.R., *Sovetskaia istoricheskaia entsiklopediia* (Soviet historical encyclopedia), vol. IV (Moscow, 1963), pp. 959–60; Eudin and North, pp. 132–33 and 209; John A. White, *The Siberian Intervention* (Princeton: Princeton University Press, 1950), p. 395; Kutakov, *Istoriia*, p. 12; Donald W. Treadgold, *Twentieth Century Russia*, second edition (Chicago: Rand McNally and Company, 1964), p. 187; J. V. Davidson-Houston, *Russia and China from the Huns to Mao Tse-tung* (London: Robert Hale, 1960), p. 101; Beckmann, pp. 375–76; Mikhail Pavlovich (Vel'tman), *Sovetskaia Rossiia i imperialisticheskaia Iaponiia* (Soviet Russia and imperialist Japan) (Moscow: Izd-vo "Krasnaia Nov'," 1923), p. 100.

[11] Japanese Foreign Office archives, temporarily seized during the Occupation and microfilmed for the Library of Congress, hereafter cited as "Japanese Archives," MT 251.106.18: 181–190.

[12] Tanaka, pp. 43–44; the Special Delegation of the Far Eastern Republic to the United States of America, *Japanese Intervention in the Russian Far East*, hereafter cited as *Japanese Intervention*, (Washington, D.C., 1922), p. 138.

[13] Tanaka, pp. 44–45.

[14] *Japanese Intervention*, p. 91; A. Morgan Young, *Japan in Recent Times 1912–1926* (New York: William Morrow, 1929), p. 270.

[15] Tanaka, pp. 45–47.

[16] Japanese Archives, MT 251.106.2:1713–1717.

[17] Japanese Archives, MT 251.102.2:1711–1712.

[18] M. A. Persits, *Dal'nevostochnaia respublika i Kitai. Rol' DVR v bor'be sovetskoi vlasti za druzhbu s Kitaem v 1920–1922 gg.* (The Far Eastern Republic and China. The role of the F.E.R. in the struggle of the Soviet regime for friendship with China in the years 1920–1922) (Moscow: Izdatel'stvo Vostochnoi Literatury, 1962), p. 236.

[19] Tanaka, p. 47; Kajima, p. 399; *Japan Advertiser*, April 21, 1922.

[20] George Alexander Lensen (comp.), *Japanese Diplomatic and Consular Officials in Russia* (Tokyo and Tallahasse: Sophia University in cooperation with the Diplomatic Press, 1968), pp. 34, 49; White, pp. 410–11; Tanaka, pp. 47–48; Young, p. 269; *Sovetskaia istoricheskaia entsiklopediia*, vol. IV, p. 947; Persits, pp. 236–37; B. Semenov, "Iapono-sovetskoe soglashenie" (The Japanese-Soviet agreement), *Novyi Vostok*, Moscow 1925, No. 7, p. 20.

[21] F. N. Petrov, *65 let v riadakh Leninskoi partii. Vospominaniia* (65 yars in the ranks of Lenin's party. Memoirs) (Moscow: Gosudarstvennoe Izdatel'stvo Politicheskoi Literatury, 1962), p. 87.

[22] Japanese Archires, MT 251.106.2:463–471; Tanaka, pp. 47–48; *Diplomaticheskii slovar'* (Diplomatic dictionary), vol. I (Moscow, 1960), p. 419; Morinosuke Kaji-

ma, *The Emergence of Japan as a World Power* (Tokyo: Charles E. Tuttle Co., 1968), p. 295.

23 *Diplomaticheskii slovar'*, vol. I, p. 419.
24 Japanese Archives, MT 251.106.3 : 505–510.
25 Tanaka, p. 48; Young, pp. 269–70 and 273.
26 Japanese Archives, MT 251.106.2 :1092–1095.
27 Tanaka, p. 48.
28 Petrov, p. 92.
29 Tanaka, pp. 48–49; Vel'tman, p. 74.
30 Persits, pp. 236–37; *Sovetskaia istoricheskaia entsiklopediia*, vol. IX, pp. 157–58.
31 Petrov, p. 91.
32 Tanaka, p. 48.
33 Japanese Archives, MT 251.106.3 : 612–613.
34 Mikhail Krichevskii, "Razryv russko-iaponskikh peregovorov v Dairene" (Rupture of the Russo-Japanese negotiations in Dairen), *Mezhdunarodnaia zhizn'*, Moscow 1922, No. 6 pp. 4–7.
35 *Japan Advertiser*, April 21, 1922 and April 22, 1922.
36 Persits, p. 239.
37 *North China Star*, May 19, 1922.
38 Tanaka, pp. 49–50.
39 *Peking Daily News*, April 25, 1922.
40 Tanaka, pp. 50–51; *Deutsche Allgemeine Zeitung*, October 4, 1922.
41 Young, pp. 270–72.
42 Krichevskii, pp. 4–7.
43 A. Ioffe, "Rossiia i Iaponiia (Chan'chunskaia konferentsiia)" (Russia and Japan [The Changchun Conference]), *Novyi Vostok* 1923, No. 4, p. 1.
44 Japanese Archives, MT 251.106.3 : 642; see also *Japan Advertiser*, April 21, 1922.
45 *Japan Advertiser*, April 21, 1922.
46 Krichevskii, p. 6.
47 Japanese Archives, MT 251.106.2 : 1596–1600.
48 Japanese Archives, MT 251.106.7 : 005–007; Eudin and North, pp. 214–15; Vel'tman, pp. 77–78.
49 Japanese Archives, MT 251.106.7 : 009–010.
50 *North China Star*, May 19, 1922.
51 *North China Standard*, April 20, 1922.
52 Tanaka, pp. 50–52.

388   *Japanese Recognition of the U.S.S.R.*

CHAPTER TWO: The Changchun Conference

1 Tanaka, pp. 65–66.
2 Grivenko, "K russko-iaponskim otnosheniiam" (Concerning the Russo-Japanese relations), *Nash put'*, Khabarovsk 1922, No. 1, pp. 17–23.
3 D.V.P., vol. v (Moscow 1961) pp. 473–74; Japanese Archives, MT 251.106.7:581–583.
4 Japanese Archives, MT 251.106.7:268–269, 596–597 and 1105–1106; Tanaka, pp. 63, 66–67; D.V.P., vol. v, pp. 529–31; *The Nation*, vol. 115, No. 2983 (Sept. 6, 1922), pp. 237–38.
5 Japanese Archives, MT 251.106.7:271–272.
6 The *Peking Tientsin Times*, July 20, 1922.
7 D.V.P., vol. v, p. 535.
8 Japanese Archives, MT 251.106.7:591–592 and 1104–1105; D.V.P., vol. v, pp. 529–30; *The Nation*, Sept. 6, 1922, p. 238; Tanaka, p. 67.
9 D.V.P., vol. v, p. 535.
10 D.V.P., vol. v, pp. 534–35; Japanese Archives, MT 215.106.7: 598–599.
11 Japanese Archives, MT 251.106.7:593–595.
12 Japanese Archives, MT 251.106.7:1046–1047.
13 D.V.P., vol. v, pp. 569–70.
14 Tanaka, p. 63; Young, pp. 273–74; White, pp. 412–13; Vel'tman, pp. 81–83.
15 The *Peking Tientsin Times*, Sept. 7, 1922.
16 *North China Star*, Sept. 7, 1922.
17 D.V.P., vol. v, p. 756; Ioffe, pp. 1–4.
18 Tanaka, p. 63; Young, pp. 273–74. For a copy of the plenary powers given to Ioffe by the Russian government, see Japanese Archives, MT 251.106.7: 2261–2263.
19 Lensen, *Revelations*, p. 302.
20 Japanese Archives, MT 251.106.7: 2603.
21 Japanese Archives, MT 251.106.7: 3335–3338.
22 *L'Asie Française*, May 1923, as quoted in Japanese Archives, MT 251.106.14: 389.
23 Eudin and North, p. 459.
24 Japanese Archives, MT 251.106.7: 2101–2103.
25 Ioffe, pp. 1–4.
26 D.V.P., vol. v, p. 578.

SOURCE NOTES 389

27 D.V.P., vol. v, p. 587; Tanaka, pp. 67–69.
28 D.V.P., vol. v, pp. 572–73.
29 News release in *Izvestiia*, dated Chita, September 15, published on September 17, 1922, as quoted in D.V.P., vol. v, pp. 584–85; Tanaka, pp. 67–69; Ioffe, p. 216; Eudin and North, pp. 215–16.
30 Japanese Archives, MT 251.106.7: 2664–2665.
31 Japanese Archives, MT 251.106.7: 2661–2663.
32 Tanaka, pp. 67–69.
33 Telegram from Ioffe to the Foreign Commissariat, dated September 15, received on September 16, in D.V.P., vol. v, pp. 583–84.
34 Tanaka, pp. 68–69.
35 D.V.P., vol. v, pp. 589–90.
36 D.V.P., vol. v, p. 586.
37 News dispatch, dated Chita, Sept. 20, published in *Izvestiia* on Sept. 23, 1922, in D.V.P., vol. v, pp. 590–92.
38 D.V.P., vol. v, pp. 592–93.
39 Tanaka, pp. 68–69.
40 News dispatch, dated September 25, 1922, published in *Izvestiia* on September 28, in D.V.P., vol. v, pp. 600–601.
41 Tanaka, pp. 69–71.
42 D.V.P., vol. v, pp. 601–604; Tanaka, pp. 69–71.
43 Japanese Archives, MT 251.106.7: 3350–3360.
44 Japanese Archives, MT 251.106.7: 1979–1981.
45 Tanaka, pp. 71–72.
46 *North China Star*, Aug. 20, 1922.
47 Ioffe, pp. 8–10.
48 *Ibid.*, pp. 4–5.
49 *Ibid.;* Young, p. 270.
50 Ioffe, pp. 6–8.
51 D.V.P., vol. v, pp. 629–30.
52 D.V.P., vol. v, p. 673; Tanaka, p. 72.
53 The *Peking Daily News*, Sept. 30, 1922.
54 Letter dated September 9, 1922, Japanese Archives, MT 251.106.7: 1492–1494 and 1519–1523.
55 The *Peking Daily News*, Sept. 28, 1922.
56 The *North China Standard*, Sept. 28, 1922.
57 The *North China Daily News*, Sept. 20 and Sept. 28, 1922.

390   *Japanese Recognition of the U.S.S.R.*

⁵⁸ Ioffe, pp. 10–11; White, pp. 412–13.
⁵⁹ Declaration of the Popular Assembly of the Far Eastern Republic, dated Chita, November 14, 1922, in D.V.P., vol. V, p. 676.

CHAPTER THREE: The Gotō-Ioffe Talks

1 Tsurumi Yūsuke 鶴見祐輔, *Gotō Shimpei* 後藤新平, vol. IV (Tokyo, 1967), p. 390.
2 Kutakov, *Istoriia*, pp. 15–18; Tanaka, p. 72.
3 Tsurumi, vol. IV, pp. 390–95.
4 Kutakov, *Istoriia*, pp. 18–19.
5 Tsurumi, vol. IV, pp. 393–95.
6 *Los Angeles Examiner*, October 8, 1922.
7 Tsurumi, vol. IV, pp. 395–400; Ken Shen Weigh, *Russo-Chinese Diplomacy* (Shanghai: The Commercial Press, 1928), pp. 281–83; Kutakov, *Istoriia*, pp. 18–19; *Izvestiia*, February 3, 1923.
8 Tsurumi, vol. IV, pp. 385–400; Kutakov, *Istoriia*, p. 20.
9 Tsurumi, vol. IV, pp. 396–97, 454–57.
10 Japanese Archives, MT 251.106.12: 249–266.
11 Japanese Archives, MT 251.106.15: 363.
12 Japanese Archives, MT 251.106.15: 549–550.
13 Kutakov, *Istoriia*, p. 20.
14 *Ibid.*, pp. 20–21.
15 *Ibid.*, p. 15.
16 *Ibid.*, pp. 21–26; Eudin and North, p. 251.
17 Kutakov, *Istoriia*, p. 26.
18 *Ibid.*, pp. 26–28; Tanaka, pp. 78–79; Lensen, *Japanese*, p. 212.
19 Tsurumi, vol. IV, pp. 48, 454; Kutakov, *Istoriia*, pp. 27–28.
20 Tanaka, pp. 79–80.
21 Communication of the Commissariat of Foreign Affairs, dated April 29, 1923, D.V.P., vol. VI (Moscow 1962), p. 273.
22 Japanese Archives, MT 251.106.15: 1083–1084.
23 Kutakov, *Istoriia*, p. 28.
24 *Ibid.*, pp. 28–29; Tanaka, p. 73; Tsurumi, vol. IV, pp. 454–56.
25 Japanese Archives, MT 251.106.15: 1031.
26 *Japan Advertiser*, April 14, 1923.
27 Kutakov, *Istoriia*, pp. 28–29; Tanaka, p. 73.
28 Tanaka, p. 73.

SOURCE NOTES

29 D.V.P., vol. VI, pp. 273-74; Kutakov, *Istoriia*, p. 30; Tsurumi, vol. IV, pp. 472-73.
30 Telegram from Ioffe to Foreign Secretariat, dated Atami, March 2, 1923, in Japanese Archives, MT 251.106.15: 549-553.
31 *Chicago Tribune* dispatch, dated May 8, 1923, in Japanese Archives, MT 251.106: 1243.
32 Kutakov, *Istoriia*, pp. 31, 34-35, 39; Japanese Archives, MT 251.106.15: 2080.
33 Tsurumi, vol. IV, pp. 404-06.
34 Japanese Archives, MT 251.106.15: 574 and 1605.
35 Japanese Archives, MT 251.106.15: 1405.
36 Japanese Archives, MT 251.106.15: 1471 and 1475.
37 Japanese Archives, MT 251.106.15: 1832.
38 Japanese Archives, MT 251.106.15: 2104.
39 Japanese Archives, MT 251.106.15: 1717.
40 *Chicago Daily News* dispatch from Tokyo, dated May 22, 1923, in Japanese Archives, MT 327.251.106: 1244.
41 Japanese Archives, MT 251.106.15: 2247-2250. For a Japanese summary of some of the points in Ioffe's letter to Gotō of May 10, see Tsurumi, vol. IV, p. 473.
42 Japanese Archives, MT 327.251.106: 1248.
43 Japanese Archives, MT 251.106.15: 2301.
44 Tanaka, pp. 73-74; Kutakov, *Istoriia*, pp. 32-35.

CHAPTER FOUR: The Ioffe-Kawakami Talks

1 Tanaka, pp. 74-75; Japanese Archives, MT 251.106.11: 732.
2 "Correspondence Exchanged between the Japanese and Russian Delegates concerning Informal Preliminary Negotiations between Japan and Russia," printed compilation in the English language in Japanese Archives, MT 251.106.11: 452-481, pp. 1-15; Tanaka, pp. 75-76; Kutakov, *Istoriia*, p. 38.
3 "Correspondence," p. 17.
4 Tanaka, pp. 75-76; Kutakov, *Istoriia*, p. 38.
5 "Correspondence," pp. 22-24.
6 *Ibid.*, pp. 7-10, 25-27.
7 *Ibid.*, p. 28- Tanaka, pp. 75-77; Kutakov, *Istoriia*, pp. 36-37.
8 Kutakov, *Istoriia*, pp. 38-39.
9 Japanese Archives, MT 251.106.11: 386.
10 Japanese Archives, MT 251.106.11: 823-825 and 478-479.

11 Japanese Archives, MT 251.106.11: 468–469.
12 *Japan Advertiser*, August 8, 1923.
13 D.V.P., vol. VI, p. 550.
14 D.V.P., vol. VI, pp. 550–51.
15 Tanaka, pp. 82–85; Kutakov, *Istoriia*, p. 40; D.V.P., vol. VI, pp. 49–50.
16 Tanaka, pp. 85–86; D.V.P., vol. VI, p. 624.
17 D.V.P., vol. VI, pp. 456–57; Tanaka, pp. 85–86.
18 D.V.P., vol. VII (Moscow 1963), pp. 127–29.

CHAPTER FIVE: The Karakhan-Yoshizawa Talks

1 Tanaka, pp. 86–87; Kutakov, *Istoriia*, p. 41.
2 D.V.P., vol. VI, pp. 466–73.
3 D.V.P., vol. VI, p. 549.
4 D.V.P., vol. VI, p. 551.
5 *Japan Advertiser*, February 20, 1924.
6 Tanaka, pp. 86–87.
7 Telegram of Karakhan to Foreign Commissariat, dated Peking, March 22, 1924, in D.V.P., vol. VII, pp. 160–62; also note of Karakhan, presented to Yoshizawa on May 5, 1924, in D.V.P., vol. VII, p. 240.
8 D.V.P., vol. VII, pp. 160–62; Tanaka, p. 87.
9 D.V.P., vol. VII, p. 706.
10 Note from Karakhan to Yoshizawa, dated Peking, May 5, 1924, in D.V.P., vol. VII, pp. 240–43; Japanese Archives, MT 251.106.19: 1309–1312 and 1486–1492.
11 D.V.P., vol. VII, pp. 240–42.
12 News release, published in *Izvestiia* on May 6, 1924, in D.V.P., vol. VII, p. 251.
13 Japanese Archives, MT 251.106.19: 1891–1894; D.V.P., vol. VII, pp. 275–76.
14 D.V.P., vol. VII, p. 275.
15 *Peking Leader*, May 30, 1924.
16 Tanaka, p. 89.
17 Japanese Archives, MT 251.106.19: 472–475; D.V.P., vol. VII, pp. 306–308.
18 D.V.P., vol. VII, pp. 305–306; Tanaka, pp. 94–95.
19 Letter from Karakhan to Chicherin, dated June 2, 1924, in D.V.P., vol. VII, pp. 365–68.
20 D.V.P., vol. VII, pp. 711–12.
21 Tanaka, p. 172.
22 D.V.P., vol. VII, pp. 376–81.

SOURCE NOTES 393

23 Kutakov, *Istoriia*, p. 47.
24 Roy Hidemichi Akagi, *Japan's Foreign Relations 1542-1936. A Short History* (Tokyo: The Hokuseido Press, 1936), pp. 423-24.
25 Japanese Archives, MT 251.106.19: 3307; *Peking Daily News*, July 30, 1924.
26 *Peking Leader*, July 7, 1924; D.V.P., vol. VII, pp. 411-12.
27 Yoshizawa Kenkichi 芳澤謙吉, *Gaikō rokujū-nen* 外交六十年 (60 years of diplomacy) (Tokyo: Jiyū Ajia-sha, 1958), p. 77.
28 D.V.P., vol. VII, pp. 715-17, 415-17; Tanaka, pp. 89, 95-96, 173; Kutakov, *Istoriia*, p. 48.
29 Japanese Archives, MT 251.106:1351; D.V.P., vol. VII, pp. 415-17.
30 *The Japan Advertiser*, August 12, 1924.
31 D.V.P., vol. VII, pp. 415-17.
32 D.V.P., vol. VII, pp. 717, 507.
33 Statement by Karakhan to a correspondent of ROSTA on October 8, printed in *Izvestiia* on October 10, 1924, in D.V.P., vol. VII, pp. 480-81.
34 D.V.P., vol. VII, p. 483.
35 D.V.P., vol. VII, p. 716.
36 D.V.P., vol. VII, pp. 483-85.
37 Japanese Archives, MT 251.106.19; 5051-5052.
38 Japanese Archives, MT 251.106.19; 5050; D.V.P., vol. VII, p. 717.
39 D.V.P., vol. VII, p. 717.
40 Kutakov, *Istoriia*, p. 49.
41 D.V.P., vol. VII, pp. 526-29, 721; Tanaka, pp. 92-94.
42 Louis Fischer, *The Soviets in World Affairs*, p. 411.
43 Morinosuke Kajima, *The Emergence of Japan as a World Power 1895-1925* (Tokyo: Charles E. Tuttle Co., 1968), p. 302.
44 Kutakov, *Istoriia*, pp. 52-53; Tanaka, pp. 89-90, 92-97; ROSTA dispatch, dated Peking, January 2, 1925, published in *Investiia* on January 4, in D.V.P., vol. VIII (Moscow, 1963), p. 9.
45 Tanaka, pp. 89-90, 92-93, 96-97; D.V.P., vol. VIII, p. 66.
46 Lensen, *Revelations*, p. 306.
47 Yoshizawa, pp. 77-78.

CHAPTER SIX: The Basic Convention

1 League of Nations, *Treaty Series*, vol. XXXIV (Geneva 1925), pp. 32-52; Japanese Archives, Russo-Japanese Treaties, 30/15-30/49.

2 Japanese Archives, MT 251.106: 1360.
3 *Peking Leader*, May 30, 1924.
4 The *Statesman*, January 29, 1925.
5 *The New York Times*, April 9, 1925.
6 Japanese Archives, MT 251.106.21: 163–164.
7 *Washington Evening Star*, July 18, 1925.
8 Japanese Archives, MT 251.106.21: 1039.
9 *Los Angeles Times*, June 5, 1925.
10 *China Press*, January 29, 1925.
11 *Ibid.*, April, 1925.
12 The *North-China Daily News*, January 23, 1925.
13 *Ibid.*
14 The *Tokyo Nichi Nichi Shimbun*, January 23, 1925.
15 *Yomiuri*, January 22, 1925.
16 *Kokumin*, January 22, 1925.
17 *Japan Advertiser*, July 17, 1923.
18 E. J. Harrison, *The Red Camarilla*. London: George Allen and Unwin, 1925.
19 *Progrès*, February 10, 1925.
20 Albert W. Fox, in the *Post*, April 7, 1925.
21 Albett W. Fox, in the *Post*, April 8, 1925.
22 *Public Ledger*, April 9, 1925.
23 *Evening Star*, April 8, 1925.
24 *Japan Advertiser*, July 17, 1923.
25 The *San Francisco Examiner*, April 25, 1925.
26 *Argonaut*, May 23, 1925.
27 K. K. Kawakami, "Japan's Treaty with Russia," *The American Review of Reviews*, No. 307, April 1925, p. 410.

CHAPTER SEVEN: Exchange of Official Representatives

1 Tanaka, pp. 101–102; Satō Naotake 佐藤尚武, *Kaiko hachi-jū nen* 回顧八十年 (Recollections of eighty years) (Tokyo: Jiji Tsushinsha, 1963), pp. 176–80.
2 Tanaka, pp. 103–104.
3 *Ibid.*, pp. 102–103; D.V.P., vol. VIII, p. 237 and vol. IX (Moscow 1964), pp. 640–41.
4 D.V.P., vol. VIII, p. 237.
5 D.V.P., vol. IX, pp. 640–41; Lensen, *Japanese*, p. 57.

SOURCE NOTES 395

6 D.V.P., vol. VIII, pp. 436–37.
7 Tanaka, pp. 102–103.
8 Lensen, *Japanese*, p. 57.
9 D.V.P., vol. VIII, p. 479; Lensen, *Japanese*, p. 98.
10 D.V.P., vol. XII (Moscow 1967), p. 231.
11 D.V.P., vol. XII, p. 317.
12 D.V.P., vol. XII, p. 317.
13 Tanaka, pp. 104–106; George Alexander Lensen (comp.), *Russian, Diplomatic and Consular Officials in East Asia* (Tokyo and Tallahassee: Sophia University in cooperation with the Diplomatic Press, 1968), p. 244; Lensen, *Japanese*, p. 60.
14 Lensen, *Revelations*, pp. 257–59.
15 *Ibid.*, pp. 297–98.
16 *Ibid.*, p. 306.
17 *Ibid.*
18 *Ibid.*, p. 316.
19 *Ibid.*, pp. 316–17; Tanaka, p. 103.
20 Japanese Archives, MT 251.106.23: 207; D.V.P., vol. VIII, p. 97.
21 Lensen, *Revelations*, pp. 316–17.
22 Japanese Archives, MT 251.106.23:190.
23 Japanese Archives, MT 251.106.23:187–200.
24 Lensen, *Revelations*, p. 319.
25 Japanese Archives, MT 251.106.23:204–205.
26 Tanaka, pp. 101–102; D.V.P., vol. IX, pp. 640–41; Lensen, *Russian*, p. 225.
27 Lensen, *Japanese*, p. 227; Tanaka, p. 103; Japanese Archives MT 251.106.23: 591.
28 Tanaka, p. 103; D.V.P., vol. VIII, pp. 358–59.
29 D.V.P., vol. IX, p. 682.
30 *Japan Weekly Chronicle*, February 24, 1926, p. 149.
31 D.V.P., vol. IX, pp. 157–59.
32 D.V.P., vol. X (Moscow 1965), pp. 482–83.
33 D.V.P., vol. IX, p. 682.
34 D.V.P., vol. X, pp. 592–93; Lensen, *Japanese*, p. 236.
35 Besedovskii, vol. II, pp. 23–25, 106–107.
36 Paul W. Blackstock, "'Books for Idiots': False Soviet 'Memoirs,'" *The Russian Review*, vol. XXV (Hanover, N. H., 1966), pp. 285–86.
37 Besedovskii, vol. II, p. 38.
38 *Ibid.*, p. 48.

39 Ibid., p. 31.
40 Ibid., pp. 106–108, 120.
41 D.V.P., vol. VIII, pp. 238–39; Kutakov, Istoriia, pp. 67–68.
42 D.V.P., vol. VIII, pp. 274–75; Tanaka, p. 107.
43 Tanaka, p. 107; Kutakov, Istoriia, p. 68.
44 Tanaka, pp. 107–10.
45 Kutakov, Istoriia, pp. 68–69.
46 D.V.P., vol. VIII, p. 456.
47 D.V.P. vol. VIII, p. 551.
48 Tanaka, pp. 109–11; Kutakov, Istoriia, p. 69.
49 Japanese Archives, Russo-Japanese Treaties, 31/1–31/4; D.V.P., vol. IX, pp. 322–24; Tanaka, pp. 111–12.
50 *Japan Weekly Chronicle*, July 1, 1926.

CHAPTER EIGHT: Concession Contracts

1 D.V.P., vol. IX, pp. 640–41.
2 D.V.P., vol. VIII, p. 286.
3 *Izvestiia*, December 15, 1925, p. 2.
4 Japanese Archives, MT 17.10.37.3:36–42.
5 Tanaka, pp. 111–13; D.V.P., vol. VIII, p. 809.
6 Tanaka, pp. 114–19.
7 Tanaka, pp. 120–25.
8 Ibid., pp. 111–13; D.V.P., vol. VIII, p. 809; *Japan Weekly Chronicle*, December 31, 1925, p. 853.
9 *Japan Weekly Chronicle*, December 17, 1925, p. 803.
10 *Izvestiia*, December 15, 1925, p. 2.
11 D.V.P., vol. VIII, p. 808; Iu. Davydov, "Ekonomicheskie otnosheniia Iaponii i SSSR" (Economic relations of Japan and the U.S.S.R.), *Mirovoe khoziaistvo i mirovaia politika*, Moscow 1938, No. 9, p. 61; Tanaka, pp. 119–20.
12 Tanaka, p. 125.
13 Tanaka, pp. 127–37; D.V.P., vol. IX, p. 681.
14 Tanaka, p. 137; D.V.P., vol. IX, pp. 12–13.
15 Tanaka, p. 137.
16 *Japan Weekly Chronicle*, December 31, 1925, p. 853.
17 Ibid.

SOURCE NOTES 397

CHAPTER NINE: Fishery Talks

[1] Tanaka, pp. 137–38.
[2] Kutakov, *Istoriia*, p. 42; D.V.P., vol. VII, p. 178.
[3] Tanaka, pp. 137–38.
[4] Minutes of the first plenary session ("Soiuzno-iaponskaia konferentsiia po peresmotru rybolovnoi konventsii 1907 goda. Protocol No. 1"), Japanese Archives, Russo-Japanese Treaties, pp. 32/72–32/73.
[5] Minutes of the second plenary session (protocol No. 2), Russo-Japanese Treaties, pp. 32/80–32/83; D.V.P., vol. IX, pp. 8–9.
[6] Tanaka, p. 138.
[7] Minutes of the third plenary session (protocol No. 3), Russo-Japanese Treaties, pp. 32194–32/97; D.V.P., vol. IX, pp. 163–65.
[8] Russo-Japanese Treaties, pp. 32/116–32/145.
[9] Minutes of the fourth plenary session (protocol 4), Russo-Japanese Treaties, pp. 32/136–32/137; Russian and Japanese drafts, the latter in English translation, 32/116–32/134, 32/138–32/145.
[10] Minutes of the fifth plenary session (protocol No. 5), Russo-Japanese Treaties, pp. 32/175–32/179.
[11] Russo-Japanese Treaties, pp. 32/179–32/182.
[12] Russo-Japanese Treaties, 32/176–32/177.
[13] D.V.P., vol. X, p. 624.
[14] D.V.P., vol. X, pp. 19–20.
[15] Minutes of the sixth plenary session (protocol 6), Russo-Japanese Treaties, pp. 32/398–32/401.
[16] Russo-Japanese Treaties, 32/239–32/259.
[17] Minutes of the sixth plenary session (protocol 6), Russo-Japanese Treaties, pp. 32/398–32/401.
[18] D.V.P., vol. X, pp. 114–16.
[19] D.V.P., vol. X, pp. 121–22.
[20] D.V.P., vol. X, p. 122.
[21] D.V.P., vol. X, pp. 326–27.
[22] D.V.P., vol. X, pp. 465–66.
[23] D.V.P., vol. X, p. 466.
[24] Tanaka, pp. 138–39.
[25] D.V.P., vol. XI (Moscow 1967), pp. 13–15; Tsurumi, vol. IV, pp. 844–45.

398   *Japanese Recognition of the U.S.S.R.*

26 D.V.P., vol. XI, pp. 693, 41–42.
27 D.V.P., pp. 20–22.
28 D.V.P., vol. XI, pp. 22–29.
29 D.V.P., vol. XI, pp. 41–42.
30 Tanaka, p. 138.
31 Russo-Japanese Treaties, pp. 32/420–32/421.

CHAPTER TEN: The Fishery Convention

1 Russo-Japanese Treaties, pp. 32/1–32/29.
2 *Ibid.*, pp. 32/420–32/424.
3 Kutakov, *Istoriia*, p. 91.
4 D.V.P., vol. XI, pp. 137–47; Tanaka, pp. 139, 165; conversation between Premier Tanaka and Ambassador Troianovskii on March 8, 1928, in D.V.P., vol. XI, pp. 137–47.

CHAPTER ELEVEN: Expanding Contacts

1 D.V.P., vol. VIII, pp. 162–63.
2 *Japan Weekly Chronicle*, December 24, 1925, p. 271.
3 D.V.P., vol. IX, p. 682; Besedovskii, vol. II, pp. 68–69, 80–81.
4 B. Boldyrev, "Iaponiia i Sovetskii Dal'nii Vostok" (Japan and the Soviet Far East), *Sibirskie ogni*, Novosibirsk 1925, No. 1, pp. 190–91.
5 Tanaka, pp. 215–18; D.V.P., vol. IX, p. 331; vol. X, pp. 593, 630; vol. XI, pp. 338–39; vol. XII, p. 227; Vl. Braude, "Sovetsko-iaponskie ekonomicheskie vzaimootnosheniia" (Soviet-Japanese economic relations), *Novyi Vostok* 1928, No. 22, p. 132.
6 *Japan Weekly Chronicle*, September 17, 1925, p. 367.
7 *Japan Weekly Chronicle*, September 10, 1925, pp. 332–33; Tanaka, pp. 216–17.
8 D.V.P., vol. X, p. 644.
9 *Japan Weekly Chronicle*, February 12, 1931, p. 166.
10 Tanaka, pp. 218–20.
11 K. Popov, *Iaponiia. Ocherki geografii i ekonomiki* (Japan. Outlines of geography and economy) (Moscow: Sotsekgiz, 1931), p. 401.
12 "K voprosu ob ekonomicheskom sblizhenii Rossii s Iaponiei" (Concerning the question of an economic rapprochement between Russia and Japan), *Zapiski Priamurskogo Otdela Imperatorskogo Obshchestva Vostokovedeniia* (Khabarovsk, 1915), pp. 260–61.

13 Braude, p. 149; A. Galperin, "Dal'nevostochnyi Krai i tikhookeanskii rynok" (The Far Eastern region and the Pacific market), *Voprosy torgovli* 1930, No. 10, pp. 22–33.
14 Davydov, pp. 52–53.
15 D.V.P., vol. XII, pp. 708–709.
16 Tanaka, p. 165.
17 *Ibid.*, pp. 166, 168–70.
18 *Ibid.*, pp. 170–71.
19 D.V.P., vol. XII, pp. 228–29.
20 *Ibid.*, p. 230.
21 Tanaka, pp. 170–71.
22 *Ibid.*, pp. 171–74.
23 *Japan Weekly Chronicle*, March 26, 1931, p. 327.
24 *Japan Weekly Chronicle*, May 14, 1931, p. 521.
25 Tanaka, pp. 174–81; Kutakov, *Istoriia*, p. 92.
26 Tanaka, pp. 187–89.
27 Kutakov, *Istoriia*, pp. 91–92.
28 Tanaka, pp. 192–94; *Pravda*, Feb. 19, 1927; U.S.Army Map Service maps, compiled from Japanese Imperial Land Survey.
29 *Ibid.*, pp. 195–97.
30 *Ibid.*, pp. 198–207.
31 *Ibid.*, pp. 210–13.
32 *Ibid.*, pp. 213–14.
33 *Ibid.*, pp. 210–13.
34 *Japan Weekly Chronicle*, January 15, 1931, p. 49.
35 *Ibid.*; Tanaka, pp. 210–13.
36 D.V.P., vol. VIII, pp. 629–31 and vol. IX, p. 267.
37 D.V.P., vol. VIII, pp. 664–65.
38 D.V.P., vol. VIII, p. 666.
39 Tanaka, p. 197.
40 D.V.P., vol. IX, pp. 267–68.
41 D.V.P., vol. IX, p. 725: Tanaka, pp. 197–98.
42 Tanaka, pp. 223–27.
43 D.V.P., vol. VIII, p. 374.
44 *Ibid.*; D.V.P., vol. IX, p. 641.
45 D.V.P., vol. VIII, pp. 374–75.
46 Tanaka, pp. 227–28; D.V.P., vol. VIII, p. 516.

⁴⁷ D.V.P., vol. VIII, pp. 516–17; Tanaka, p. 228.
⁴⁸ Tanaka, p. 228; *Pravda*, Oct. 20, 1925.
⁴⁹ D.V.P., vol. VIII, p. 563.
⁵⁰ D.V.P., vol. VIII, pp. 562–63, 802, 805; Tanaka, pp. 228–29.

CHAPTER TWELVE: Lingering Mistrust

¹ Tanaka, pp. 220–22.
² D.V.P., vol. VIII, pp. 381–82.
³ Anna Marie Anderson Clayberg, "Soviet Policy Toward Japan," MS (microfilm), Slavic Studies, University of California, 1962, pp. 45–46.
⁴ Tanaka, pp. 158–59.
⁵ D.V.P., vol. VIII, pp. 296–97.
⁶ Japanese Archives, MT 251.106.17:47–49.
⁷ D.V.P., vol. VIII, pp. 541–44; Tanaka, pp. 216–17.
⁸ D.V.P., vol. VIII, p. 574.
⁹ D.V.P., vol. VIII, pp. 636–38.
¹⁰ Tanaka, pp. 155–56.
¹¹ D.V.P., vol. IX, pp. 735–36.
¹² D.V.P., vol. X, p. 624.
¹³ D.V.P., vol. X, pp. 626–28.
¹⁴ D.V.P., vol. XI, pp. 137–47.
¹⁵ Xenia Joukoff Eudin and Robert M. Slusser, *Soviet Foreign Policy 1928–34* (University Park: Pennsylvania State University Press, 1966), vol. I, pp. 35, 94–98.
¹⁶ D.V.P., vol. XI, pp. 145–46.
¹⁷ D.V.P., vol. XI, pp. 240–42.
¹⁸ D.V.P., vol. XI, p. 405.
¹⁹ D.V.P., vol. XI, p. 734.
²⁰ D.V.P., vol. XI, pp. 405–06.
²¹ Eudin and Slusser, vol. I, pp. 35–36, 235–37.
²² E. Navron (transl.) "Iz istorii kommunisticheskoi partii Iaponii" (From the history of the Communist Party of Japan), *Tikhii Okean*, Moscow 1934, No. 1, pp. 116, 126–27.
²³ Eudin and Slusser, vol. I, pp. 35–36.

EPILOGUE

1 Boris Ivanovich Nikolaevskii, "Sovetsko-iaponskoe soglashenie 1925 goda, *Novyi zhurnal*, vol. V (1943)," p. 203.

2 D.V.P., vol. VI, p. 256; Kutakov, *Istoriia*, pp. 14–15.

3 Eudin and North, p.

4 M. Kolobov, "Dairen i Chan'chun' v russko-iaponskikh otnosheniiakh" (Dairen and Changchun in Russo-Japanese relations), *Ekonomicheskaia zhizn' Dal'nego Vostoka*, Chita 1922, No. 3–4, p. 91.

5 Louis Fischer, *The Soviets in World Affairs: A History of Relations between the Soviet Union and the Rest of the World* (New York: Vintage Books, 1960, originally published in 1930), p. 406.

6 B. Semenov, "Iapono-sovetskoe soglashenie" (The Japanese-Soviet agreement), *Novyi vostok*, Moscow 1925, No. 7, pp. 22–37; Grigorii Shmigel'skii, "Sovetsko-iaponskoe soglashenie" (The Soviet-Japanese agreement), *Vostokovedenie*, Kiev 1925, p. 50.

7 Telegram dated January 22, 1925, D.V.P., vol. VIII, p. 85.

8 Semenov, p. 42.

9 *Ibid.*, p. 43.

10 Shmigel'skii, "Sovetsko-iaponskoe soglashenie," p. 50.

11 D.V.P., vol. IX, pp. 414–15.

12 Eudin and North, p. 336.

13 Hirota Kōki Denki Kankokai 広田弘毅伝記刊行会 *Hirota Kōki* 広田弘毅 (Tokyo, 1966), p. 367.

14 Nikolaevskii, p. 200.

15 *Ibid.*, pp. 211, 238.

16 Japanese Archives, MT 251.106.8:80.

17 Adachi Kinnosuke, "Japan Eager to Renew Russian Friendship if Right to obtain Oil Supplies is Assured," in the *New York Herald Tribune*, Sundey, August 3, 1924.

Blackstock, Paul W. " 'Books for Idiots': False Soviet 'Memoirs,' " *The Russian Review*, vol. 25 (Hanover, N. H., 1966), No. 1, pp. 285–96.

Bibliography

Akagi, Roy Hidemichi. *Japan's Foreign Relations 1542–1936. A Short History.* Tokyo: The Hokuseido Press, 1936.

Argonaut.

Beckmann, George M. *The Modernization of China and Japan.* New York: Harper and Row, 1962.

Beckmann, George M. and Okubo Genji, *The Japanese Communist Party 1922–1945* (Stanford: Stanford University Press, 1969)

Besedovskii, G.Z. *Na putiakh k termidoru (Iz vospominanii b. sovetsk. diplomata)* (On the road to the Thermidor [From the recollections of a former Soviet diplomat] (Paris: Izdatel'stvo "Mishen'," 1930. 2 vols.)

Blackstock, Paul W. "'Books for Idiots': False Soviet 'Memoirs,'" *The Russian Review,* vol. 25 (Hanover, N.H., 1966), No. 1, pp. 285–96.

Boldyrev, B. "Iaponiia i Sovetskii Dal'nii Vostok" (Japan and the Soviet Far East), *Sibirskie ogni,* No. 1, pp. 187–94.

Braude, Vl. "Sovetsko-iaponskie ekonomicheskie vzaimootnosheniia" (Soviet-Japanese economic relations), *Novyi Vostok* 1928, No. 22, pp. 131–51.

Chicago Daily News.

Chicago Tribune.

China Press.

D'Avigdor, D.C.H. "The Siberian Situation," *The Contemporary Review,* No. 676 (April 1922), pp. 482–90.

Clayberg, Anna Marie Anderson. "Soviet Policy Toward Japan," MS (microfilm), doctoral dissertation in Slavic Studies, University of California, 1962.

Davidson-Houston, J.V. *Russia and China from the Huns to Mao Tse-tung.* London: Robert Hale, Ltd., 1960.

Davydov, Iu. "Ekonomicheskie otnosheniia Iaponii i SSSR" (Economic relations of Japan and the U.S.S.R.), *Mirovoe khoziaistvo i mirovaia politika,* Moscow 1938, No. 9, pp. 50–64.

Deutsche Allgemeine Zeitung.

Diplomaticheskii slovar' (Diplomatic dictionary). Moscow, 1960–64. 3 vols.

Eudin, Xenia Joukoff and Robert C. North. *Soviet Russia and the East 1920–1927. A Documentary Survey.* Stanford: Stanford University Press, 1957.

Eudin, Xenia Joukoff and Robert M. Slusser. *Soviet Foreign Policy 1928–1934.* University Park: Pennsylvania State University Press, 1966–67. 2 vols.

Evening Star.

Far Eastern Republic, The Special Delegation of the Far Eastern Republic to the United States of America. *Japanese Intervention in the Russian Far East.* Washington, D.C., 1922.

Fischer, Louis. *Oil Imperialism. The International Struggle for Petroleum.* New York: International Publishers, 1926.

———, *The Soviets in World Affairs: A History of Relations between the Soviet Union and the Rest of the World.* New York: Vintage Books, 1960 (originally published in 1930).

Galkovich, M. "SSSR na Dal'nem Vostoke" (The U.S.S.R. in the Far East), *Mezhdunarodnaia Letopis'*, Moscow 1925, No. 3, pp. 9–20.

Gal'perin, A. "Dal'nevostochnyi Krai i tikhookeanskii rynok" (The Far Eastern region and the Pacific market), *Voprosy torgovli* 1930, No. 10, pp. 22–33.

Grivenko. "K russko-iaponskim otnosheniiam" (Concerning the Russo-Japanese relations), *Nash put'*, Khabarovsk 1922, No. 1, pp. 17–23.

Harrison, E. J. *The Red Camarilla.* London: George Allen and Unwin, 1925.

Hirota Kōki Denki Kankokai 廣田弘毅傳記刊行會. *Hirota Kōki* 廣田弘毅. Tokyo, 1966.

Ioffe, A. "Rossiia i Iaponiia (Chan'chunskaia konferentsiia)" (Russia and Japan [The Changchun Conference]), *Novyi vostok* 1923, No. 4 pp. 1–11.

Izvestiia.

Japan Advertiser.

Japan, Foreign Office. "A Historical Resumé of Japanese-Russian Negotiations." Typed MS, no date.

———. *Correspondence Exchanged between the Japanese and Russian Delegates concerning Informal Preliminary Negotiations between Japan and Russia.* No date.

———. *Nihon gaikō nempyō narabi ni shuyō bunsho* 日本外交年表竝主要文書 (Chronology and main documents of Japanese diplomacy). Tokyo, 1965. 2 vols.

Japan, Foreign Office Archives (cited as "Japanese Archives"). Microfilms made during the Occupation for the Library of Congress, MT (Meiji-Taishō documents) series.

———. Russo-Japanese Treaties series.

Japan Weekly Chronicle.
"K voprosu ob ekonomicheskom sblizhenii Rossii s Iaponiei" (Concerning the question of an economic rapprochement between Russia and Japan), *Zapiski Priamurskogo Otdela Imperatorskogo Obschestva Vostokovedeniia,* Khabarovsk, 1915, pp. 260-61.
Kawakami, K. K., "Japan's Treaty with Russia," *The American Review of Reviews,* No. 307, April, 1925, pp. 407-10.
Kajima Morinosuke 鹿島守之助. *Teikoku gaikō no kihon seisaku* 帝國外交の基本政策 (Basic policy of the [Japanese] empire's diplomacy). Tokyo, 1940.
———. *The Emergence of Japan as a World Power 1895-1925.* Tokyo: Charles E. Tuttle Co., 1968. Translation of the above, without documentation.
Khaifets, A. N. *Sovetskaia diplomatiia i narody vostoka 1921-1927* (Soviet diplomacy and the peoples of the East 1921-1927). Moscow: Izdatel'stvo "Nauka," 1968.
Kolobov, M. "Dairen i Chan'chun' v russko-iaponskikh otnosheniiakh" (Dairen and Changchun in Russo-Japanese relations), *Ekonomicheskaia zhizn' Dal'nego Vostoka,* Chita 1922, No. 3-4, pp. 84-93.
Krichevskii, Mikhail. "Razryv russko-iaponskikh peregovorov v Dairene" (The rupture of Russo-Japanese negotiations in Dairen), *Mezhdunarodnaia zhizn',* Moscow 1922, No. 6, pp. 4-7.
Kutakov, Leonid Nikolaevich. *Istoriia sovetsko-iaponskikh diplomaticheskikh otnoshenii* (History of Soviet-Japanese diplomatic relations). Moscow: Izdatel'stvo Instituta mezhdunarodnykh otnoshenii, 1962. (Dr. Kutakov is a Soviet diplomat; he served as counselor of the embassy in Tokyo in 1959-60. A three volume translation of the above study has been published in Japan under the title *Nisso gaikō kankei-shi* 日ソ外交関係史 [Tokyo, 1965-69]).
———. *Portsmutskii mirnyi dogovor 1905-1945.* (The Portsmouth Peace Treaty 1905-1945). Moscow: Izdatel'stvo sotsial'no-ekonomicheskoi literatury, 1961.
L'Asie Française.
League of Nations. *Treaty Series,* vol. XXXIV. Geneva, 1925.
Lensen, George Alexander (comp.). *Japanese Diplomatic and Consular Officials in Russia. A Handbook of Japanese Representatives in Russia from 1874 to 1968, compiled on the basis of Japanese and Russian sources with a historical introduction.* Tokyo and Tallahassee: Sophia University in cooperation with the Diplomatic Press, 1968.
——— (ed.). *Revelations of a Russian Diplomat: The Memoirs of Dmitrii I. Abrikossow.* Seattle: University of Washington Press, 1964.
——— (comp.). *Russian Diplomatic and Consular Officials in East Asia. A Handbook of the*

Representatives of Tsarist Russia and the Provisional Government in China, Japan and Korea from 1858 to 1924 and of Soviet Representatives in Japan from 1925 to 1968, compiled on the basis of Russian, Japanese and Chinese sources with a historical introduction. Tokyo and Tallahassee: Sophia University in cooperation with the Diplomatic Press, 1968.

Los Angeles Times.

Mullins, Patrick Grant. "Japanese-Soviet Relations, 1925–1940. A Study of Issues and Japanese Attitudes toward the Soviet Union, as Reflected in the *Japan Weekly Chronicle*," MS, M.A. thesis in history, The Florida State University, 1960.

The Nation.

Navron, E. (transl.). "Iz istorii kommunisticheskoi partii Iaponii" (From the history of the Communist Party of Japan), *Tikhii Okean* 1934, No. 1, pp. 113–68.

The New York Herald Tribune.

The New York Times.

Nikiforov, P. M. *Zapiski prem'era DVR. Pobeda Leninskoi politiki v bor'be s interventsiei na Dal'nem Vostoke* (1917–1922 gg.) (Memoirs of the premier of the Far Eastern Republic. Victory of the Lenin policy in the struggle with the intervention in the Far East [1917–1922]). Moscow: Gosudarstvennoe izdatel'stvo politicheskoi literatury, 1963.

Nikolaevskii, Boris Ivanovich "Sovetsko-iaponskoe soglashenie 1925 goda (Iz ocherkov po istorii vneshnei politiki Moskvy)" (The Soviet-Japanese agreement of 1925 [From sketches of the history of Moscow's foreign policy]), *Novyi zhurnal*, vol. V (1943), pp. 198–240.

The North China Daily News.

The North China Standard.

The North China Star.

The Peking Daily News.

Peking Leader.

The Peking Tientsin Times.

Persits, M. A. *Dal'nevostochnaia respublika i Kitai. Rol' DVR v bor'be sovetskoi vlasti za druzhbu s Kitaem v 1920–1922 gg.* (The Far Eastern Republic and China. The role of the F.E.R. in the struggle of the Soviet regime for friendship with China in the years 1920–1922). Moscow: Izdatel'stvo Vostochnoi Literatury, 1962.

Petrov, F. N. *65 let v riadakh Leninskoi partii. Vospominaniia* (65 years in the ranks of Lenin's party Memoirs). Moscow: Gosudarstvennoe Izdatel'stvo Politicheskoi Literatury, 1962.

Popov, K. *Iaponiia. Ocherki geografii i ekonomiki* (Japan. Outlines of geography and economy). Moscow: Sotsekgiz, 1931.
Pravda.
Public Ledger.
Saitō Yoshie. 齋藤良衞. *Sovieto Rokoku no kyokutō shinshutsu* ソヴィエト露國の極東進出 (Soviet Russia's push toward the Far East). Tokyo: Nihon hyōron-sha, 1931.
The San Francisco Examiner.
Satō Naotake 佐藤尙武. *Kaiko hachi-jū nen* 回顧八十年 (Recollections of eighty years). Tokyo: Jiji Tsushinsha, 1963.
Semenov, B. "Iapono-sovetskoe soglashenie" (The Japanese-Soviet agreement), *Novyi vostok* 1925, No. 7, pp. 20-48.
Shinobu Junpei 信夫淳平. *Taishō gaikō jūgonen-shi* 大正外交十五年史 (History of 15 years of Taishō diplomacy). Tokyo: Kokusai Remmei Kyōkai Hakkō, 1927.
Shmigel'skii, Grigorii. "Sovetsko-iaponskoe soglashenie" (The Soviet-Japanese agreement), *Vostokovedenie*, Kiev 1925, pp. 46-50.
Sovetskaia istoricheskaia entsiklopediia (Soviet historical encyclopedia). Moscow: Akademiia nauk SSSR, 1961- .
The Statesman.
Swearingen, Rodger and Paul Langer. *Red Flag in Japan, International Communism in Action 1919-1951*. Cambridge, Mass.: Harvard University Press, 1952.
Tanaka Bunichirō 田中文一郎. *Nisso koshō-shi* 日ソ交渉史 (History of negotiations between Japan and the Soviet Union). Tokyo: Foreign Office, Europe and Asia Bureau, 1942. (An official account, classified as "secret," prepared on the basis of unpublished Foreign Office documents by a Japanese Foreign Service Officer who had served in Tsarist Russia and the Soviet Union for about 15 years; microfilmed by the Library of Congress as part of the Japanese Archives project. Declassified and being reprinted in Japan in 1969.)
Tokyo Nichi-Nichi Shimbun 東京日日新聞
Treadgold, Donald W. *Twentieth Century Russia*. Second edition. Chicago: Rand McNally and Company, 1964.
Tsurumi Yūsuke 鶴見祐輔. *Gotō Shimpei* 後藤新平. Vol. IV (Tokyo, 1967).
U.S.S.R., Ministry of Foreign Affairs. *Dokumenty vneshnei politiki SSSR* (Documents of the foreign policy of the U.S.S.R.), vols. II-XII (Moscow, 1958-67).
(Vel'tman), Mikhail Pavlovich. *Sovetskaia Rossiia i imperialisticheskaia Iaponiia* (Soviet Russia and imperialist Japan). Moscow: Izd-vo "Krasnaia Nov'", 1923.
Washington Evening Star.
Weigh, Ken Shen. *Russo-Chinese Diplomacy*. Shanghai: The Commercial Press, 1928.

White, John A. *The Siberian Intervention*. Princeton: Princeton University Press, 1950.

Yoneda Minoru 米田實. *Gendai gaikō kōwa* 現代外交講話 (Lectures on modern diplomacy). Tokyo: Hakuyōsha, 1926.

Yoshizawa Kenkichi 芳澤謙吉. *Gaikō rokujū-nen* 外交六十年 (60 years of diplomacy). Tokyo: Jiyū Ajia-sha, 1958.

Young, A. Morgan. *Japan in Recent Times 1912–1926*. New York: William Morrow, 1929.

Index

Abolechef Bay, 279, 378
Aboltin, 227
Abrikossow, Dmitrii Ivanovich, 58, 175, 208–12
Adams, John Quincy, 69
Agnevo, 230
Agreements
  Basic Convention, 39, 50, 54–55, 101, 145, 160, 175–202, 211, 213, 227, 241, 271, 314, 317, 331–32, 345, 350–51, 364–68
  Draft agreement of 29 articles, 18–25
  Fishery convention (1907), 112–13, 155, 174, 178, 241
  Fishery convention (1928), 269–316, 375–84
  Provisional fishery agreement (1923), 113, 143
  German-Soviet trade, 12
  Hirota-Karakhan, 330–31
  Military, 39–40, 65
  Soviet-Chinese, 157–158
  Telegraph, 111n
  Trade and General, 34–38, 45, 69–71
  see also Treaties, under place of signature
Aian Bay, 280–81
Aigun, Treaty of, 39
Ako (Kamchatka Co.), 324, 327
Akura gumi, 323
Aleksandrovsk, 174, 183, 195, 206–207, 336–38

Alliance
  Russo-American, Japanese fear of, 10
  Russo-Japanese (1916), 5, 85, 144, 363
  Soviet-Japanese, 364, 367
Amity, Russo-Japanese, 5–9, 15, 52, 85, 96–97, 108–109, 115–16, 121, 142, 146, 169, 180, 196, 240, 321, 343, 351, 363–64, 367, 372–73
Amur River, 8, 13–14, 16, 28, 39, 81, 251, 282, 302–303, 308
Anadyr Bay, 280
Andrianov, F. I., 242n
Anglo-Japanese Alliance, 196, 267n, 352
Anokhin, 17, 345
Antonov, V. G., 38n, 43, 49–51, 54, 125
Aomori, 137
Aralov, S. I., 231, 242, 246, 269
Astakhov, Georgii Aleksandrovich, 215, 348
Atami, 89, 113, 115
Austrin, 215
Avatcha Bay, 280
Azhia Ringyō Kabushiki Kaisha, 236

Babkin, I, P., 242n
Baikal Gulf, 280
Baikal, Lake, 9
Bank of Korea (Chosen), 237, 326,

334–36, 343
Baron Korfa Gulf, 280, 378
Bechevinska Bay, 280, 378
Belgium, 12
Berlin, 339, 350
Berlin, Treaty of, 350n
Besedovskii, Grigorii Zinov'evich, 211–12, 214–17, 239, 251, 318, 331, 349–51
Blagoveshchensk, 107, 118, 206–207
Bliukher (Blücher), Vasilii Konstantinovich, 17n, 31, 31n, 32
Bolshevik, see Communist
Borah, William E., 200
Borodin, Mikhail Markovich, 350
Boxer indemnity, 207
Brest-Litovsk, 58, 59, 97, 141
Bukharin, Nikolai Ivanovich, 344

Cape Balusek, 281
Cape Bezimyanni, 280
Cape Burni, 280
Cape Butakov, 281
Cape Dalni, 280
Cape Gamova, 281
Cape Geka, 280
Cape Groto, 280
Cape Khargilakh, 279
Cape Kloster Kamp, 281
Cape Lamsdorf, 280
Cape Lazarev, 309
Cape Lissovsky, 280
Cape Mamet, 280
Cape Manevskago, 281
Cape Matveeva, 281
Cape Meetchken, 280
Cape Milyutina, 280
Cape Netchkhonone, 279
Cape Ostri, 281

Cape Pnaugun, 279
Cape Pogobi, 309
Cape Povorotni, 281
Cape Putyatina, 280
Cape St. Basilius, 280
Cape Shkhota, 281
Cape Strashni, 280
Cape Tshauno, 24, 309
Cape Vatovskago, 281
Cape Vesseli, 280
Cape Vitovta, 280
Cerruti, Vittorio, 175
Comintern, 220n, 346, 350, 358–61
Chaivo, 192–93, 232, 336–37
Chakre-Kampi Changu, 333
Changchun, 55–56, 60, 86, 90–91, 97
Changchun Conference, 49–84, 92, 97, 101–102, 119, 133, 151
Chemerin-Dagi, 333
Cherkasov, secretary, 214, 359
Mrs. Cherkasov, 214
Chernobaev, N. G., 242
Chichaev, I. A., 242
Chicherin, Georgii Vasil'evich, 6–9, 33, 45n, 81, 87, 91, 126, 130, 133, 136, 138, 144–46, 158–60, 165–71, 203–204, 209, 217, 221, 237–38, 259–60, 264–69, 317, 343–44, 367
China
 Relations with Japan, 26, 89, 339–40, 357, 370
 Relations with Soviet Russia, 12–14, 28, 39, 47, 86–88, 106, 108, 136, 157–58, 196–97, 201, 205, 207, 262, 318, 320, 339–42, 350, 357, 366–67, 371
Chinese in Russia, 319
Chinese Eastern Railway, 31, 56, 157, 158n, 169, 210, 339–42, 344, 357

Chinese National Railways, 340
Chita, 9–10, 12, 15, 33, 39, 42, 46, 50, 53–56, 60, 69, 107
Chosen, *see* Korea
Code, use of, 94, 108–111, 117n, 337
Commercial agents, 107–108, 111, 217
  see also Trade delegation
Commercial treaty, discussion of, 23, 154, 165, 172, 179, 350, 352, 358
Communist Party of Japan, 344–46, 358–60
Communist Revolution, impact on Russo-Japanese relations, 5
Communist subversion
  in Japan, 65, 67, 108–109, 125, 132, 137–39, 149, 155–56, 163, 180, 197–199, 208, 220, 344, 349, 358–61
  in Korea, 13–14n, 79
Concessions
  American in North Sakhalin, 10–11, 106, 119, 200
  Japanese in the Russian Far East, 1–2, 16, 29, 32–33, 39, 66, 81, 93, 110, 119, 128–29, 131, 149, 155, 157, 180, 229–40, 262, 332–35, 370–71
  see also North Sakhalin
Consular representation, *see* Diplomatic and consular representation
Coolidge, Calvin, 201
Czechoslovaks in Siberia, 5

Dairen (Talien, Dalny), 16, 50–51, 54–55, 62, 129, 206, 214, 339, 342, 359
Dairen Conference, 5–48, 61–63, 67, 69–70, 74–79, 119, 151
Dal'ta (Far Eastern Telegraph Agency), 38n, 43, 49

Davtian, Ia. Kh., 103
Debts, pre-revolutionary, 5, 110–12, 119–20, 126–32, 144, 149, 156–57, 163
Debuchi, 216, 225, 251, 259, 331, 347, 349–51, 360
De Castries (De-Kastri) Bay, 281
Denmark, 12
Derzhinskii, F. E., 231
Dietrichs, M. K., 66
Diplomatic and consular representation, 93, 106–10, 117, 143, 148, 178, 203–25, 336
  Old Russian embassy and consulates, 106, 154, 157, 181–82, 207–12
  Old Japanese embassy, 203
Doseikai, 328
Dovgalevskii, Valer'ian, 214, 217, 238, 260–61, 351–52, 355 Mrs. Dovgalevskii, 215
Dowakai, 328
Due mine, 194–95, 230, 233

Earthquake, 137–38, 142, 145–47, 208, 365
Economic interests, Soviet recognition of Japanese preeminent interests in Russian Far East, 7, 9–10
Economic organizations (Khozorgany), 218
Ehabi (Ekhabi), 192–93, 232, 333
Enkaishū Kaikon Kaisha 238
Enkaishū Rinyō Dan, 236
Equality and reciprocity, Soviet insistence on, 98, 100, 107, 117, 157, 179
Ergamyshev, N. A., 244, 257
Ershova, 345
Espionage, alleged Japanese, 137, 148, 150, 152, 343

Estonia, 340–41
Etefovich, 231
Ettinger, Dr., 114
Evacuation, see Intervention and North Sakhalin

Far Eastern Bank, 347
Far Eastern Republic, 9–84, 365
Far Eastern State Bank, 335, 347
Fischer, Louis, 365
Fishery, 14, 16, 23, 27, 30, 32, 54, 63, 69, 105, 110–13, 121, 139, 143, 155, 160, 165, 172, 174, 178, 241–316, 323–32, 349–50, 355, 375–84
France, 5, 12, 100, 222, 341
Fredericks Bay, 281
Fufaev, D. V., 321
Fujita, 94
Fukushima Shoten, 236
Furuno Inosuke, 60

Galen, see Bliukher
Genoa Conference, 102, 111, 119
Gensan, 100, 108
Germany, 5, 12, 47, 99, 208–200, 219, 222, 231, 318, 341, 344, 350, 356 see also Rapallo, Treaty of
Gold mining, 236
Gorkii, Maksim, 141
Gotō Ichizō, 89
Gotō Shimpei, 85–128, 142–46, 238, 261–68, 317, 319
Grab Peak, 279
Grand Duke Constantin Bay, 280, 378
Great Britain, 5, 12–13, 47, 101–107, 136, 196–97, 350, 252, 356, 364, 369–70
Gulf of Penjinsk, 280, 281
Gurevich, 232

Habomai Islands, 369
Hajiya, 237
Hakodate, 108, 208, 216, 322
Handazawa, 338
Harbin, 16–17, 50–56, 59–60, 68n, 105, 206–207, 212, 342, 345
Harrison, E. J., 200
Hatano, 321
Heifets, A. N., 1
Hikoshima, 320
Hiroshima, 213, 320
Hirota Kōki, 328–30, 367
Hokkaido, 1, 336
Hokushinkai, 192, 323
Holy Cross Gulf, 280
Hostility, Russo-Japanese, 5, 8–9, 15, 96–92, 99, 119, 145, 331, 358–59, 363
Hughes, Charles Evans, 75–76, 201
Hyōgo, 213

Iagrin, 243
Iampol'skii, 232
Iamskaia Bay, 280–81, 378
Ianel, Iakov, 215
Ianson, Iakov Davidovich, 31, 33, 39, 45–46, 50–67 passim, 76, 217–18, 220n, 221, 225
Ichikawa, 344
Ichikawa, comrade, 360
Ichikawa Sadanji, 319, 360
Ide Masataka, 242
Iijūin Hikokichi, 143
International Seamen's Club, 349
Intervention, Japanese in Russian Far East, 5–15, 26, 30–31, 39–83 passim, 92, 99, 104, 112, 130, 162, 207n, 238, 322, 363, 370 see also North Sakhalin

Index

Ioffe, Adol'f Abramovich, 3, 53-83 *passim*, 86-146, 151, 208, 217, 228
   wife Mary, 88
   daughter Nadezhda, 114
   son Vladimir, 88
Inukai Tsuyoshi, 161
Irkutsk, 14, 238, 371
Italy, 12, 47, 101, 102, 222
Itō Fumikichi, 318
Itō Hirobumi, 267
Iurin, Ignatii L., 14-17, 68
Iuzhnyi Boatasin, 333
Izvestiia, criticism of, 122

Jackson, Andrew, 368
Japanese attack on U.S., expectation of, 196, 200
Japanese diplomacy, Soviet appraisal of, 122-23
Japanese-Russian-German alliance, prediction of, 209-200
"Japanization" of Soviet railways, 321-22
Joffe, *see* Ioffe

Kadono Jukurō, 238
Kalagan Bay, 279, 378
Kalinin, Mikhail Ivanovich, 204-205
Kamakura, 216
Kamchatka, 14, 30, 65, 332
Kamchatka Co., *see* Ako
Kan-in, Prince, 317
Karafuto, *see* Sakhalin and North Sakhalin
Karafuto Kōgyō, 236
Karaga Harbor, 378
Karakhan, Lev Mikhailovich, 3, 53-55, 62, 70, 72, 91, 108, 115, 135, 141-78, 181-211 *passim*, 251, 260-71, 279, 290, 294, 329, 314, 327-30, 355, 359-60, 379-84
Katangli, 193, 194, 232
Katanoki-Noglin, 333
Katō Takaaki, 86n, 161-63, 169, 174
Katō Tomosaburō, 52, 86-87, 104, 106-108, 116-17, 124, 205
Kawaji Toshiakira, 3
Kawakami, K. K. 202
Kawakami Toshitsune, 87, 90, 103, 105, 125n, 126-39, 148, 175, 227-28, 231-32
Kawasumi Tadao, 212
Kayokai, 328
Kellogg, Frank B., 201
Kellogg-Briand pact, 352n
Kenkokukai, 359
Kenkyūkai, 121, 328
Kenseikai, 105
Kerbi, 130
Kerenskii, Aleksandr Fedorovich, 33
Khabarovsk, 130, 224, 236-37, 259, 277, 313, 318, 335-36, 342, 350
Khanka, Lake, 238
Khrushchev, Nikita Sergeevich, 371
Kita Karafuto Kōgyō Kabushiki Kaisha, 236
Kita Karafuto Sekiyu Kabushiki Kaisha, 236, 333, 337
Kita Sagaren Sekitan Kigyō Kumiai, 227, 232, 236
Kita Sagaren Sekiyu Kigyō Kumiai, 227, 232
Kiyokaze Fukumatsu, 343
Kiyoura Keigo, 146-47, 162
Kobe, 88, 108-109, 206, 213, 216, 335, 346-47
Kōchi, 213
Kodama, Lt. Gen., 321

Koji Maru, 106
Kolchak, Aleksandr Vasil'evich, 33
Kolchanovskii, 250, 257
Kolesnikov, Anatolii, 213
Konyam Bay, 279, 378
Kopp, Viktor Leont'evich, 139n, 211–15, 218–22, 320, 340, 343–49
Korea, 9, 13–14, 29–30, 111, 139, 336, 339–40, 366
Koreans in Russia, 13–14, 77, 319
Korean Communists, 349–50
Korean railways, 340
Kōseikai, 105, 328
Koshida Tukujirō, 222, 257
Kosuchina River, 230, 236
Koyu Club, 328
Kozakov, M. A., 242, 257
Kozhevnikov, I. S., 12, 16, 17
Kraga Harbor, 280
Krasnoshchekov, A., 12, 64n
Krassin (Krasin), Leonid Borisovich, 91
Krestinskii, Nikolai Nikolaevich, 350
Krestovaya Bay, 280, 378
Krichesvskii, Mikhail, 42
Krupenskii, Vasilii Nikolaevich, 207–8
Kryshov, G. A., 242
Kuhara Fusanosuke, 318, 354
Kuhara Kogyo, 236
Kuril Islands, 1, 369–70
Kutakov, Leonid Nikolaevich, 16n, 127n–28n, 133n, 331
Kuznetsov, enterpriser, 333
Kuznetsov, Nikolai Kirillovich, 212, 215, 347
Kwanchengtze, 210
Kydalan'i, 333
Kyokutō Shinrin Kōgyō Kabushiki Kaisha, 236

Kyokutō Takushoku Kabushiki Kaisha, 238

Lansing, Robert, 200
La Perouse Strait, 128
Larin, Iurii, 364
Lashkevich, G. N., 242n
Latsis, Martin Ivanovich, 242–46, 269, 272, 279, 290, 294, 299, 314
Latvia, 340–41
Lawrence, David, 201
Lebedev, chief of Vladivostok Forestry Affairs Bureau, 237
Lebedev, Nina, 11n
Lenin, Vladimir Il'ich, 11, 32, 45n, 60, 66–67, 364
Lenin, 136, 140
Levin, 88, 114–15, 137
Leningrad, 319
  see also St. Petersburg and Petrograd
Levyi mine, 236
Lishinskii mine, 236
Literary-Artistic Japanese-Russian Society, 348
Litvinov, Maksim Maksimovich, 64, 231, 252n
Loginov, Aleksandr Nikolaevich, 206, 216
Lysaya Golova, 280

Machi, 230, 233
Mail communication, 338
Malik, Iakov Aleksandrovich, 367
Mal'tsev, Iurii Vladimirovich, 216
Mamonov, 237
Manchuria, 9, 16, 29, 339, 364–67
ManchurianI Incident, 148n, 361
Markhlevskii, Iulian Iuzefovich, 32–33, 39, 61

Marumo Naotoshi, 7
Matsudaira Tsuneo, 6, 49, 51, 56, 62, 67–77, 105, 107, 127, 147–48
Matsui Keishirō, 146–47
Matsumura Sadao, 106–107
Matsumura Shinichirō, 242
Matsushima Hajime, 16–18, 31–39, 42, 56, 105, 127, 147
Matveev, N. M., 64
Maybon, Albert, 49n
Mechigme Bay, 279, 378
Meiji, Emperor, 116
Mel'nikov, B. N., 218, 269
Merkulov government, 33, 44
Mikoian, Anastas Ivanovich, 318–19
Milkachinsky Bay, 280–81, 378
Minkin, 232
Mitsubishi Company, 169, 174, 194–95, 218, 323
Mitsubishi Goshi, 236
Mitsui Company, 323
Mitsui Kozan, 236
Miyakawa Funao, 242–43
Miyake Setsurei, 115–116n, 121
Mizuno Rentarō, 88, 89
Molotov, Viacheslav Mikhailovich, 216
Mongolia, 366
Motono Ichirō, 210
Mori Kōzō, 88, 146
Moscow, *passim*
Mowrer, Edgar Ansel, 197
Mukden, 55, 56, 60
Murashiki, 237
Murom, 321
Musatov, 232
Myngi-Kongi, 333

Nabilskii Gulf, 280
Nagasaki, 88, 108, 206, 216

Nakai, 343
Nakano Kogyo, 236
Nakasato Shigetsugu, 227, 231
Nakatani Sadayori, 242
Narita, 237
Narkomindel, 6
Nationalism, revival in Russia, 57
Nichi-Ro Gyogyo Kaisha, 127n, 323–24, 326
Nikiforov, Peter Mikhailovich, 11n
Nikolaevsk Incident
  Massacre, 8–9, 129–31
  Settlement of, 14, 26, 29, 32, 39, 54, 57, 61, 65, 71–164 *passim*, 190, 207–8
Nikolaevsk-on-the-Amur, 108, 206
Nikolaevskii, Boris Ivanovich, 368
Nikol'sk-Ussuriisk, 66, 107
Nishi Haruhino, 242, 257
Nomura Masuzo, Viscount, 327
Non-aggression pact or pledge, 34, 69, 71–73, 160, 181, 350–58
North Sakhalin, 10, 16, 26, 30, 32, 39–40, 52, 65, 71–207 *passim*, 227–40, 309, 322, 333–38, 366–70
Norway, 12
Novosibirsk, 207
Nuiskii Gulf, 280
Nuivo, 192, 194, 232
Nutovo, 192–93, 232

Obata Torikichi, 81, 93, 105
Occupation, *see* Intervention and North Sakhalin
Odessa, 206–207
Oil concessions, 104, 106, 119, 157, 173–75, 192–94, 227–36, 332–33 *see also* North Sakhalin
Ogasawara, Count, 360

Okha (Oha), 192–93, 206, 232–38
Okhotsk, 69, 236, 249
Okhotsk Sea, 281
Okumura Masao, 227–28, 231
Okura Gumi, 236
Omsk, 14
Omsk Government, 213
Onor, 338
Open Door, principle of, 23–24, 69, 200–201, 354, 364
Osaka, 83, 206, 318–19, 346
Osaka Shosen Kaisha, 336, 339–40
Otaru, 216
Otomari, 336
Ozarnin, E. K., 50–52

Pacific War, 1, 5, 363, 368, 371
Pan-Pacific Congress, 318
Paris, 341, 364
Paromai (Poromai), 333
Peace Preservation Law, 358
Peking, 53–56, 59–60, 78, 81, 94, 103, 141, 146–47, 150, 161–64, 167, 174, 181–87, 196, 209, 211
Penkegunei Bay, 279
Pensacola, 369
Peter the Great Bay, 281
Petrograd, 6, 7
Petropavlovsk, 108, 206–207, 338
Petrov, Dr. Fedor Nikolaevich, 17–18, 31–33, 39, 42, 45n, 64n, 68
Petrovskoe Spit, 308
Philippines, 357
Pilutun, 192–93, 232
Podkagernaya River, 281
Poland, 202, 341
Port Arthur, 129
Port Soviet, 280
Portsmouth, Treaty of, 112–13, 119, 128, 132, 149, 155, 160, 163, 165, 173, 178, 187, 327
Possiette Bay, 281
Pravyi mine, 236
Preobrazheniya Bay, 281
Providence Bay, 280
Provisional Government, 33
Pusan, 342
Putiatin, Evfimii Vasil'evich, 3

Radek, Karl, 364
Radio-telegraph communication, 336–37
Railway communication, 338–41
  see also Chinese Eastern Railway and South Manchurian Railway
Rapallo, Treaty of, 101–103, 145, 196, 351
Recognition, Japanese of U.S.S.R., 85, 87, 102–105, 110, 116–17, 123–27, 132, 141, 147–50, 170, 201, 211, 344, 366; see also Agreements, Basic Convention
  of the People's Republic of China, 2
The Red Camarilla, 200
Riga, 342
Rigin, 14n
Rockefeller, John D., 366
Rizhinskii mine, 236
Rogatui mine, 194–95, 230
Roryō Ringyō Kabushiki Kaisha, 238
Roryō Ringyō Kumiai, 237, 238
Roryō Suisan Kumiai, 325
Roumilet Bay, 279, 378
Rudyi, 340
Russian Soviet Federated Socialist Republic, 11–83
Russo-Asian Bank, 207

Russo-Chinese-Japanese alliance, speculation about, 196–97
Russo-German-Chinese-Japanese block, speculation about, 200
Russo-Japanese Association, 86, 317
Russo-Japanese War (1904–1905), 5, 85, 86n, 99, 104, 112, 132, 216, 267n, 363–64, 369

Sabanin, A. V., 269
St. Lawrence Bay, 279
St. Marks, 369
St. Nicholas Gulf, 280
St. Olga Bay, 281
St. Pavla Bay, 280, 378
St. Peterbsurg, 17, 127, 203, 267
St. Vladimir Bay, 281
Saitō Hiroshi, 318
Sakai Kumiai, 227, 230, 232, 333
Sakamoto Toshiatsu, 327
Sakhalin, 29, 100, 368–69
   see also North Sakhalin
Sako Shuichi, 242, 246–48, 257
Salzmann, Erich von, 13–14n, 59, 88n
Sasaki, vice president of Nichi-Ro Fisheries Company, 328
Sasaki Seigo, 203
Sasaki Yukitada, 327
Satō Naotake, 203–206, 217–20
Sawada, interpreter, 353
Sawada, member of the Mitsubishi combine, 174
Schastiya Gulf, 23
Secret police
   Japanese, 95–96, 346–49
   Russian, 96, 350
Seiyūkai, 121, 135
Sekkabōshidan, 89
Selenga River, 13, 14

Semenov, B., 366
Semenov, Grigorii Mikhailovich, 10, 14, 213
Seoul, 208, 213
Seventeen Demands, 26–32
Severnaia Okha, 333
Severnyi Boatosin, 333
Shanghai, 39, 87, 88, 94
Shestakov, S. A., 321
Shibuya, 343
Shidehara Kijurō, 162, 169, 174, 200, 213–14, 219–22, 317, 328, 347–51
Shima Tokuzo, 324
Shimada Masaharu, 16–17, 105, 169, 242n
Shimonoseki, 320
Shindō Shintarō, 323
Shirahama Fuku, 343
Shliupochnaya Harbor, 280
Shōwa Kinkō Kabushiki Kaisha, 236
Shurukumu, 237
Siberia, Japanese development of, 1, 50, 62, 86, 104, 137, 146, 208, 237–38, 317, 332, 345, 354, 370–72
Siberian Veterans Association, 200
Sinclair, Harry Ford, company, 106, 119, 200
Six Feet Lake, 280
Skvirskii, Boris Evseevich, 365
Somov, 16
South Manchurian Railway, 56, 85, 127n, 339–40, 347
South Sakhalin, 369
Sovet Natsional'no-Gosudarstvennykh Ob'edinenii, 52
Soviet-Japanese Society, 317, 319
   see also Russo-Japanese Association
Sovtorgflot, 340
Soya, 336

Sugiyama, General, 321
Spain, 369
Spaask, 118
Spal'vin, Evgenii Genrikhovich, 215, 222, 348–49
Mrs. Spal'vin, 215
Stakheev (Staheeff) Co., 196–97, 333
Stalin, Joseph, 318, 363, 367
Starka Bay, 280
Stepukhovich, 232
Stomoniakov, B. S., 246, 256–58, 268
Stresemann, Gustav, 350
Sun Yat-sen, 87
Sungari River, 13, 16, 28, 39, 210
Suzuki Kisaburō, 359
Sweden, 12

Taguchi Unzō, 94, 116
Taiku, 320
Taishō, Emperor (Yoshihito), 318
Takayanagi, General, 17, 41
Takiguchi, 237
Tanaka Bunichirō, 6n, 47–18, 72, 77, 127n–28n, 133n, 205
Tanaka, consul general, 87–88, 94–95
Tanaka Giichi, 205, 214, 261, 267, 325–26, 351–58
Tanaka Tokichi, 104, 204–206, 231–71 *passim*, 290, 294, 308, 314, 327, 352n, 379–84
Tanaka Yotarō, 236
Taneda, 340
Tashkent, 14
Tatar Strait, 128
Technical aid, Japanese, 322
Terne Bay, 280
Third International, 198–199, 344
Tkachef, Major General, 82
Toki Chinjirō, 212

Tokushima, 213
Tokyo, *passim*
Tomsk, 14, 238
Tottori, 213
Toyohara, 336
Trade, 2, 6, 45, 50, 108, 344, 356
Trade and General Agreement proposal, 34–38, 69, 322–23
Trade delegation (torgpredstvo), 217–24,
Shimoda, Treaty of, 3
Triapitsyn, 11n, 130–31
Troianovskii, Aleksandr Antonovich, 2, 205, 214, 319, 322, 325, 352n, 353–60
Troianovskii, Oleg Aleksandrovich, 2
Trotskii, Leon, 58
Tsalemchuk, I. Iu., 269
Tsarist Russia, relations with Japan, 5, 85, 104–105, 129, 131, 144–45, 178, 187, 213, 322, 356, 383, 368, 370
Tsiurp, D. A., 212
Tsukahara Association, 230, 236
Tsuruga, 108, 206, 338
Tuilen, Lake, 280
Turkey, 222
Twenty-one Demands, 26

Uchida Kōsai, 8, 34, 39, 45, 72, 76–77, 87–89, 105, 108, 110, 113, 124, 126, 130, 132
Uchida Yasuya, 6
Uda Kanichirō, 324–25
Ueda Sentarō, 6
Uiglekuty (Vuigrektui), 193–94, 232
Ulan-Ude, *see* Verkhneudinsk
Umeura Kenkichi, 237
Ungern-Shternberg, Baron, 14
Union of Soviet Socialist Republics,

formation of, 83
United States
  relations with China, 2, 86n
  relations with Japan, 5, 10–13, 45n, 104–105, 137, 196–97, 200, 344–45, 357, 363–69, 373
  relations with Russia, 5, 10–13, 47, 86, 106–107, 136, 197, 200–202, 345, 356–57, 363–69, 373
Usami, 322

Vanderbilt, Cornelius, Jr., 88
Vanina Bay, 280
Vengri-Bol'shaia Khuzi (Daifuji), 333
Verkhneudinsk (Ulan-Ude), 9
Versailles, Peace Conference, 137, 364
Vilenskii-Sibiriakov, V. D., 6, 8–10
Visas, 106, 205, 217–18, 224
Vladimirskii mine, 230, 233, 236
Vladivostok, 13–14, 16, 27, 29, 33, 40, 43–44, 65–66, 77–78, 82, 106–13, 127, 130, 138, 143, 148, 152, 206, 224, 241, 253–54, 272–73, 326, 332, 335–39, 342–43, 349
Vladivostok Nippō, 336
Vol'f, Lev Il'ich, 217, 348
Vologda, 7
Volkoveiov, 320
Volunteer Fleet, 339
Vuigrektui (Uiglekuty), 193–94, 232

War debts, *see* Debts
Washington, 2, 365
Washington Conference, 10, 13, 42, 45, 56, 76, 137, 197, 200, 364
Watanabe Riye, 106–107, 110, 206
White Russians
  harassment of Soviet representatives, 213–14
  protest against Japanese dealings with Soviets, 52–82
  sailed vessels into exile, 112
  support by Japanese, 14, 31, 43–44, 50, 66–75, 80, 98, 100, 106, 113, 142, 156, 180, 207n, 213

Yalta Conference, 369
Yamaguchi, 213
Yamaguchi, T., 222, 224
Yamamoto Gombei, 141, 146n–47n
Yamamoto Teijirō, 262, 325–26
Yamanouchi Shirō, 50–54
Yamazaki Jirō, 242
Yokohama, 88–89, 95, 108, 137, 142
Yoshida, 205
Yoshizawa Kenkichi, 141, 147–78, 181, 183, 186, 188, 190, 191, 195, 202–8, 211, 218, 327

Zetlin, 44